Mercede
Owners
Workshop
Manual

A K Legg T Eng (CEI), AMIMI

Models covered
UK: 250 and 250 long wheelbase Saloons; 2525 cc
       250 T Estate; 2525 cc
       280 and 280 E Saloons; 2746 cc
       280 TE Estate; 2746 cc
       280 C and 280 CE Coupes; 2746 cc

USA: 280 E Sedan; 167.6 cu in (2746 cc)
       280 CE Coupe; 167.6 cu in (2746 cc)

ISBN 0 85696 677 0
ISBN 0 85696 983 4 (US)

ABCDE
FGHIJ
KLMNO
PQr

Printed in England

THE
BOOK

AUTOMOTIVE
PARTS &
ACCESSORIES
ASSOCIATION MEMBER

HAYNES PUBLISHING GROUP
SPARKFORD YEOVIL SOMERSET BA22 7JJ ENGLAND
distributed in the USA by
HAYNES PUBLICATIONS INC
861 LAWRENCE DRIVE
NEWBURY PARK
CALIFORNIA 91320
USA

Acknowledgements

Special thanks are due to Mercedes-Benz for the supply of technical information and certain illustrations. Castrol Limited provided lubrication data, and the Champion Sparking Plug Company supplied the illustrations showing the various spark plug conditions. Sykes-Pickavant provided some of the workshop tools. Thanks are also due to all those people at Sparkford who helped in the production of this manual.

About this manual

Its aim

The aim of this manual is to help you get the best value from your vehicle. It can do so in several ways. It can help you decide what work must be done (even should you choose to get it done by a garage), provide information on routine maintenance and servicing, and give a logical course of action and diagnosis when random faults occur. However, it is hoped that you will use the manual by tackling the work yourself. On simpler jobs it may even be quicker than booking the car into a garage and going there twice, to leave and collect it. Perhaps most important, a lot of money can be saved by avoiding the costs a garage must charge to cover its labour and overheads.

The manual has drawings and descriptions to show the function of the various components so that their layout can be understood. Then the tasks are described and photographed in a step-by-step sequence so that even a novice can do the work.

Its arrangement

The manual is divided into twelve Chapters, each covering a logical sub-division of the vehicle. The Chapters are each divided into Sections, numbered with single figures, eg 5; and the Sections into paragraphs (or sub-sections), with decimal numbers following on from the Section they are in, eg 5.1, 5.2, 5.3 etc.

It is freely illustrated, especially in those parts where there is a detailed sequence of operations to be carried out. There are two forms of illustration: figures and photographs. The figures are numbered in sequence with decimal numbers, according to their position in the Chapter – eg Fig. 6.4 is the fourth drawing/illustration in Chapter 6. Photographs carry the same number (either individually or in related groups) as the Section or sub-section to which they relate.

There is an alphabetical index at the back of the manual as well as a contents list at the front. Each Chapter is also preceded by its own individual contents list.

References to the 'left' or 'right' of the vehicle are in the sense of a person in the driver's seat facing forwards.

Unless otherwise stated, nuts and bolts are removed by turning anti-clockwise, and tightened by turning clockwise.

Vehicle manufacturers continually make changes to specifications and recommendations, and these, when notified, are incorporated into our manuals at the earliest opportunity.

Whilst every care is taken to ensure that the information in this manual is correct, no liability can be accepted by the authors or publishers for loss, damage or injury caused by any errors in, or omissions from, the information given.

Introduction to the Mercedes-Benz 250 and 280

This manual covers the Mercedes-Benz 123 body style fitted with the 123 engine (2525 cc) and the 110 engine (2746 cc). The 123 engine incorporates a single overhead camshaft, but the 110 engine is of double overhead camshaft design. The cylinder block components on both engines are very similar.

The overall design of the Mercedes-Benz is undoubtedly rugged and carefully constructed with attention to detail and safety aspects. Although the car gives an impression of being complicated, it is, in fact, quite conventional and should not present the home mechanic with any problems. However, the engine and transmission are of considerable weight and it is therefore important that any lifting and jacking equipment is adequate.

Contents

Mercedes-Benz 280 TE

Mercedes-Benz 250

General dimensions, weights and capacities

Dimensions

Overall length:
    250, 280 and 280 E:
        UK .... 4725 mm (186.0 in)
        USA .... 4848 mm (190.9 in)
    280 C and 280 CE:
        UK .... 4640 mm (182.7 in)
        USA .... 4763 mm (187.5 in)
    250 (LWB) .... 5355 mm (210.8 in)
    250 T .... 4725 mm (186.0 in)
    280 TE .... 4725 mm (186.0 in)

Overall width:
    All models .... 1786 mm (70.3 in)

Overall height:
    250, 280, 280 E .... 1438 mm (56.6 in)
    280 C, 280 CE .... 1395 mm (54.9 in)
    250 (LWB) .... 1480 mm (58.3 in)
    250 T (14 in wheels, no top rail) .... 1425 mm (56.1 in)
    250 T (15 in wheels, no top rail) .... 1470 mm (57.9 in)
    250 T (14 in wheels, with top rail) .... 1470 mm (57.9 in)
    250 T (15 in wheels, with top rail) .... 1515 mm (59.6 in)
    280 TE (14 in wheels, no top rail) .... 1425 mm (56.1 in)
    280 TE (14 in wheels, with top rail) .... 1470 mm (57.9 in)

Wheelbase:
    250, 280, 280 E, 250 T, 280 TE .... 2795 mm (110.0 in)
    280 C, 280 CE .... 2710 mm (106.7 in)
    250 (LWB) .... 3425 mm (134.8 in)

Track:

	Front	Rear
250, 280, 280 E, 280 C, 280 CE	1488 mm (58.6 in)	1446 mm (56.9 in)
250 (LWB)	1477 mm (58.1 in)	1430 mm (56.3 in)
250 T (14 in wheels)	1488 mm (58.6 in)	1453 mm (57.2 in)
250 T (15 in wheels)	1477 mm (58.1 in)	1435 mm (56.5 in)
280 TE	1488 mm (58.6 in)	1453 mm (57.2 in)

Turning circle:
    250, 280, 280 E:
        With power steering .... 11.29 m (37.0 ft)
        Without power steering .... 11.25 m (36.9 ft)
    280 C, 280 CE .... 11.0 m (36.1 ft)
    250 (LWB) .... 13.35 m (43.8 ft)
    250 T and 280 TE .... 11.29 m (37.0 ft)

Ground clearance:
    250, 280, 280 E, 280 C, 280 CE .... 164 mm (6.5 in)
    250 (LWB) .... 200 mm (7.9 in)
    250 T (14 in wheels) and 280 TE .... 150 mm (5.9 in)
    250 T (15 in wheels) .... 194 mm (7.6 in)

Weights

250 Special (LWB)	1690 kg (3726 lb)
280 E Special (LWB)	1740 kg (3836 lb)
250	1410 kg (3108 lb)
250 (LWB)	1570 kg (3461 lb)
280	1455 kg (3208 lb)
280 E:	
UK	1475 kg (3252 lb)
USA	1565 kg (3450 lb)
280 CE:	
UK	1460 kg (3219 lb)
USA	1560 kg (3439 lb)
250 T	1510 kg (3329 lb)
250 T (heavy duty)	1535 kg (3384 lb)
280 TE	1560 kg (3439 lb)
280 C	1445 kg (3186 lb)
Maximum trailer weight (with brakes)	1500 kg (3307 lb)
Maximum roof rack load	100 kg (220 lb)

Capacities

Engine oil (including filter)	7.0 litre (12.3 Imp pt; 7.4 US qt)
Cooling system (including heater)	10.0 litre (17.6 Imp pt; 10.6 US qt)
Fuel tank:	
Total	65, 70 or 80 litre (14.3, 15.4 or 17.6 Imp gal; 69, 74 or 85 US qt)
Reserve	9.5, 11.0 or 11.5 litre (2.1, 2.4 or 2.5 Imp gal; 10.0, 11.6 or 12.2 US qt)
Manual gearbox	1.6 litre (2.8 Imp pt; 1.7 US qt)
Automatic transmission:	
Complete refill:	
Early models	6.6 litre (11.6 Imp pt; 7.0 US qt)
Late models	6.1 litre (10.7 Imp pt; 6.4 US qt)
Service:	
Early models	5.3 litre (9.3 Imp pt; 5.6 US qt)
Late models	4.8 litre (8.5 Imp pt; 5.1 US qt)
Final drive	1.0 litre (1.8 Imp pt; 1.1 US qt)
Steering gear:	
Manual	0.3 litre (0.5 Imp pt; 0.3 US qt)
Powered	1.4 litre (2.5 Imp pt; 1.5 US qt)

Use of English

As this book has been written in England, it uses the appropriate English component names, phrases, and spelling. Some of these differ from those used in America. Normally, these cause no difficulty, but to make sure, a glossary is printed below. In ordering spare parts remember the parts list may use some of these words:

English	American	English	American
Aerial	Antenna	Motorway	Freeway, turnpike etc
Accelerator	Gas pedal	Number plate	License plate
Anti-roll bar	Stabiliser or sway bar	Paraffin	Kerosene
Bonnet (engine cover)	Hood	Petrol	Gasoline (gas)
Boot (luggage compartment)	Trunk	Petrol tank	Gas tank
Bulkhead	Firewall	'Pinking'	'Pinging'
Cam follower or tappet	Valve lifter or tappet	Propeller shaft	Driveshaft
Carburettor	Carburetor	Quarter light	Quarter window
Catch	Latch	Retread	Recap
Choke/venturi	Barrel	Reverse	Back-up
Circlip	Snap-ring	Rocker cover	Valve cover
Clearance	Lash	Saloon	Sedan
Crownwheel	Ring gear (of differential)	Seized	Frozen
Disc (brake)	Rotor/disk	Side indicator lights	Side marker lights
Drop arm	Pitman arm	Side light	Parking light
Drop head coupe	Convertible	Silencer	Muffler
Dynamo	Generator (DC)	Spanner	Wrench
Earth (electrical)	Ground	Sill panel (beneath doors)	Rocker panel
Engineer's blue	Prussian blue	Split cotter (for valve spring cap)	Lock (for valve spring retainer)
Estate car	Station wagon	Split pin	Cotter pin
Exhaust manifold	Header	Steering arm	Spindle arm
Fault finding/diagnosis	Trouble shooting	Sump	Oil pan
Float chamber	Float bowl	Tab washer	Tang; lock
Free-play	Lash	Tappet	Valve lifter
Freewheel	Coast	Thrust bearing	Throw-out bearing
Gudgeon pin	Piston pin or wrist pin	Top gear	High
Gearchange	Shift	Trackrod (of steering)	Tie-rod (or connecting rod)
Gearbox	Transmission	Trailing shoe (of brake)	Secondary shoe
Halfshaft	Axleshaft	Transmission	Whole drive line
Handbrake	Parking brake	Tyre	Tire
Hood	Soft top	Van	Panel wagon/van
Hot spot	Heat riser	Vice	Vise
Indicator	Turn signal	Wheel nut	Lug nut
Interior light	Dome lamp	Windscreen	Windshield
Layshaft (of gearbox)	Countershaft	Wing/mudguard	Fender
Leading shoe (of brake)	Primary shoe		
Locks	Latches		

Miscellaneous points

An 'oil seal', is also fitted to components lubricated by grease!

A 'damper' is a 'shock absorber', it damps out bouncing, and absorbs shocks of bump impact. Both names are correct, and both are used haphazardly.

Note that British drum brakes are different from the Bendix type that is common in America, so different descriptive names result. The shoe end furthest from the hydraulic wheel cylinder is on a pivot; interconnection between the shoes as on Bendix brakes is most uncommon. Therefore the phrase 'Primary' or 'Secondary' shoe does not apply. A shoe is said to be 'Leading' or 'Trailing'. A 'Leading' shoe is one on which a point on the drum, as it rotates forward, reaches the shoe at the end worked by the hydraulic cylinder before the anchor end. The opposite is a 'Trailing' shoe and this one has no self servo from the wrapping effect of the rotating drum.

Buying spare parts and vehicle identification numbers

Buying spare parts

Spare parts are available from many sources, for example: Mercedes-Benz garages, other garages and accessory shops, and motor factors. Our advice regarding spare parts is as follows:

Officially appointed Mercedes-Benz garages – This is the best source for parts which are peculiar to your car and otherwise not generally available (eg. complete cylinder heads, internal gearbox components, badges, interior trim etc). To be sure of obtaining the correct parts it will always be necessary to give the storeman your car's engine and chassis number, and if possible, to take the old part along for positive identification. Remember that many parts are available on a factory exchange scheme – any parts returned should always be clean. It obviously makes good sense to go to the specialists on your car for this type of part for they are best equipped to supply you.

Other garages and accessory shops – These are often very good places to buy material and components needed for the maintenance of your car (eg. oil filters, spark plugs, bulbs, drivebelts, oils and grease, touch-up paint, filler paste etc). They also sell general accessories, usually have convenient opening hours, charge lower prices and can often be found not far from home.

Motor factors – Good factors will stock all of the more important components which wear out relatively quickly (eg. clutch components, pistons, valves, exhaust systems, brake cylinders, pipes, hoses, seals, pads etc). Motor factors will often provide new or reconditioned components on a part exchange basis – this can save a considerable amount of money.

Vehicle identification numbers

Modifications are a continuing and unpublicised process in vehicle manufacture quite apart from major model changes. Spare parts manuals and lists are compiled upon a numerical basis, the individual vehicle number being essential to correct identification of the component required. The accompanying illustrations show the location of the identification numbers (photo).

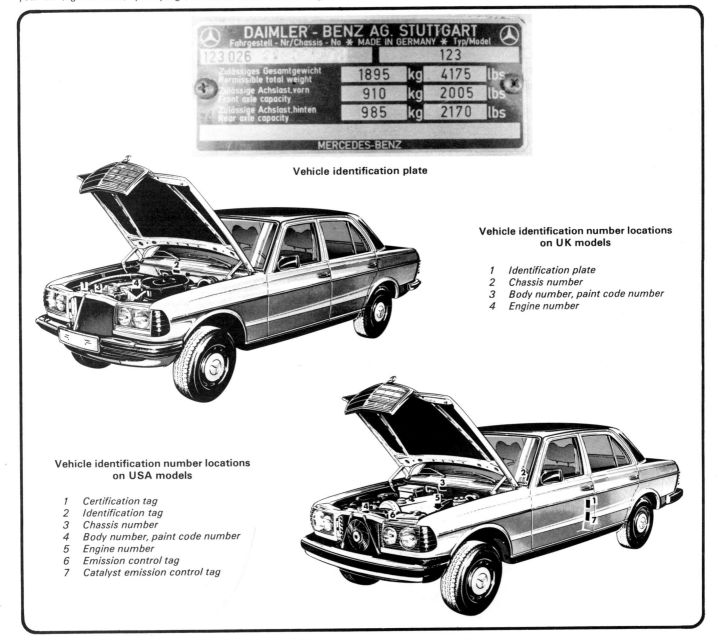

Vehicle identification plate

Vehicle identification number locations on UK models

1 Identification plate
2 Chassis number
3 Body number, paint code number
4 Engine number

Vehicle identification number locations on USA models

1 Certification tag
2 Identification tag
3 Chassis number
4 Body number, paint code number
5 Engine number
6 Emission control tag
7 Catalyst emission control tag

Tools and working facilities

Introduction

A selection of good tools is a fundamental requirement for anyone contemplating the maintenance and repair of a motor vehicle. For the owner who does not possess any, their purchase will prove a considerable expense, offsetting some of the savings made by doing-it-yourself. However, provided that the tools purchased are of good quality, they will last for many years and prove an extremely worthwhile investment.

To help the average owner to decide which tools are needed to carry out the various tasks detailed in this manual, we have compiled three lists of tools under the following headings: *Maintenance and minor repair, Repair and overhaul,* and *Special.* The newcomer to practical mechanics should start off with the *Maintenance and minor repair* tool kit and confine himself to the simpler jobs around the vehicle. Then, as his confidence and experience grow, he can undertake more difficult tasks, buying extra tools as, and when, they are needed. In this way, a *Maintenance and minor repair* tool kit can be built-up into a *Repair and overhaul* tool kit over a considerable period of time without any major cash outlays. The experienced do-it-yourselfer will have a tool kit good enough for most repair and overhaul procedures and will add tools from the *Special* category when he feels the expense is justified by the amount of use to which these tools will be put.

It is obviously not possible to cover the subject of tools fully here. For those who wish to learn more about tools and their use there is a book entitled *How to Choose and Use Car Tools* available from the publishers of this manual.

Maintenance and minor repair tool kit

The tools given in this list should be considered as a minimum requirement if routine maintenance, servicing and minor repair operations are to be undertaken. We recommend the purchase of combination spanners (ring one end, open-ended the other); although more expensive than open-ended ones, they do give the advantages of both types of spanner.

Combination spanners - 10, 11, 12, 13, 14 & 17 mm
Adjustable spanner – 9 inch
Gearbox/rear axle drain plug key
Spark plug spanner (with rubber insert)
Spark plug gap adjustment tool
Set of feeler gauges
Brake bleed nipple spanner
Screwdriver - 4 in long x $\frac{1}{4}$ in dia (flat blade)
Screwdriver - 4 in long x $\frac{1}{4}$ in dia (cross blade)
Combination pliers - 6 inch
Hacksaw (junior)
Tyre pump
Tyre pressure gauge
Oil can
Fine emery cloth (1 sheet)
Wire brush (small)
Funnel (medium size)

Repair and overhaul tool kit

These tools are virtually essential for anyone undertaking any major repairs to a motor vehicle, and are additional to those given in the *Maintenance and minor repair* list. Included in this list is a comprehensive set of sockets. Although these are expensive they will be found invaluable as they are so versatile - particularly if various drives are included in the set. We recommend the $\frac{1}{2}$ in square-drive type, as this can be used with most proprietary torque wrenches. If you cannot afford a socket set, even bought piecemeal, then inexpensive tubular box spanners are a useful alternative.

The tools in this list will occasionally need to be supplemented by tools from the *Special* list.

Sockets (or box spanners) to cover range in previous list
Reversible ratchet drive (for use with sockets)
Extension piece, 10 inch (for use with sockets)
Universal joint (for use with sockets)
Torque wrench (for use with sockets)
'Mole' wrench - 8 inch
Ball pein hammer
Soft-faced hammer, plastic or rubber
Screwdriver - 6 in long x $\frac{5}{16}$ in dia (flat blade)
Screwdriver - 2 in long x $\frac{5}{16}$ in square (flat blade)
Screwdriver - 1$\frac{1}{2}$ in long x $\frac{1}{4}$ in dia (cross blade)
Screwdriver - 3 in long x $\frac{1}{8}$ in dia (electricians)
Pliers - electricians side cutters
Pliers - needle nosed
Pliers - circlip (internal and external)
Cold chisel - $\frac{1}{2}$ inch
Scriber
Scraper
Centre punch
Pin punch
Hacksaw
Valve grinding tool
Steel rule/straight-edge
Allen keys
Selection of files
Wire brush (large)
Axle-stands
Jack (strong scissor or hydraulic type)

Special tools

The tools in this list are those which are not used regularly, are expensive to buy, or which need to be used in accordance with their manufacturers' instructions. Unless relatively difficult mechanical jobs are undertaken frequently, it will not be economic to buy many of these tools. Where this is the case, you could consider clubbing together with friends (or joining a motorists' club) to make a joint purchase, or borrowing the tools against a deposit from a local garage or tool hire specialist.

The following list contains only those tools and instruments freely available to the public, and not those special tools produced by the vehicle manufacturer specifically for its dealer network. You will find occasional references to these manufacturers' special tools in the text of this manual. Generally, an alternative method of doing the job without the vehicle manufacturers' special tool is given. However, sometimes, there is no alternative to using them. Where this is the case and the relevant tool cannot be bought or borrowed, you will have to entrust the work to a franchised garage.

Valve spring compressor
Piston ring compressor
Balljoint separator
Universal hub/bearing puller
Impact screwdriver
Micrometer and/or vernier gauge
Dial gauge
Stroboscopic timing light

Dwell angle meter/tachometer
Universal electrical multi-meter
Cylinder compression gauge
Lifting tackle
Trolley jack
Light with extension lead

Buying tools

For practically all tools, a tool factor is the best source since he will have a very comprehensive range compared with the average garage or accessory shop. Having said that, accessory shops often offer excellent quality tools at discount prices, so it pays to shop around.

Remember, you don't have to buy the most expensive items on the shelf, but it is always advisable to steer clear of the very cheap tools. There are plenty of good tools around at reasonable prices, so ask the proprietor or manager of the shop for advice before making a purchase.

Care and maintenance of tools

Having purchased a reasonable tool kit, it is necessary to keep the tools in a clean serviceable condition. After use, always wipe off any dirt, grease and metal particles using a clean, dry cloth, before putting the tools away. Never leave them lying around after they have been used. A simple tool rack on the garage or workshop wall, for items such as screwdrivers and pliers is a good idea. Store all normal wrenches and sockets in a metal box. Any measuring instruments, gauges, meters, etc, must be carefully stored where they cannot be damaged or become rusty.

Take a little care when tools are used. Hammer heads inevitably become marked and screwdrivers lose the keen edge on their blades from time to time. A little timely attention with emery cloth or a file will soon restore items like this to a good serviceable finish.

Working facilities

Not to be forgotten when discussing tools, is the workshop itself. If anything more than routine maintenance is to be carried out, some form of suitable working area becomes essential.

It is appreciated that many an owner mechanic is forced by circumstances to remove an engine or similar item, without the benefit of a garage or workshop. Having done this, any repairs should always be done under the cover of a roof.

Wherever possible, any dismantling should be done on a clean, flat workbench or table at a suitable working height.

Any workbench needs a vice: one with a jaw opening of 4 in (100 mm) is suitable for most jobs. As mentioned previously, some clean dry storage space is also required for tools, as well as for lubricants, cleaning fluids, touch-up paints and so on, which become necessary.

Another item which may be required, and which has a much more general usage, is an electric drill with a chuck capacity of at least $\frac{5}{16}$ in (8 mm). This, together with a good range of twist drills, is virtually essential for fitting accessories such as mirrors and reversing lights.

Last, but not least, always keep a supply of old newspapers and clean, lint-free rags available, and try to keep any working area as clean as possible.

Spanner jaw gap comparison table

Jaw gap (in)	Spanner size
0.250	$\frac{1}{4}$ in AF
0.276	7 mm
0.313	$\frac{5}{16}$ in AF

Jaw gap (in)	Spanner size
0.315	8 mm
0.344	$\frac{11}{32}$ in AF; $\frac{1}{8}$ in Whitworth
0.354	9 mm
0.375	$\frac{3}{8}$ in AF
0.394	10 mm
0.433	11 mm
0.438	$\frac{7}{16}$ in AF
0.445	$\frac{3}{16}$ in Whitworth; $\frac{1}{4}$ in BSF
0.472	12 mm
0.500	$\frac{1}{2}$ in AF
0.512	13 mm
0.525	$\frac{1}{4}$ in Whitworth; $\frac{5}{16}$ in BSF
0.551	14 mm
0.563	$\frac{9}{16}$ in AF
0.591	15 mm
0.600	$\frac{5}{16}$ in Whitworth; $\frac{3}{8}$ in BSF
0.625	$\frac{5}{8}$ in AF
0.630	16 mm
0.669	17 mm
0.686	$\frac{11}{16}$ in AF
0.709	18 mm
0.710	$\frac{3}{8}$ in Whitworth; $\frac{7}{16}$ in BSF
0.748	19 mm
0.750	$\frac{3}{4}$ in AF
0.813	$\frac{13}{16}$ in AF
0.820	$\frac{7}{16}$ in Whitworth; $\frac{1}{2}$ in BSF
0.866	22 mm
0.875	$\frac{7}{8}$ in AF
0.920	$\frac{1}{2}$ in Whitworth; $\frac{9}{16}$ in BSF
0.938	$\frac{15}{16}$ in AF
0.945	24 mm
1.000	1 in AF
1.010	$\frac{9}{16}$ in Whitworth; $\frac{5}{8}$ in BSF
1.024	26 mm
1.063	$1\frac{1}{16}$ in AF; 27 mm
1.100	$\frac{5}{8}$ in Whitworth; $\frac{11}{16}$ in BSF
1.125	$1\frac{1}{8}$ in AF
1.181	30 mm
1.200	$\frac{11}{16}$ in Whitworth; $\frac{3}{4}$ in BSF
1.250	$1\frac{1}{4}$ in AF
1.260	32 mm
1.300	$\frac{3}{4}$ in Whitworth; $\frac{7}{8}$ in BSF
1.313	$1\frac{5}{16}$ in AF
1.390	$\frac{13}{16}$ in Whitworth; $\frac{15}{16}$ in BSF
1.417	36 mm
1.438	$1\frac{7}{16}$ in AF
1.480	$\frac{7}{8}$ in Whitworth; 1 in BSF
1.500	$1\frac{1}{2}$ in AF
1.575	40 mm; $\frac{15}{16}$ in Whitworth
1.614	41 mm
1.625	$1\frac{5}{8}$ in AF
1.670	1 in Whitworth; $1\frac{1}{8}$ in BSF
1.688	$1\frac{11}{16}$ in AF
1.811	46 mm
1.813	$1\frac{13}{16}$ in AF
1.860	$1\frac{1}{8}$ in Whitworth; $1\frac{1}{4}$ in BSF
1.875	$1\frac{7}{8}$ in AF
1.969	50 mm
2.000	2 in AF
2.050	$1\frac{1}{4}$ in Whitworth; $1\frac{3}{8}$ in BSF
2.165	55 mm
2.362	60 mm

General repair procedures

Whenever servicing, repair or overhaul work is carried out on the car or its components, it is necessary to observe the following procedures and instructions. This will assist in carrying out the operation efficiently and to a professional standard of workmanship.

Joint mating faces and gaskets

Where a gasket is used between the mating faces of two components, ensure that it is renewed on reassembly, and fit it dry unless otherwise stated in the repair procedure. Make sure that the mating faces are clean and dry with all traces of old gasket removed. When cleaning a joint face, use a tool which is not likely to score or damage the face, and remove any burrs or nicks with an oilstone or fine file.

Make sure that tapped holes are cleaned with a pipe cleaner, and keep them free of jointing compound if this is being used unless specifically instructed otherwise.

Ensure that all orifices, channels or pipes are clear and blow through them, preferably using compressed air.

Oil seals

Whenever an oil seal is removed from its working location, either individually or as part of an assembly, it should be renewed.

The very fine sealing lip of the seal is easily damaged and will not seal if the surface it contacts is not completely clean and free from scratches, nicks or grooves. If the original sealing surface of the component cannot be restored, the component should be renewed.

Protect the lips of the seal from any surface which may damage them in the course of fitting. Use tape or a conical sleeve where possible. Lubricate the seal lips with oil before fitting and, on dual lipped seals, fill the space between the lips with grease.

Unless otherwise stated, oil seals must be fitted with their sealing lips toward the lubricant to be sealed.

Use a tubular drift or block of wood of the appropriate size to install the seal and, if the seal housing is shouldered, drive the seal down to the shoulder. If the seal housing is unshouldered, the seal should be fitted with its face flush with the housing top face.

Screw threads and fastenings

Always ensure that a blind tapped hole is completely free from oil, grease, water or other fluid before installing the bolt or stud. Failure to do this could cause the housing to crack due to the hydraulic action of the bolt or stud as it is screwed in.

When tightening a castellated nut to accept a split pin, tighten the nut to the specified torque, where applicable, and then tighten further to the next split pin hole. Never slacken the nut to align a split pin hole unless stated in the repair procedure.

When checking or retightening a nut or bolt to a specified torque setting, slacken the nut or bolt by a quarter of a turn, and then retighten to the specified setting.

Locknuts, locktabs and washers

Any fastening which will rotate against a component or housing in the course of tightening should always have a washer between it and the relevant component or housing.

Spring or split washers should always be renewed when they are used to lock a critical component such as a big-end bearing retaining nut or bolt.

Locktabs which are folded over to retain a nut or bolt should always be renewed.

Self-locking nuts can be reused in non-critical areas, providing resistance can be felt when the locking portion passes over the bolt or stud thread.

Split pins must always be replaced with new ones of the correct size for the hole.

Special tools

Some repair procedures in this manual entail the use of special tools such as a press, two or three-legged pullers, spring compressors etc. Wherever possible, suitable readily available alternatives to the manufacturer's special tools are described, and are shown in use. In some instances, where no alternative is possible, it has been necessary to resort to the use of a manufacturer's tool and this has been done for reasons of safety as well as the efficient completion of the repair operation. Unless you are highly skilled and have a thorough understanding of the procedure described, never attempt to bypass the use of any special tool when the procedure described specifies its use. Not only is there a very great risk of personal injury, but expensive damage could be caused to the components involved.

Jacking and towing

The jack supplied with the car should only be used for changing roadwheels and must always be engaged with the special recesses on the sills. When using a trolley jack, the front of the car can be raised beneath the crossmember and the rear raised either beneath the semi-trailing arms or beneath the final drive unit. Always support the body with axle stands (photos).

Towing eyes are provided at the front and rear of the car on the right-hand side (photo). The ignition key must be inserted and turned to position 1 or 2. On automatic transmission models the transmission must contain the correct quantity of fluid, the towing speed must not exceed 30 mph (50 kph) and the towing distance must not exceed 75 miles (120 km). The selector lever must be in position N. For longer distances the rear of the car must be lifted from the ground or, alternatively, the propeller shaft disconnected.

Spare wheel and jack

Tool kit jack in position

Front towing eye

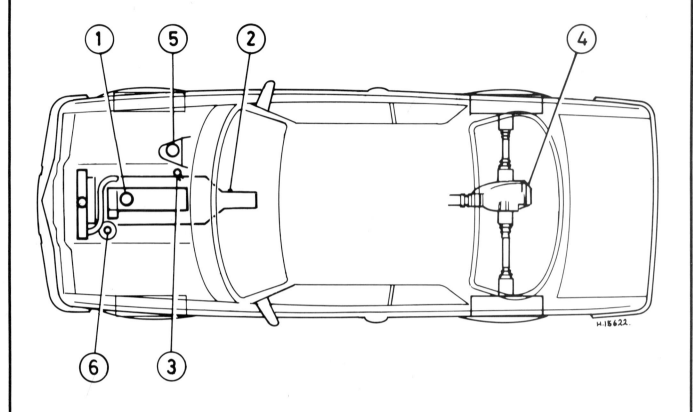

H.15622.

Recommended lubricants and fluids

Component or system	Lubricant type or specification	Castrol product
Engine (1)	Multigrade oils: 10W/40, 10W/50, 15W/40 or 15W/50	GTX
Manual gearbox (2)	Automatic transmission fluid (ATF)	TQ Dexron® R11
Automatic transmission (3)	Automatic transmission fluid (ATF)	TQT
Final drive (4)	Hypoid SAE 90	Hypoy B EP90
Brake (5) and clutch hydraulic system	Hydraulic fluid to SAE J1703 or US FMVSS Dot 3	Castrol Girling Universal Brake and Clutch Fluid
Manual steering	Hypoid SAE 90	None specified
Power steering (6)	Automatic transmission fluid (ATF)	TQ Dexron® R11 or TQT

Safety first!

Professional motor mechanics are trained in safe working procedures. However enthusiastic you may be about getting on with the job in hand, do take the time to ensure that your safety is not put at risk. A moment's lack of attention can result in an accident, as can failure to observe certain elementary precautions.

There will always be new ways of having accidents, and the following points do not pretend to be a comprehensive list of all dangers; they are intended rather to make you aware of the risks and to encourage a safety-conscious approach to all work you carry out on your vehicle.

Essential DOs and DON'Ts

DON'T rely on a single jack when working underneath the vehicle. Always use reliable additional means of support, such as axle stands, securely placed under a part of the vehicle that you know will not give way.

DON'T attempt to loosen or tighten high-torque nuts (e.g. wheel hub nuts) while the vehicle is on a jack; it may be pulled off.

DON'T start the engine without first ascertaining that the transmission is in neutral (or 'Park' where applicable) and the parking brake applied.

DON'T suddenly remove the filler cap from a hot cooling system – cover it with a cloth and release the pressure gradually first, or you may get scalded by escaping coolant.

DON'T attempt to drain oil until you are sure it has cooled sufficiently to avoid scalding you.

DON'T grasp any part of the engine, exhaust or catalytic converter without first ascertaining that it is sufficiently cool to avoid burning you.

DON'T syphon toxic liquids such as fuel, brake fluid or antifreeze by mouth, or allow them to remain on your skin.

DON'T inhale brake lining dust – it is injurious to health.

DON'T allow any spilt oil or grease to remain on the floor – wipe it up straight away, before someone slips on it.

DON'T use ill-fitting spanners or other tools which may slip and cause injury.

DON'T attempt to lift a heavy component which may be beyond your capability – get assistance.

DON'T rush to finish a job, or take unverified short cuts.

DON'T allow children or animals in or around an unattended vehicle.

DO wear eye protection when using power tools such as drill. sander, bench grinder etc, and when working under the vehicle.

DO use a barrier cream on your hands prior to undertaking dirty jobs – it will protect your skin from infection as well as making the dirt easier to remove afterwards; but make sure your hands aren't left slippery.

DO keep loose clothing (cuffs, tie etc) and long hair well out of the way of moving mechanical parts.

DO remove rings, wristwatch etc, before working on the vehicle – especially the electrical system.

DO ensure that any lifting tackle used has a safe working load rating adequate for the job.

DO keep your work area tidy – it is only too easy to fall over articles left lying around.

DO get someone to check periodically that all is well, when working alone on the vehicle.

DO carry out work in a logical sequence and check that everything is correctly assembled and tightened afterwards.

DO remember that your vehicle's safety affects that of yourself and others. If in doubt on any point, get specialist advice.

IF, in spite of following these precautions, you are unfortunate enough to injure yourself, seek medical attention as soon as possible.

Fire

Remember at all times that petrol (gasoline) is highly flammable. Never smoke, or have any kind of naked flame around, when working on the vehicle. But the risk does not end there – a spark caused by an electrical short-circuit, by two metal surfaces contacting each other, or even by static electricity built up in your body under certain conditions, can ignite petrol vapour, which in a confined space is highly explosive.

Always disconnect the battery earth (ground) terminal before working on any part of the fuel system, and never risk spilling fuel on to a hot engine or exhaust.

It is recommended that a fire extinguisher of a type suitable for fuel and electrical fires is kept handy in the garage or workplace at all times. Never try to extinguish a fuel or electrical fire with water.

Fumes

Certain fumes are highly toxic and can quickly cause unconsciousness and even death if inhaled to any extent. Petrol (gasoline) vapour comes into this category, as do the vapours from certain solvents such as trichloroethylene. Any draining or pouring of such volatile fluids should be done in a well ventilated area.

When using cleaning fluids and solvents, read the instructions carefully. Never use materials from unmarked containers – they may give off poisonous vapours.

Never run the engine of a motor vehicle in an enclosed space such as a garage. Exhaust fumes contain carbon monoxide which is extremely poisonous; if you need to run the engine, always do so in the open air or at least have the rear of the vehicle outside the workplace.

If you are fortunate enough to have the use of an inspection pit, never drain or pour petrol, and never run the engine, while the vehicle is standing over it; the fumes, being heavier than air, will concentrate in the pit with possibly lethal results.

The battery

Never cause a spark, or allow a naked light, near the vehicle's battery. It will normally be giving off a certain amount of hydrogen gas, which is highly explosive.

Always disconnect the battery earth (ground) terminal before working on the fuel or electrical systems.

If possible, loosen the filler plugs or cover when charging the battery from an external source. Do not charge at an excessive rate or the battery may burst.

Take care when topping up and when carrying the battery. The acid electrolyte, even when diluted, is very corrosive and should not be allowed to contact the eyes or skin.

If you ever need to prepare electrolyte yourself, always add the acid slowly to the water, and never the other way round. Protect against splashes by wearing rubber gloves and goggles.

When jump starting a car using a booster battery, for negative earth (ground) vehicles, connect the jump leads in the following sequence: First connect one jump lead between the positive (+) terminals of the two batteries. Then connect the other jump lead first to the negative (–) terminal of the booster battery, and then to a good earthing (ground) point on the vehicle to be started, at least 18 in (45 cm) from the battery if possible. Ensure that hands and jump leads are clear of any moving parts, and that the two vehicles do not touch. Disconnect the leads in the reverse order.

Mains electricity

When using an electric power tool, inspection light etc, which works from the mains, always ensure that the appliance is correctly connected to its plug and that, where necessary, it is properly earthed (grounded). Do not use such appliances in damp conditions and, again, beware of creating a spark or applying excessive heat in the vicinity of fuel or fuel vapour.

Ignition HT voltage

A severe electric shock can result from touching certain parts of the ignition system, such as the HT leads, when the engine is running or being cranked, particularly if components are damp or the insulation is defective. Where an electronic ignition system is fitted, the HT voltage is much higher and could prove fatal.

Routine maintenance

Maintenance is essential for ensuring safety, and desirable for the purpose of getting the best in terms of performance and economy from the car. Over the years the need for periodic lubrication — oiling, greasing and so on — has been drastically reduced, if not totally eliminated. This has unfortunately tended to lead some owners to think that because no such action is required the items either no longer exist or will last forever. This is certainly not the case; it is essential to carry out regular visual examination as comprehensively as possible in order to spot any possible defects at an early stage before they develop into major expensive repairs.

Every 250 miles (400 km) or weekly — whichever comes first

Engine
    Check the oil level, and top up if necessary (photos)
    Check the coolant level, and top up if necessary (photo)

Tyres
    Check the tyre pressures, and adjust if necessary (photo)

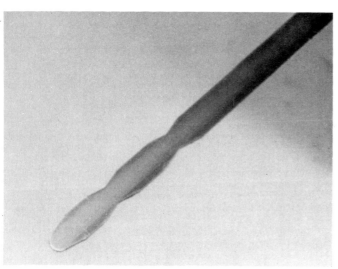

Engine oil level dipstick markings

Topping-up engine oil level

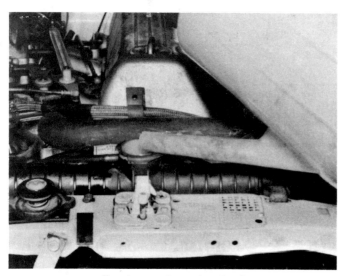

Topping-up the coolant level

Checking tyre pressures

Under-bonnet view (250 model)

1 Throttle cable
2 Carburettor
3 Brake fluid reservoir filler cap
4 Low brake fluid wiring
5 Heater/central locking vacuum valves
6 Automatic transmission filler/dipstick tube
7 Heater return hose
8 Heater supply hose
9 Battery filler cap
10 Battery
11 Front shock absorber top mounting
12 Fuel feed and return pipes
13 Engine damper/mounting
14 Spark plug HT leads
15 Ignition pre-resistors
16 Diagnostic socket
17 Electronic ignition control unit
18 Coil
19 Windscreen washer fluid reservoir
20 Power steering pump and fluid reservoir
21 Spark plug
22 Crankcase ventilation outlet
23 Engine oil filler cap
24 Radiator filler cap
25 Radiator top hose
26 Radiator
27 Vehicle identification plate
28 Fan belt
29 Alternator
30 Fuel return pressure valve

View of front underside of car

1 Engine/transmission rear mounting crossmember
2 Exhaust system
3 Exhaust system support bracket
4 Automatic transmission oil pan
5 Automatic transmission filler/dipstick tube
6 Automatic transmission fluid cooler pipes
7 Automatic transmission
8 Suspension support tube
9 Steering gear drop arm (Pitman arm)
10 Steering gear
11 Coil spring seat
12 Lower control arm
13 Lower control arm inner mounting
14 Crossmember
15 Drag link
16 Engine sump oil pan
17 Sump housing
18 Engine oil drain plug
19 Steering damper
20 Brake caliper
21 Track rod end
22 Steering idler
23 Engine earth strap
24 Speedometer cable

View of rear underside of car

1 Final drive unit
2 Stabiliser bar (anti-roll bar)
3 Brake hydraulic fluid hose
4 Handbrake/parking brake cable
5 Driveshaft
6 Propeller shaft
7 Exhaust system intermediate silencer
8 Rear suspension crossmember front mounting
9 Rear suspension crossmember
10 Semi-trailing arm
11 Rear shock absorber lower mounting
12 Exhaust system rubber mounting rings
13 Exhaust system rear silencer

Engine sump drain plug

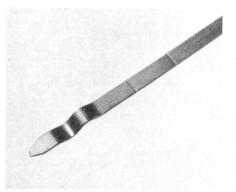

Automatic transmission fluid level dipstick markings

Checking the tyre tread depth

Every 5000 miles (8000 km) on UK models, every 7500 miles (12 000 km) on USA models

Engine
Change oil and filter (photo)
Lubricate engine controls

Every 10 000 miles (16 000 km) on UK models, every 15 000 miles (24 000 km) on USA models

Engine
Check for leaks of fuel, water and oil
Check the condition of all hoses
Check compressions
Adjust valve clearances
Adjust idling
Clean the air filter element and fuel filter
Check all drivebelt tensions, and adjust if necessary
Renew speark plugs
Renew the contact points, where applicable
Check and adjust the ignition timing

Transmission
Check oil/fluid level of gearbox/automatic transmission, and top up if necessary (photo)
Check oil level of final drive, and top up if necessary
Check clutch fluid level, and top up if necessary

Suspension and steering
Check level control for leaks and fluid level, and top up if necessary
Check all joints and rubbers for wear
Check tyres for wear and damage (photo)
Rotate tyre positions
Check power steering fluid level, and top up if necessary
Check steering balljoints and linkages for wear and damage
Check all suspension and steering fastenings for tightness

Brakes
Check hydraulic fluid level, and top up if necessary
Check all brake lines for damage and leakage
Check disc pads and shoes for wear, and renew if necessary
Adjust the handbrake/parking brake

Electrical system
Check the function of all electrical components
Check battery electrolyte level, and top up if necessary

Body
Check seat belts for condition and security
Lubricate door and bonnet hinges and locks
Check windscreen washer fluid level, and top up if necessary
Check air conditioning and automatic climate control fluid level
Lubricate exterior mirror

Every 12 months

Brakes
Renew the hydraulic fluid

Body
Clean and grease the sliding roof rails

Every 30 000 miles (48 000 km)

Engine
Renew air filter element
Renew Lambda oxygen sensor

Transmission
Check clutch disc for wear
Change automatic transmission fluid and renew filter
Check propeller shaft flange bolts for tightness

Brakes
Check handbrake/parking brake cables and linkage for damage and ease of operation

Body
Clear all water drain holes

Every 36 months

Engine
Change antifreeze solution

Every 60 000 miles (96 000 km)

Engine
Renew the fuel filter on fuel injection models

Fault diagnosis

Introduction

The vehicle owner who does his or her own maintenance according to the recommended schedules should not have to use this section of the manual very often. Modern component reliability is such that, provided those items subject to wear or deterioration are inspected or renewed at the specified intervals, sudden failure is comparatively rare. Faults do not usually just happen as a result of sudden failure, but develop over a period of time. Major mechanical failures in particular are usually preceded by characteristic symptoms over hundreds or even thousands of miles. Those components which do occasionally fail without warning are often small and easily carried in the vehicle.

With any fault finding, the first step is to decide where to begin investigations. Sometimes this is obvious, but on other occasions a little detective work will be necessary. The owner who makes half a dozen haphazard adjustments or replacements may be successful in curing a fault (or its symptoms), but he will be none the wiser if the fault recurs and he may well have spent more time and money than was necessary. A calm and logical approach will be found to be more satisfactory in the long run. Always take into account any warning signs or abnormalities that may have been noticed in the period preceding the fault – power loss, high or low gauge readings, unusual noises or smells, etc – and remember that failure of components such as fuses or spark plugs may only be pointers to some underlying fault.

The pages which follow here are intended to help in cases of failure to start or breakdown on the road. There is also a Fault Diagnosis Section at the end of each Chapter which should be consulted if the preliminary checks prove unfruitful. Whatever the fault, certain basic principles apply. These are as follows:

Verify the fault. This is simply a matter of being sure that you know what the symptoms are before starting work. This is particularly important if you are investigating a fault for someone else who may not have described it very accurately.

Don't overlook the obvious. For example, if the vehicle won't start, is there petrol in the tank? (Don't take anyone else's word on this particular point, and don't trust the fuel gauge either!) If an electrical fault is indicated, look for loose or broken wires before digging out the test gear.

Cure the disease, not the symptom. Substituting a flat battery with a fully charged one will get you off the hard shoulder, but if the underlying cause is not attended to, the new battery will go the same way. Similarly, changing oil-fouled spark plugs for a new set will get you moving again, but remember that the reason for the fouling (if it wasn't simply an incorrect grade of plug) will have to be established and corrected.

Don't take anything for granted. Particularly, don't forget that a 'new' component may itself be defective (especially if it's been rattling round in the boot for months), and don't leave components out of a fault diagnosis sequence just because they are new or recently fitted. When you do finally diagnose a difficult fault, you'll probably realise that all the evidence was there from the start.

Electrical faults

Electrical faults can be more puzzling than straightforward mechanical failures, but they are no less susceptible to logical analysis if the basic principles of operation are understood. Vehicle electrical wiring exists in extremely unfavourable conditions – heat, vibration and chemical attack – and the first things to look for are loose or corroded connections and broken or chafed wires, especially where the wires pass through holes in the bodywork or are subject to vibration.

All metal-bodied vehicles in current production have one pole of the battery 'earthed', ie connected to the vehicle bodywork, and in nearly all modern vehicles it is the negative (–) terminal. The various electrical components – motors, bulb holders etc – are also connected to earth, either by means of a lead or directly by their mountings. Electric current flows through the component and then back to the battery via the bodywork. If the component mounting is loose or corroded, or if a good path back to the battery is not available, the circuit will be incomplete and malfunction will result. The engine and/or gearbox are also earthed by means of flexible metal straps to the body or subframe; if these straps are loose or missing, starter motor, generator and ignition trouble may result.

Assuming the earth return to be satisfactory, electrical faults will be due either to component malfunction or to defects in the current supply. Individual components are dealt with in Chapter 10. If supply wires are broken or cracked internally this results in an open-circuit, and the easiest way to check for this is to bypass the suspect wire temporarily with a length of wire having a crocodile clip or suitable connector at each end. Alternatively, a 12V test lamp can be used to verify the presence of supply voltage at various points along the wire and the break can be thus isolated.

If a bare portion of a live wire touches the bodywork or other earthed metal part, the electricity will take the low-resistance path thus formed back to the battery: this is known as a short-circuit. Hopefully a short-circuit will blow a fuse, but otherwise it may cause burning of the insulation (and possibly further short-circuits) or even a fire. This is why it is inadvisable to bypass persistently blowing fuses with silver foil or wire.

Spares and tool kit

Most vehicles are supplied only with sufficient tools for wheel changing; the *Maintenance and minor repair* tool kit detailed in *Tools and working facilities,* with the addition of a hammer, is probably sufficient for those repairs that most motorists would consider attempting at the roadside. In addition a few items which can be fitted without too much trouble in the event of a breakdown should be carried. Experience and available space will modify the list below, but the following may save having to call on professional assistance:

Spark plugs, clean and correctly gapped
HT lead and plug cap – long enough to reach the plug furthest from the distributor
Distributor rotor, condenser and contact breaker points
Drivebelt(s) – emergency type may suffice
Spare fuses
Set of principal light bulbs
Tin of radiator sealer and hose bandage
Exhaust bandage
Roll of insulating tape
Length of soft iron wire
Length of electrical flex
Torch or inspection lamp (can double as test lamp)
Battery jump leads
Tow-rope
Ignition waterproofing aerosol
Litre of engine oil
Sealed can of hydraulic fluid
Emergency windscreen
Worm drive clips
Tube of filler paste

If spare fuel is carried, a can designed for the purpose should be used to minimise risks of leakage and collision damage. A first aid kit and a warning triangle, whilst not at present compulsory in the UK, are obviously sensible items to carry in addition to the above.

When touring abroad it may be advisable to carry additional spares which, even if you cannot fit them yourself, could save having to wait while parts are obtained. The items below may be worth considering:

Throttle cable
Cylinder head gasket
Alternator brushes
Tyre valve core

One of the motoring organisations will be able to advise on availability of fuel etc in foreign countries.

Using a spark plug to check for HT spark – do not remove plug from engine otherwise fuel/air mixture may explode

Checking for fuel delivery at the carburettor

Engine will not start

Engine fails to turn when starter operated
Flat battery (recharge, use jump leads, or push start)
Battery terminals loose or corroded
Battery earth to body defective
Engine earth strap loose or broken
Starter motor (or solenoid) wiring loose or broken
Automatic transmission selector in wrong position, or inhibitor switch faulty
Ignition/starter switch faulty
Major mechanical failure (seizure)
Starter or solenoid internal fault (see Chapter 10)

Starter motor turns engine slowly
Partially discharged battery (recharge, use jump leads, or push start)
Battery terminals loose or corroded
Battery earth to body defective
Engine earth strap loose
Starter motor (or solenoid) wiring loose
Starter motor internal fault (see Chapter 10)

Engine turns normally but fails to start
Damp or dirty HT leads and distributor cap (crank engine and check for spark) (photo)
Dirty or incorrectly gapped distributor points (if applicable)
No fuel in tank (check for delivery) (photo)
Excessive choke (hot engine) or insufficient choke (cold engine)
Fouled or incorrectly gapped spark plugs (remove, clean and regap)
Other ignition system fault (see Chapter 4)
Other fuel system fault (see Chapter 3)
Poor compression (see Chapter 1)
Major mechanical failure (eg camshaft drive)

Engine fires but will not run
Insufficient choke (cold engine)
Air leaks at inlet manifold
Fuel starvation (see Chapter 3)
Ignition fault (see Chapter 4)

Engine cuts out and will not restart

Engine cuts out suddenly – ignition fault
Loose or disconnected LT wires
Wet HT leads or distributor cap (after traversing water splash)

Coil or condenser failure (check for spark)
Other ignition fault (see Chapter 4)

Engine misfires before cutting out – fuel fault
Fuel tank empty
Fuel pump defective or filter blocked (check for delivery)
Fuel tank filler vent blocked (suction will be evident on releasing cap)
Carburettor needle valve sticking
Carburettor jets blocked (fuel contaminated)
Other fuel system fault (see Chapter 3)

Engine cuts out – other causes
Serious overheating
Major mechanical failure (eg camshaft drive)

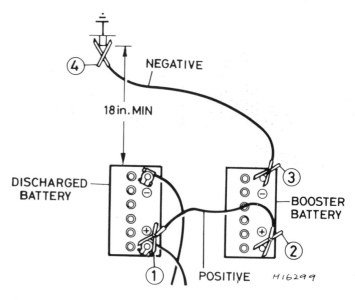

Jump start lead connections for negative earth vehicles – connect leads in order shown

Engine overheats

Ignition (no-charge) warning light illuminated
Slack or broken drivebelt – retension or renew (Chapter 2)

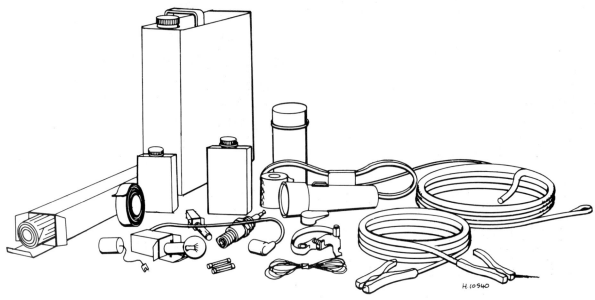

Carrying a few spares can save you a long walk!

Ignition warning light not illuminated
Coolant loss due to internal or external leakage (see Chapter 2)
Thermostat defective
Low oil level
Brakes binding
Radiator clogged externally or internally
Engine waterways clogged
Ignition timing incorrect or automatic advance malfunctioning
Mixture too weak

Note: *Do not add cold water to an overheated engine or damage may result*

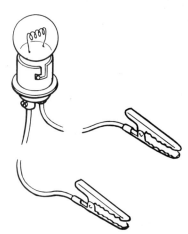

A simple test lamp is useful for tracing electrical faults

Low engine oil pressure

Gauge reads low or warning light illuminated with engine running
Oil level low or incorrect grade
Defective gauge or sender unit
Wire to sender unit earthed

Engine overheating
Oil filter clogged or bypass valve defective
Oil pressure relief valve defective
Oil pick-up strainer clogged
Oil pump worn or mountings loose
Worn main or big-end bearings

Note: *Low oil pressure in a high-mileage engine at tickover is not necessarily a cause for concern. Sudden pressure loss at speed is far more significant. In any event, check the gauge or warning light sender before condemning the engine.*

Engine noises

Pre-ignition (pinking) on acceleration
Incorrect grade of fuel
Ignition timing incorrect
Distributor faulty or worn
Worn or maladjusted carburettor/fuel injection
Excessive carbon build-up in engine

Whistling or wheezing noises
Leaking vacuum hose
Leaking manifold gaskets
Blowing head gasket

Tapping or rattling
Incorrect valve clearances
Worn valve gear
Worn timing chain
Broken piston ring (ticking noise)

Knocking or thumping
Unintentional mechanical contact (eg fan blades)
Worn fanbelt
Peripheral component fault (alternator, water pump etc)
Worn big-end bearings (regular heavy knocking, perhaps less under load)
Worn main bearings (rumbling and knocking, perhaps worsening under load)
Piston slap (most noticeable when cold)

Chapter 1 Engine

Contents

Specifications

General
Type .... Six-cylinder in-line, single overhead camshaft (123 engine) or double overhead camshafts (110 engine)

Firing order 1-5-3-6-2-4
Bore .... 86.0 mm (3.3858 in)
Stroke:
    123 Engine .... 72.45 mm (2.8524 in)
    110 Engine .... 78.8 mm (3.1024 in)
Cubic capacity:
    123 Engine .... 2525 cc (154 cu in)
    110 Engine .... 2746 cc (168 cu in)
Compression ratio .... 8.0 : 1 to 9.4 : 1, according to model

Cylinder block
Standard bore .... 85.998 to 86.028 mm (3.3858 to 3.3869 in)
Oversize 1 .... 86.498 to 86.528 mm (3.4054 to 3.4066 in)
Oversize 2 .... 86.998 to 87.028 mm (3.4251 to 3.4263 in)
Minimum block height after machining .... 212.80 mm (8.3780 in)

Cylinder head
Minimum height after machining:
    123 Engine .... 84.0 mm (3.3071 in)
    110 Engine .... 93.1 mm (3.6654 in)

Crankshaft and connecting rods
Main bearings:
    Maximum running clearance .... 0.08 mm (0.0031 in)
    Maximum endfloat .... 0.30 mm (0.0118 in)
Big-end bearings:
    Maximum running clearance .... 0.08 mm (0.0031 in)
    Maximum side float .... 0.50 mm (0.0197 in)
Maximum crankpin/journal out-of-true .... 0.01 mm (0.0004 in)
Main bearing journal diameter (standard) .... 59.965 to 59.955 mm (2.3608 to 2.3604 in)
Crankpin diameter (standard) .... 47.965 to 47.955 mm (1.8884 to 1.8880 in)
Undersizes .... Four, at increments of 0.25 mm (0.010 in)
Connecting rod stud minimum diameter .... 8.0 mm (0.3150 in)

Pistons
Maximum difference in weight of any two pistons .... 10 g (0.353 oz)
Piston ring side clearance (maximum):
    Top .... 0.15 mm (0.006 in)
    Middle .... 0.10 mm (0.004 in)
    Bottom .... 0.10 mm (0.004 in)
Piston ring gap:
    Top .... 0.3 to 1.0 mm (0.012 to 0.039 in)
    Middle .... 0.3 to 0.8 mm (0.012 to 0.031 in)
    Bottom .... 0.25 to 0.8 mm (0.010 to 0.031 in)
Piston crown-to-block surface dimension:
    123 Engine .... 0.0 mm (0.0 in) to 0.55 mm (0.022 in) protrusion
    110 Engine (normal compression) .... 0.20 mm (0.008 in) recess to 1.50 mm (0.059 in) recess
    110 Engine (low compression) .... 0.25 mm (0.010 in) protrusion to 0.15 mm (0.006 in) recess

Flywheel/driveplate
Maximum run-out .... 0.05 mm (0.002 in)

	Manual gearbox	Automatic transmission
Mounting bolt minimum diameter:		
123 Engine	7.6 mm (0.299 in)	7.3 mm (0.287 in)
110 Engine	8.1 mm (0.319 in)	7.3 mm (0.287 in)

Valves
Head-to-gasket surface dimension (maximum):
123 Engine:
    Inlet .... 1.5 mm (0.059 in)
    Exhaust .... 16.0 mm (0.630 in)
110 Engine:
    Inlet .... 4.2 mm (0.165 in)
    Exhaust .... 0.94 mm (0.037 in)
Seat angle .... 45°

Valve clearances:	Cold	Warm
Inlet	0.10 mm (0.004 in)	0.15 mm (0.006 in)
Exhaust:		
123 Engine	0.20 mm (0.008 in)	0.25 mm (0.010 in)
110 engine	0.25 mm (0.010 in)	0.30 mm (0.012 in)

Valve timing:

	123 engine	110 engine (except USA)	110 engine (USA)
Inlet opens	15° ATDC	7° ATDC	7° ATDC
Inlet closes	21° ABDC	21° ABDC	21° ABDC
Exhaust opens	21° BBDC	30° BBDC (to 1982) 35° BBDC (1982 onwards)	34° BBDC
Exhaust closes	11° BTDC	12° BTDC (to 1982) 17° BTDC (1982 onwards)	16° BTDC

Camshaft
Maximum bearing running clearance:
    123 Engine .... 0.09 mm (0.0035 in)
    110 Engine .... 0.11 mm (0.0043 in)
Maximum endfloat .... 0.15 mm (0.0059 in)

Lubricating system
Type .... Double gear pump driven by intermediate shaft
Oil capacity (including filter) .... 7.0 litre; 12.3 Imp pt; 7.4 US qt
Oil pressure:
    Idling .... 0.3 bar (4.4 lbf/in^2)
    At 3000 rpm .... 3.0 bar (44 lbf in^2) minimum
Pressure relief valve opening pressure:
    123 Engine .... 4.0 bar (58 lbf/in^2)
    110 Engine .... 5.0 bar (73 lbf/in^2)

Torque wrench settings

	lbf ft	Nm
Camshaft gear	59	80
Connecting rod nuts	30 to 37	41 to 50
Main bearing bolts	59	80
Crankshaft front flange bolt	295 to 332	400 to 450
Flywheel/driveplate	22 to 30	30 to 41
Intermediate plate	37	50
Oil pan	8	11
Oil filter housing:		
123 Engine	19	26
110 Engine	26	35
Oil filter bowl	26 to 30	35 to 41
Oil pressure relief valve	30	41
Timing chain tensioner:		
123 Engine	66	89
110 Engine	37	50
Camshaft housing – 110 Engine	19	26
Oil drain plug	30	41
Valve cover:		
123 Engine	11	15
110 Engine	4	5
Cylinder head bolts:		
Hexagon socket type:		
Stage 1	30	41
Stage 2	52	71
Stage 3 (after 10 minutes setting)	81	110
Double hexagon socket type:		
Stage 1	30	41
Stage 2	52	70
Stage 3 (after 10 minutes setting)		Tighten further 90°
Stage 4		Tighten further 90°

1 General description

The engine is of six-cylinder in-line type mounted at the front of the car. The 123 engine has a single overhead camshaft, and the 110 engine has double overhead camshafts.

The cylinder block is of cast iron construction while the cylinder head and sump housing are of aluminium.

The crankshaft incorporates four main bearings on the 123 engine and seven main bearings on the 110 engine. The endfloat is controlled on No 2 bearing.

The camshaft(s) is (are) driven by a double row timing chain which also drives an intermediate shaft for the distributor, oil pump and fuel pump, where applicable.

Lubrication is by means of a double gear pump which draws oil from the sump and forces it through a full-flow filter into the engine oil galleries where it is distributed to the crankshaft, camshaft and intermediate shaft. An oil cooler is fitted to models equipped with air conditioning.

A closed crankcase ventilation system is employed whereby piston blow-by gases are drawn back into the engine via the inlet manifold.

2 Major operations possible with the engine in the car

The following operations can be carried out without having to remove the engine from the car:

(a) *Removal and servicing of the cylinder head and camshaft(s)*
(b) *Removal of the lower oil pan and oil pump*
(c) *Removal of the engine mountings*
(d) *Removal of the flywheel/driveplate*
(e) *Renewal of the crankshaft front oil seal*
(f) *Removal of the intermediate gear and shaft*

3 Major operations only possible after removal of the engine from the car

The following operations can only be carried out after removal of the engine from the car:

(a) *Removal of the pistons and connecting rods*
(b) *Removal of the big-end bearings*
(c) *Removal of the crankshaft main bearings*
(d) *Removal of the crankshaft*
(e) *Renewal of the crankshaft rear oil seal*

4 Method of engine removal

The engine may be lifted out either on its own or together with the manual gearbox or automatic transmission, however the combined weight of the engine and transmission is considerable and it is therefore recommended that the engine is removed separately. The latter method is described in Section 5.

5 Engine – removal

1 Either completely remove the bonnet, as described in Chapter 12, or lock the bonnet in a vertical position.
2 Disconnect the battery negative lead.
3 Remove the radiator and cooling fan, with reference to Chapter 2.
4 Where applicable, remove the air conditioning compressor, with reference to Chapter 12, and place it to one side.
5 On models with rear suspension automatic level control, remove the pump from the engine, with reference to Chapter 11.
6 Disconnect the power steering pump hoses from the steering gear, with reference to Chapter 11, and drain the fluid into a suitable container.
7 Remove the air cleaner and disconnect the throttle controls, also, where applicable, remove the fuel injection equipment, with reference to Chapter 3.
8 Disconnect all wires from the engine, but identify them first for location and routing (photos).
9 Disconnect the heater hoses and remaining coolant hoses, also disconnect all vacuum hoses (photos).
10 Disconnect the fuel supply and return hoses, and the oil pressure line (photos).
11 Apply the handbrake/parking brake then jack up the front of the car and support on axle stands.
12 On automatic transmission models drain the fluid, with reference to Chapter 6, and unbolt the dipstick tube from the inlet manifold. Disconnect the oil cooler pipes and unbolt them from the engine and transmission. Also unbolt the transmission front cover and remove the driveplate-to-torque converter bolts, with reference to Chapter 6 (photos).

5.8A Engine wiring harness connector

5.8B Water temperature sensor and wiring (123 engine)

5.8C Disconnecting the TDC sensor and wiring

5.9A Top hose connection to the thermostat housing

5.9B Automatic transmission vacuum line location (arrowed)

5.10A Fuel supply and return hose location on a carburettor model (123 engine)

5.10B Disconnecting the oil pressure line

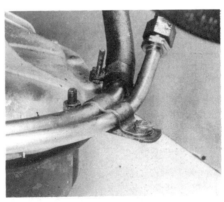

5.12A Oil cooler pipe front bracket (automatic transmission models)

5.12B Oil cooler pipe right-hand side bracket (automatic transmission models)

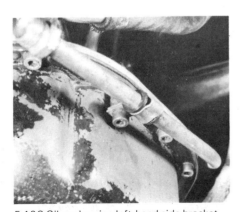

5.12C Oil cooler pipe left-hand side bracket (automatic transmission models)

5.12D Remove the automatic transmission front cover ...

5.12E ... and unscrew the torque converter bolts

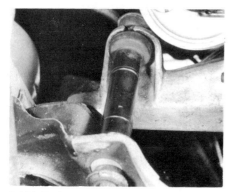

5.13A Engine mounting damper

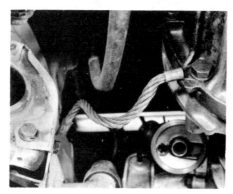

5.13B Engine earth strap location

5.16 Using an extension socket to unscrew the top gearbox/transmission bolts

5.17 Removing the engine mounting through-bolts

5.19A Removing the engine

5.19B Guiding the downshift rod from the inlet manifold as the engine is being removed (123 engine)

13 Unscrew the nuts from the engine dampers on the crossmember and also disconnect the earth strap (photos).

14 Remove the exhaust system, as described in Chapter 3.

15 Remove the starter motor, as described in Chapter 10.

16 Support the gearbox/transmission with a trolley jack then unbolt the rear mounting crossmember from the underbody and lower the unit slightly. Unscrew all the bolts securing the gearbox/transmission to the engine, using extension socket bars from the rear to reach the upper bolts (photo). With all the bolts removed, refit the rear mounting crossmember to the underbody.

17 Using an Allen key, unscrew the engine mounting bolts from below (photo). If they are seized it will be necessary to unbolt the mountings from the body. Note the exhaust shield on the right-hand mounting.

18 Attach a suitable hoist to the engine hangers so that the front of the engine is slightly raised.

19 With the gearbox/transmission supported with the trolley jack, raise the engine from the mountings then ease it forwards until clear of the gearbox input shaft or torque converter, as applicable. On automatic transmission models make sure that the torque converter remains fully engaged with the transmission primary oil pump and guide the downshift rod from the inlet manifold (photos).

20 Lift the engine from the car being careful not to damage the surrounding components. Tie the gearbox/transmission to the body and remove the trolley jack.

6 Engine dismantling – general

It is best to mount the engine on a dismantling stand, but, if this is not available, stand the engine on a strong bench at a comfortable working height. Failing this it will have to be stripped down on the floor.

Cleanliness is most important, and if the engine is dirty it should be cleaned first with paraffin. Avoid working with the engine directly on a concrete floor, as grit presents a real source of trouble.

As parts are removed, clean them in a paraffin bath. However do not immerse parts with internal oilways in paraffin as it is difficult to remove, usually requiring a high pressure hose.

It is advisable to have suitable containers to hold small items according to their use, as this will help when reassembling the engine and also prevent possible losses.

Always obtain complete sets of gaskets when the engine is being dismantled, but retain the old gaskets with a view to using them as a pattern to make a replacement if a new one is not available.

When possible refit nuts, bolts and washers in their location after being removed as this helps protect the threads and will also be helpful when reassembling the engine.

Retain unserviceable components in order to compare them with the new parts supplied.

7 Ancillary components – removal

Before dismantling the main engine components, the following externally mounted ancillary components can be removed. The removal sequence need not necessarily follow the order given:

Power steering pump (Chapter 11) (photos)
Alternator (Chapter 10)
Inlet and exhaust manifolds (Chapter 3)
Fuel hoses and, where applicable, fuel pump (Chapter 3)
Distributor, HT leads and spark plugs (Chapter 4)
Engine mounting brackets (photos)
Clutch (Chapter 5)
Oil filter (Section 18 of this Chapter) and housing (photo)
Thermostat (Chapter 2) and housing
Air conditioning compressor, where applicable (Chapter 12)
Oil dipstick tube
Water pump (Chapter 2) and housing (photos)

8 Cylinder head – removal

If the engine is still in the car, first carry out the following operations:-

(a) Disconnect the battery negative lead
(b) Remove the inlet and exhaust manifolds (Chapter 3)
(c) Remove the air conditioning compressor, where applicable (Chapter 12)
(d) Remove the distributor, HT leads and spark plugs (Chapter 4)
(e) Remove the rear suspension automatic level control pump, where applicable (Chapter 11)
(f) Disconnect all wires and hoses – drain the cooling system (Chapter 2) (photo)
(g) Remove the oil dipstick tube, where applicable

123 Engine

1 Unscrew the nuts and remove the valve cover (photo).

2 Loosen the clips and remove the by-pass hose from between the water pump and thermostat housing. Also remove the housing (photo).
3 On automatic transmission models unbolt the strut between the right-hand engine mounting and cylinder head (photo).
4 Turn the crankshaft pulley bolt until both the valves in No 1 cylinder are closed and the TDC mark on the vibration damper is aligned with the timing pointer.
5 Mark the timing chain and camshaft gear in relation to each other.
6 Unscrew the timing chain tensioner plug and remove the spring, then unscrew the nuts and withdraw the tensioner body, together with the plunger (photos).
7 Unscrew the bolt from the camshaft gear while holding the gear stationary with a metal rod through one of the holes.
8 Pull off the gear, remove it from the timing chain and tie the chain to one side (photo). Note that the writing on the gear is on the outer facing surface.
9 Unscrew the union bolts and remove the vent tube from between the water pump and cylinder head (photo).

7.1A Power steering pump side bracket ...

7.1B ... and front bracket

7.1C Left-hand engine mounting bracket

7.1D Right-hand engine mounting bracket

7.1E Oil filter housing

7.1F Water pump housing

7.1G Using an Allen key to unscrew the water pump housing bottom bolt

8.0 Heater hose connection on the cylinder head

8.1 Valve cover nut (123 engine)

10 Unscrew the cylinder head bolts in the reverse order to that shown in Fig. 1.11 using an Allen key socket. Do not forget the two bolts in the timing chain aperture (photo). Note that the longer bolts are located on the camshaft pedestals.
11 Have an assistant lift the timing chain and hold the chain guide inwards, then lift the cylinder head from the block (photo). If it is stuck tap it free with a wooden mallet. Do not insert a lever into the gasket joint, otherwise the mating surfaces will be damaged. Place the cylinder head on blocks of wood to prevent damage to the valves.
12 Remove the cylinder head gasket from the block.

110 Engine
13 Where applicable, on North American models, remove the vacuum pump.
14 Using an Allen key unscrew the bolts and remove the camshaft front covers (photo).
15 Unbolt the oil return pipe.

16 Loosen the clips and remove the by-pass hose from between the water pump and thermostat housing. Also remove the housing.
17 Unscrew the nuts and remove the valve cover.
18 Using a screwdriver, prise the springs from the cam followers.
19 Turn the crankshaft pulley bolt until No 1 cylinder cam lobe peaks are pointing upwards, then lever the valves down sufficiently to extract the cam followers (photo). Keep the followers identified for position. Repeat the procedure on the remaining valves.
20 Turn the crankshaft pulley bolt until No 1 cylinder cam lobe peaks are pointing upwards, and the TDC mark on the vibration damper is aligned with the timing pointer. Check that the marks on the camshaft gears and camshaft housing are aligned (photo).
21 Unscrew the bolts from the camshaft gears while holding the gears stationary with a metal rod through one of the holes (photo).
22 Remove the radiator, as described in Chapter 2 – although not essential this gives more working room.
23 Using an Allen key, unscrew the timing chain tensioner plug and loosen the inner plug about two turns. Unscrew the outer ring and

8.2 Removing the by-pass hose and thermostat housing (123 engine)

8.3 Right-hand engine mounting and cylinder head strut (123 engine with automatic transmission)

8.6A Unscrew the timing chain tensioner plug and remove the spring (123 engine) ...

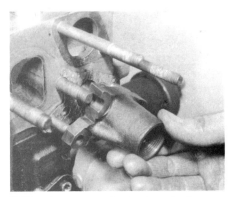
8.6B ... then remove the tensioner body

8.8 Removing the camshaft gear (123 engine)

8.9 Removing the vent tube (123 engine)

8.10 Small cylinder head bolts located in the timing chain aperture (123 engine) – arrowed

8.11 Removing the cylinder head (123 engine)

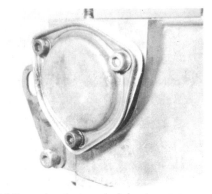
8.14 Removing the camshaft front covers (110 engine)

8.19 Removing a cam follower (110 engine)

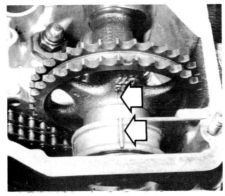

8.20 Camshaft gear and housing TDC marks – arrowed (110 engine)

8.21 Removing a camshaft gear bolt (110 engine)

8.24A Using a slide hammer to extract the upper guide rail pins (110 engine)

8.24B Removing the upper guide rail (110 engine)

8.25A From the 110 engine remove the camshaft spacers ...

8.25B ... the right-hand camshaft gear ...

8.25C ... and the left-hand camshaft gear

8.25D Front of the camshaft with gear removed (110 engine)

8.26 Removing the timing chain guide gear bearing pin (110 engine)

8.27 Removing the side guide rail pins (110 engine)

8.29 Removing the cylinder head (110 engine)

withdraw the tensioner. If it is stuck unscrew the inner plug and use a bolt to withdraw the assembly.

24 Using a slide hammer extract the pins and withdraw the upper guide rail from the camshaft housing (photos).

25 Push the camshafts fully to the rear, then pull off the spacers and gears, remove them from the timing chain, and tie the chain to one side (photos).

26 Unscrew the cover plug then using a slide hammer, extract the bearing pin and withdraw the timing chain guide gear (photo).

27 Using the slide hammer, extract the pins and withdraw the side guide rail from the cylinder head (photo).

28 Unscrew the cylinder head bolts in the reverse order to that shown in Fig. 1.8 using an Allen key socket. Do not forget the two bolts in the timing chain aperture.

29 Have an assistant lift the timing chain and hold the right-hand chain guide inwards, then lift the cylinder head from the block (photo). If it is stuck tap it free with a wooden mallet. Do not insert a lever into the gasket joint, otherwise the mating surfaces will be damaged. Place the cylinder head on blocks of wood to prevent damage to the valves.

30 Remove the cylinder head gasket from the block.

9 Camshaft – removal

123 Engine

1 If the engine is still in the car it is not necessary to remove the cylinder head, although the camshaft gear must be removed, as described in Section 8, but first prise the springs from the cam followers and, working on each side valve in turn, lever the valve down sufficiently far to extract the cam follower while turning the engine so that the lobe peak is pointing upwards (photos).

2 Remove the thrust washer from the front of the camshaft (photo).

3 Using an Allen key, unbolt and remove the bearing pedestals complete with the camshaft and oil pipe from the cylinder head (photo). If necessary use a wooden mallet to release the pedestals.

4 Withdraw the camshaft rearwards from the pedestals and, if required, unbolt the oil pipe (photos).

110 Engine

5 If the engine is still in the car it is not necessary to remove the cylinder head, however the cam followers and cam gears must be removed, as described in Section 8. If the right-hand camshaft only is to be removed, the left-hand cam gear may be left on the front of the camshaft.

6 Unscrew the camshaft housing and cylinder head bolts in the reverse order of that shown in Fig. 1.1 and lift the housing from the cylinder head (photo). Do not remove the 7 bolts indicated by arrows.

7 Unbolt the rear covers from the housing (photo).

8 Remove the thrust washers from the front of the camshafts.

9 Withdraw the camshafts rearwards from the housing (photo).

10 Remove the bearings from the front of the housing (photo).

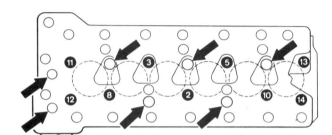

Fig. 1.1 Camshaft housing bolt removal sequence – 110 engine (Sec 9)

10 Cylinder head – dismantling

Note: All components must be kept identified for location to ensure correct reassembly

1 Remove the pressure pads from the tops of the valves (photo).

2 Using a valve spring compressor, compress the valve springs in

9.1A Cam follower and retaining spring (123 engine)

9.1B Levering down the valve to remove the cam follower (123 engine)

9.2 Thrust washer on front of camshaft (123 engine)

9.3 Camshaft bearing pedestal location dowels on the cylinder head (123 engine)

9.4A Removing the camshaft (123 engine)

9.4B Showing front of camshaft being removed from the bearing pedestal (123 engine)

9.4C Camshaft oil pipe centre mounting (123 engine)

9.4D Camshaft oil pipe front mounting (123 engine)

9.6 Removing the camshaft housing (110 engine)

9.7 Removing the camshaft housing rear covers (110 engine)

9.9 Removing a camshaft (110 engine)

9.10 Removing a camshaft front bearing (110 engine)

10.1 Removing a pressure pad (123 engine)

10.2A Using a compressor to remove the split collets (110 engine)

10.2B Removing the spring retainer (123 engine)

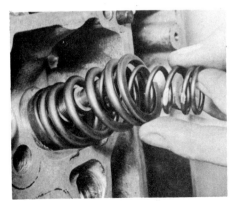

10.2C Removing the valve springs (110 engine)

10.3A Removing an inlet valve (123 engine)

10.3B Removing an exhaust valve (123 engine)

10.3C Removing an exhaust valve (110 engine)

10.3D Removing an inlet valve (110 engine)

10.4A Removing an inlet valve stem seal (123 engine)

turn until the split collets can be removed. Release the compressor and remove the retainer and spring. If the retainer is difficult to release do not continue to tighten the compressor, but gently tap the top of the tool with a hammer. Always make sure that the compressor is held firmly over the retainer (photos).

3   Remove the valves from the cylinder head (photos).
4   Prise the valve stem oil seals from the top of the valve guides and remove the spring seats (photos).
5   If necessary unscrew the cam follower ball-pins from the head (photo).

10.4B Removing an exhaust valve stem seal (123 engine)

10.4C Ball-bearing spring seat on the inlet valve (123 engine)

10.4D Rigid spring seat on the exhaust valve (123 engine)

10.4E Rigid spring seat (left) and ball-bearing spring seat (right) (123 engine)

10.4F Inlet valve stem seal (110 engine)

10.4G Exhaust valve stem seal (110 engine)

10.5 A cam follower ball-pin (110 engine)

11 Timing chain – renewal

1   Remove the spark plugs (Chapter 4) and also remove the valve cover (right-hand side on 110 engine).
2   If required the cam followers can be removed, with reference to Sections 8 or 9, to enable the engine to turn smoothly.
3   Turn the engine two complete turns and check whether the timing chain includes a connecting link. If not, place rag around the cam gear and grind away the pin ends of one single link.
4   Remove the timing chain tensioner, with reference to Section 8.

5   With the removable link on the cam gear, remove the link and connect the new timing chain using the new link (photo). Keep the chain engaged with the gear then have an assistant rotate the engine while the new chain is fed onto the gears.
6   With the free ends on the cam gear insert the link from the rear and fit the washers and clips. If a single clip is supplied, the closed end must face the direction of rotation.
7   Refit the timing chain tensioner, with reference to Section 38.
8   Refit the cam followers and check the valve timing, with reference to Sections 37 and 38.
9   Refit the valve cover and spark plugs.

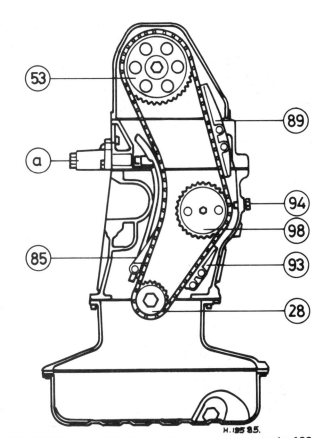

Fig. 1.2 Diagram of the timing chain components on the 123 engine (Sec 11)

28 Crankshaft sprocket	93 Lower guide
53 Camshaft gear	94 Limit pin
85 RH guide	98 Intermediate gear
89 Upper guide	a Tensioner

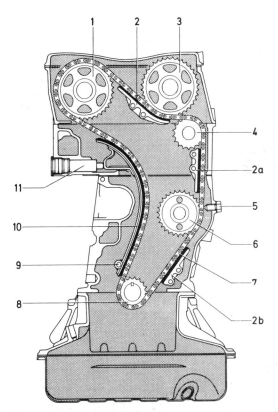

Fig. 1.3 Diagram of the timing chain components on the 110 engine (Sec 11)

1 Exhaust camshaft gear	6 Intermediate gear
2 Upper guide	7 Timing chain
2a Intermediate gear	8 Crankshaft sprocket
2b Lower guide	9 Pivot pin
3 Inlet camshaft gear	10 RH guide
4 Guide wheel	11 Hydraulic chain
5 Limit pin	tensioner

11.5 Removing the timing chain link (110 engine)

12 Intermediate gear and shaft – removal

If the engine is still in the car, first carry out the following operations:-

(a) Remove the radiator (Chapter 2)
(b) Remove the air filter (Chapter 3)
(c) Remove the timing chain tensioner, with reference to Section 8
(d) Remove the distributor (Chapter 4)
(e) Remove the inlet manifold on the 110 engine (Chapter 3)
(f) Remove the water pump/alternator drivebelt (Chapter 2)

123 Engine

1 Set the engine at TDC on No 1 cylinder.
2 Unscrew the bolt and remove the distributor guide housing and spacer (photo).
3 Note the position of the slot in the driveshaft then extract it with long-nosed pliers from the cylinder block (photos).
4 Remove the rear suspension level control pump, where applicable, with reference to Chapter 11.
5 Using an Allen key, unbolt the cover plate from the front of the cylinder block and remove the gasket (photo).
6 Unscrew the bolt from the camshaft gear while holding the gear stationary with a metal rod through one of the holes.
7 Pull off the gear, remove it from the timing chain and tie the chain to one side.
8 Using an Allen key, unbolt the pulley and vibration damper from the flange on the front of the crankshaft.
9 Using a slide hammer or puller through the hole in the flange, extract the bottom pivot pin of the right-hand timing chain guide, then withdraw the guide upwards (photos). If no hole is provided the flange must be removed.
10 Unscrew the bolt from the intermediate gear while holding it stationary with a metal rod through the hole in the gear (photo).
11 Unscrew the timing chain limit pin from the left-hand side of the cylinder block (photo).
12 Push the intermediate shaft rearwards, then withdraw the gear upwards (photo).
13 Unscrew the bearing retaining bolt and remove the washer (photo).
14 Using a suitable bolt, pull out the intermediate shaft, together with the front bearing (photo). Remove the bearing from the shaft.

110 Engine

15 Using a slide hammer extract the plug from the left-hand side of the cylinder block (photos).
16 Pull out the oil pump driveshaft using a bolt (photo).
17 Using an Allen key, unbolt the pulley and vibration damper from the flange on the front of the crankshaft.

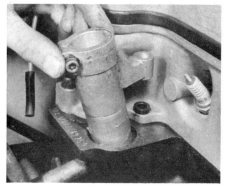

12.2 Removing the distributor guide housing and spacer (123 engine)

12.3A Note the position of the slot ...

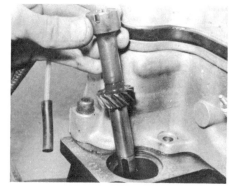

12.3B ... then extract the distributor driveshaft (123 engine)

12.5 Removing the intermediate gear cover plate (123 engine)

12.9A Extract the pivot pin (123 engine) ...

12.9B ... and remove the timing chain guide (123 engine)

12.9C Using a socket and bolt to extract the timing chain guide pivot pin (123 engine)

12.10 Unscrewing the intermediate gear bolt (123 engine)

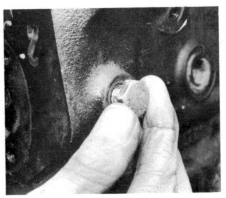

12.11 Removing the timing chain limit pin (123 engine)

12.12 Intermediate gear being removed from the shaft (123 engine)

12.13 Unscrew the bolt and retaining washer ...

12.14 ... and withdraw the intermediate shaft and bearing (123 engine)

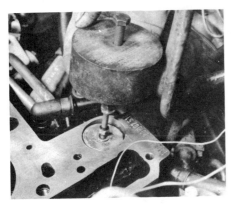

12.15A Using a slide hammer ...

12.15B ... to remove the plug (110 engine)

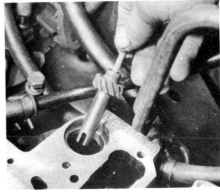

12.16 Removing the oil pump driveshaft (110 engine)

12.19A Removing the distributor housing ...

12.19B ... and drive dog (110 engine)

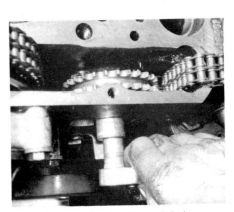

12.20A Unscrewing the oil supply bolt ...

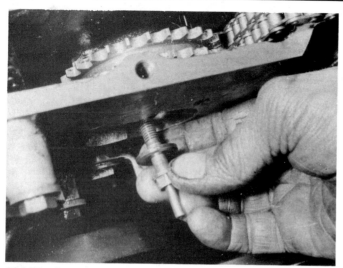

12.20B ... from the intermediate gear (110 engine)

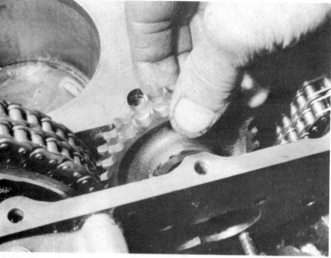

12.22 Removing the intermediate gear (110 engine)

18 Unscrew the upper plug from the TDC sensor bracket then unscrew and remove the oil pressure relief valve.
19 Unbolt the distributor housing and remove the gasket. Remove the drive dog (photos).
20 Hold the intermediate gear stationary then unscrew the oil supply bolt and washer (photos).
21 Unscrew the timing chain limit pin from the left-hand side of the cylinder block.
22 Tap the intermediate shaft rearwards and withdraw the gear upwards (photo).
23 Cover the bottom of the timing case with rags.
24 Unscrew the bearing retaining bolt and remove the circlip and washer.
25 Using a suitable bolt, pull out the intermediate shaft, together with the front bearing. Remove the bearing from the shaft.
26 If necessary, use an extractor to remove the rear bearing from the cylinder block. Alternatively it may be possible to remove the bearing by filling the internal cavity with grease and tapping the intermediate shaft or close fitting dowel rod into the bearing.

13 Flywheel/driveplate – removal

If the engine is still in the car, remove the clutch (Chapter 5) or the automatic transmission (Chapter 6), as applicable.

13.1A Automatic transmission driveplate ring ...

13.1B ... driveplate ...

13.1C ... and flywheel

1 Hold the flywheel/driveplate stationary using a wide-bladed screwdriver inserted in the starter ring gear, then unscrew the bolts and withdraw the unit from the crankshaft. Note that, on the 123 engine, the unit locates on a dowel, and on the 110 engine alignment marks are provided. Remove the plates where applicable (photos).

14 Crankshaft front oil seal – renewal

1 Remove the radiator and cooling fan, as described in Chapter 2. Also remove the drivebelts, as applicable.
2 Using an Allen key, unbolt the pulley and vibration damper from the flange on the front of the crankshaft (photos).
3 Hold the crankshaft stationary by removing the starter and inserting a wide-bladed screwdriver in the ring gear. If the flywheel/driveplate has been removed re-insert two bolts in the crankshaft and use a lever.
4 Unscrew the crankshaft front flange bolt and remove the special washers (photo).
5 Mark the flange (balance disc) in relation to the crankshaft, then use a pulley to withdraw it (photo). Remove the location dowels.
6 Lever out the oil seal with a screwdriver (photo).
7 If necessary extract the spacer and renew it (photo).
8 Clean the oil seal recess and tap the spacer into position.
9 Smear a little oil on the oil seal lip then use a metal tube to drive it squarely into the recess until flush.
10 Locate the flange on the crankshaft and tap in the location dowels (photos).
11 Fit the special washers on the flange bolt with their concave sides against the head, then insert the bolt and tighten to the specified torque (photo).
12 Refit the vibration damper and pulley, and tighten the bolts.
13 Refit the drivebelts, radiator and cooling fan, with reference to Chapter 2.

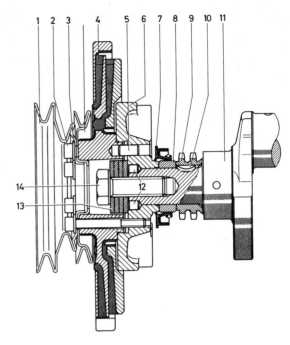

Fig. 1.4 Cross-section of the crankshaft vibration damper and pulley (Sec 14)

1 Pulley
2 Bolts
3 Washers
4 Vibration damper
5 Dowels
6 Flange
7 Oil seal
8 Spacer
9 Crankshaft sprocket
10 Woodruff key
11 Crankshaft
12 Set pin
13 Cup spring
14 Screw

14.2A Unscrew the bolts ...

14.2B ... and remove the pulley and vibration damper

14.4 Crankshaft front flange and bolt

14.5 Using a puller to remove the crankshaft flange

14.6 Removing the crankshaft front oil seal

14.7 Removing the oil seal spacer from the crankshaft

14.10A Fit the flange to the crankshaft ...

14.10B ... and insert the dowels

14.11 Tightening the crankshaft flange bolt

15 Oil pump – removal

1   Where applicable, remove the fuel pump with reference to Chapter 3, and drain the engine oil.

15.3 Oil pump mounting bolt locations

2   Unbolt the oil pan from the bottom of the housing and remove the gasket.
3   Unscrew the mounting bolts from the crankcase and main bearing cap bolt (photo).
4   Withdraw the oil pump from the cylinder block (photo).

16 Pistons and connecting rods – removal

1   Remove the cylinder head (Section 8), crankshaft front oil seal (Section 14), and oil pump (Section 15).
2   Extract the oil return pipe or dipstick tube from the sump housing. If necessary use a soft metal drift from below.
3   Unbolt the alternator mounting bracket if applicable (photo).
4   Unscrew the bolts and nuts and remove the sump housing from the crankcase (photos). Prise out the lower half of the crankshaft rear oil seal.
5   Check the big-end caps for identification marks and, if necessary, use a centre-punch to mark them in relation to the connecting rods and cylinder.
6   Turn the crankshaft so that No 1 crankpin is at its lowest point, then unscrew the nuts and tap off the cap. Keep the bearing shells in the cap and connecting rod.
7   Using the handle of a hammer, push the piston and connecting rod up the bore and withdraw from the top of the cylinder block. Loosely refit the cap to the connecting rod.
8   Repeat the procedure in paragraphs 6 and 7 on No 6 piston and connecting rod, then repeat the procedure on pistons 2 and 5, and 3 and 4.

15.4 Removing the oil pump

16.3 The alternator mounting bracket

16.4A Unscrew the bolts and nuts ...

16.4B ... and remove the sump housing

17 Crankshaft and main bearings – removal

1   Remove the pistons, as described in Section 16, or alternatively disconnect the big-end bearings if it is not required to work on the piston and bores. Also remove the camshaft gear(s), as described in Section 8, the crankshaft front oil seal, as described in Section 14, and the flywheel/driveplate, as described in Section 13.
2   Unbolt the intermediate plate from the rear of the cylinder block (photo).
3   Release the timing chain from the crankshaft front sprocket then

lever off the sprocket. Remove the timing chain (photos).
4   If necessary, unbolt the timing bracket from the front of the cylinder block and remove the oil pressure relief valve (photos). Also remove the lower timing chain guide, if required.
5   Check the main bearing caps for identification marks and, if necessary, mark them for position.
6   Before removing the crankshaft, check that the endfloat is within the specified limits by inserting a feeler blade between the crankshaft web and the thrust face of No 2 main bearing shell (photo).
7   Unscrew the bolts and tap off the main bearing caps complete with bearing shells (photo).

17.2 Removing the intermediate plate

17.3A Lever the sprocket from the crankshaft ...

17.3B ... release the timing chain ...

17.3C ... and remove the sprocket and timing chain

17.4A Unscrew the plug ...

17.4B ... remove the oil pressure relief valve ...

17.4C ... and remove the timing bracket and guide

8   Lift the crankshaft from the crankcase (photo).
9   Extract the bearing shells from the caps and crankcase, keeping them identified for location (photo). Also prise the upper half of the crankshaft rear oil seal from the crankcase.

18 Oil filter – renewal

1   The oil filter should be renewed every 6250 miles (10 000 km) on pre-1980 models and every 5000 miles (8000 km) on models 1980 onwards.
2   Place a container directly beneath the oil filter, then unscrew the filter bowl centre bolt and empty the oil and filter element into the container (photo).
3   Clean the filter bowl with paraffin and wipe dry. Prise the sealing ring from the groove in the bowl and fit a new one. If necessary, remove the spring retainer and bolt from the bowl and renew the O-ring seal.
4   Insert the new element then fit the bowl and tighten the centre bolt, while turning the bowl to make sure that the sealing ring is seated correctly.

17.6 Checking the crankshaft endfloat

17.7 Removing No 2 main bearing cap

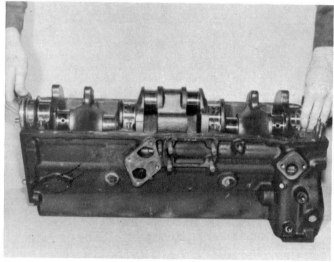

17.8 Removing the crankshaft

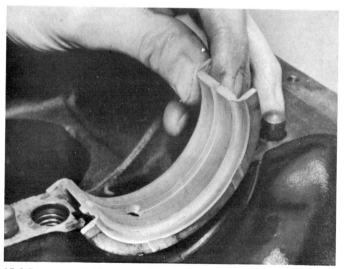

17.9 Removing No 2 main bearing shell from the crankcase

18.2 Removing the oil filter bowl and element

19.6 Removing an engine mounting

19 Engine mountings – renewal

1 Apply the handbrake/parking brake then jack up the front of the car and support on axle stands.
2 Using an Allen key, unscrew the mounting through-bolt.
3 Unscrew the nut and remove the washer and rubber from the bottom of the damper.
4 Position a trolley jack and block of wood beneath the sump oil pan and raise the engine slightly. Take care not to damage the power steering hoses.
5 Where applicable on the right-hand mounting remove the guard plate.
6 Unbolt the mounting from the body (photo).

7 Fit the new mounting using a reversal of the removal procedure.

20 Crankcase ventilation system – description and maintenance

The closed crankcase ventilation system draws blow-by gases from the crankcase through the air cleaner to be burnt in the combustion chambers together with the fuel/air mixture. The system is shown in Figs. 1.5 and 1.6. On 123 engines a water separator is included whereas, on the 110 engine, a vent valve or vent jet assists circulation.

There are no specific maintenance procedures, but periodically the system hose should be checked for condition and security.

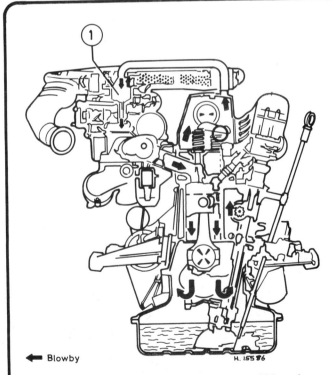

Blowby

Fig. 1.5 Crankcase ventilation system on the 123 engine (Sec 20)

1 Water separator

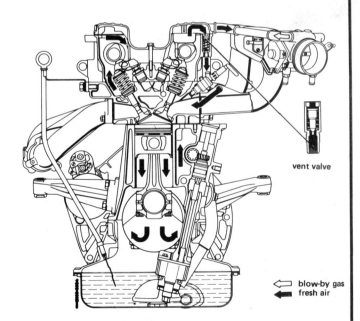

vent valve

blow-by gas
fresh air

Fig. 1.6 Crankcase ventilation system on the 110 engine with fuel injection and electronic ignition (Sec 20)

21 Examination and renovation – general

With the engine completely stripped, clean all the components and examine them for wear. Each part should be checked and, where necessary, renewed or renovated, as described in the following Sections. Renew main and big-end shell bearings as a matter of course, unless you know that they have had little wear and are in perfect condition.

22 Crankshaft and bearings – examination and renovation

1   Examine the crankpin and journal surfaces for signs of scoring or scratches. Check the ovality of the crankpins at several different positions using a micrometer. If more than 0.005 mm (0.0002 in) out of round, the crankshaft will have to be reground. Check the journals in the same manner.
2   If it is necessary to regrind the crankshaft and to fit new bearings, your Mercedes dealer will decide how much to grind off and he will supply new oversize shell bearings to suit. Details of regrinding tolerances and bearings are given in the Specifications.
3   If the endfloat is outside the specified tolerance, renew the main bearing shells. It is recommended that the bearing shells are always renewed at the time of a major engine overhaul, even if they appear to

be in good condition. If the crankshaft has been checked and found to be fit for further service without regrinding, make sure that any new bearing shells are identical to those being discarded, either standard or undersize.
4   An accurate method of determining bearing wear is by the use of Plastigage. The plastic filament is located across the journal which must be dry. The cap is then fitted and the bolts/nuts tightened to the specified torque. On removal of the cap the width of the filament is checked with a gauge and the running clearance compared with that given in the Specifications (photos).
5   On manual gearbox models, if the spigot bearing in the rear of the crankshaft is rough or noisy when rotated, extract it with a suitable puller and drive in a new bearing and cover.

23 Connecting rods and bearings – examination and renovation

1   Big-end bearing failure is indicated by a knocking from within the crankcase and a slight drop in oil pressure.
2   Examine the big-end bearing surfaces for pitting and scoring. Renew the shells where necessary with ones of exact size to the originals. Where the crankshaft has been reground, the correct undersize big-end shell bearings will be supplied by the repairer (photo).

22.4A Place a filament of Plastigage on the crankshaft journal, tighten the cap ...

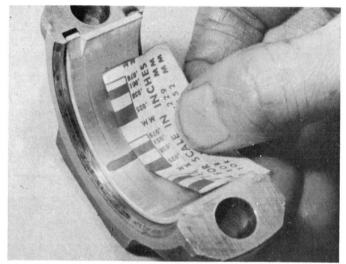

22.4B ... then check the running clearance with the gauge

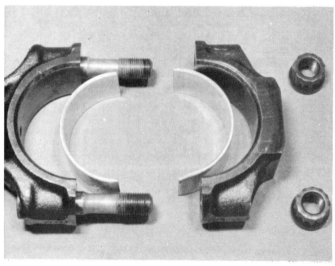

23.2 Big-end bearing components

23.3 Checking the connecting rod studs for stretching

23.5 Gudgeon pin retaining circlip location

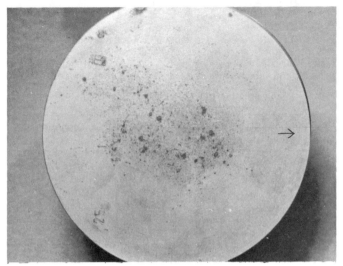
23.7 Front facing arrow on the piston crown

3   Check each connecting rod for bending or twisting and check that the stud width is not less than the specified minimum.

4   Fit each connecting rod to its crankpin on the crankshaft, complete with bearing shells, and tighten the cap bolts to the specified torque setting. Now check the side float which should be within the specified limits. Excessive side float will mean that new connecting rods must be fitted.

5   The piston may be removed from the connecting rod after extracting the circlip from each end of the gudgeon pin and pressing the pin from the connecting rod small end. The pistons do not need to be warmed as the gudgeon pins are a floating fit in them (photo).

6   Renew the small end bush and gudgeon pin as necessary. The weight deviation between any two of the six connecting rods must not exceed 5.0g (0.18 oz).

7   Refit the piston so that, with the arrow on the crown facing forwards, the shell tab locations are to the left-hand side of the engine (photo).

24 Piston and piston rings – examination and renovation

1   If the original pistons are to be refitted, carefully remove the piston rings by opening each of them in turn, just enough to enable them to ride over the lands of the piston body.

24.6 Checking the piston ring side clearance

2   In order to prevent the lower rings dropping into an empty groove higher up the piston as they are removed, it is helpful to use two or three narrow strips of tin or old feeler blades inserted behind the ring at equidistant points and then to employ a twisting motion to slide the ring from the piston.

3   Clean the grooves and rings free from carbon, taking care not to scratch the aluminium surfaces of the pistons.

4   If new rings are to be fitted, the top compression ring should be stepped to prevent it impinging on the 'wear ring' which will almost certainly have been formed at the top of the cylinder bore.

5   Before fitting the rings to the pistons, push each ring in turn down to the bottom of its respective cylinder bore (use an inverted piston to do this so that the ring is kept square in its bore) and then measure the ring end gap. The gaps should be as given in the Specifications.

6   Each ring should now be tested in its respective groove for side clearance. Using a feeler gauge, the clearances should be checked against those given in the Specifications (photo). Where the side clearance is excessive, renew the piston as it will be the groove (width) that is worn.

7   Refit the rings and space the gaps evenly around the piston.

25 Cylinder bores – examination and renovation

1   The cylinder bores must be examined for taper, ovality, scoring and scratches. Start by carefully examining the top of the cylinder bores. If they are at all worn, a very slight ridge will be found on the thrust side. This marks the top of the piston ring travel. The owner will have a good indication of the bore wear prior to dismantling the engine, or removing the cylinder head. Excessive oil consumption accompanied by blue smoke from the exhaust is a sure sign of worn cylinder bores and piston rings.

2   Measure the bore diameter just under the ridge with a micrometer and compare it with the diameter at the bottom of the bore, which is not subject to wear. If the difference between the two measurements is more than 0.15 mm (0.006 in) then it will be necessary to fit special pistons and rings or to have cylinders rebored and fit oversize pistons.

3   Oversize pistons are available and these are machined to provide the correct running clearance in the new oversize bores. The weight deviation between any two of the six pistons must not exceed that specified.

4   If the bores are slightly worn, but not so badly as to justify reboring them, then special oil control rings and pistons can be fitted which will restore compression and stop the engine burning oil. Several different types are available and the manufacturer's instructions concerning their fitting must be followed closely.

5   If new pistons or rings are being fitted and the bores have not been reground, it is essential to slightly roughen the hard glaze on the sides of the bores with fine glass paper so the new piston rings will have a chance to bed in properly.

6   Check the cylinder block and crankcase for cracks and damage and check that all the waterways and oilways are clear. Check the security of all the small cover plates on the side of the crankcase and cylinder block. Where any of the gaskets are suspect or leakage is evident, unscrew the cover plate socket screws, and remove the plate. Clean the plate and mating surface, fit a new gasket and insert and retighten the screws. Also check the water jacket plugs for leakage (photo).

26 Camshaft and timing components – examination and renovation

1   Check the camshaft journals for scoring and then measure them at several different points to detect taper or out-of-round. Use a micrometer to do this.
2   Inspect the bearing surfaces in the pedestals or housing for grooving or scoring.
3   Where any of the foregoing conditions are evident, renew the camshaft and pedestals or housing.
4   Renew the camshaft if the lobes are worn excessively, and renew the cam followers at the same time (photo).
5   Examine the camshaft gear(s), crankshaft sprocket, intermediate shaft and gear, and the distributor and oil pump drivegears and renew them if worn excessively.
6   Wash the timing chain in paraffin and examine it for wear. Support the chain at both ends so that the rollers are vertical. A worn chain will take on a deeply bowed appearance while an unworn one will dip only slightly at its centre point.
7   Check the chain tensioner for wear, also the chain guides and renew if necessary.
8   Check the camshaft oil pipe(s) and holes for blockage and, on the 110 engine, check the distributor drivegears for wear (photos).

27 Flywheel/driveplate and ring gear – examination and renovation

1   On manual gearbox models, examine the friction contact surface of the flywheel for scoring and discolouration caused by overheating. If evident the surface may be ground by an engineering works or the flywheel renewed.
2   If the starter ring gear is worn, remove it either by drilling and splitting with a cold chisel or by heating it quickly and tapping it from the flywheel.
3   Heat the new ring gear to 200°C (392°F) until it is a light straw colour in appearance and drop it onto the flywheel making sure that the lead-in chamfer on the teeth is nearer the engine side.

25.6 Water jacket plug

26.4 Check the cam followers for wear

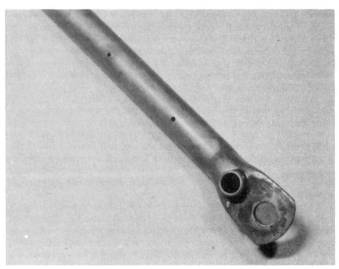

26.8A Camshaft oil pipe supply holes

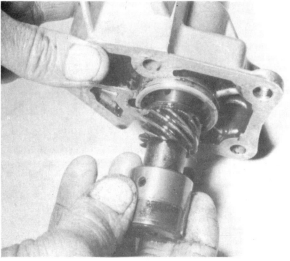

26.8B Distributor drivegear

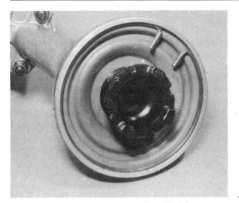

28.1A Extract the clip from the oil pick-up tube ...

28.1B ... and remove the filter and rubber stand

28.3A Removing the oil pump pick-up housing ...

28 Oil pump – examination and renovation

1   Extract the spring clip from the pick-up tube and remove the filter and rubber stand (photos).

2   Note the location of the mounting bracket, then unscrew and remove the through-bolts and unscrew the bolt from the pick-up housing.

3   Separate the housings and remove the driven gear, while identifying it for fitted position (photos).

4   Wash the components in paraffin and wipe dry. Examine the gears and end facings for wear and, if excessive, renew the oil pump. If the components are serviceable refit them in reverse order and tighten the bolts (photos).

5   Prime the oil pump with oil by turning the driveshaft anti-clockwise while pouring oil into the pick-up tube.

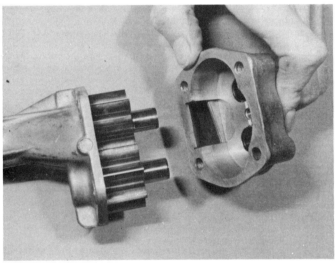

28.3B ... intermediate housing ...

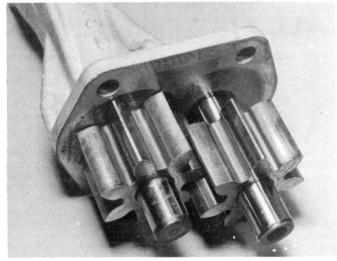

28.3C ... and driven gear

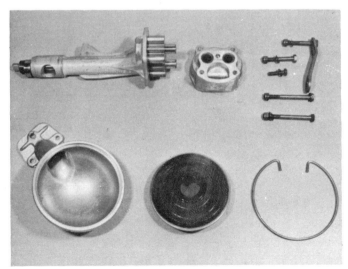

28.4A Oil pump components

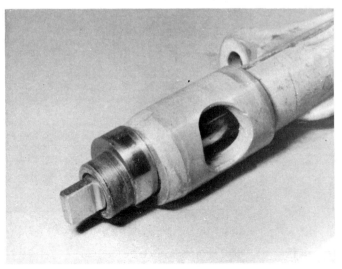

28.4B Oil pump outlet and shaft

29 Cylinder head – decarbonising, valve grinding and renovation

1   With the cylinder head removed, use a blunt scraper to remove all trace of carbon and deposits from the combustion spaces and ports. A wire brush in an electric drill will speed up the carbon removal operation. Scrape the cylinder head free from scale or old pieces of gasket or jointing compound. Clean the cylinder head by washing it in paraffin and take particular care to pull a piece of rag through the ports and cylinder head bolt holes. Any dirt remaining in these recesses may well drop onto the gasket or cylinder block mating surface as the cylinder head is lowered into position and could lead to a gasket leak after reassembly is complete.

2   With the cylinder head clean, check for distortion if a history of coolant leakage has been apparent. Carry out this test using a straight-edge and feeler gauges or a piece of plate glass. If the surface shows any warping in excess of 0.08 mm (0.003 in) then the cylinder head will have to be resurfaced which is a job for a specialist engineering company. Make sure that the minimum distance of the valve heads from the gasket surface is maintained as given in the Specifications. Use a straight-edge and vernier calipers to check the dimension (photo).

3   Clean the pistons and top of the cylinder bores. If the pistons are still in the block then it is essential that great care is taken to ensure that no carbon gets into the cylinder bores as this could scratch the cylinder walls or cause damage to the piston and rings. To ensure this does not happen, first turn the crankshaft so that the end two pistons are at the top of their bores. Stuff rag into the other bores or seal them off with paper and masking tape to prevent particles of carbon entering the cooling system and damaging the water pump.

4   Rotate the crankshaft and repeat the carbon removal operations on the remaining pistons and cylinder bores.

5   Thoroughly clean all particles of carbon from the bores and then inject a little light oil round the edges of the pistons to lubricate the piston rings.

6   Examine the heads of the valves for pitting and burning, especially the exhaust valves (photo). The valve seats should be examined at the same time. If the pitting on the valve and seat is very slight, the marks can be removed by grinding the valves and seats together using first coarse and then fine valve grinding paste. Where the valve seats are badly pitted, it will be necessary to re-cut them to give a finished seat angle of 45°. Unless you have the correct valve cutting equipment, it is best to leave this to the local dealer. Normally it is the valves that are too badly worn or burned away and have to be renewed and then ground into their seats. Fitting of new valve seats should be left to your dealer.

7   Valve grinding is carried out as follows. Smear a trace of coarse carborundum paste on the seat face and apply a suction grinder tool to the valve head. With a semi-rotary motion, grind the valve head to its seat, lifting the valve occasionally to redistribute the grinding paste. When a dull matt, even surface finish is produced on both the valve seat and the valve, wipe off the paste and repeat the process with fine carborundum paste, lifting and turning the valve to distribute the paste as before. A light spring placed under the valve head will greatly ease this operation. When a smooth unbroken ring of light grey matt finish is produced, on both valve and valve seat faces, the grinding operation is completed.

8   Scrape away all carbon from the valve head and the valve stem. Carefully clean away every trace of grinding compound, taking great care to leave none in the ports or in the valve guides. Clean the valves and valve seats with a paraffin-soaked rag then with a dry rag, and finally, if an air line is available, blow the valves, valve guides and valve ports clean.

9   To test for wear in a valve guide, insert a new unworn valve and check to see whether it rocks from side to side. If it does, the guide must be driven out of the cylinder head using a suitable mandrel. Always fit an oversize guide (+ 0.012 mm) in order to maintain the interference fit of the guide in the head. Before fitting the guide, heat the cylinder head to between 80 and 90°C (176 and 194°F) and cool the guide in liquid nitrogen or dry ice if possible. Drive in the guide until the circlip is tight against the upper surface of the cylinder head.

10   Check the valve springs for free length by comparison with a new spring and renew them if necessary.

11   Check the spring seat bearings, where applicable, and renew them if necessary.

30 Engine reassembly – general

1   To ensure maximum life with minimum trouble from a rebuilt engine, not only must everything be correctly assembled, but it must also be spotlessly clean. All oilways must be clear, and locking washers and spring washers must be fitted where indicated. Oil all bearings and other working surfaces thoroughly with engine oil during assembly.

2   Before assembly begins, renew any bolts or studs with damaged threads.

3   Gather together a torque wrench, oil can, clean rag and a set of engine gaskets and oil seals, together with a new oil filter.

31 Crankshaft and main bearings – refitting

1   Fit the upper half of the crankshaft rear oil seal to the groove in the crankcase. Note that after fitting, the seal ends must protrude by 0.5 mm (0.020 in). Use an oiled hammer handle to press in the seal and cut it off as necessary (photos).

2   Wipe clean the main bearing shell locations, the crankshaft journals and the backs of the main bearing shells.

3   Fit the main bearing upper shells to the crankcase and lubricate them with oil (photo).

29.2 Checking the valve head-to-gasket surface dimension

29.6 A badly burnt exhaust valve

Fig. 1.7 Checking the intermediate plate centering (Sec 31)

31.1B Pressing in the crankshaft rear oil seal in the crankcase prior to cutting

4   Lower the crankshaft onto the bearing shells (photo).

5   Fit the main bearing lower shells to the main bearing caps and lubricate them with oil.

6   Fit the main bearing caps and insert the bolts, noting that the oil pump mounting bolt is located on the front cup (photo).

7   Lightly tighten all the main bearing cap bolts, then fully tighten them to the specified torque in a progressive manner (photo).

8   Check that the crankshaft rotates freely, then check that the endfloat is within the specified limits.

9   Fit the timing bracket (and lower timing chain guide if removed) to the cylinder block, fit the oil pressure relief valve and tighten the plugs.

10 Locate the timing chain loosely on the crankshaft then check that the Woodruff key is in the groove and tap the timing sprocket on until the timing chain can be located on it (photo). If the sprocket was tight to remove, heat it to 80°C (176°F) before fitting it.

11 Fit the intermediate plate to the rear of the cylinder block, insert the bolts and lightly tighten. Check that the plate is central over the crankshaft preferably using a dial gauge (see Fig. 1.7) then fully tighten the bolts.

12 Refit the flywheel/driveplate (Section 34), the crankshaft front oil seal (Section 14), the camshaft gear(s) (Section 38) and the pistons (Section 32), where applicable.

31.3 Lubricating the main bearing upper shells

31.1A Rear oil seal groove and spike in crankcase

31.4 Crankshaft in the rear main bearing showing rear oil seal (arrowed)

31.6 Front main bearing cap showing oil pump mounting bolt

31.7 Tightening the main bearing cap bolts

31.10 Locate the timing chain loosely on the crankshaft

32 Pistons and connecting rods – refitting

1   Clean the backs of the big-end bearing shells and the recesses in the connecting rods and big-end caps (photo).

2   Press the bearing shells into the connecting rods and caps with the tabs in the cut-outs and oil them liberally.

3   Lubricate the cylinder bores with engine oil.

4   Fit a ring compressor to No 1 piston then insert the piston and connecting rod into No 1 cylinder. With No 1 crankpin at its lowest point, drive the piston carefully into the cylinder with the wooden handle of a hammer, and at the same time guide the connecting rod onto the crankpin (photos). Make sure that the arrow on the piston crown is facing the front of the engine.

5   Oil the crankpin then fit the big-end bearing cap in its previously noted position, and tighten the nuts to the specified torque (photos). Check that the crankshaft turns freely.

6   With the piston at TDC use vernier calipers to determine the distance between the piston crown and the cylinder block top surface (photo). It should be as given in the Specifications.

7   Repeat the procedures given in paragraphs 4 to 6 inclusive on the remaining pistons.

8   Fit the lower half of the crankshaft rear oil seal to the groove in the sump housing (photo). Note that after fitting, the seal ends must protrude by 0.5 mm (0.020 in). Use an oiled hammer handle to press in the seal, and cut it off as necessary.

9   Clean the mating surfaces of the sump housing and crankcase then smear them with sealing compound.

10   Locate the sump housing on the crankcase, then insert and tighten the bolts (photo).

11   If applicable, fit the alternator bracket and tighten the bolts.

12   Apply sealing compound to the oil return pipe or dipstick tube and press it into the sump housing.

13   Refit the oil pump (Section 33), crankshaft front oil seal (Section 14) and cylinder head (Section 38).

32.2 The bearing shell recesses must be cleaned thoroughly

32.4A Fit the ring compressor to the piston ...

32.4B ... and drive the piston into the cylinder with the handle of a hammer

32.5A Fit the big-end bearing cap ...

32.5B ... and tighten the nuts with a torque wrench

32.6 Checking the piston height

32.8 Rear oil seal groove and spike in the sump housing

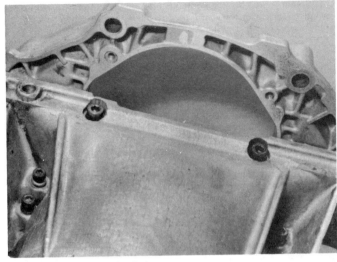

32.10 Rear sump housing bolts

33 Oil pump – refitting

1   Insert the oil pump into the bottom of the cylinder block.
2   Insert the mounting bolts into the crankcase and main bearing cap bolt, and tighten.
3   Refit the oil pan, together with a new gasket, then insert and tighten the bolts.
4   Refit the fuel pump (Chapter 3) and fill the engine with oil.

34 Flywheel/driveplate – refitting

1   Using vernier calipers check that the narrow section of the retaining bolts is not less than the Specified minimum. Renew the bolts if necessary.
2   Wipe the mating faces then locate the flywheel/driveplate on the crankshaft with the alignment marks, where applicable.
3   Insert the bolts and tighten them in diagonal sequence to the specified torque while holding the flywheel/driveplate stationary using a wide-bladed screwdriver inserted in the starter ring gear (photo).
4   Refit the automatic transmission (Chapter 6) or clutch (Chapter 5), as applicable.

34.3 Tightening the flywheel/driveplate bolts

35 Intermediate gear and shaft – refitting

110 Engine

1   Using a soft metal drift, drive the shaft rear bearing into the cylinder block until flush. Note that the groove must be uppermost.
2   Locate the front bearing on the intermediate shaft then oil the rear bearing and insert them into the block. Make sure that the Woodruff key is in the shaft groove.
3   Fit the retaining washer, together with the bolt and circlip, and tighten the bolt.
4   Locate the intermediate gear on the shaft, and pull out the shaft with a bolt (photo). Make sure that the timing chain is engaged with the gear teeth.
5   Insert the oil supply bolt and washer, and tighten to the specified torque while holding the intermediate gear stationary.
6   Insert the timing chain limit pin in the cylinder block and tighten.
7   Engage the drive dog with the intermediate gear then fit the distributor housing, with the drivegear slot aligned with the drive dog, together with a new gasket (photo). Insert and tighten the bolts.
8   If applicable, insert the oil pressure relief valve in the TDC sensor bracket. Coat the plug threads with sealing compound then insert and tighten.
9   Fit the vibration damper and pulley, then insert and tighten the bolts.
10 Using a bolt, insert the oil pump driveshaft so that it engages the oil pump.

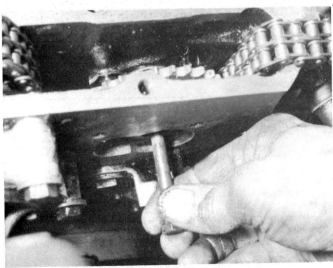

35.4 Pulling the intermediate shaft into the gear (110 engine)

11 Smear a little sealing compound on the plug then drive it into the cylinder block over the oil pump driveshaft (photo).

123 Engine
12 Oil the intermediate shaft front bearing and locate it on the intermediate shaft, then insert them into the block with the bearing recess towards the bolt hole. Make sure that the Woodruff key is in the shaft groove.
13 Fit the retaining washer and tighten the bolt.
14 Locate the intermediate gear on the shaft, and pull out the shaft with a bolt. Make sure that the timing chain is engaged with the gear teeth.
15 Insert the bolt and tighten while holding the intermediate gear stationary.
16 Insert the timing chain limit pin in the cylinder block and tighten.
17 Insert the right-hand timing chain guide and align the pivot hole. Apply a little sealing compound to the pivot pin flange then use a slide hammer to drive it into the block.
18 Fit the vibration damper and pulley, then insert and tighten the bolts.
19 Engage the camshaft gear with the timing chain then push it onto the camshaft. Insert the bolt and tighten it while holding the gear stationary with a metal rod through one of the holes.
20 Fit the cover plate to the front of the cylinder block, together with a new gasket, insert the bolts and tighten them evenly.
21 Where applicable, refit the rear suspension level control pump, with reference to Chapter 11.
22 Check that the engine is still set at TDC on No 1 cylinder, then insert the distributor driveshaft so that the slot is approximately parallel with the cylinder block with the wide segment towards the engine. This setting should be checked again after refitting the timing chain tensioner.
23 Refit the distributor guide housing and spacer then insert and tighten the bolt.

All engines
24 If the engine is in the car reverse the introductory procedure given in Section 12.

---

36 Cylinder head – reassembly

1   Grease the threads then insert the cam follower ball-pin in the cylinder head and tighten.
2   Locate the bottom spring seats and bearings over the valve guides. On the 110 engine both the inlet and exhaust valves are provided with bearings, but on the 123 engine the exhaust valves have a rigid seat.
3   Lubricate the valve stem oil seals and press them onto the guides.
4   Oil the valve stems and insert the valves in their correct guides.
5   Working on each valve in turn, fit the valve spring(s) and retainer (photo), then compress the spring(s) with the compressor and insert the split collets. Release the compressor and remove it. Tap the end of the valve stem with a wooden mallet to settle the collets.
6   Locate the pressure pads in the tops of the valves.

---

37 Camshaft – refitting

110 Engine
1   Fit the bearings into the front of the camshaft housing (photo).
2   Locate the thrust washers on the front of the camshafts, then oil the bearings and insert the camshafts from the rear of the housing (photo).
3   Fit the housing rear covers, together with new gaskets, then insert and tighten the bolts.
4   Clean the mating faces of the camshaft housing and cylinder head, and locate the metal foil gasket on the cylinder head.
5   Lower the camshaft housing onto the head then dip the bolts in engine oil and insert them with the washers.
6   Tighten the bolts in three stages to the specified torques in the reverse order to that shown in Fig. 1.1. Check that both camshafts are free to be turned.
7   Refit the cam gears and cam followers, as described in Section 38.

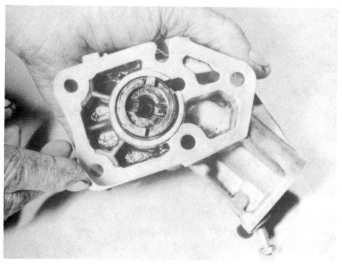

35.7 Gasket located on the distributor housing (110 engine)

35.11 Fitting the oil pump driveshaft plug (110 engine)

36.5 The valve spring retainer must be fitted this way round

37.1 Fitting the camshaft front bearings (110 engine)

37.2 Lubricating the camshaft bearings (110 engine)

123 Engine

8   If removed, refit the oil pipe to the camshaft pedestals and tighten the bolts.

9   Oil the pedestal bearings and insert the camshaft from the rear (photo).

10 Locate the pedestals on the cylinder head dowels, and insert the bolts.

11 Tighten the bolts evenly to the specified torque, working from the centre outwards, then slightly loosen the other head bolts and tighten them to the specified torque, again working from the centre outwards.

12 Check that the camshaft turns freely. If not the bolts have been tightened unevenly and the tightening procedure should be carried out again.

13 Locate the thrust washer on the front of the camshaft.

14 Refit the camshaft gear, as described in Section 38, if the engine is in the car.

15 Working on each valve in turn, rotate the engine or camshaft so that the lobe peak is pointing upwards, then dip the cam follower in oil and fit it while levering the valve downwards. Hook the spring on the clip and lever it over the cam follower with a screwdriver (photo).

16 Note that valve clearances must be adjusted *after* refitting the head, otherwise the clearances will be reduced when the head is tightened down.

17 Using a feeler blade, check that the camshaft endfloat is as given in the Specifications (photo).

37.9 Lubricating the camshaft bearings (123 engine)

37.15 Fitting the cam follower retaining spring (123 engine)

37.17 Checking the camshaft endfloat (123 engine)

38 Cylinder head – refitting

1   Clean the faces of the cylinder head and cylinder block, then locate the new gasket on the dowels on the block (photos). *Do not use jointing compound.*
2   Set No 1 piston at TDC and check that the camshaft TDC marks are aligned and/or No 1 camshaft lobes are pointing upwards.

110 Engine

3   Place two lengths of wood on the front and rear of the gasket (photo).
4   Have an assistant insert the timing chain up through the aperture in the cylinder head, and hold the right-hand chain guide inwards, then lower the cylinder head onto the lengths of wood.
5   Remove the front length of wood and lower the cylinder head onto the dowel, then similarly lower the rear of the head onto the rear dowel.
6   Dip the head bolts in oil and insert them, together with the washers.
7   Tighten the bolts evenly in three or four stages to the specified torque, using the sequence shown in Fig. 1.8 (photos).
8   Check that both camshafts can be turned freely.
9   Locate the side guide rail in the cylinder head and align the holes

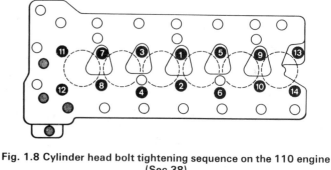

Fig. 1.8 Cylinder head bolt tightening sequence on the 110 engine (Sec 38)

then drive in the retaining pins with a slide hammer making sure that the timing chain is located correctly.
10   Using a length of welding wire, lower the guide gear into position engaged with the timing chain (photo). Oil the bearing pin then drive it through the gear using a slide hammer. Remove the wire.
11   Insert and tighten the cover plug. Fit a new washer if necessary.
12   Move the camshafts to the rear and fit the gears and spacers, making sure that the timing chain is correctly located.
13   Insert the bolts with spacers into the camshafts and screw them in finger tight.

38.1A Cylinder head gasket fitted to block (110 engine)

38.1B Location dowel position on the block (110 engine)

38.1C Cylinder head gasket fitted to block (123 engine)

38.1D Location dowel position on the block (123 engine)

38.3 Place two lengths of wood on the gasket when fitting the cylinder head (110 engine)

38.7A Cylinder head bolt at the front (110 engine)

38.7B Tightening the cylinder head bolts (110 engine)

38.7C Tightening the small cylinder head bolts (110 engine)

38.10 Lowering the guide gear into position (110 engine)

38.20 Tightening a camshaft bolt (110 engine)

14 Check that the TDC mark on the vibration damper is aligned with the timing pointer, and that the TDC marks on the camshaft gears and camshaft housing are also aligned.

15 Locate the upper guide rail in the camshaft bearing then use a slide hammer to drive in the pins.

16 Using a metal rod through the timing chain tensioner aperture, depress the guide rail to tension the chain then recheck that the TDC marks are still aligned, as in paragraph 14.

17 On the early type tensioner it must be dismantled and reset to the starting point – do not fully tighten the spring tension plug, but turn it one or two turns. On the later type dismantle the unit and then assemble it during refitting.

18 Insert the tensioner components and tighten the plugs and outer ring.

19 Rotate the engine two complete turns and recheck the TDC timing marks.

20 Working on each camshaft in turn, hold the gear stationary with a metal rod through one of the holes and tighten the bolt (photo).

21 Refit the radiator, if applicable (Chapter 2).

22 Working on each valve in turn, rotate the engine so that the lobe peak is pointing upwards, then dip the cam follower in oil and fit it while levering the valve downwards. Hook the spring on the clip and lever it over the cam follower with a screwdriver.

23 Adjust the valve clearances, as described in Section 41.

24 Fit the valve cover, together with a new gasket, and tighten the nuts.

25 Fit the thermostat housing with a new gasket and tighten the bolts.

26 Fit the by-pass hose between the water pump and thermostat housing, and tighten the clips.

27 Fit the oil return pipe with a new gasket and tighten the bolt.

28 Fit the camshaft front covers with new gaskets and tighten the bolts.

29 Where applicable, on North American models, refit the vacuum pump.

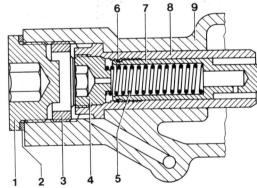

Fig. 1.10 Cross-section of the later type timing chain tensioner set for refitting (Sec 38)

1 Plug
2 Washer
3 Ring
4 Plug
5 Spring
6 Clip
7 Plunger
8 Tensioner body
9 Cylinder head

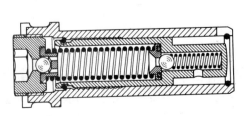

Fig. 1.9 Cross-section of the early type timing chain tensioner set for refitting (Sec 38)

123 Engine

30 Have an assistant insert the timing chain up through the aperture in the cylinder head and hold the chain guide inwards, then lower the cylinder head onto the gasket and locating dowel.

31 Dip the head bolts in oil, then insert them together with the washers.

32 Tighten the bolts evenly in two stages to the specified torques using the sequence shown in Fig. 1.11 (photo). Check that the camshaft can be turned freely. Do not forget the two bolts in the timing chain aperture.

33 Fit the vent tube between the water pump and cylinder head, insert the union bolts with new washers and tighten.

34 Check that the TDC mark on the vibration damper is aligned with the timing pointer, and that the camshaft TDC mark is aligned with the mark on the front pedestal (photo).

35 Engage the camshaft gear with the timing chain so that the Woodruff key is aligned, then push it onto the camshaft. Insert the bolt and spacer and screw in the bolt finger tight.

36 Using a metal rod through the timing chain tensioner aperture depress the guide rail to tension the chain then recheck that the TDC marks are still aligned, as in paragraph 34.

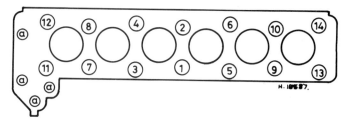

Fig. 1.11 Cylinder head bolt tightening sequence on the 123 engine (Sec 38)

37 Refit the timing chain tensioner housing, then insert the plunger and spring and tighten the plug (photo).

38 Hold the camshaft gear stationary using a metal rod through one of the holes, then tighten the bolt to the specified torque (photo).

39 On automatic transmission models refit the strut between the right-hand engine mounting and cylinder head.

40 Fit the thermostat housing with a new gasket and tighten the bolts.

38.32 Tightening the cylinder head bolts (123 engine)

38.34 Camshaft TDC alignment marks – arrowed (123 engine)

38.37 Inserting the timing chain tensioner plunger (123 engine)

38.38 Tightening the camshaft gear bolt (123 engine)

41 Fit the by-pass hose between the water pump and thermostat housing and tighten the clips.
42 Adjust the valve clearances, as described in Section 41.
43 Fit the valve cover, together with a new gasket, and tighten the nuts.

110 and 123 engines
44 If the engine is in the car reverse the introductory procedure given in Section 8.

39 Ancillary components – refitting

Refer to Section 7 and refit the listed components with reference to the Chapters indicated.

Apply a little sealing compound to the oil dipstick tube before pressing it into the sump housing.

40 Engine – refitting

Reverse the removal procedure given in Section 5, but note the following additional points:

(a) *The rear mounting should be freed of any tension by shaking the engine with the mounting through-bolt loosened. Tighten the bolt after*
(b) *Fill the automatic transmission with fluid and adjust the downshift rod, with reference to Chapter 6*
(c) *Fill the power steering system, with reference to Chapter 11*
(d) *Fill the engine with oil*
(e) *Adjust the throttle controls, with reference to Chapter 3*

41 Valve clearances – adjustment

1 The valve clearances can be checked and adjusted with the engine warm or cold. First remove the valve cover and the spark plugs.
2 Turn the engine on the crankshaft pulley bolt until the inlet valve for No 1 cylinder is closed with the peak of the cam lobe pointing upwards.
3 Insert a feeler blade of the correct thickness between the cam lobe and the cam follower, and check that it is a firm sliding fit (photo). If not, turn the ball-pin as necessary using an open-ended spanner or a special tool available from Mercedes.
4 If there is insufficient adjustment on the ball-pin a pressure pad of different thickness may be fitted between the cam follower and valve stem.
5 Repeat the procedure given in paragraphs 2 to 4 on the remaining inlet valves using the following cylinder sequence: 1-5-3-6-2-4; then

adjust the exhaust valves in the same manner. Note the layout of the valves as shown in Figs. 1.12 and 1.13.
6 Refit the spark plugs and valve cover, renewing the gasket if necessary.

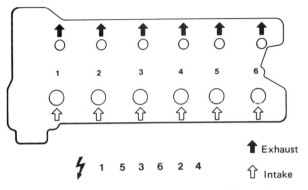

Fig. 1.13 Valve layout for the 110 engine (Sec 41)

41.3 Checking the valve clearances (123 engine)

42 Engine – adjustment after major overhaul

1 With the engine refitted to the car, make a final check to ensure that everything has been reconnected and that no rags or tools have been left in the engine compartment.
2 If new pistons or crankshaft bearings have been fitted, turn the idling speed screw (Chapter 3) in about half a turn to compensate for the initial tightness of the new components.
3 Start the engine. This may take a little longer than usual, especially on carburettor models where the float chamber may be empty.
4 As soon as the engine starts, check that the oil pressure light goes out.
5 Check the oil filter, fuel hoses and water hoses for leaks.
6 Run the engine to normal operating temperature then adjust the slow running, as described in Chapter 3.
7 On the 110 engine stop the engine then, working on the cylinder head bolts in the order shown in Fig. 1.8, first loosen the bolt $\frac{1}{4}$ of a turn then retighten it to the specified final torque. It is not necessary to re-adjust the valve clearances.
8 If new pistons or crankshaft bearings have been fitted, the engine must be run-in for the first 500 miles (800 km).

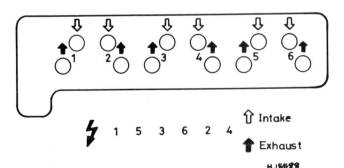

Fig. 1.12 Valve layout for the 123 engine (Sec 41)

43 Fault diagnosis – engine

Symptom	Reason(s)
Engine fails to start	Discharged battery
	Loose battery connection
	Loose or broken ignition leads
	Moisture on spark plugs, distributor cap or HT leads
	Incorrect spark plug gap
	Cracked distributor cap or rotor
	Dirt or water in fuel
	Empty fuel tank
	Faulty fuel pump
	Faulty starter motor
	Low cylinder compression
Engine idles erratically	Inlet manifold air leak
	Leaking cylinder head gasket
	Worn camshaft lobes
	Incorrect valve clearances
	Incorrect slow running adjustment
	Uneven cylinder compressions
	Incorrect ignition timing
Engine misfires	Incorrect spark plug gap
	Faulty coil or ignition system
	Dirt or water in fuel
	Incorrect slow running adjustment
	Leaking cylinder head gasket
	Distributor cap cracked
	Incorrect valve clearances
	Uneven cylinder compressions
	Moisture on spark plugs, distributor cap or HT leads
Engine stalls	Incorrect slow running adjustment
	Inlet manifold air leak
	Incorrect ignition timing
Excessive oil consumption	Worn pistons and cylinder bores
	Valve guides and valve stem seals worn
	Oil leaking from gasket or oil seal
Engine runs on after switching off	Excessive carbon build-up in combustion chambers
	Incorrect slow running adjustment

Chapter 2 Cooling system

Contents

Specifications

System type	Pressurised, with belt-driven pump, automatically controlled fan and thermostat
Radiator cap pressure	
Pressure release	14.5 lbf/in^2 (1.0 kgf/cm^2)
Vacuum release	1.5 lbf/in^2 (0.1 kgf/cm^2)
Thermostat	
Opening temperature	85 to 89°C (185 to 193°F)
Fully open temperature	102°C (216°F)
Minimum lift at fully open temperature	8.0 mm (0.3 in)
Water pump/alternator drivebelt tension	10.0 mm (0.4 in) deflection midway between water pump and alternator pulleys under firm thumb pressure
System capacity (including heater)	10.0 litre; 17.6 Imp pt; 10.6 US qt
Antifreeze/water mixture	
Protection down to −30°C (−22°F)	45%/55%
Protection down to −40°C (−40°F)	52.5%/47.5%

Torque wrench settings	lbf ft	Nm
Radiator drain plug	1.1 to 1.5	1.5 to 2.0
Water pump	7	9
Magnetic fan	15 to 18	20 to 24

1 General description

The cooling system is of pressurised type and includes a front-mounted radiator, belt-driven water pump, automatically controlled fan and a thermostat. On automatic transmission models a transmission fluid cooler is incorporated in the radiator, and on some models an expansion tank is mounted on the side of the engine compartment. The thermostat is located in a housing on the front of the cylinder head, and its purpose is to ensure rapid engine warm-up by restricting the flow of coolant in the engine when cold, and also to assist in regulating the normal operating temperature of the engine. The system is pressurised by the filler cap which incorporates a spring tensioned valve – as the coolant temperature rises, the pressure increases which has the effect of increasing the boiling point temperature of the coolant.

The system functions as follows: Cold water in the bottom of the radiator circulates through the bottom hose to the water pump where the pump impeller forces the water through the passage within the cylinder block, cylinder head, inlet manifold and, where applicable, the carburettor. After cooling the cylinder bores, combustion surfaces and valve seats, the water reaches the underside of the thermostat, which is initially closed, and passes through the by-pass hose to the water pump. Water also circulates through the car interior heater when the controls are on. When the coolant reaches the predetermined temperature the thermostat opens and hot water passes through the top hose to the top of the radiator. As the water circulates down through the radiator it is cooled by the passage of air when the car is in forward motion, supplemented by the action of the cooling fan as necessary. Having reached the bottom of the radiator, the water is now cooled and the cycle is repeated.

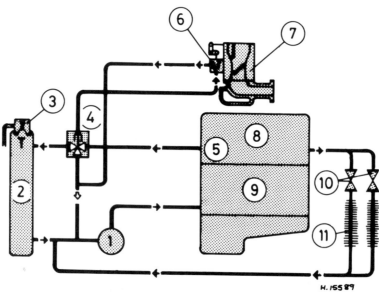

Fig. 2.1 Diagram of cooling system on carburettor engines
(Sec 1)

1 Water pump	4 Thermostat	6 Automatic choke	9 Cylinder block
2 Radiator	5 Temperature gauge	7 Carburettor	10 Heater valves
3 Pressure cap	transmitter	8 Cylinder head	11 Heater matrix

The cooling fan is either of magnetic or temperature-controlled type. The magnetic type consists of two magnetic plates which effectively transmit torque up to an engine speed of approximately 1700 rpm. The temperature-controlled type works on a hydraulic principle, transmitting torque through a film of oil controlled by a bi-metallic strip of metal.

2 Cooling system – draining

1   It is preferable to drain the cooling system with the engine cold. If this is not possible, place a thick cloth over the filler cap on the radiator or expansion tank (as applicable) and turn the cap slowly to the first detent, then wait until all the pressure has been released. Be prepared for the emission of very hot steam, as the release of pressure may cause the coolant to boil.
2   Turn the filler cap to the second detent then remove it.
3   Place a suitable container beneath the radiator.
4   Set the heater controls to the hot air position.
5   Using a screwdriver unscrew the drain plug from the bottom of the radiator and drain the coolant (photo). Refit and tighten the plug when all the coolant has drained.
6   Place the container beneath the right-hand side of the cylinder block then unscrew the drain plug and drain the coolant from the block (photo). Refit the plug.

3 Cooling system – flushing

1   After some time the radiator and engine waterways may become restricted or even blocked with scale or sediment which reduces the efficiency of the cooling system. If this occurs, the coolant will appear rusty and dark in colour and the system should then be flushed. In severe cases reverse flushing may be required, as described later.
2   Disconnect the top hose from the radiator, then insert a hose and allow water to circulate through the radiator until it runs clear from the drain hole. For more effective flushing also disconnect the bottom hose from the radiator.
3   In severe cases of contamination the system should be reverse flushed. To do this, remove the radiator, invert it, and insert a hose in

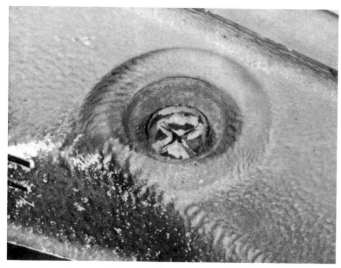

2.5 Radiator bottom drain plug

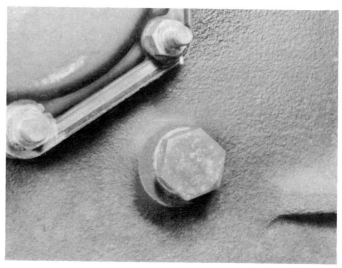

2.6 Cylinder block drain plug

the outlet. Continue flushing until clear water runs from the inlet.

4   The engine should also be flushed. To do this, remove the thermostat and check that the heater controls are set to the hot air position. Insert the hose in the thermostat housing waterway to the cylinder head and continue flushing until clear water runs from the cylinder block drain plug and bottom hose. Also disconnect and flush the hoses to the carburettor/inlet manifold (if applicable).

5   The use of chemical cleaners should only be necessary as a last resort. The regular renewal of the antifreeze/corrosion inhibitor solution should prevent the contamination of the system.

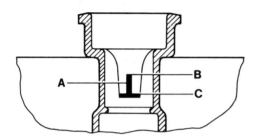

Fig. 2.2 Cross-section of the radiator filler neck level indicator (Sec 4)

A   Indicator pin   B   Warm full mark   C   Cold full mark

4   Cooling system – filling

1   Refit the radiator and thermostat, and reconnect all the hoses.

2   Refit and tighten the radiator and cylinder block drain plugs.

3   With the heater controls set to the hot air position pour the coolant into the radiator or expansion tank until full. In the radiator filler neck there are two level positions, the lower one for a cold engine and the upper one for a hot engine.

4   Refit the filler cap then run the engine at a fast idling speed for several minutes, then stop the engine and check the coolant level. Top up as necessary then refit the cap.

5   Run the engine to its normal operating temperature then check the level again, being careful to release pressure from the system before removing the filler cap.

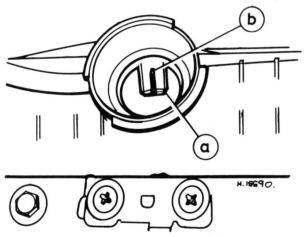

Fig. 2.3 Radiator filler neck level indicator (Sec 4)

a   Cold full mark
b   Warm full mark

5   Antifreeze/corrosion inhibitor mixture – general

Note: *The antifreeze/corrosion inhibitor mixture is toxic and must not be allowed to contact the skin. Precautions must also be taken to prevent the mixture contacting the bodywork and clothing.*

1   The antifreeze/corrosion inhibitor should be renewed every three years. Always use an approved antifreeze which is suitable for engines with aluminium heads.

2   Before adding the mixture, the cooling system should be completely drained and flushed , and all hose connections checked for tightness.

3   Mix the quantity required in a clean container using the concentration given in the Specifications, then fill the cooling system with reference to Section 4.

4   After filling, a label should be attached to the radiator stating the type of antifreeze and the date installed. Any subsequent topping up should be made with the same type and concentration of antifreeze.

6   Radiator – removal, inspection, cleaning and refitting

1   Drain the cooling system, as described in Section 2. Unless the coolant is to be renewed there is no need to drain the cylinder block.

2   Prise out the two clips and lift the fan shroud from the rear of the radiator, then place it over the fan (photo).

3   On some models equipped with air conditioning unbolt the air cooler from the side of the radiator and tie it to one side. On some models it may be necessary to completely remove the air cooler, in which case the air conditioning system should be evacuated by a qualified engineer.

4   On automatic transmission models place a clean container beneath the fluid cooler at the bottom of the radiator, disconnect the hoses and drain the transmission fluid. Cover the cooler apertures with masking tape and also cover the drained fluid to prevent contamination by dirt and dust.

5   Disconnect the top and bottom hoses from the radiator (photos).

6   Prise up the upper mounting clips and lift out the radiator, taking care not to damage the matrix or to spill coolant on the bodywork (photos).

7   Radiator repair is best left to a specialist, however, minor repairs may be made using a proprietary repair kit or coolant additive.

8   Clear the matrix of flies and small leaves with a soft brush or by hosing. Reverse flush the radiator, as described in Section 3. Examine the hoses and clips and renew them if they are damaged or deteriorated. Also check the lower mounting rubbers. Check the filler cap for damage and make sure that the vacuum valve seats correctly on the rubber seal. If necessary the cap can be tested for pressure and vacuum by a garage and the results compared with the figures given in the Specifications.

9   Refitting is a reversal of removal, but fill the cooling system as described in Section 4. Top up the automatic transmission fluid, with reference to Chapter 6, and have the air conditioning system recharged, as applicable.

6.2 Fan shroud clip location on the radiator

6.5A Radiator top hose

6.5B Radiator bottom hose, also showing automatic transmission cooler hose

6.6A Remove the upper mounting clips ...

6.6B ... and lift out the radiator

7.4 Withdraw the thermostat

7.6 The thermostat

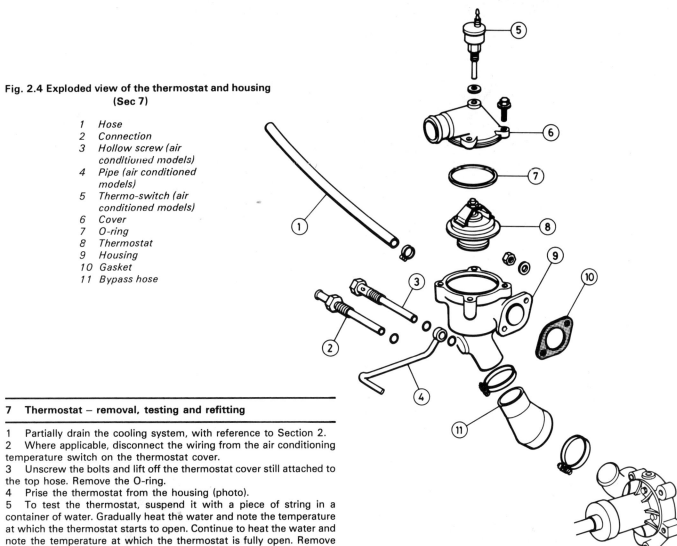

Fig. 2.4 Exploded view of the thermostat and housing (Sec 7)

1 Hose
2 Connection
3 Hollow screw (air conditioned models)
4 Pipe (air conditioned models)
5 Thermo-switch (air conditioned models)
6 Cover
7 O-ring
8 Thermostat
9 Housing
10 Gasket
11 Bypass hose

7 Thermostat – removal, testing and refitting

1 Partially drain the cooling system, with reference to Section 2.
2 Where applicable, disconnect the wiring from the air conditioning temperature switch on the thermostat cover.
3 Unscrew the bolts and lift off the thermostat cover still attached to the top hose. Remove the O-ring.
4 Prise the thermostat from the housing (photo).
5 To test the thermostat, suspend it with a piece of string in a container of water. Gradually heat the water and note the temperature at which the thermostat starts to open. Continue to heat the water and note the temperature at which the thermostat is fully open. Remove the thermostat from the water and check that it is fully closed when cold.
6 Renew the thermostat if the temperatures noted are not as given in the Specifications or if the unit does not fully close when cold (photo).
7 Clean the mating faces of the housing and cover and obtain a new O-ring.
8 Refitting is a reversal of removal, but fit the new O-ring and make sure that the ball vent valve is located at the highest point on 123 engines. Fill the cooling system, as described in Section 4.

8 Water pump – removal and refitting

1 Drain the cooling system, as described in Section 2.
2 On models equipped with a magnetic fan coupling remove the radiator, as described in Section 6.
3 Loosen the alternator mounting and pivot bolts, swivel the alternator towards the engine and release the drivebelt from the pulleys. If it is necessary to completely remove the alternator drivebelt on models equipped with power steering, air conditioning and/or an air pump, the relevant drivebelts must be removed first.
4 On models with a magnetic fan coupling, hold the unit stationary and unscrew the central bolt, then withdraw the fan unit and unbolt the pulley from the water pump (photos). Hold the pulley stationary with a screwdriver jammed between the central shaft and one of the bolt heads.
5 On models with a viscofan coupling unscrew the bolts and withdraw the fan unit and pulley from the water pump.
6 Unscrew the bolts and withdraw the water pump from the housing

8.4A Unscrew the centre bolt ...

8.4B ... remove the magnetic fan unit ...

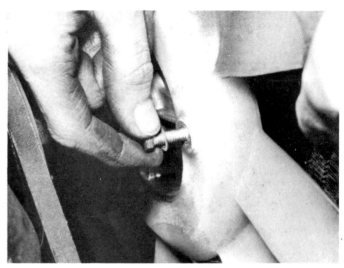

8.4C ... then remove the screws ...

8.4D ... and withdraw the fan

8.4E Removing the water pump pulley

on the front of the cylinder block (photo). If it is required to remove the housing also, it may be necessary to first remove the crankshaft damper if the damper does not have an access hole. It will also be necessary to disconnect the hoses and vent pipe (photos).

7   Clean the mating faces of the water pump and housing.
8   Refitting is a reversal of removal, but fit a new gasket and tighten the bolts to the specified torque. Fill the cooling system, as described in Section 4, and tension the drivebelt, as described in Section 10.

8.6A Removing the water pump

8.6B Water pump return hose

8.6C Removing the water pump housing

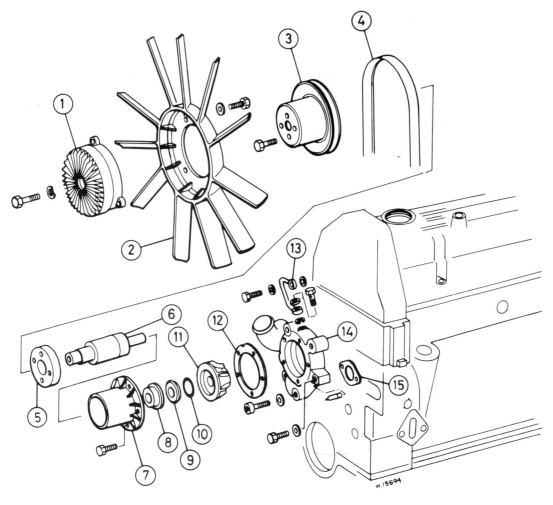

Fig. 2.5 Exploded view of the water pump and magnetic coupling fan (Sec 8)

1	Magnetic coupling	6	Shaft and bearings	11	Impeller
2	Fan	7	Housing	12	Gasket
3	Pulley	8	Sliding ring seal	13	Vent pipe
4	Drivebelt	9	Counter ring	14	Housing
5	Hub	10	O-ring	15	Gasket

9 Water pump – overhaul

Note: *If the water pump develops a fault it is generally best to renew the compete unit, however, it is possible to renew the seal and shaft/bearings.*

1 Support the water pump in a piece of metal tube with the impeller facing upwards, then use a soft metal drift to drive the shaft through the impeller and the shaft and bearings through the pump body. Remove the impeller.

2 Using the drift from the outer end of the pump, drive out the sliding ring seal.

3 Prise the center ring and O-ring seal from the impeller.

4 Clean the pump body and impeller with paraffin and wipe dry. Note that the shaft and bearings, together with a new fan hub and sealing components must always be renewed.

5 Support the pump housing with the impeller end downwards, then using a metal tube on the bearing outer track drive the new shaft and bearing into the housing until the track is flush with the end of the housing.

6 Support the pump housing with the impeller end upwards, and apply sealing compound to the sliding ring seal bore in the housing.

7 Using a metal tube drive the sliding ring seal squarely into the housing.

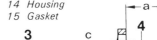

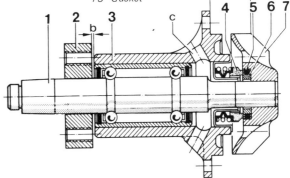

Fig. 2.6 Cross-sectional view of the water pump (Sec 9)

1	Shaft and bearings	7	Impeller
	(magnetic fan type	a	= 25.8 to 26.2 mm
	shown – viscofan		(1.016 to 1.031 in) for
	type is longer)		magnetic type fan
2	Hub	a	= 22.8 to 23.2 mm
3	Housing		(0.898 to 0.913 in) for
4	Sliding ring seal		viscofan type
5	O-ring	b	= 2.0 mm (0.079 in)
6	Counter ring	c	= vent bore

Fig. 2.7 Prising the counter ring and O-ring seal from the impeller (Sec 9)

Fig. 2.8 Using a 2.0 mm (0.079 in) spacer to position the fan hub on the shaft (Sec 9)

8   Fit the new O-ring to the counter ring, then coat the O-ring with brake cylinder paste and press the ring into the impeller, chamfered side first.

9   Clean the shaft and impeller bore, and also the sealing surfaces, then support the shaft and drive on the impeller until flush with the shaft end. Refer to Fig. 2.6 and check the dimension 'a'.

10   Heat the new fan hub on a hot plate to approximately 300°C (572°F) until it turns blue in colour. Clean the shaft and obtain a 2.0 mm (0.08 in) metal spacer in order to position the hub correctly. Position the hub on a metal tube then insert the shaft and press it up against the shim. Wait until the hub is firmly on the shaft then dip it in water and remove the spacer.

10 Water pump/alternator drivebelt – checking, renewal and adjustment

1   The drivebelt should be checked and, if necessary, re-tensioned every 15 000 miles (24 000 km). Check the full length of the drivebelt for cracks and deterioration and turn the engine in order to check the sections in contact with the pulleys. If the drivebelt is unserviceable renew it.

2   On models equipped with power steering, air conditioning and/or an air pump, the relevant drivebelts must first be removed with reference to Chapters 11, 12 and 3 respectively.

3   Disconnect the battery negative lead.

4   Loosen the alternator mounting bolts/nuts and swivel the alternator in towards the cylinder block.

5   Slip the drivebelt from the alternator, water pump pulley, and crankshaft pulley and ease it over the fan blades.

6   Fit the new drivebelt over the pulleys and tension it by turning the bolt head with the toothed gear in contact with the rack until the specified tension is obtained (photo).

7   Tighten the alternator mounting bolts/nuts and reconnect the battery negative lead.

8   Run the engine for several minutes with all electrical accessories connected, then stop the engine and re-tension the drivebelt.

11 Cooling fan coupling – checking

Magnetic fan coupling

1   With the engine stopped, rotate the fan by hand and check that there is a clear even resistance, free of any noise which would indicate internal parts touching.

2   If there is no resistance or if the unit emits noises, it should be renewed.

Temperature-controlled viscofan clutch coupling

3   Run the engine to normal operating temperature then hold the engine speed at 4000 to 4500 rpm. Do not obstruct the radiator, otherwise the coupling unit will not sense the correct temperature.

10.6 Tensioning the water pump/alternator drivebelt

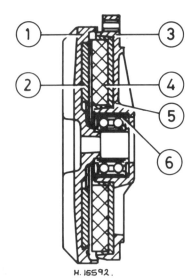

H. 16592.

Fig. 2.9 Cross-section of the magnetic fan coupling (Sec 11)

1 Primary disc	4 Permanent magnet
2 Hysteresis disc	5 Steel disc
3 Secondary disc	6 Ball-bearing

4 Using a thermometer or the temperature gauge check that when the temperature reaches 90 to 95°C (194 to 203°F) the fan speed increases by approximately 1000 rpm. This can be clearly heard if the unit is functioning correctly. Renew the unit if it is faulty.

12 Temperature gauge transmitter – removal and refitting

1 The temperature gauge transmitter is located on the cylinder head, on the left-hand side on 123 engines (photo) and the right-hand side on 110 engines. To remove it, first make sure that the engine is cold.
2 Remove the cooling system filler cap to release any remaining pressure, then refit it.
3 Disconnect the wire from the terminal on the transmitter.
4 Unscrew transmitter from the cylinder head, and temporarily plug the aperture with a suitable rubber or cork bung.
5 Remove the bung and screw it in the new transmitter. Tighten it and refit the wire.
6 Top up the cooling system, if necessary.

12.1 Temperature gauge transmitter on a 123 engine

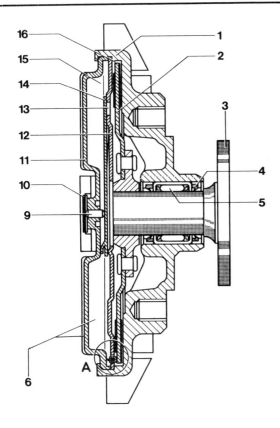

Detail A

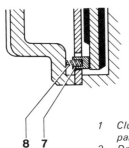

Fig. 2.10 Cross-section of the viscofan coupling (Sec 11)

1 Clutch body (secondary part)	5 Needle bearing	11 Cover with holder
2 Driveplate (primary part)	6 Cooling fins	12 Intermediate washer
3 Flanged shaft	7 Oil scraper	13 Feed bore
4 Seal	8 Spring	14 Valve lever
	9 Thrust pin	15 Reservoir
	10 Bi-metallic strip	16 Working chamber

13 Fault diagnosis – cooling system

Symptom	Reason(s)
Overheating	Low coolant level
	Faulty pressure cap
	Thermostat sticking shut
	Drivebelt slipping
	Clogged radiator matrix
	Faulty cooling fan coupling
	Retarded ignition timing
Slow warm-up	Thermostat sticking open
	Locked cooling fan coupling
Coolant loss	Deteriorated hose
	Leaking water pump or thermostat housing gasket
	Blown cylinder head gasket
	Leaking radiator
	Cracked cylinder head
	Leaking core plug

Chapter 3 Fuel, exhaust and emission control systems

Contents

Specifications

Air cleaner

Type	Thermostatically-controlled, with renewable paper element
Operating temperature	15° to 35°C (59° to 95°F)

Fuel pump

See also 'Fuel injection'

Type:

Carburettor engine	Mechanical, diaphragm; operated by pushrod and eccentric on oil pump shaft
Fuel injection engine	Electric, roller cell

Operating vacuum and pressure:

Mechanical:

Suction	0.332 to 0.465 bar (4.8 to 6.7 lbf/in^2)
Pressure	0.250 to 0.380 bar (3.6 to 5.5 lbf/in^2)
Electric	5.0 to 5.6 bar (72.5 to 81.2 lbf/in^2)

Fuel tank

Capacity:

Total	65, 70 or 80 litres, according to model (14.3, 15.4 or 17.6 Imp gal; 68.7, 74.0 or 84.5 US qt)
Reserve	9.5, 11.0 or 11.5 litres, according to model (2.1, 2.4 or 2.5 Imp gal; 10.0, 11.6 or 12.2 US qt)

Carburettor

Idling speed:

pre September 1981	800 to 900 rpm
September 1981 onwards	700 to 800 rpm
CO% at idle	0.2 to 1.2
Carburettor type	Solex 4 A 1
Main jet (stage 1)	x97.5
Idling air jet (stage 1)	100
Idling fuel jet (stage 1)	45

Float level:

110.923, 110.924 engines	2.0 mm (0.079 in)
Except 110.923, 110.924 engines	7.0 mm (0.276 in)

Vacuum governor:

Engine speed with vacuum hose off	2000 rpm
Throttle lever gap (manual transmission)	1.0 mm (0.04 in)

Fuel injection

Idling speed:	
110.984 engine	750 to 850 rpm
110.988 engine	700 to 800 rpm
CO% at idle	0.5 to 1.5
Injection valve opening pressure	3.0 bar (43.5 lbf/in²)
Fuel pump delivery	1.0 litre (1.8 pt; 1.1 US qt) minimum in 30 seconds (fuel tank at least half-full)

Torque wrench settings

	lbf ft	Nm
Carburettor	4 to 6	5 to 8
Fuel gauge sender unit	15 to 22	20 to 30
Fuel tank	15 to 18	20 to 24
Exhaust manifold flange nut	15 to 18	20 to 24
Exhaust system support bracket	5	7
Fuel injection lines	7 to 9	9 to 12
Mixture regulator	6 to 7	8 to 9

1 General description

The fuel system consists of a rear-mounted fuel tank, downdraught carburettor, continuous fuel injection system (CIS) or electronic fuel injection system, and a thermostatically-controlled air cleaner.

The exhaust system is in three sections. The fuel supply is of the feed and return type (photos).

Before working on the fuel system read the precautions given in 'Safety First' at the front of this manual.

2 Air cleaner and element – removal and refitting

1 Disconnect the inlet hose and warm air hose, where applicable.
2 Disconnect the crankcase ventilation hose.
3 Unscrew the wing nuts and release the spring clips, then remove the cover and lift out the element (photos).
4 Clean the inside of the air cleaner and cover.

1.2A Fuel return pressure valve

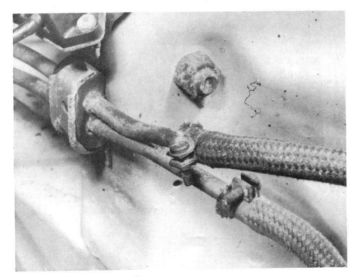

1.2B Fuel feed and return lines

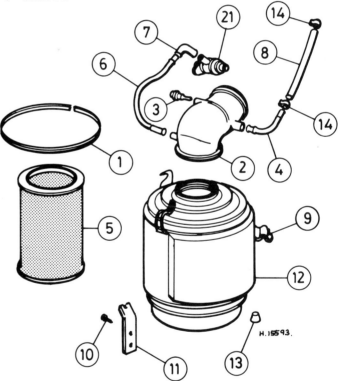

Fig. 3.1 Air cleaner components for electronic fuel injection models (Sec 2)

1	Rubber ring	9	Rubber buffer
2	Rubber scoop	10	Screw
3	Air temperature sensor	11	Holding angle
4	Plastic tube	12	Air filter
5	Air filter element	13	Rubber buffer
6	Supplementary air line	14	Hose clip
7	Contour hose	21	Supplementary air valve
8	Rubber hose to idle speed air duct on intake pipe		

2.3A Air cleaner cover clip

2.3B Removing the air cleaner element

2.5A Air cleaner hose connections (123 engine)

2.5B Disconnect this hose ...

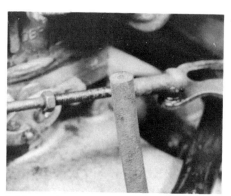

2.5C ... and this hose from the air cleaner

2.6 Air cleaner sealing ring location (arrowed)

5   To remove the air cleaner body, unscrew the mounting nuts, where necessary, and lift the unit from the carburettor or fuel metering unit. Disconnect the hoses, as required (photos). The air cleaner on electronic fuel injection models is shown in Fig. 3.1.

6   Refitting is a reversal of removal, but check the sealing ring and renew it, if necessary (photo).

3   Air intake preheater – description, dismantling and reassembly

1   On carburettor models the air cleaner inlet incorporates a preheater control which maintains the inlet air at a stable temperature. The control consists of a flap regulated by a wax-filled thermostat, which regulates and mixes air at ambient temperature with air from a shroud on the exhaust manifold as required.

2   With the engine cold, the control flap should initially admit warm air only, provided the ambient air temperature is below 15°C (59°F); but as the air temperature increases, the flap will gradually open the cold air inlet. With the ambient air temperature above 35°C (95°F) the flap will only admit cold air.

3   To remove the thermostat, first remove the element, as described in Section 2.

4   On the Knecht type, compress the spring and ease the guide from the bracket and flap control arm, then remove the guide from the thermostat pin. Unscrew the locknut then unscrew the thermostat from inside the air cleaner, or simply remove the thermostat (photos).

5   On the Mann and Hunnel type push the guide against the spring and remove it from the thermostat pin. If necessary, extract the clip and disconnect the coiled rod from the flap control arm and bracket. Unscrew the locknut, then unscrew the thermostat from inside the air cleaner.

6   Refitting is a reversal of removal, but where applicable adjust the thermostat position with reference to Figs. 3.2 and 3.3.

Fig. 3.2 Knecht type air preheater control (Sec 3)

1	Thermostat	8	Control arm
2	Internal nut	9	Extension
3	Locknut	a	= 7 to 8 mm (0.28 to
4	Guide		0.31 in)
5	Spring		

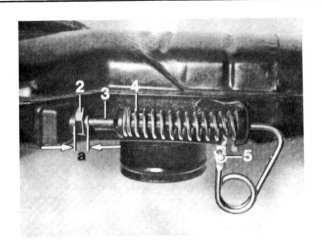

Fig. 3.3 Mann and Hummel type air preheater control (Sec 3)

2	Locknut	5	Clip
3	Guide	a	= 7 to 8 mm (0.28 to
4	Spring		0.31 in)

3.4A Air intake preheater unit

3.4B Removing the preheater guide ...

3.4C ... and thermostat

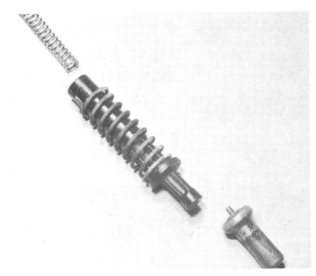

3.4D Air intake preheater control components

4 Fuel pump (mechanical) – testing, servicing, removal and refitting

1   The fuel pump is located on the front left-hand side of the cylinder block, and is driven by an eccentric on the oil pump driveshaft. To test its operation, disconnect the outlet hose and hold a wad of rag near the pump. Disconnect the low tension negative wire from the ignition coil.

2   Have an assistant spin the engine on the starter and check that well defined spurts of fuel are ejected from the fuel pump outlet.

3   If a pressure gauge or vacuum gauge is available the fuel pump can be checked more accurately. With the pressure gauge connected to the outlet, spin the engine on the starter and check that the pressure is as given in the Specifications. Similarly check the vacuum on the pump inlet. If the readings are low, first check the cover seal, but if this is in good condition renew the fuel pump.

4   At the intervals given in Routine Maintenance the fuel pump filter must be renewed. To do this, unscrew the cover screw, withdraw the cover and remove the gauze filter (photos).

5   Clean the cover and pump body with fuel, and wipe dry. Obtain a repair kit consisting of a filter, sealing ring, screw and washer.

6   Fit the new filter using a reversal of the removal procedure, but make sure that the alignment marks on the cover and body are together.

7   To remove the fuel pump, disconnect the inlet and outlet hoses, and plug the inlet hose (photos).

8   Unscrew the two bolts and withdraw the fuel pump and gasket from the cylinder block (photo). Note that on some 110 engines O-rings may be fitted instead of a gasket.

9   Clean the mating faces of the pump and cylinder block.

10 Refitting is a reversal of removal, but always fit a new gasket or O-rings, and coat the threads of the mounting bolts with sealing compound prior to inserting them and tightening.

5   Fuel pump (electric) — testing, servicing, removal and refitting

1   An electric fuel pump is fitted in conjunction with the fuel injection system on certain 110 engine models. It is located beneath the rear underbody, near the final drive unit. To test the fuel pump delivery on the mechanical CIS system, unscrew the return hose from the fuel distributor and connect a further hose from the outlet to a graduated container. On the electronic injection system, disconnect the return hose after the pressure regulator and connect a further hose using an adaptor to a graduated container. Pull off the fuel pump relay (Fig. 3.5) and connect a link between terminals 1 and 3.

2   Switch on the ignition for 30 seconds (on the CIS system also disconnect the safety switch plug on the mixture regulator). If the specified quantity of fuel is not delivered, check that battery voltage is

4.4A Removing the fuel pump cover ...

4.4B ... and gauze filter

4.7A Fuel pump location

4.7B Disconnecting the fuel pump hoses

4.8 Removing the fuel pump

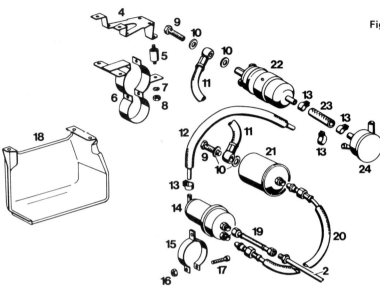

Fig. 3.4 Exploded view of the fuel pump, filter and reservoir (Sec 5)

2   Fuel feed line
4   Holder
5   Vibration dampening buffer
6   Holder
7   Snap-ring
8   Nut
9   Hollow screw
10 Sealing ring
11 Fuel hose
12 Fuel hose
13 Hose clip
14 Fuel reservoir
15 Holder
16 Nut
17 Screw
18 Protective box
19 Fuel hose
20 Fuel hose
21 Fuel filter
22 Fuel pump
23 Fuel hose
24 Damper

reaching the pump, the fuel lines are clear and the fuel filter is not blocked.

3   Servicing consists of renewing the fuel filter at the intervals given in Routine Maintenance.

4   To remove the fuel pump, jack up the rear of the car and support it on axle stands, and chock the front wheels.

5   Remove the guard plate and use a brake hose clamp to block the supply hose.

6   On CIS models, disconnect the hoses and retaining clamp and remove the fuel reservoir, fuel filter and fuel pump. Disconnect the wiring from the fuel pump.

7   On electronic injection models, disconnect the hoses and wiring, release the retaining clamp and remove the fuel filter and fuel pump.

8   Refitting is a reversal of removal, but, where applicable, check that the packing is located centrally in the retaining clamp.

6   Fuel tank (Saloon) – removal and refitting

Note: *For safety the fuel tank must always be removed in a well ventilated area, never over a pit.*

1   Disconnect the battery negative lead.

2   Jack up the rear of the car and support on axle stands. Chock the front wheels.

3   Remove the tank filler cap.

4   Position a suitable container beneath the fuel tank.

5   On carburettor models, loosen the clip and disconnect the outlet hose (photo). On fuel injection models, loosen the clip and disconnect the supply hose from the damper by the fuel pump. Drain all the fuel from the tank.

6   Loosen the clips and disconnect the vent and return hoses from the bottom of the tank (photo).

7   Remove the rubber mat from the luggage compartment and also the side panel and jack.

8   Remove the screws and withdraw the tank rear panel.

9   Unscrew the mounting nuts or bolts and withdraw the fuel tank sufficiently far to disconnect the wiring from the tank sender unit (photos). Tie the wiring to one side.

10 Release the vent hose from the neck, then withdraw the fuel tank from the car.

11 Unscrew the supply hose from the tank.

12 If the tank is contaminated with sediment or water, swill it out with clean fuel. If the tank leaks or is damaged, it should be repaired by specialists or renewed. *Do not under any circumstances solder or weld a fuel tank.*

13 Refitting is a reversal of removal, but check that the rubber strips are firmly glued in position, and, after fitting, brush suitable sealant to hose apertures in the underbody (photo).

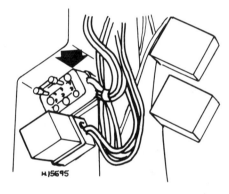

Fig. 3.5 Fuel pump relay link connection when checking the fuel pump delivery on the electronic ignition system (Sec 5)

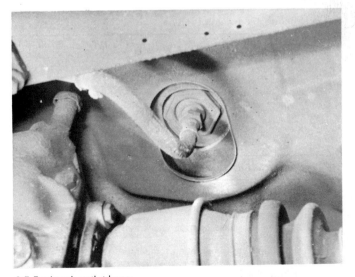

6.5 Fuel tank outlet hose

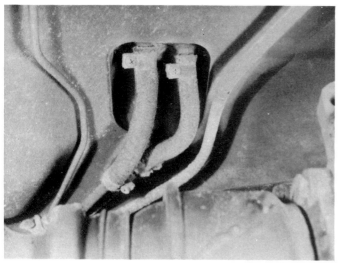

6.6 Fuel tank vent and return hoses

6.9A Fuel tank mounting nuts

6.9B Fuel gauge sender unit location in the fuel tank

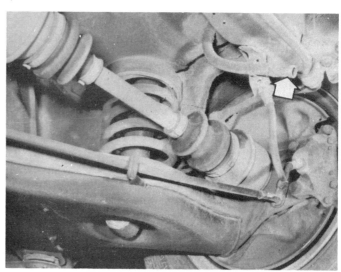

6.13 Fuel tank vent hose outlet (arrowed)

7   Fuel gauge sender unit (Saloon) – removal and refitting

1   Remove the first aid kit and tray from the shelf behind the rear seat backrest.
2   Disconnect the wiring plug from the sender unit and tie it to one side to prevent it slipping out of reach (photo).
3   Unscrew the sender unit and withdraw it from the fuel tank. Using masking tape, seal the aperture to prevent fuel fumes escaping.
4   Refitting is a reversal of removal, but use a new sealing ring. On early models make sure that the locating pin is pointing rearwards.

8   Carburettor – idle adjustment

1   Connect a tachometer and CO meter to the engine (photo).
2   Switch off the air conditioner, where fitted, and select P on automatic transmission models.
3   On models with cruise control, check that the operating cable is free of tension.
4   Run the engine to its operating temperature.
5   Check that the throttle valve lever is resting on the idle speed adjusting screw, then start the engine and check that the idle speed is as given in the Specifications. If not, turn the screw as required.
6   Turn the mixture adjustment screw(s) until the CO content is

7.2 Fuel gauge sender unit viewed through the first aid kit aperture

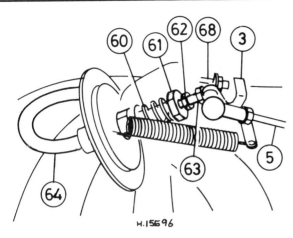

Fig. 3.6 Carburettor idle adjustment (Sec 8)

3	Throttle valve lever	63	Vacuum governor
5	Opening rod		adjusting screw
60	Spring	64	Vacuum hose
61	Nut	68	Idle speed adjusting
62	Nut		screw

correct – turning the screw(s) out enrichens the mixture, turning them in weakens the mixture. Where there are two screws set them to the same position by turning clockwise to the stop then unscrewing by equal amounts.

7   Accelerate the engine briefly, then recheck the adjustment.

8   Now adjust the carburettor vacuum governor. With the engine running, pull off the vacuum hose and turn the screw until the engine runs at 2000 rpm, then reconnect the hose.

9   On automatic transmission models, engage D and turn the adjusting nut on the vacuum governor so that the engine speed is 600 to 700 rpm.

10 On manual gearbox models, turn the large adjusting nut on the vacuum governor so that there is approximately 1.0 mm (0.04 in) between the Idle speed adjusting screw and the throttle valve lever.

9   Carburettor – removal and refitting

1   Remove the air cleaner, as described in Section 2.

2   With the engine cold, temporarily remove the radiator cap and refit it in order to release any pressure.

3   Disconnect the fuel supply and return hoses, and plug them.

4   Disconnect and plug the coolant hoses to the automatic choke and bracket (photo).

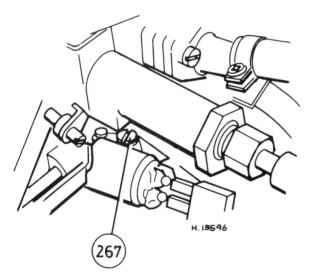

Fig. 3.7 Carburettor mixture screw (267) location (Sec 8)

Fig. 3.8 Location of double mixture screws on some carburettors (Sec 8)

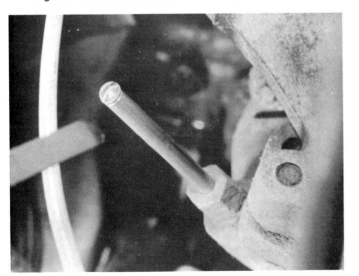

8.1 CO meter take-off point on the exhaust manifold

9.4 Coolant hose connections on the carburettor

5   Disconnect the wiring from the various components on the carburettor; and identify each wire for location with adhesive tape (photos).

6   Disconnect the vacuum lines.

7   Disconnect the throttle rod.

8   Unscrew the mounting nuts on the top cover, and withdraw the carburettor up over the studs. Remove the gasket (photos).

9   Refitting is a reversal of removal, but make sure that the mating faces are clean and always fit a new gasket. Tighten the nuts progressively to the specified torque. Finally adjust the idling speed, as described in Section 8.

10 Carburettor – cleaning

1   Remove the air cleaner, as described in Section 2.

2   Clean the exterior of the carburettor with fuel.

3   Remove the cover screw and carburettor mounting nuts.

4   Disconnect the vacuum hoses and the vacuum control rod.

5   Disconnect the choke operating rod.

6   Remove the air cleaner screw, where applicable, then withdraw the cover from the carburettor. If it is stuck, lever it only at the special recess provided.

7   Unscrew the fuel supply hose union and extract the filter (photo). Clean the filter using compressed air, then refit it and tighten the bolt.

8   Remove the fuel enrichment device, together with the air correction needles, then unscrew the idle speed air and fuel jets.

9   Unscrew the main jets.

10 Using compressed air, clean the internal channels and components removed then refit all items, but do not fit the carburettor cover at this stage.

11 Prise out the clip, and remove the float and needle valve.

12 On 123 engine models remove the accelerator pump cover.

13 Extract the plug from the accelerator pump intake port and remove the ball with a length of greased welding rod or a magnet.

14 Using compressed air, clean the float chamber and internal channels.

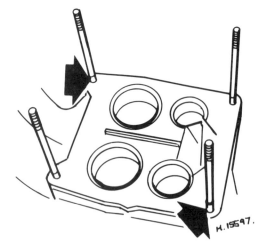

Fig. 3.9 Inlet manifold with carburettor removed (Sec 9)

Note the centering sleeves (arrowed)

15 Refit the ball, plug, cover (123 engine), needle valve, float and clip.

16 With the gasket removed, use a screwdriver to depress the short end of the float arm so that the needle valve is shut, then use vernier calipers to measure the float height in relation to the top surface of the carburettor. If the dimension is not as given in the Specifications, bend the arm as shown in Fig. 3.16.

17 Check that the open end of the clip from the needle valve faces the front of the carburettor.

18 Refit the carburettor cover with a new gasket, using a reversal of the removal procedure, and finally adjust the idling speed, as described in Section 8.

9.5A Wiring and hose connections to the carburettor

9.5B Fuel cut-off solenoids on the carburettor

9.5C Wiring connector on the carburettor

9.8A Carburettor mounting nuts (arrowed)

9.8B View of the carburettor

10.7 Removing the inlet filter from the carburettor

Fig. 3.10 Carburettor cover showing choke operating rod (43) (Sec 10)

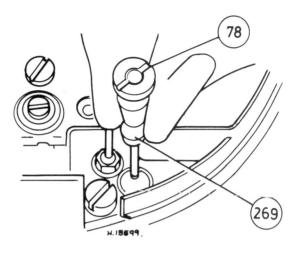

Fig. 3.11 Removing the idle speed air (78) and fuel (269) jets (Sec 10)

Fig. 3.12 Carburettor jet locations (Sec 10)

79   Main jets stages I
149 Jet needles stage II
158 Riser pipes bypass
     system stage II
193 Riser pipes starting
     mixture enrichment

224 Riser pipe TN choke
     (thermostatically
     controlled bypass choke)

Fig. 3.13 Float chamber components (Sec 10)

32 Float   34 Clip

Fig. 3.15 Checking the float level on the curved top float (Sec 10)

Fig. 3.14 Checking the float level on the flat top float (Sec 10)

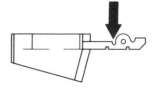

Fig. 3.16 Float adjustment bending point (Sec 10)

Fig. 3.17 Solex 4 A 1 carburettor (Sec 10)

   57   *Vacuum governor*
  198   *Actuating lever –*
          accelerating pump
  210   *Pulldown cover*
  214   *Float chamber vent*
          valve
  233   *Coolant connection for*
          TN starter
  236   *TN starter*
          (thermostatically
          controlled bypass choke)
  237   *Vacuum connection for*
          vacuum booster of EGR
          (Venturi connection)
          (USA models)
  240   *Plastic guide piece*

11 Carburettor automatic choke – adjusting

1   Remove the three screws and withdraw the ring and automatic choke from the housing after marking the choke for position (photo).
2   Check the operating lever behind the housing is at right-angles to the housing – if not, bend as required.
3   Half open the throttle valve lever, then push the choke lever to the left against the stop.
4   Check that the choke valves are fully shut and that there is a gap of 1.0 mm (0.04 in) between the operating lever and the housing. If necessary, disconnect the choke rod and bend it as required.
5   Half open the throttle valve lever again and push the choke lever to the left against the stop.
6   Mark the housing in line with the operating lever, then refit the automatic choke so that the marks are aligned (photo).

11.1 Automatic choke location (arrowed)

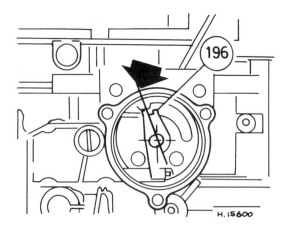

Fig. 3.18 Marking the automatic choke housing in relation to the operating lever (196) (Sec 11)

11.6 Automatic choke alignment marks (arrowed)

12.1 Vacuum governor location (arrowed)

12.3 Accelerator pump location (arrowed)

12 Carburettor accelerator pump – adjusting

1   With the engine running, disconnect the hose from the vacuum governor on the carburettor, then stop the engine (photo).
2   Check that the throttle valve lever is resting on the idle speed adjusting screw.
3   Adjust the nut on the pump lever so that the lever just contacts the diaphragm bolt (photo).
4   Adjust the stroke limiting screw so that the gap between it and the pump cover is 3.0 mm (0.118 in).
5   On automatic transmission models fitted with the throttle lever shown in Fig. 3.19, screw in the adjusting nut by 1 to 1½ turns.
6   Reconnect the vacuum governor hose.

13 Throttle control rods and cable – adjusting

1   Adjust the rods to the lengths shown in Figs. 3.20 to 3.24 (photos).
2   With the accelerator pedal fully depressed, check that the throttle valve is fully open. Where fitted, the cable should be adjusted as required (photo). Note that on automatic transmission models the throttle valve must be open without depressing the kickdown switch.

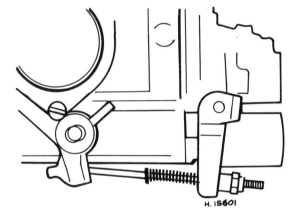

Fig. 3.19 Early accelerator pump pushrod on automatic transmission models (Sec 12)

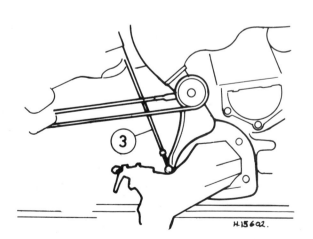

Fig. 3.20 123 engine throttle control rods (Sec 13)

3 = 252 mm (9.92 in)

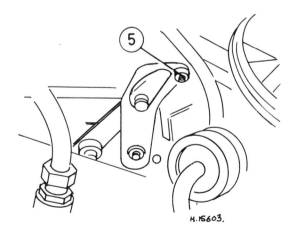

Fig. 3.21 123 engine throttle control rods (Sec 13)

5 = 139 mm (5.47 in)
     Manual transmission
     shown

Fig. 3.22 110 engine throttle control rods (Sec 13)

2 = 343 mm (13.5 in)
5 = 186 mm (7.32 in)
LHD shown

Fig. 3.23 110 engine throttle control rods (Sec 13)

10 = 306 mm (12.05 in)
LHD shown

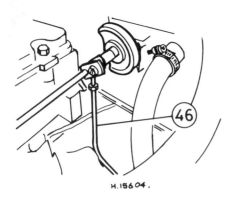

Fig. 3.24 110 engine throttle control rods (Sec 13)

46 = 186 mm (7.32 in)
RHD shown

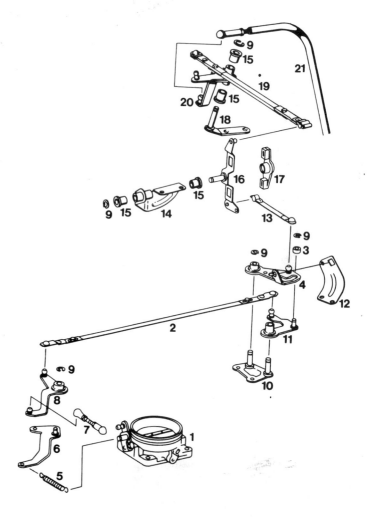

Fig. 3.25 Throttle control for 110 fuel injection engines
(Sec 13)

1   Throttle valve housing
2   Control rod
3   Roller
4   Gate lever
5   Return spring
6   Lever
7   Control rod
8   Guide lever
9   Lock
10 Bearing bracket
11 Guide lever
12 Holder
13 Control rod
14 Holder
15 Plastic sleeve
16 Lever
17 Plastic link
18 Bearing bracket
19 Control rod
20 Guide lever
21 Control pressure rod
LHD shown

13.1A Throttle control rod

13.1B Throttle control intermediate lever

13.1C Downshift rod connected to the intermediate lever on automatic transmission models

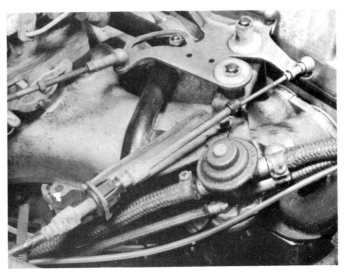

13.2 Throttle control rods and cable adjustment

14 Fuel injection system (CIS) – general

The system measures the amount of air entering the engine and determines the amount of fuel which needs to be mixed with the air to give the correct combustion mixture for the particular conditions of engine operation. The fuel is sprayed continuously by an injection nozzle to the intake channel of each cylinder. This fuel and air is drawn into the cylinders when the intake valves open.

The following paragraphs describe the system and its various elements. Later Sections describe the tests which can be carried out to ensure whether a particular unit is functioning correctly, but dismantling and repair procedures of units are not generally given because repairs are not possible.

Air flow meter

The airflow meter consists of an air funnel with a sensor plate mounted on a lever which is supported at its fulcrum. The weight of the air flow sensor plate and its lever are balanced by a counterweight and the upward force on the sensor plate is opposed by a plunger. The plunger, which moves up and down as a result of the variations in air flow, is surrounded by a sleeve having vertical slots in it. The vertical movement of the plunger uncovers a greater or lesser length of the slots, which meters the fuel to the injection valves.

The sides of the air funnel are not a pure cone because optimum operation of the engine requires a different air/fuel ratio under different conditions such as idling, part load and full load. By making parts of the funnel steeper than the basic shape, a richer mixture can be provided for at idling and full load. By making the funnel flatter than the basic shape, a leaner mixture can be provided.

Fuel supply

Fuel is pumped continuously while the engine is running by a roller cell pump running at constant speed; excess fuel is returned to the tank. The fuel pump is operated when the ignition switch is in the Start position, but once the starter is released a switch connected to the air plate prevents the pump from operating unless the engine is running.

The fuel line to the fuel supply valve incorporates a filter and also a fuel accumulator. The function of the accumulator is to maintain pressure in the fuel system after the engine has been switched off and so give good hot re-starting.

Associated with the fuel accumulator is a pressure regulator which is an integral part of the fuel metering device. When the engine is switched off, the pressure regulator lets the pressure to the injection valves fall rapidly to cut off the fuel flow through them and so prevent the engine from 'dieseling' or 'running on'. The valve closes at just below the opening pressure of the injector valves and this pressure is then maintained by the pressure accumulator.

Fuel distributor

The fuel distributor is mounted on the air metering device and is controlled by the vertical movement of the air flow sensor plate. It consists of a spool valve which moves vertically in a sleeve, the sleeve having as many vertical slots around its circumference as there are cylinders on the engine.

The spool valve is subjected to hydraulic pressure on the upper end and this balances the pressure on the air plate which is applied to the bottom of the valve by a plunger. As the spool valve rises and falls it uncovers a greater or lesser length of metering slot and so controls the volume of fuel fed to each injector.

Each metering slot has a differential pressure valve, which ensures that the difference in pressure between the two sides of the slot is always the same. Because the drop in pressure across the metering slot is unaffected by the length of slot exposed, the amount of fuel flowing depends only on the exposed area of the slots.

Compensation units

For cold starting and during warming up, additional devices are required to adjust the fuel supply to the differential fuel requirements of the engine under these conditions.

Cold start valve

The cold start valve is mounted in the intake manifold and sprays additional fuel into the manifold during cold starting. The valve is solenoid operated and is controlled by a thermotime switch in the engine cooling system (photo). The thermotime switch is actuated for a period which depends upon coolant temperature, the period decreasing with rise in coolant temperature. If the coolant temperature is high enough for the engine not to need additional fuel for starting, the switch does not operate.

14.12 Thermo-switches for the CIS system on 110 engines

Warm-up regulator

While warming up, the engine needs a richer mixture to compensate for fuel which condenses on the cold walls of the inlet manifold and cylinder walls. It also needs more fuel to compensate for

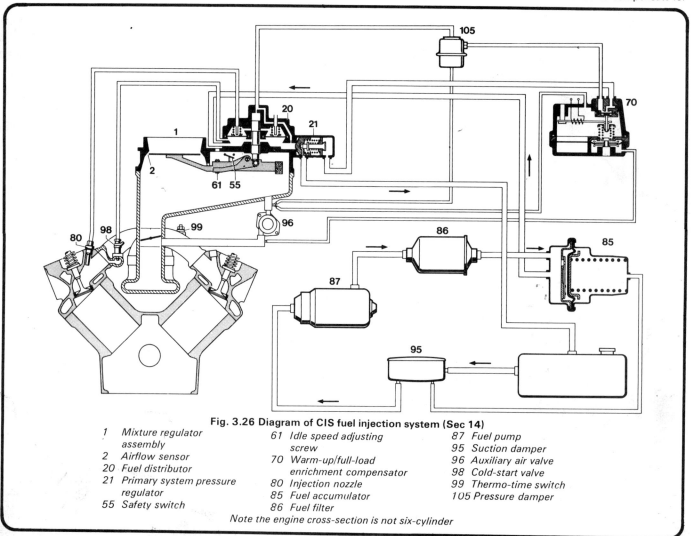

Fig. 3.26 Diagram of CIS fuel injection system (Sec 14)

1 Mixture regulator assembly	61 Idle speed adjusting screw	87 Fuel pump
2 Airflow sensor	70 Warm-up/full-load enrichment compensator	95 Suction damper
20 Fuel distributor		96 Auxiliary air valve
21 Primary system pressure regulator	80 Injection nozzle	98 Cold-start valve
55 Safety switch	85 Fuel accumulator	99 Thermo-time switch
	86 Fuel filter	105 Pressure damper

Note the engine cross-section is not six-cylinder

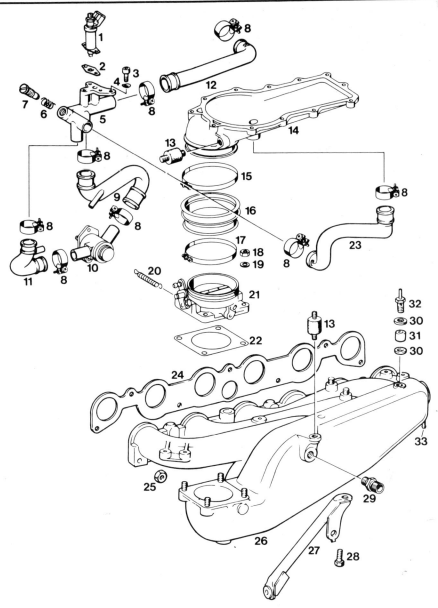

Fig. 3.27 CIS fuel injection components (Sec 14)

1	Cold-starting valve	10	Auxiliary air valve
2	Gasket	11	Shaped hose
3	Hex socket screw	12	Shaped hose
4	Wave washer	13	Vibration dampening
5	Idle speed air distributor		buffer
6	Compression spring	14	Air guide housing
7	Idle speed air screw	15	Hose clip
8	Hose clip	16	Rubber sleeve
9	Shaped hose	17	Hose clip
18	Nut	27	Support
19	Washer	28	Hex screw
20	Return spring	29	Double connection
21	Throttle valve housing	30	Sealing ring
22	Gasket	31	Spacing sleeve
23	Shaped hose	32	Vacuum connection
24	Gasket	33	Vacuum connection for
25	Nut		full load enrichment
26	Intake pipe		

power lost because of increased friction losses and increased oil drag in a cold engine. The mixture is made richer during warming up by the warm-up regulator. This is a pressure regulator which lowers the pressure applied to the control plunger of the fuel regulator during warm-up. This reduced pressure causes the airflow plate to rise higher than it would do otherwise, thus uncovering a greater length of metering slot and making the mixture richer.

The valve is operated by a bi-metallic strip which is heated by an electric heater. When the engine is cold the bi-metallic strip presses against the delivery valve spring to reduce the pressure on the diaphragm and enlarge the discharge cross-section. This increase in cross-section results in a lowering of the pressure fed to the control plunger.

When the engine is started, the electrical heater of the bi-metallic strip is switched on. As the strip warms it rises gradually until it ultimately rises free of the control spring plate and the valve spring becomes fully effective to give normal control pressure.

Auxiliary air device

Compensation for power lost by greater friction is compensated for by feeding a larger volume of fuel/air mixture to the engine than is supplied by the normal operating of the throttle. The auxiliary air device bypasses the throttle with a channel having a variable aperture valve in it. The aperture is varied by a pivoted plate controlled by a spring and a bi-metallic strip.

During cold starting the channel is open and increases the volume of fuel/air mixture passing to the engine, but as the bi-metallic strip bends it allows a control spring to pull the plate over the aperture until, at normal operating temperature, the aperture is closed. The heating of the bi-metallic strip is similar to that of the warm-up regulator.

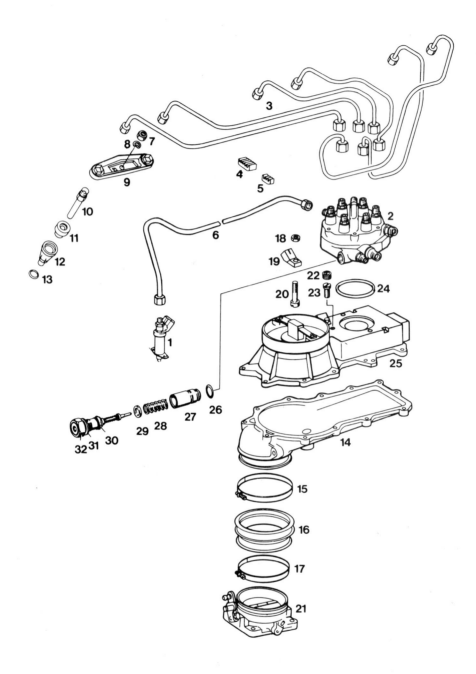

Fig. 3.28 CIS fuel injection distributor and airflow meter components (Sec 14)

1	Cold-starting valve	12	Plastic sleeve	23	Closing screw
2	Fuel distributor	13	O-ring	24	O-ring
3	Injection lines	14	Air guide housing	25	Airflow meter
4	Plastic clip	15	Hose clip	26	O-ring
5	Plastic clip	16	Rubber sleeve	27	Regulating piston
6	Fuel line	17	Hose clip	28	Compression spring
7	Nut	18	Polystop nut	29	Adjusting washers
8	Undulated washer	19	Safety switch	30	O-ring
9	Fastening bridge	20	Screw	31	Copper sealing ring
10	Injection valve	21	Throttle valve housing	32	Closing screw
11	Rubber ring	22	Closing plug		

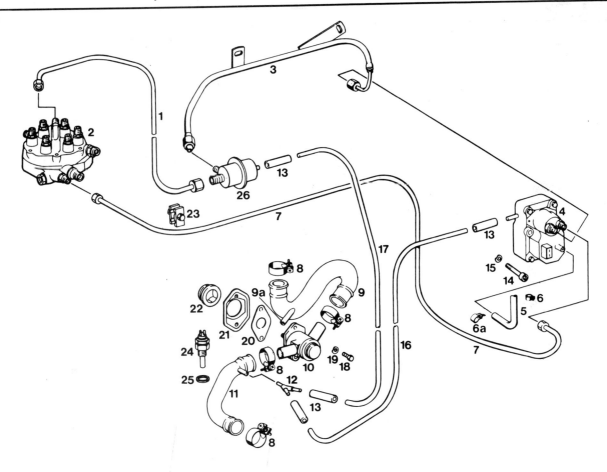

Fig. 3.29 CIS fuel injection warm-up compensator components (Sec 14)

1	Control pressure line	
2	Fuel distributor	
3	Control pressure line with Tecal device	
4	Warm-up compensator	
5	Vacuum hose for full load enrichment	
6	Hose clip	
6a	Hose clip for emission control versions only	
7	Fuel return line	
8	Hose clip	
9	Shaped hose	
10	Auxiliary air valve	
11	Shaped hose	
12	Distributor	
13	Connecting hose	
14	Screw	
15	Wave washer	
16	Leak line	
18	Screw	
19	Wave washer	
20	Gasket	
21	Flange	
22	Closing plug	
23	Fastener	
24	Thermo-time switch	
25	Sealing ring	
26	Pressure damper	

15 Starting devices (CIS) – checking

1 Test the battery and alternator for proper operation. Be sure the cables and electrical terminals are clean and securely fastened.

Cold-start valve

2 Ensure that the coolant temperature is below 15°C (59°F) and that the car battery is fully charged.

3 Pull the high tension lead off the centre of the distributor and connect the lead to ground.

4 Pull the connectors off the warm-up valve and the auxiliary air unit.

5 Remove the two bolts securing the cold-start valve to the intake manifold and remove the valve, taking care not to damage the gasket.

6 With fuel line and electrical connections connected to the valve, hold the valve over a glass jar and operate the starter for 10 seconds. The cold-start valve should produce an even cone of spray during the time the thermotime switch is on.

7 After completing the checks, refit the valve and reconnect the leads that were disturbed.

Thermotime switch

8 The thermotime switch energizes the cold start valve for a short time on starting and the time for which the valve is switched on depends upon engine temperature.

9 Pull the connector off the cold start valve and connect a test lamp or voltmeter across the contacts of the connector.

10 Pull the high tension lead off the centre of the distributor and connect the lead to ground.

11 Operate the starter for 10 seconds and note the interval before the test lamp lights and the period for which it remains lit. The switching time should increase approximately 1.5 seconds for each drop in temperature of 5°C (9°F) below 15°C (59°F).

12 Connect an ohmmeter to the thermotime switch. With the contacts of the switch closed (engine temperature below 15°C (59°F), group connection G, the ohmmeter should read 48 ohms. Next ground connection W, the ohmmeter should read 0 ohms.

13 With the engine temperature above 15°C (59°F), (contacts in the switch opened), grounding the G connection should register as 62 ohms while grounding the W connection should read 270 ohms on the ohmmeter.

14 Install the high tension lead onto the distributor, and reconnect the lead to the cold start valve.

16 Injection valves (CIS) – testing

1   There is one injection valve fitted per cylinder.
2   The injection valve may give trouble for one of four reasons. The spray may be irregular in shape; the nozzle may not close when the engine is shut down, causing flooding when restarting; the nozzle filter may be choked giving less than the required ration of fuel; or the seal may be damaged allowing an air leak.
3   If the engine is running roughly and missing on one cylinder, allow it to idle and pull each spark plug lead off and refit it. *This test should not be carried out on engines fitted with transistorised ignition.* If that cylinder's injection valve is working properly, there will be an even more adverse effect on the idling speed when the lead is pulled off, which will promptly improve once the lead is refitted. If there is little difference when the lead is removed then that is the cylinder giving trouble. Stop the engine and check and service the spark plug. Now have a look at the injection valve. Remove the injection valve, as described in Section 18. Take the injection valve to an authorised Mercedes mechanic to be tested.

17 Fuel distributor (CIS) – removal and refitting

1   Disconnect the battery terminals.
2   Ensure that the vehicle is in a well ventilated space and that there are no naked flames or other possible sources of ignition.
3   While holding a rag over the joint to prevent fuel from being sprayed out, loosen the control pressure line from the warm-up valve. The control pressure line is the one connected to the large union of the valve.
4   Mark each fuel line, and its port of the fuel distributor. Carefully clean all dirt from around the fuel unions and distributor ports, and then disconnect the fuel lines.
5   Unscrew and remove the connection of the pressure control line to the fuel distributor.
6   Remove the locking plug from the CO adjusting screw, then remove the screws securing the fuel distributor.
7   Lift off the fuel distributor, taking care that the metering plunger does not fall out. Some later model distributors come with a sheet-metal lock to keep the plunger from falling out. This sheet-metal lock should not be removed. If the plunger does fall out accidentally, clean it in gasoline and re-insert it with its chamfered end downwards.
8   Before installing the distributor, ensure that the plunger moves up and down freely. If the plunger sticks, the distributor must be replaced, because the plunger cannot be repaired or replaced separately.
9   Install the distributor, using a new slightly lubricated sealing ring, and after tightening the screws, lock them with paint.
10 Install the fuel lines and the cap of the CO adjusting screw and tighten the union on the warm-up valve.

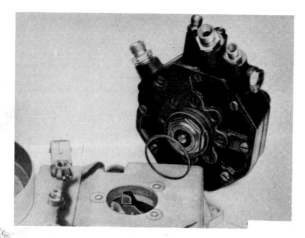

Fig. 3.30 Removing the CIS fuel distributor (Sec 17)

18 Injection valves (CIS) – removal and refitting

1   Remove the air cleaner assembly, as described in Section 2.
2   Place the appropriate wrench on the injection valve to use as a counterhold and unscrew the metal injection lines going to the injection valve.
3   Unscrew the other end of the injection line from the fuel distributor.
4   Unscrew the fuel line running to the cold starting valve.
5   Loosen the screws that mount the bridges to the injector lines. Place a wrench on the injector valve as a counterhold while removing the bridges so the injection valve and the insulating sleeves are not jarred or damaged.
6   Push down on the insulating sleeve and pull the injection valve out of its position. If the insulating sleeves are pulled out, install them with new O-rings.
7   Check the insulator sleeve, the O-ring and the injector sealing ring for wear or cracks. Replace them if necessary. The injector valve sealing ring should be replaced any time the injector valve is removed.
8   Moisten the O-rings and injector valve seals with fuel before installing them into the intake manifold and likewise moisten the injector valve before inserting it into the seal.
9   Install the injection lines to the fuel distributor and the injector valves. Use the appropriate wrench on the injector valve as a counterhold, while tightening the line to it.
10 Install the fuel line for the cold starting valve.
11 Start the engine and check all of the fuel connections for leaks.
12 Install the air cleaner assembly connecting the hoses and electrical terminals to their designated locations.

19 Mixture controller (CIS) – removal and refitting

1   Remove the air cleaner assembly, as described in Section 2.
2   Using a wrench to counterhold the injection valves, loosen the fuel injection lines to the injector valves and disconnect the fuel lines to the fuel distributor.
3   Unscrew the return line and fuel feed holder. Plug the lines to prevent leaks and to keep dirt out of the system.
4   Unplug the electrical connecting cable from the safety switch.
5   Loosen the hose clamp on the rubber sleeve between the valve housing and the air guide housing.
6   Slide the contoured hose from the supplementary air valve to the air guide housing.
7   Remove the nuts that secure the rubber buffers to the injection unit.
8   Remove the mixture controller along with the air guide housing.
9   Installation of the mixture controller is the reverse of the removal procedure. Be sure to tighten the hex nuts to the specified torque. When installing the fuel lines, use a wrench on the injector valve to counterhold it from turning.
10 Check the adjusting lever in the air volume sensor for ease of operation. To do so, pull the plug from the safety switch and switch the ignition to the On position to establish a control pressure. Switch the ignition Off again and push the retaining disc downward. Resistance to movement should be uniform through the complete throw of the adjusting lever. During a fast upwards motion there should be no resistance felt because the control piston lifts off the adjusting lever. The control piston should follow smoothly during this slow upwards motion.
11 Start the engine and check all of the fuel connections for leaks.
12 Install the air cleaner assembly, as described in Section 2.
13 Adjust the idle speed, if necessary, as described in Section 22.

20 Throttle valve housing (CIS) – removal and refitting

1   Remove the mixture controller unit, as described in Section 19.
2   Loosen the clamps and remove the rubber sleeve from between the air guide housing and the throttle valve housing.
3   Separate the linkage return spring and the regulating linkage from the throttle valve housing.
4   Label and remove the vacuum hoses connected to the throttle valve housing.

5 Remove the bolts securing the throttle valve housing and lift the housing away.

6 Installation is the reverse of the removal procedure.

7 Adjust the regulating linkage, as described in Section 13.

8 Adjust the ignition timing, as described in Chapter 4.

9 Adjust the idle speed, as described in Section 22.

21 Warm-up governor (CIS) – removal and refitting

1 The warm-up governor is located on the cylinder block, next to the oil filter. First note the location of the connections.

2 Disconnect the wiring plug, the fuel and vacuum lines.

3 Using an Allen key, unbolt and remove the warm-up governor.

4 Refitting is a reversal of removal.

22 Fuel injection system (CIS) – idle adjustment

1 Connect a tachometer and CO meter to the engine.

2 Switch off the air conditioner, where fitted, and select P on automatic transmission models. Switch off the automatic climate control where fitted.

3 Remove the air cleaner, as described in Section 2.

4 Note that where a catalyst is fitted connect the CO meter to the exhaust back pressure line (Fig. 3.31).

5 Run the engine to its normal operating temperature only – do not make the adjustment with the engine very hot.

6 On models with cruise control, check that the operating cable is free of tension.

7 Check that the roller is against the end stop in the linkage plate and, if necessary, adjust the connecting rod.

8 Start the engine and check that the idling speed is as given in the Specifications. If not, turn the adjusting screw as required.

9 Check that the CO content is as given in the Specifications. If not, remove the tamperproof plug (check first that local legislation permits this) and use an Allen key to turn the adjustment as required. Turning anti-clockwise weakens the mixture, and clockwise enrichens the mixture.

10 Fit a new tamperproof plug.

11 Refit the air cleaner (Section 2) then make any fine adjustments to the idle speed and mixture, as required.

12 As applicable, select D, switch on the air conditioner and turn the power steering on full lock – the engine should continue to run smoothly.

Fig. 3.31 Exhaust back pressure line location on 110 engines fitted with a catalyst – connect the CO meter here (Sec 22)

23 Fuel injection system (electronic) – general

Early 110 engines may be fitted with an electronic fuel injection system. Fuel is injected into each induction duct by the intake valve. There are a number of sensors attached to the engine which relay information to an electronic control unit, which determines the

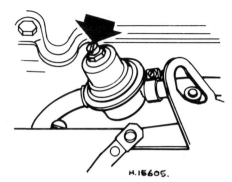

Fig. 3.32 Electronic fuel injection idle speed screw location (Sec 23)

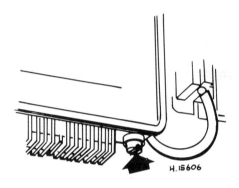

Fig. 3.33 Electronic fuel injection mixture screw location on the control unit (Sec 23)

quantity of fuel to deliver to each injector valve in relation to engine load and speed.

Testing most components of the electronic fuel injection system requires the use of special equipment designed specifically for Bosch fuel injection systems. The expense and availability of this equipment places the inspection of the fuel injection system beyond the scope of the home mechanic. If your fuel injection system is in need of repair, you should entrust the inspection of the system to an authorized Mercedes dealer or an expert on Bosch fuel injection systems.

The idle adjustment procedure is identical to that for the CIS system, described in Section 22, and the adjustment screws are shown in Figs. 3.32 and 3.33.

24 Emission control systems – general

On UK models emission control consists only of the crankcase ventilation system described in Chapter 1. However, on USA models, the following systems are employed; depending on the model year and territory.

Exhaust gas recirculation (EGR)

This device returns exhaust gases to the throttle valve housing where they are drawn into the engine again. The effect is to lower the temperature of combustion and reduce the oxides of nitrogen content of the exhaust.

Afterburning (air injection) system

An air pump is used to pump fresh air into the exhaust ports in order to allow unburnt gases to continue to burn. This reduces hydrocarbon and carbon monoxide. A diverter valve is mounted on the air pump to route the air into the atmosphere during deceleration.

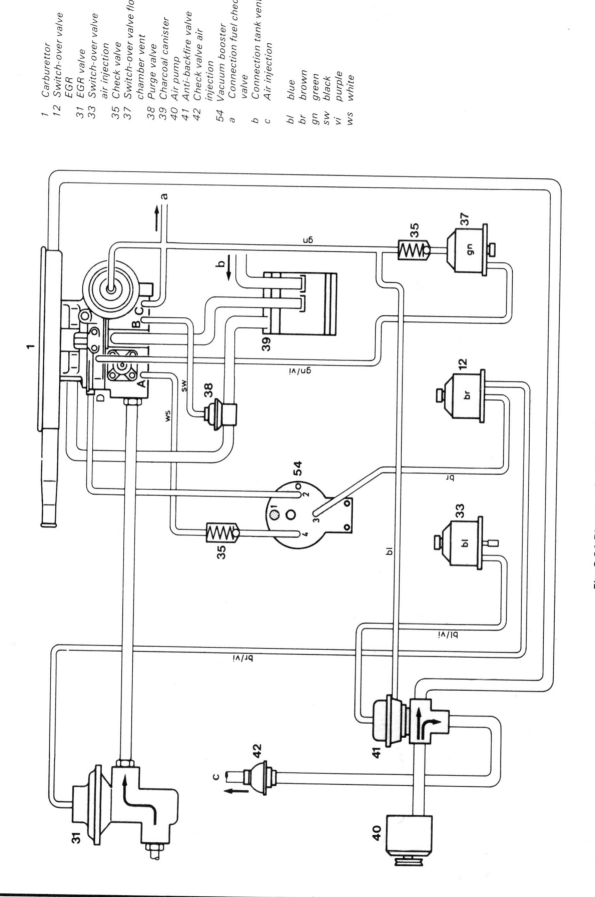

1   Carburettor
12 Switch-over valve
    EGR
31 EGR valve
33 Switch-over valve
    air injection
35 Check valve
37 Switch-over valve float
    chamber vent
38 Purge valve
39 Charcoal canister
40 Air pump
41 Anti-backfire valve
42 Check valve air
    injection
54 Vacuum booster
a   Connection fuel check
    valve
b   Connection tank vent
c   Air injection

bl blue
br brown
gn green
sw black
vi purple
ws white

Fig. 3.34 Diagram of early emission control system (Sec 24)

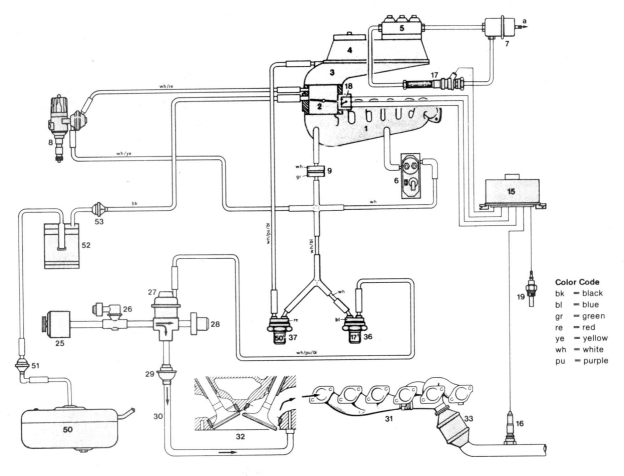

Fig. 3.35 Diagram of late emission control system (Sec 24)

1	Intake manifold	9	Restricting orifice
2	Throttle valve housing	15	Electronic control unit
3	Air duct housing	16	Oxygen sensor
4	Airflow sensor	17	Frequency valve
5	Fuel distributor	18	Throttle valve switch
6	Warm-up enrichment	19	Temperature switch, oil
	compensator		16°C (60°F)
7	Pressure damper	25	Air pump
8	Ignition distributor	26	Pressure relief valve

27	Diverter valve	37	Thermo-vacuum valve
28	Muffler (air filter)		50°C (122°F)
29	Check valve	50	Fuel tank
30	Air injection line	51	Vent valve
31	Exhaust manifold	52	Charcoal canister
32	Cylinder head	53	Purge valve
33	Primary catalyst	a	Leak-off connection
36	Thermo-vacuum valve		
	17°C (63°F)		

Catalyst

The catalyst is flanged to the exhaust manifold on early models and in the exhaust system on later models; it contains ceramic material which assists in the oxidation of carbon monoxide and hydrocarbon into carbon dioxide and water. The unit can be rendered ineffective by lead and other fuel additions, so it is important that only unleaded fuel is used, and that the fuel contains no harmful additives.

Fuel evaporation control

Fuel tank vapours are stored in a charcoal canister in the engine compartment. As the throttle valve opens, a vacuum-operated purge valve opens and the fuel vapours are drawn into the intake manifold.

Lambda control

An oxygen sensor located in the front exhaust pipe relays information to the electronic control unit which determines the quantity of fuel supplied by the fuel distributor. The oxygen sensor must be renewed every 30 000 miles (48 000 km).

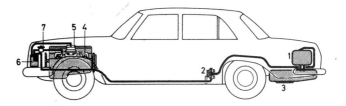

Fig. 3.36 Diagram of fuel evaporation control system (Sec 24)

1	Expansion tank	5	Carburettor with vent
2	Valve system		valve
3	Fuel tank	6	Charcoal canister
4	Intake pipe	7	Purge valve

25 Inlet/exhaust manifolds (123 engines) – removal and refitting

1   Drain the cooling system, as described in Chapter 2.
2   Remove the air cleaner, as described in Section 2.
3   Disconnect the throttle controls.
4   Note the location of all wiring and hoses.
5   Disconnect the coolant and vacuum hoses, and the wiring from the carburettor (photos).
6   Unbolt the heater return pipe (photo).
7   Unscrew the nuts from the downpipe flanges and tap the flanges free (photo).
8   Note the location of the brackets on the manifolds.
9   Disconnect the hot spot control linkage (photos).
10 Unscrew the nuts and withdraw the inlet and exhaust manifolds from the cylinder head. Remove the gaskets (photo).
11 Remove the carburettor, with reference to Section 9.
12 Unbolt the hot air shrouds (photos).
13 Refitting is a reversal of removal, but use new gaskets and finally adjust the idling speed as described in Section 8.

25.5A Vacuum valve hose connections on the inlet manifold

25.5B Vacuum take-off on the inlet manifold for heater/central locking controls and automatic transmission control

25.5C Brake servo vacuum line connection to the inlet manifold

25.6 Heater return pipe fitting to the inlet manifold

25.7 Exhaust downpipe flange on the 123 engine

25.9A Exhaust manifold hot spot control linkage on the 123 engine

25.9B Exhaust manifold hot spot vacuum control

25.10 Removing the manifold gasket (123 engine)

25.12A Front exhaust manifold shroud

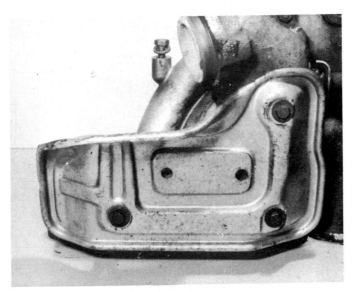

25.12B Rear exhaust manifold shroud

25.12C Manifold hot spot shaft and
inlet/exhaust manifold nuts (arrowed)

26 Inlet/exhaust manifolds (110 engine) – removal and refitting

Inlet manifold

1   Remove the carburettor (Section 9) or throttle valve housing (Section 20).
2   Drain the cooling system, as described in Chapter 2.
3   Disconnect the throttle controls.
4   Note the location of all wiring and hoses, then disconnect them as required.
5   Unscrew the mounting nuts/bolts and withdraw the inlet manifold from the cylinder head. Remove the gasket. On some models it may be necessary to detach the engine mounting and damper, and raise the engine before removing the manifold.
6   Refitting is a reversal of removal, but use a new gasket. Fill the cooling system, with reference to Chapter 2, and finally adjust the idling speed, as described in Section 22.

Exhaust manifolds (UK)

7   Unscrew the nuts from the downpipe flanges and separate the downpipes from the exhaust manifolds. Remove the gaskets.
8   Note the location of brackets, then unscrew the nuts and withdraw the manifolds from the cylinder head. Remove the gaskets.

9   Refitting is a reversal of removal, but use new gaskets, noting that the raised bead must face the manifold.

Exhaust manifold (USA)

10   Unbolt the catalyst from the manifolds and downpipes.
11   Remove the air cleaner and disconnect the throttle linkage, as required.
12   Unbolt the catalyst mounting and shield, and withdraw the catalyst.
13   Unscrew the EGR pipe and where applicable the afterburn pipe.
14   Note the location of brackets, then unscrew the nuts and withdraw the manifolds from the cylinder head. Remove the gaskets.
15   Refitting is a reversal of removal, but use new gaskets, noting that the raised bead must face the manifold.

27 Exhaust system – checking, removal and refitting

1   The exhaust system should be examined for leaks, damage and security at the intervals given in Routine Maintenance. To do this apply the handbrake/parking brake firmly and allow the engine to idle. Lie down on each side of the car in turn and check the full length of the exhaust system for leaks while an assistant temporarily places a wad

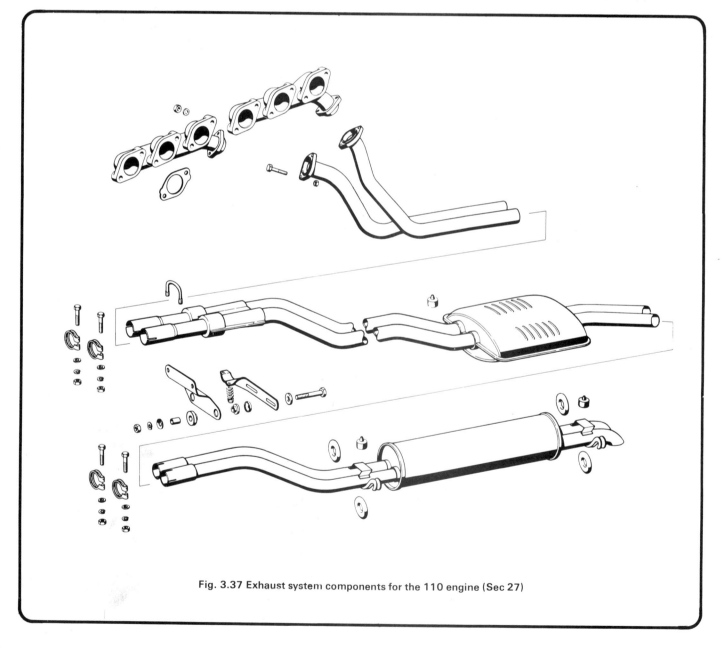

Fig. 3.37 Exhaust system components for the 110 engine (Sec 27)

27.4A Exhaust system support bracket

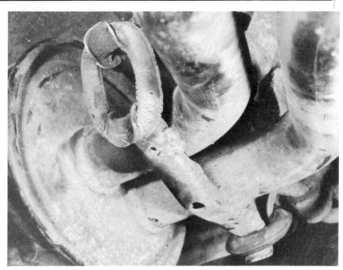

27.4B Exhaust system intermediate mounting rings

27.4C Exhaust system rear mounting rings

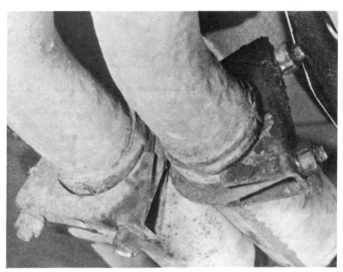

27.6A Exhaust system front joints

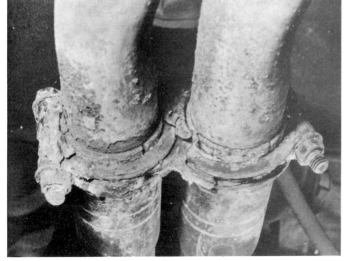

27.6B Exhaust system intermediate joints

of cloth over the tailpipe. If a leak is evident, stop the engine and use a proprietary repair kit to seal it. If the leak is excessive, or damage is evident, renew the section. Check the rubber mountings, and renew them if necessary.

2   To remove the exhaust system, jack up the front and rear of the car and support on axle stands.

3   Unscrew the nuts from the downpipe flanges, tap the flanges free, and separate the downpipes from the manifolds.

4   Unbolt the bracket from the gearbox/transmission and, with the help of an assistant, support the exhaust system while unhooking the rubber mounting rings (photos).

5   Withdraw the exhaust system from under the car.

6   To separate the sections, unscrew the clamp bolts and tap the clamps from the joints (photos). Tap around the joints to release the accumulated rust then separate the sections. If necessary, heat the joint with a blowlamp.

7   Refitting is a reversal of removal, but mount the exhaust system loosely before finally tightening the clamps and mountings. Always renew the flange gaskets. Make sure that there is sufficient clearance between the exhaust system and the underbody.

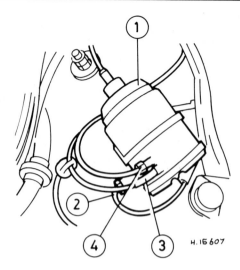

Fig. 3.38 Cruise control system throttle servo unit (Sec 28)

1	Servo unit	3	Vacuum line
2	Wiring harness	4	Vent line

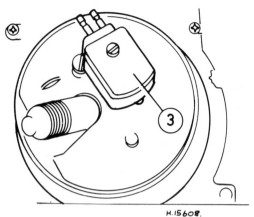

Fig. 3.39 Cruise control system transducer (3) location
(Sec 28)

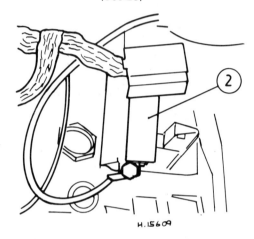

Fig. 3.40 Cruise control system control unit (2) location
(Sec 28)

28 Cruise control – general

A cruise control system is fitted to some models and it allows the driver to maintain a constant speed without touching the accelerator pedal. The system is operated by a lever on the steering column and comprises a switch, transducer, control unit and throttle servo unit. The transducer is incorporated in the speedometer cable on early models or on the rear of the speedometer head on later models. The control unit is located beneath the facia panel.

The throttle control cable should be adjusted so that there is a minimum of endplay.

29 Fault diagnosis – fuel, exhaust and emission control systems

Symptom	Reason(s)
Excessive fuel consumption	Mixture setting incorrect Air cleaner element blocked Fuel leak Incorrect float level (carburettor) Warm-up governor or fuel distributor faulty (CIS)
Insufficient fuel supply or weak mixture	Fuel pump faulty Mixture setting incorrect Fuel leak Air leak Automatic choke faulty (carburettor) Sticking needle valve (carburettor) Accelerator pump faulty (carburettor) Cold start valve faulty (CIS)

Chapter 4 Ignition system

Contents

Specifications

System type .... Conventional contact breaker or transistorised, with coil

Distributor
Rotor rotation .... Clockwise
Firing order 1-5-3-6-2-4
Basic points gap (conventional ignition) .... 0.3 mm (0.012 in)

Dwell angle
123 engine with conventional ignition .... 35° to 41° (at idling speed)
123 engine with transistorised ignition .... 39° to 51° (at 1500 rpm)
110 engine with conventional ignition .... 39° to 42° (at idling speed)
110 engine with transistorised ignition:
    With pre-resistors .... 33° to 51° (at 1500 rpm)
    Without pre-resistors .... 7° to 25° (at starting speed)

Coil
Primary winding resistance:
    Conventional ignition .... 1.2 to 1.6 ohm
    Transistorised ignition with pre-resistors .... 0.38 to 0.43 ohm
    Transistorised ignition without pre-resistors .... 0.5 to 0.9 ohm

Ignition timing
123 engine:
    Static .... 8° BTDC
    Dynamic .... 32° BTDC at 4500 rpm without vacuum
110 engine (UK) – static:
    110.923 (except with distributors 0237302021 and
    0237302015) .... 5° BTDC
    110.923 (with distributors 0237302021 and
    0237302015) .... 10° BTDC
    110.984 .... 10° BTDC
    110.988 .... 12° BTDC
110 engine (UK) – dynamic:
    110.923 (except with distributors 0237302021 and
    0237302015) .... 28° BTDC at 4500 rpm without vacuum
    110.923 (with distributors 0237302021 and 0237302015) .... 32° BTDC at 4500 rpm without vacuum
    110.984 (pre 1979) .... 32° BTDC at 3500 rpm without vacuum
    110.984 (1979 onwards) .... 30° BTDC at 3500 rpm without vacuum
    110.988 .... 30° BTDC at 3500 rpm without vacuum
110 engine (US):
    Static .... 10° BTDC
    Dynamic:
        Pre 1979 .... TDC at idling speed with vacuum
        1979 onwards .... 10° BTDC at idling speed with vacuum and with the engine at normal operating temperature (ie vacuum retard off)

Spark plugs
Type .... Bosch W8D or W7D
Gap .... 0.8 mm (0.031 in)

Torque wrench settings

	lbf ft	Nm
Spark plugs	18 to 22	24 to 30

1   General description

The ignition system consists of the battery, coil, distributor and spark plugs. On early models the system is of conventional type incorporating contact breaker points and a condenser, but later models are fitted with a transistorised system incorporating a magnetic sensor and control unit (photo).

The conventional system functions as follows: Low tension voltage is fed to the coil primary windings and then to the contact breaker points. When the contact points open, the electro magnetic field in the coil induces high tension voltage in the coil secondary windings. The high tension (HT) voltage is then fed, via the carbon brush in the centre of the distrbutor cap, to the rotor arm and then via the metal segments in the cap to each spark plug in turn. The condenser prevents arcing across the contact points and helps collapse the electro magnetic field in the coil, thus ensuring the correct high tension voltage.

The transistorised system functions in a similar manner to the conventional system, but the contact points and condenser are replaced by a magnetic sensor in the distributor and a control unit mounted separately. As the distributor driveshaft rotates, the magnetic impulses are fed to the control unit which switches the primary circuit on and off. No condenser is necessary as the circuit is switched electronically with semiconductor components. To prevent damage to the system, or personal injury, observe the precautions given in Section 6.

The ignition advance on both systems is controlled mechanically by centrifugal weights and by a vacuum capsule mounted on the side of the distributor. The vacuum capsule also incorporates a section which retards the ignition under certain circumstances.

2   Routine maintenance

1   Every 10 000 miles (16 000 km) renew the spark plugs, excepting US Federal versions where the spark plugs should be cleaned at 15 000 miles (24 000 km) and renewed at 30 000 miles (48 000 km).
2   Check and, if necessary, adjust the ignition timing every 10 000 miles (16 000 km). Where applicable, on models with conventional ignition, first renew the contact breaker points. Also check the ignition advance and retard mechanism and vacuum unit. Where applicable, check the contact points dwell angle before adjusting the ignition timing.

1.1 Control unit for electronic transistorised ignition system

3   Contact breaker points – removal, refitting and adjustment

1   Release the two clips securing the distributor cap and remove the cap.
2   Pull the rotor arm off the cam spindle and, where applicable, remove the dust cover.
3   Remove the cap from the contact points and disconnect the low tension wire.
4   Remove the screw and withdraw the contact points from the distributor.
5   Before fitting the new points, smear the distributor cam and moving contact pivot with the grease supplied with the new points, and also wipe clean the contact points.
6   Fit the new points using a reversal of the removal procedure, but only lightly tighten the securing screw.

Fig. 4.1 Contact breaker points location in the distributor (Sec 3)

1   Protective cap

Fig. 4.2 Contact breaker points set (Sec 3)

1   Contact points   2   Protective cap   3   Grease capsule

7 Using a socket on the crankshaft pulley bolt turn the engine until the heel of the moving contact is on the highest point of one of the cam lobes.

8 Check that the gap between the two points is as given in the Specifications using a feeler blade which should be a firm sliding fit. If necessary, adjust the position of the fixed contact point using a screwdriver between the two pips on the baseplate. When the setting is correct, tighten the screw fully.

9 Using a dwell meter check that the dwell angle is as given in the Specifications. If the angle is too small the points gap must be decreased, if too large the gap must be increased.

10 Refit the dust cover, rotor arm and cap.

4 Condenser – testing, removal and refitting

1 A faulty condenser will cause misfiring or complete failure of the ignition system. Its purpose is to produce arcing across the contact points, and if the points are discoloured and excessively pitted the condenser is probably at fault.

2 Accurate testing requires special instruments, however, a simple test can be made by separating the closed points by hand with the ignition switched on. If this is accompanied by a blue flash the condenser is faulty, but a small white flash is normal. Testing for a short circuit can be made by connecting a test lamp from the battery positive terminal in series with the condenser – with the contact points disconnected. If the test lamp lights up the condenser has an internal short circuit.

3 To remove the condenser, first remove the distributor cap, rotor and dust cap, then disconnect the supply and contact point leads. Remove the retaining screw and withdraw the condenser together with the lead and grommet.

4 Refitting is a reversal of removal.

5 Distributor – removal and refitting

1 Disconnect the battery negative lead.

2 Release the two clips securing the distributor cap and remove the cap.

3 Remove the rotor arm and dust cover, then refit the rotor arm.

4 Turn the engine with a socket on the crankshaft pulley bolt until the rotor arm is aligned with the mark on the rim of the distributor body (photo). No 1 piston is now at TDC compression, and therefore the TDC (%) mark on the vibration damper should be aligned with the pointer on the crankcase (photo).

5 Mark the distributor body in relation to the cylinder block or driveshaft housing (as applicable).

6 Unscrew the retaining screw and disconnect the vacuum hoses and wiring (photos).

7 Withdraw the distributor from the engine (photo). Do not remove the driveshaft except for inspection; in which case first note the position of the drive groove and segments.

Fig. 4.3 Rotor arm aligned with the TDC mark on the distributor body rim (arrowed) (Sec 5)

Fig. 4.4 Distributor retaining screw on the 110 engine (arrowed) (Sec 5)

5.4A Distributor rotor arm at No 1 cylinder TDC position (arrowed)

5.4B Ignition timing pointer aligned with TDC mark on the vibration damper

5.6A Distributor wiring plug and bracket

5.6B Distributor vacuum advance hose

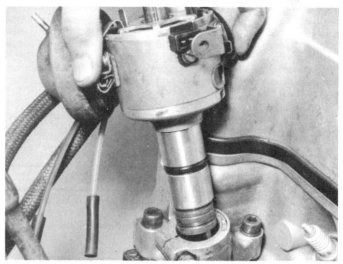

5.7 Removing the distributor from a 123 engine

8　Refitting is a reversal of removal, but make sure that the TDC marks are aligned, and, after fitting, adjust the ignition timing as described in Section 8. Note that the red vacuum hose is connected to the top of the vacuum advance unit.

6　Transistorised ignition system – precautions

To prevent personal injury and damage to the ignition system, the following precautions must be observed when working on the ignition system.
1　Do not attempt to disconnect any plug lead or touch any of the high tension cables when the engine is running, or being turned by the starter motor.
2　Ensure that the ignition is switched off before disconnecting any of the ignition wiring.
3　Ensure that the ignition is switched off before connecting or disconnecting any ignition testing equipment such as a timing light.
4　Do not connect a suppression condenser or test lamp to the coil negative terminal '1'.
5　Do not connect any test appliance or stroboscopic lamp requiring a 12 volt supply to the coil positive terminal '15'.
6　If the coil HT cable is disconnected from the distributor terminal it must be connected to earth if the engine is to be rotated by the starter motor, for example if a compression test is to be done.
7　The ignition coil of a transistorised system must never be replaced by one from a contact breaker type ignition system.

7.2 Transistorised ignition pre-resistances

7　Transistorised ignition system – testing

1　First check that all the wiring is secure and undamaged.

Voltage test
2　Connect a voltmeter to the input side of the pre-resistance and check that the reading is approximately 12 volts with the ignition switched on (photo).
3　Connect the voltmeter to terminals '15' and '1' on the coil and check that the readings are approximately 4.5 volts and 0.5 to 2.0 volts respectively at an ambient temperature of 20°C (68°F). If the terminal '1' reading is excessive, renew the switch gear control unit. If the reading is correct, but there is no HT spark, check that the coil secondary winding resistance is between 7k and 12k ohm, then check the transmitter, as described in paragraph 5 to 8.

Dwell angle test
4　Using a dwell meter check that the dwell angle is as given in the Specifications. If incorrect first check the transmitter, as described in paragraphs 5 to 8, and if still incorrect renew the switch gear control unit.

7.7 Using a brass (ie non-magnetic) feeler gauge to check the air gaps

Measuring plug gap. A feeler gauge of the correct size (see Ignition system specifications) should have a slight 'drag' when slid between the electrodes. Adjust gap if necessary

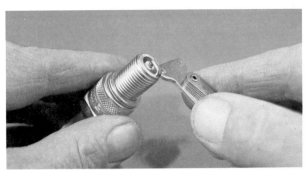

Adjusting plug gap. The plug gap is adjusted by bending the earth electrode inwards, or outwards, as necessary until the correct clearance is obtained. Note the use of the correct tool

Normal. Grey-brown deposits, lightly coated core nose. Gap increasing by around 0.001 in (0.025 mm) per 1000 miles (1600 km). Plugs ideally suited to engine, and engine in good condition

Carbon fouling. Dry, black, sooty deposits. Will cause weak spark and eventually misfire. Fault: over-rich fuel mixture. Check: carburettor mixture settings, float level and jet sizes; choke operation and cleanliness of air filter. Plugs can be re-used after cleaning

Oil fouling. Wet, oily deposits. Will cause weak spark and eventually misfire. Fault: worn bores/piston rings or valve guides; sometimes occurs (temporarily) during running-in period. Plugs can be re-used after thorough cleaning

Overheating. Electrodes have glazed appearance, core nose very white – few deposits. Fault: plug overheating. Check: plug value, ignition timing, fuel octane rating (too low) and fuel mixture (too weak). Discard plugs and cure fault immediately

Electrode damage. Electrodes burned away; core nose has burned, glazed appearance. Fault: pre-ignition. Check: as for 'Overheating' but may be more severe. Discard plugs and remedy fault before piston or valve damage occurs

Split core nose (may appear initially as a crack). Damage is self-evident, but cracks will only show after cleaning. Fault: pre-ignition or wrong gap-setting technique. Check: ignition timing, cooling system, fuel octane rating (too low) and fuel mixture (too weak). Discard plugs, rectify fault immediately

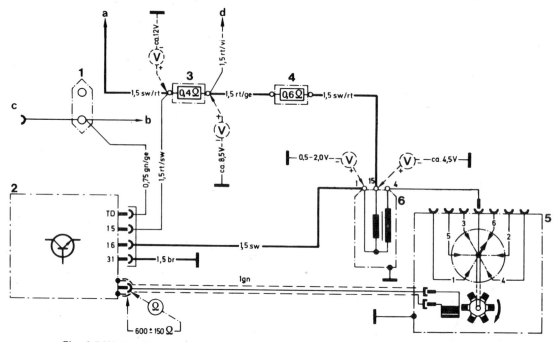

Fig. 4.5 Wiring diagram for the transistorised ignition system with pre-resistors (Sec 7)

1 Cable connector
2 Switch gear (control unit)
3 Pre-resistance – 0.4 ohm

4 Pre-resistance – 0.6 ohm
5 Distributor, incorporating transmitter
6 Coil

a Ignition switch terminal 15
b Instrument panel rev counter

c Diagnostic socket
d Starter motor terminal 16

Transmitter test

5 Disconnect the distributor sensor wiring from the control unit and connect an ohmmeter across the connector terminals. A reading of 500 to 700 ohm should be obtained.

6 Connect the ohmmeter between the central terminal (terminal 7) and earth. The reading should be infinity. If not, there is a short circuit to earth in the wiring or transmitter coil.

7 Remove the distributor cap and check that the air gaps between the rotor and stator are correct and even (photos).

8 If the transmitter is proved faulty the complete distributor must be renewed.

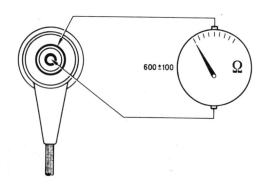

Fig. 4.6 Ohmmeter connection for testing the transistorised ignition transmitter (Sec 7)

8 Ignition timing – adjustment

Static (initial setting)

1 Note the position of No 1 HT lead on the distributor cap, then remove the distributor cap and turn the engine with a socket on the crankshaft pulley bolt until the rotor arm is approaching the No 1 position.

2 Continue turning the engine until the correct timing mark (see Specifications) is aligned with the pointer on the crankcase. This is the point at which the HT spark should occur in No 1 cylinder.

3 Check that the contact points have just separated on the conventional ignition system, or that the sensor arm is aligned with the stator on the transistorised ignition system. If not, loosen the distributor retaining screw and move the distributor body as required, then retighten the screw. On the conventional ignition system the exact point at which the contact points separate can be determined by connecting a 12 volt test lamp from the LT points terminal in the distributor to earth – with the ignition switched on the test lamp will light up when the points separate.

4 Refit the distributor cap.

Dynamic

5 Refer to the Specifications and, if necessary, disconnect and plug the vacuum advance hose from the distributor capsule.

6 Wipe clean the timing marks on the crankshaft vibration damper and the pointer on the crankcase. If necessary use white paint or chalk to highlight the marks.

7 Connect a stroboscopic timing light and tachometer to the engine in accordance with the manufacturer's instructions.

8 Start the engine and run it at the specified speed.

9 Point the timing light at the vibration damper and check that the specified mark is aligned with the pointer on the crankcase.

10 If adjustment is necessary (ie the specified mark and pointer are not aligned) loosen the distributor retaining screw and turn the distributor body anti-clockwise to advance the timing or clockwise to retard the timing. As a safety precaution the engine can be switched off before adjusting the distributor. Note that the distributor movement will be half of the crankshaft movement (eg adjustment of 5° on the vibration damper will require the distributor to be turned 2.5°). Tighten the retaining screw when the setting is correct.

11 An approximate check of the distributor centrifugal advance mechanism can be made by disconnecting the vacuum hoses and checking that the ignition timing advances as the engine speed is increased. Similarly the operation of the vacuum advance and retard can be checked by noting the change of ignition timing while disconnecting and connecting the vacuum hoses – advance should be checked at 3000 rpm and retard at idle speed. Make sure that the hoses are reconnected correctly after making the check.

12 Remove the timing light and tachometer.

9.1 Ignition coil

9 Coil – description and testing

1 The coil is located on the left-hand side of the engine compartment (photo). It should be kept clean at all times to prevent possible arcing across the high tension tower.

2 To ensure the correct HT polarity at the spark plugs, the LT coil leads must always be connected correctly. On the conventional ignition system the contact points wire from the distributor must be connected to the negative terminal on the coil (terminal 1). On the transistorised ignition system the wire from terminal 16 on the control unit must be connected to the negative terminal on the coil (terminal 1) (photo).

3 Testing of the coil is by the use of an ohmmeter. Disconnect all wiring and connect the ohmmeter across terminals 1 and 15 to check the primary winding resistance, and across terminals 1 and 4 to check the secondary winding resistance. The primary resistance should be as given in the Specifications, and the secondary resistance between 6k and 15k ohm. Reconnect the wiring after making the test.

9.2 Ignition coil terminals

10 Spark plugs and HT leads – general

1 The correct functioning of the spark plugs is vital for the correct running and efficiency of the engine. Clean and/or renew the spark plugs at the intervals given in Section 2. However, if misfiring or bad starting is experienced before the end of the service period the spark plugs must be removed, cleaned and regapped.

2 To remove the spark plugs first disconnect the HT leads. If necessary, identify each lead for position to ensure correct refitting.

3 Clean the area around each spark plug using a small brush, and, on 110 type engines, blow the accumulated dirt from the cavities in the cylinder head using air pressure.

4 Using a plug spanner (preferably with a rubber insert) unscrew and remove the plugs (photo). Cover the spark plug holes with a clean rag to prevent the ingress of any foreign matter.

5 The condition of the spark plugs will tell much about the overall condition of the engine.

6 If the insulator nose of the spark plug is clean and white, with no deposits, this is indicative of a weak mixture, or too hot a plug. (A hot plug transfers heat away from the electrodes slowly – a cold plug transfers it away quickly).

7 If the top and insulator nose is covered with hard black looking deposits, then this is indicative that the mixture is too rich. Should the plug be black and oily, then it is likely that the engine is fairly worn, as well as the mixture being too rich.

8 If the insulator nose is covered with light tan to greyish brown deposits, then the mixture is correct and it is likely that the engine is in good condition.

9 If there are any traces of long brown tapering stains on the outside of the white portion of the plug, then the plug will have to be renewed, as this shows that there is a faulty joint between the plug body and the insulator, and compression is being allowed to leak away.

10 Plugs should be cleaned by a sand blasting machine, which will free them from carbon more thoroughly than cleaning by hand. The machine may also test the condition of the plugs under compression. Any plug that fails to spark at the recommended pressure should be renewed.

11 The spark plug gap is of considerable importance, as if it is too large or too small the size of the spark and its efficiency will be seriously impaired. The spark plug gap should be set to the clearance given in the Specifications. To set it, measure the gap with a feeler gauge, and then bend open, or close, the outer plug electrode until the correct gap is achieved. The centre electrode should never be bent as this may crack the insulation and cause plug failure, if nothing worse.

10.4 Removing a spark plug

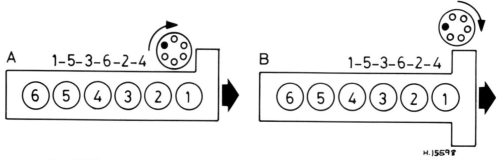

Fig. 4.7 Diagram showing distributor rotor rotation and HT lead positions (Sec 10)

A   123 engine
B   110 engine

Filled-in HT lead position
is for No 1 cylinder

12 Before fitting the spark plugs check that the threaded connector sleeves are tight and that the plug exterior surfaces are clean. Also make sure that the threads and seats are clean.
13 Screw in the spark plugs and tighten them to the specified torque.
14 Wipe clean the HT leads and distributor cap then reconnect the leads to their respective plugs.

11 Fault diagnosis – ignition system

There are two distinct symptoms of ignition faults. Either the engine will not start or fire, or it starts with difficulty and does not run normally. If the starter motor spins the engine satisfactorily and there is adequate fuel, but the engine will not start, the fault is likely to be on the LT side. If the engine starts, but does not run satisfactorily, it is more likely to be an HT fault.

Engine fails to start
1 If the starter motor spins the engine satisfactorily, but the engine does not start, first check that the fuel supply to the engine is in order, with reference to Chapter 3.
2 Check for broken or disconnected wires to the coil and distributor, and for a damp distributor cap and HT leads.
3 For models with transistorised ignition follow the procedure detailed in Section 7.
4 For models with conventional ignition, disconnect the LT lead from the coil terminal 1 and connect a 12 volt test lamp between the lead and the terminal. Spin the engine and check that the lamp flashes on and off as the engine turns. If it fails to flash, but either remains alight or fails to light, check the contact points, condenser and LT wiring.

Engine starts, but misfires
5 Bad starting and misfiring can be caused by an intermittent connection in the LT circuit, but if the previously described tests have been made the fault must be in the HT circuit.
The following tests should not be done if transistorised ignition is fitted.
6 Run the engine at a fast idling speed, then pull off each of the plug HT leads in turn and listen to the note of the engine. *Hold the plug leads with a well insulated pair of pliers as protection against a shock from the HT supply.* No difference in the engine running will be noticed when the lead from the defective circuit is removed, however, the engine speed will drop when a lead from a good firing circuit is removed.
7 Disconnect the defective plug lead and hold it about 5 mm (0.2 in) away from the cylinder head. Restart the engine. If the sparking is strong and regular, the fault must be in the spark plug. The plug may be loose, the insulation may be cracked, or the points may have burnt away giving too wide a gap for the spark to jump. Worse still, one of the points may have broken off. Either renew the plug or clean and reset it.
8 If there is no spark at the end of the plug lead, or if it is weak and intermittent check the HT lead from the distributor cap to the plug and renew it if necessary. Also check the HT connections in the distributor cap.
9 If there is still no spark, examine the distributor cap carefully for tracking. This can be recognised by a very thin black line running between two or more electrodes, or between an electrode and some other part of the cap. These lines are paths which conduct HT current and cause the misfiring, if evident the cap should be renewed. Tracking will also occur if the inside or outside of the cap is damp, and in this case a proprietary water repellant spray should be used, or alternatively the cap thoroughly dried out.

Chapter 5 Clutch

Contents

Specifications

Type .... Single dry plate, diaphragm spring, hydraulically-operated

Clutch plate (disc)
Lining thickness (new) .... 3.9 to 4.1 mm (0.154 to 0.161 in)
Lining thickness (minimum) .... 1.9 to 2.1 mm (0.075 to 0.083 in)
Run-out (maximum) .... 0.5 mm (0.02 in)

Clutch pedal
Dead centre spring dimension between retainers .... 47.5 mm (1.87 in)
Total movement at pad .... 150.0 mm (5.9 in)
Pushrod-to-master cylinder clearance .... 0.2 mm (0.008 in)

Torque wrench settings

	lbf ft	Nm
Clutch cover	18	24

1 General description

The clutch is of single dry plate type with a diaphragm spring pressure plate. The pressure plate is actuated hydraulically by a release arm and sealed ball-bearing.

The clutch plate (or disc) is free to slide along the splined gearbox input shaft, and is held in position between the flywheel and the pressure plate by the pressure of the diaphragm spring. Friction lining material is riveted to the clutch plate and it has a spring cushioned hub to absorb transmission shocks and help ensure a smooth take-off.

The circular diaphragm spring is mounted on shoulder pins and held in the cover by two fulcrum rings. The spring is also held to the pressure plate by three steel spring clips which are riveted in position.

The clutch is actuated by a hydraulic master and slave cylinder. Wear of the friction linings is compensated for automatically by the hydraulic system.

Depressing the clutch pedal actuates the slave cylinder piston which moves the release arm. The release bearing on the arm is forced against the centre fingers of the diaphragm spring and the pressure plate is released from the clutch plate.

When the clutch pedal is released, the diaphragm spring forces the pressure plate onto the clutch plate linings, and the clutch plate is also forced onto the flywheel. Drive from the engine is now transmitted directly through the clutch to the gearbox.

2 Clutch pedal assembly – removal, refitting and adjustment

1 Remove the panel covering the lower part of the steering column.
2 Remove the floor mat beneath the pedal assembly.
3 Remove the filler cap from the combination brake and clutch fluid reservoir and tighten it down onto a piece of polythene sheeting. This will reduce any subsequent loss of fluid. Alternatively syphon out the fluid into a clean container.
4 Unscrew the union nut securing the outlet pipe to the clutch master cylinder, and plug the outlet.
5 Disconnect the clutch master cylinder supply hose at the reservoir and plug the outlet if necessary.
6 Disconnect the pushrod from the brake pedal by unscrewing the pivot bolt. Remove the bush.
7 Disconnect the plug from the stop-light switch.
8 Unscrew the mounting nuts then withdraw the assembly rearwards and downwards while feeding the supply hose through the bulkhead.

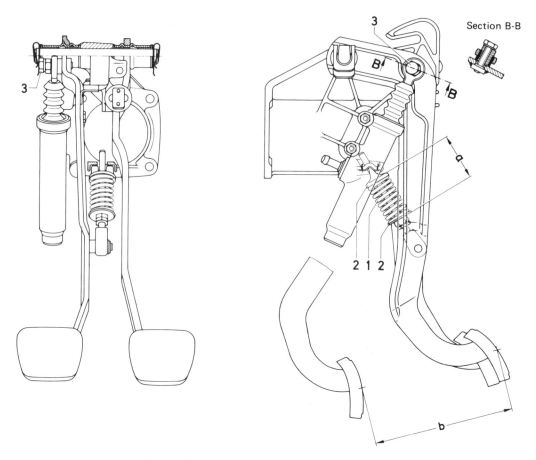

Fig. 5.1 Diagrams of the clutch pedal assembly (Sec 2)

1	Dead centre spring	a	Dead centre spring
2	Retainers		dimension
3	Eccentric bolt	b	Clutch pedal travel

9   The clutch pedal may be removed after removing the clutch master cylinder and disconnecting the dead centre spring.

10   Refitting is a reversal of removal, but refit the master cylinder with reference to Section 3. Check that the distance across the the dead centre spring retainers is as given in the Specifications with the pedal released. If not, loosen the locknut and turn the adjusting nut as necessary. Tighten the locknut when the dimension is correct. Finally bleed the hydraulic system, as described in Section 5.

3   Master cylinder – removal, refitting and adjustment

1   Remove the floor covering beneath the pedals, and remove the panel covering the lower part of the steering column.

2   Syphon the fluid from the combination brake and clutch fluid reservoir until it is below the level of the clutch outlet.

3   Disconnect the clutch supply hose from the reservoir.

4   Unscrew the union nut securing the outlet pipe to the master cylinder and plug the outlet.

5   Unscrew the mounting bolt and withdraw the master cylinder downwards, leaving the pushrod connected to the pedal. At the same time withdraw the supply hose through the bulkhead.

6   Disconnect the supply hose.

7   If the master cylinder is faulty it should be renewed complete, although it may be possible to obtain a kit of rubber seals from certain motor factors.

8   Refitting is a reversal of removal, but the pushrod must be adjusted so that there is a clearance between it and the master cylinder piston with the pedal fully released. The clearance is given in the Specifications, however, as it is not accessible, an approximate adjustment can be made by checking that the pad on the end of the pedal moves approximately 1.0 mm (0.04 in) before resistance is felt.

If necessary loosen the locknut on the eccentric adjuster bolt connecting the pushrod to the pedal, turn the bolt as required, and re-tighten the locknut. A further method is to completely drain the system, disconnect the supply hose from the fluid reservoir, and connect a hose from the supply hose to a container of water. A 1.5 mm (0.06 in) spacer is then placed between the pedal and the pedal stop, and air pressure (0.5 bar, 7.3 lbf/in²) supplied to the slave

Fig. 5.2 Clutch master cylinder supply hose connected to the combination brake and clutch fluid reservoir (Sec 3)

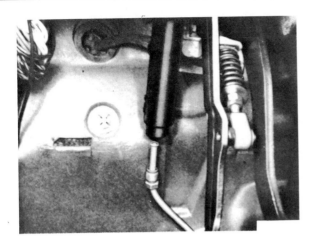

Fig. 5.3 Disconnecting the outlet pipe from the master cylinder (Sec 3)

Fig. 5.4 Using a bottle of water and hose to set the clutch master cylinder pushrod clearance (Sec 3)

cylinder or master cylinder outlet. With air passing through the system, bubbles will be seen in the water, but the eccentric bolt must be adjusted so that the bubbles just cease, then the locknut tightened. With the spacer removed, the bubbles should start again. Finally bleed the hydraulic system, as described in Section 5.

4 Slave cylinder – removal and refitting

1 Jack up the front of the car and support it on axle stands. Apply the handbrake/parking brake.
2 Working beneath the car, disconnect the hydraulic pipe from the slave cylinder and quickly cap the end of the pipe to prevent loss of fluid.
3 Unbolt and remove the slave cylinder, together with the slotted spacer.
4 If the master cylinder is faulty it should be renewed complete, although it may be possible to obtain a kit of rubber seals from certain motor factors.
5 Refitting is a reversal of removal, but make sure that the slotted side of the spacer is against the gearbox housing, and that the pushrod is correctly seated in the release lever. Finally bleed the hydraulic system, as described in Section 5.

5 Clutch hydraulic system – bleeding

1 The clutch hydraulic system should be bled in reverse flow by forcing fluid through the slave cylinder via the master cylinder to the fluid reservoir. First jack up the front of the car and support it on axle stands.

Method 1
2 Syphon fluid from the reservoir to the minimum level.
3 Using a proprietary *pressurised* brake bleeding kit, connect the supply line to the bleed screw on the slave cylinder and open the screw half a turn.
4 Allow the fluid to fill the system until it reaches the maximum level in the reservoir then tighten the bleed screw.
5 Check the operation of the clutch. If necessary, bleed the system again to remove all the air.

Method 2
6 Top up the fluid in the reservoir to the maximum level mark.
7 Connect a hose to the right-hand front brake caliper bleed screw long enough to reach the clutch slave cylinder bleed screw. Fill the hose with fluid by temporarily loosening the bleed screw and having an assistant depress the brake pedal slowly. Tighten the bleed screw.
8 Connect the hose to the clutch slave cylinder bleed screw, and loosen both bleed screws.
9 Have the assistant fully depress the brake pedal, then tighten the clutch bleed screw before releasing the pedal. Continue bleeding until

the fluid reaching the reservoir is free of air bubbles, then tighten both bleed screws and remove the hose. Only use the minimum number of strokes, otherwise there is a possibility of allowing aerated fluid to enter the brake hydraulic circuit. Also, do not allow the fluid level to drop below the maximum mark – this may occur if the clutch hydraulic circuit is initially empty.
10 Finally top up the fluid in the reservoir to the maximum level mark, and lower the car to the ground.

6 Clutch – removal

1 The clutch may be removed by two alternative methods. Either remove the engine (Chapter 1) or remove the gearbox (Chapter 6). Unless the engine requires a major overhaul, it is easier and quicker to remove the gearbox.
3 With a file or scriber, mark the relative position of the clutch cover and flywheel to ensure identical positioning on refitting. This is not necessary if a new clutch is to be fitted.
3 Unscrew, in diagonal and progressive manner, the six bolts and spring washers securing the clutch cover to the flywheel. This will prevent distortion of the cover and also prevent the cover from suddenly flying off due to binding on the dowels.
4 With all the bolts removed lift the assembly from the locating dowels. Note which way round the friction disc is fitted and lift it from the clutch cover.

7 Clutch – inspection

1 It is possible to check the wear of the friction disc linings before removing the clutch. Fig. 5.5 shows the special gauge obtainable from the manufacturers in use. If the notches on the gauge enter the slave cylinder spacer, the linings are still serviceable, however, if the notches remain visible, the friction disc is worn excessively and should be renewed. If the gauge is not available, use a knife or thin file to mark the slave cylinder pushrod then remove the cylinder and check where it is marked – if it is on the high section of the pushrod, the linings are worn excessively.
2 With the clutch removed examine the surfaces of the pressure plate and flywheel for scoring. If this is only light, the parts may be re-used, but if scoring is excessive the clutch cover must be renewed and the flywheel friction face reground; provided the amount of metal being removed is minimal. If any doubt exists, renew the flywheel.
3 Renew the friction disc if the linings are worn down to or near the specified minimum thickness. If the linings appear oil stained, the cause of the oil leak must be found and rectified. This is most likely to be a failed gearbox input shaft oil seal or crankshaft rear oil seal. Check the hub and centre splines for wear, and check that the specified maximum run-out is not exceeded with the disc mounted on the gearbox input shaft.
4 Examine the clutch cover and diaphragm spring for wear which will be indicated by loose components. If the diaphragm spring has any

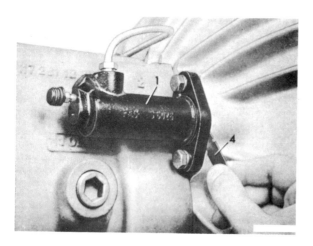

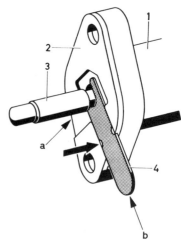

Fig. 5.5 Using the special gauge to check the friction disc linings (Sec 7)

1	Slave cylinder	a	Shoulder on pushrod	Arrow shows checking
2	Slotted spacer	b	Press gauge in this	notches
3	Pushrod		direction	
4	Gauge			

blue discoloured areas, the clutch has probably been overheated at some time and the clutch cover should be renewed.

5   Remove the release bearing from the clutch housing, as described in Section 8, and spin it to check for roughness. Also attempt to move the thrust surface laterally against the bearing housing. If any excessive movement or roughness is evident, renew the release bearing, as described in Section 8.

8   Clutch release bearing and arm – removal and refitting

1   With the gearbox and engine separated to provide access to the clutch, attention can be given to the release bearing located in the clutch housing over the input shaft.
2   Withdraw the release bearing from the guide sleeve.
3   Withdraw the release arm from the slave cylinder pushrod position, then pull it sideways from the ball-pin to disengage the spring clip.
4   Check the release bearing, as described in Section 7. Renew the bearing if there are any signs of grease leakage. Do not wash the bearing in solvent. Check the release arm for damage and wear.
5   Smear a little high melting-point grease on the guide sleeve, ball-pin, and the release bearing contact areas on the release arm.
6   Refitting is a reversal of removal, but make sure that the release bearing seats correctly in the arm.

9   Clutch – refitting

1   It is important that no oil or grease contacts the friction disc linings, or the pressure plate and flywheel faces. Refit the clutch with clean hands, and wipe down the pressure plate and flywheel faces with a clean rag before assembly begins. First smear a little high melting-point grease to the spigot bearing in the centre of the crankshaft and also to the splines on the gearbox input shaft.
2   Place the friction disc against the flywheel with the projecting torsion spring hub to the rear.
3   Fit the clutch cover assembly loosely on the dowels with the previously made marks aligned where applicable. Insert the six bolts and spring washers and tighten them finger tight so that the friction disc is gripped, but can still be moved.
4   The friction disc must now be centralised so that when the engine and gearbox are mated, the input shaft splines will pass through the splines in the friction disc into the spigot bearing. Ideally a universal clutch centralising tool should be used or, if available, an old gearbox input shaft. Alternatively a mandrel should be made – masking tape can be used to obtain the correct diameters if necessary.

5   With the friction disc correctly centralised, tighten the cover bolts progressively in a diagonal sequence to the specified torque, then remove the tool.
6   Refit the gearbox (Chapter 6) or engine (Chapter 1).

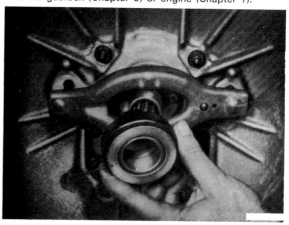

Fig. 5.6 Removing the release bearing (1) (Sec 8)

Fig. 5.7 Using a friction disc centralising tool (Sec 9)

10 Fault diagnosis – clutch

Symptom	Reason(s)
Judder when taking up drive	Worn clutch plate friction linings or contamination with oil Worn splines on clutch plate (disc) or gearbox input shaft Loose engine or gearbox mountings
Clutch drag (failure to disengage)	Clutch plate sticking on input shaft splines Spigot bearing in crankshaft seized Air in hydraulic system Faulty master or slave cylinder seals
Clutch slip	Worn clutch plate friction linings or contamination with oil Weak diaphragm spring due to overheating
Noise evident on depressing clutch pedal	Dry or worn release bearing

Chapter 6
Manual gearbox and automatic transmission

Contents

Specifications

Manual gearbox
Type .... Four or five forward speeds and reverse, synchromesh on all forward speeds

Ratios

	Four-speed (716.005)	Four-speed (716.006)	Five-speed (717.400)
1st	3.90 : 1	3.98 : 1	3.82 : 1
2nd	2.30 : 1	2.29 : 1	2.202 : 1
3rd	1.41 : 1	1.45 : 1	1.398 : 1
4th	1.1 : 1	1 : 1	1 : 1
5th	–	–	0.813 : 1
Reverse	3.66 : 1	3.74 : 1	3.705 : 1

Oil capacity .... 1.6 litre; 2.8 Imp pt; 1.7 US qt

Torque wrench settings

	lbf ft	Nm
Drive flange nut:		
Four-speed	110	150
Five-speed	118	160
Mainshaft nut	59	80
Countershaft nut	110	150
Filler and drain plugs	44	60
Detent plug	18	24
Cover bolts (four-speed)	11	15
Front and rear cover bolts (five-speed)	15	20
Intermediate plate (five-speed)	20	27
Shift cover (five-speed)	7	9

Automatic transmission
Type .... Four forward speeds and one reverse, epicyclic geartrain with hydraulic control and torque converter

Ratios

	Early models	Later models
1st	3.98 : 1	3.68 : 1
2nd	2.39 : 1	2.41 : 1
3rd	1.46 : 1	1.44 : 1
4th	1 : 1	1 : 1
Reverse	5.47 : 1	5.14 : 1

Fluid capacity

	Early models	Later models
Complete refill	6.6 litre; 11.6 Imp pt; 7.0 US qt	6.1 litre; 10.7 Imp pt; 6.5 US qt
Service fluid change	5.3 litre; 9.3 Imp pt; 5.6 US qt	4.8 litre; 8.5 Imp pt; 5.1 US qt

Torque wrench settings

	lbf ft	Nm
Transmission to engine	40	54
Torque converter	30	41
Oil pan	5	7

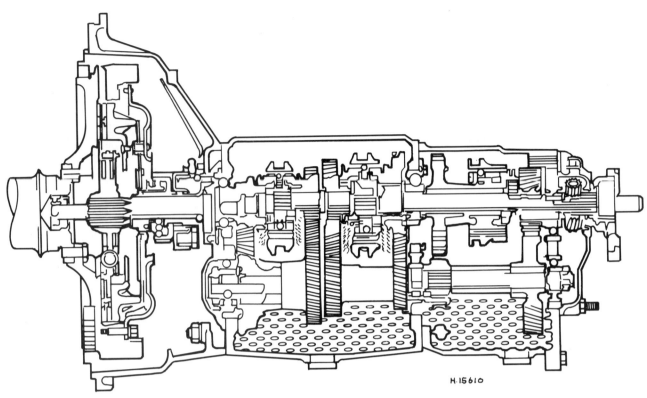

Fig. 6.1 Cross-section of the five-speed gearbox (Sec 1)

MANUAL GEARBOX

1 General description

The manual gearbox is of four- or five-speed type with synchromesh on all forward speeds. The five-speed version has been adapted from the four-speed version with the 5th gear in a housing on the rear of the gearbox, because of this some of the repair procedures are identical.

When overhauling the gearbox, due consideration should be given to the costs involved, since it is often more economical to obtain a service exchange or good secondhand gearbox rather than fit new parts to the existing gearbox.

2 Removal and refitting

The gearbox can be removed in unit with the engine, as described in Chapter 1, then separated from the engine on the bench. However, if work is only necessary on the gearbox or clutch it is better to remove the gearbox from under the car. The latter method is described in this Section.

1 Position the car over an inspection pit or alternatively on car ramps and/or axle stands so that there is sufficient working room beneath the car.

2 Disconnect the battery negative lead.

3 Remove the exhaust system, as described in Chapter 3.

4 Where applicable on four-speed models disconnect the throttle rod at the carburettor.

5 Support the gearbox with a trolley jack, then unscrew the rear mounting nut and unbolt the crossmember from the underbody.

6 Unscrew the nuts and clamp, and remove the exhaust bracket from the rear of the gearbox, noting the position of the rubbers where applicable.

7 Remove the propeller shaft with reference to Chapter 7.

8 Disconnect the gear shift rods from the levers by prising off the clips.

9 Unscrew the bolt from the rear cover and pull out the speedometer cable. Tie it to one side.

10 Remove the clutch slave cylinder and hydraulic line, with reference to Chapter 5, and tie to one side.

11 Remove the starter motor, as described in Chapter 10.

12 Lower the trolley jack a little and support the engine with a further jack or blocks of wood.

13 Unscrew all the bolts securing the gearbox to the engine, then, with the help of an assistant, withdraw the gearbox from the engine and remove it from under the car. Do not allow the weight of the gearbox to hang on the input shaft and make sure that the car is adequately supported, since a little rocking may be necessary to free the gearbox.

14 Refitting is a reversal of removal, but check the clutch release arm and bearing and the centralisation of the disc, with reference to Chapter 5. Lightly grease the input shaft splines with high melting-point grease. Finally check and, if necessary, top up the gearbox oil level. When engaging the input shaft with the clutch disc it will be helpful to temporarily engage top gear and to turn the rear drive flange.

Fig. 6.2 Speedometer cable retaining bolt – arrowed (Sec 2)

3   Dismantling into major assemblies

1   Clean the exterior of the gearbox with paraffin and wipe dry.
2   Remove the clutch release arm and bearing with reference to Chapter 5, then unscrew the nuts and remove the clutch housing from the front of the gearbox using a wooden mallet, if necessary.
3   Unscrew the drain plug and drain the oil into a suitable container. Refit and tighten the drain plug.
4   From the left-hand side of the gearbox loosen the clamp bolt on the centre shift lever for reverse gear (and, on five-speed versions, 5th gear), mark the lever in relation to the shaft then withdraw it from the splines.
5   Prise off the circlip and remove the washer from the shaft.
6   Unscrew the shift cover bolts and tap the cover from the locating dowels while at the same time tapping the reverse (and 5th if applicable) shaft inwards. Insert the fingers behind the cover and disconnect the shift forks from the rockers, then tilt the top of the cover outwards and lift it from the gearbox.
7   Unbolt the front cover from the gearbox casing, noting the location of the shims for adjustment of the bearing endfloat. Remove the gasket. Leave the clutch release bearing guide tube attached to the cover at this stage.
8   Hold the rear drive flange stationary with a metal bar bolted to it then use a slotted box spanner to unscrew the special nut.
9   Remove the drive flange from the splines with a suitable puller.

Fig. 6.3 View inside the gearbox with the shift cover removed (Sec 3)

63 Reverse/5th selector dog
65 Reverse/5th selector rod
106 3rd/4th selector fork
107 1st/2nd selector fork

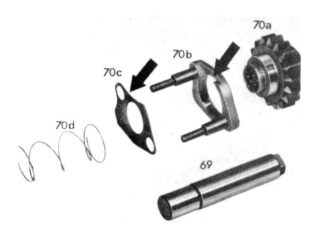

Fig. 6.4 Reverse idler gear synchroniser brake components (Sec 3)

69 Idler shaft
70a Reverse idler gear
70b Synchro ring
70c Thrust plate
70d Spring

Fig. 6.5 Removing the mainshaft assembly (Sec 3)
11a Synchro sleeve in 3rd speed position

Fig. 6.6 Extracting the input shaft bearing from the casing (Sec 3)

1a Slotted nut
3a Bearing
6   Oil thrower
7a Input shaft

Fig. 6.7 Driving the countershaft with taper roller bearing from the casing (Sec 3)

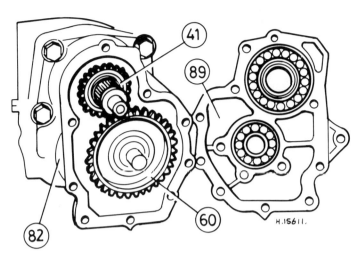

Fig. 6.8 Removing the intermediate plate on the five-speed gearbox (Sec 3)

41 5th gear (mainshaft)   82 Intermediate housing
60 5th gear (countershaft)   89 Intermediate plate

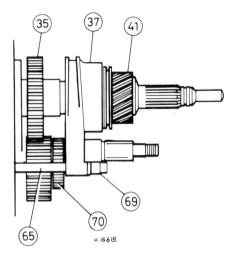

Fig. 6.9 Gears with the intermediate housing removed on the five-speed gearbox (Sec 3)

35 Reverse gear (mainshaft)   65 Reverse/5th selector rod
37 5th synchro unit   69 Reverse idler gear shaft
41 5th gear (mainshaft)   70 Reverse idler gear

10 Unscrew the bolts from the rear cover and tap it from the gearbox casing. Remove the gasket.

11 Pull the speedometer worm drive gear from the rear end of the mainshaft.

Four-speed version

12 Pull the reverse gear from the mainshaft.

13 Pull out the reverse idler shaft then disconnect the idler gear from the fork on the selector rod. If necessary, screw a slide hammer into the end of the shaft to remove it. On some models the idler gear is fitted with a synchroniser brake which must be withdrawn from the casing together with the thrust plate and spring.

14 Unscrew the nut from the rear of the countershaft and lever off the reverse gear. In order to hold the countershaft stationary, temporarily refit the drive flange and bolt a length of bar to it, then select top gear.

15 With neutral engaged, remove the selector forks from the grooves in the synchro sleeves.

16 Using a pin punch drive the roll pin from the reverse selector dog then withdraw the selector shaft and remove the dog.

17 Move the synchro unit sleeves to select two gears at the same time, then bend back the peening, if applicable, and unscrew the bearing nut from the front of the countershaft using a slotted box spanner, if applicable.

18 Flatten the tab washers and unbolt the bearing retaining plate from the rear of the casing.

19 *On versions with a ball-bearing on the front of the countershaft follow paragraphs 20 to 25. On versions with a taper roller bearing follow paragraphs 26 to 33.*

20 Using a bearing puller, extract the countershaft front and rear bearings from the casing.

21 Similarly extract the mainshaft rear bearing.

22 Locate a suitable length of metal tube over the rear of the mainshaft and retain with the drive flange nut, in order to retain the 1st gear on the needle bearing.

23 Lift the rear of the mainshaft and withdraw the input shaft from the front of the casing. Recover the 4th synchro ring and the needle bearing.

24 Push the 3rd/4th synchro sleeve into 3rd speed position, then move the mainshaft assembly rearwards and withdraw it through the side aperture.

25 Move the countershaft rearwards, then withdraw it through the side aperture.

26 Use a bearing puller to extract the countershaft rear bearing from the casing.

27 Using a slotted box spanner unscrew the special nut from the input shaft. Grip the input shaft in a soft jawed vice to hold it stationary.

28 Lever the input shaft bearing from the casing and shaft with two screwdrivers.

29 Using a bearing puller, extract the mainshaft rear bearing from the casing.

30 With the help of an assistant lift the input shaft and mainshaft together and use a soft-faced mallet to drive the countershaft and taper roller bearing rearwards from the casing — temporarily refit the nut on the front of the shaft first.

31 With the countershaft in the bottom of the casing, withdraw the input shaft and bearing. Recover the 4th synchro ring and the needle bearing.

32 Push the 3rd/4th synchro sleeve into 3rd speed position, then move the mainshaft assembly rearwards and withdraw it through the side aperture.

33 Move the countershaft rearwards, then withdraw it through the side aperture.

Five-speed version

34 Remove the selector forks from the grooves in the synchro sleeves.

35 Unscrew the nut from the rear of the countershaft using a slotted box spanner where applicable. In order to hold the countershaft stationary, temporarily move the synchro unit sleeves to select two gears at the same time.

36 Unbolt the intermediate plate and withdraw it together with the bearings, using a soft-faced mallet to release it from the shafts. The countershaft bearing may in fact remain on the shaft if tight.

37 Using a two-legged puller, remove the 5th gear (and bearing if tight) from the countershaft.

38 Unbolt the intermediate housing from the casing, and remove the gasket.

39 Using a pin punch, drive the roll pin from the reverse/5th selector dog and move the dog forward as far as possible.

40 Extract the reverse/5th detent holder together with the detent spring and ball from the side of the casing.

41 Pull out the reverse idler shaft then disconnect the idler gear from the fork on the selector rod.

42 Slide the 5th gear, together with the needle bearing and synchro ring, from the mainshaft.

43 Using a two-legged puller on the reverse gear, pull the reverse gear and 5th synchro unit from the mainshaft. At the same time withdraw the reverse/5th selector rod from the casing and remove the dog. Also at the same time remove the 5th gear needle bearing race. Note the spacer between the synchro unit and reverse gear.

44 Prise the Woodruff key from the countershaft and slide off the spacer. Remove the reverse gear from the splines, using a puller if necessary.

45 Prise both Woodruff keys from the mainshaft.

46 Move the synchro unit sleeves to select two gears at the same time, then bend back the peening, if applicable, and unscrew the bearing nut from the front of the countershaft, using a slotted box spanner if applicable.

47 Unbolt the bearing retaining plate from the rear of the casing and recover the endfloat shims.

48 Extract the inner circlip from the input shaft then use a bearing puller to remove the bearing from the casing and input shaft. Remove the oil thrower.

49 Similarly remove the mainshaft rear bearing.

50 Locate a suitable length of metal tube over the rear of the mainshaft and retain with the drive flange nut, in order to retain the 1st gear on the needle bearing.

51 On versions with a ball-bearing on the front of the countershaft use a bearing puller to extract the bearing from the casing and countershaft.

52 Using a soft-faced mallet drive the countershaft (and front tapered

roller bearing, if applicable) rearwards while an assistant lifts the mainshaft and input shaft. When the rear countershaft bearing is out of the casing use two levers to remove the bearing from the shaft.

53 With the countershaft in the bottom of the casing, withdraw the input shaft and bearing. Recover the 4th synchro ring and the needle bearing.

54 Push the 3rd/4th synchro sleeve into 3rd speed position then move the mainshaft assembly rearwards and withdraw it through the side aperture.

55 Move the countershaft rearwards then withdraw it through the side aperture.

---

4   Mainshaft – dismantling and reassembly

1   Temporarily refit the drive flange to the rear of the mainshaft and grip the flange in a vice with the mainshaft vertical.

2   Unscrew the nut from the front of the mainshaft using a slotted

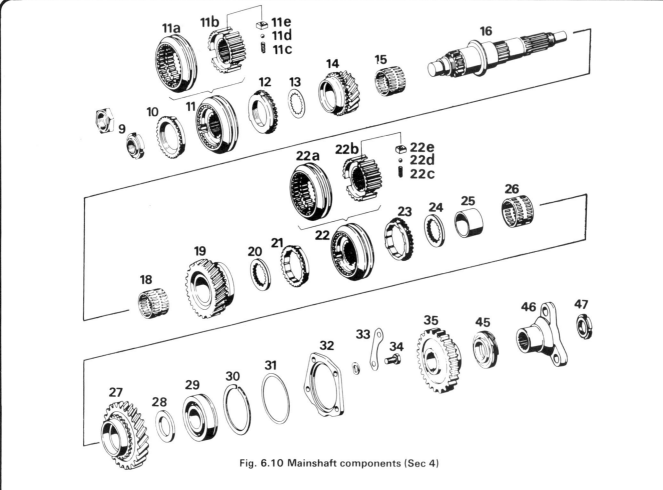

Fig. 6.10 Mainshaft components (Sec 4)

9	Slot nut or hex nut mainshaft front	13	Thrust washer for 3rd gear
10	Synchronizing ring for 4th gear	14	Helical gear 3rd gear
11	Synchronizing body with sliding sleeve for 3rd and 4th gear	15	Needle cage for 3rd gearwheel
11a	Sliding sleeve	16	Mainshaft
11b	Synchronizing body	18	Needle cage for 2nd gearwheel
11c	Compression springs synchronizing body	19	Helical gear 2nd gear with synchronizing cone
11d	Steel ball	20	Thrust washer
11e	Key	21	Synchronizing ring for 2nd gear
12	Synchronizing ring for 3rd gear	22	Synchronizing body with sliding sleeve 1st and

	2nd gear	28	Thrust washer
22a	Sliding sleeve	29	Radial ball-bearing
22b	Synchronizing body	30	Circlip
22c	Compression spring synchronizing body	31	Compensating washer
22d	Steel ball	32	Holding ring rear bearing mainshaft
22e	Key	33	Locking plate or spring washer
23	Synchronizing ring for 1st gear	34	Hex bolt
24	Thrust washer	35	Reversing gear mainshaft
25	Race 1st gearwheel	45	Helical gear tachometer drive
26	Needle cage for 1st gearwheel	46	Universal flange
27	Helical gear for 1st gear	47	Locking nut universal flange on mainshaft

box spanner where necessary and remove the 3rd/4th synchro unit and synchro-ring.

3   Remove the serrated thrust washer (if fitted) followed by 3rd gear and the needle bearing.

4   Remove the mainshaft from the vice then, from the rear, remove the thrust washer, 1st gear and the needle bearing rollers.

5   Place the mainshaft upright in the open vice with the 2nd gear at the bottom, then use a soft-faced mallet to drive the mainshaft down until the 1st gear needle bearing inner race is free.

6   Remove the mainshaft from the vice and withdraw the inner race followed by the thrust washer (if fitted), 1st synchro-ring, 1st/2nd synchro unit and 2nd synchro-ring.

7   Remove the thrust washer (if fitted), 2nd gear and needle bearing.

8   Clean all components in paraffin and wipe dry, then examine them for wear and damage. Press each synchro-ring onto its respective gear

Fig. 6.11 Checking the synchro-ring wear (Sec 4)

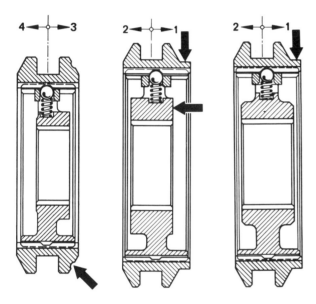

Fig. 6.12 Cross-section of coil spring type synchro units (Sec 4)

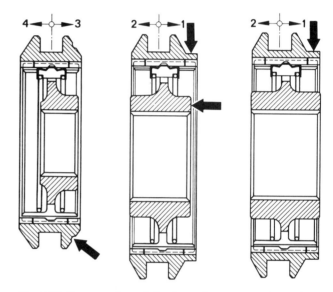

Fig. 6.13 Cross-section of circular spring type synchro units (Sec 4)

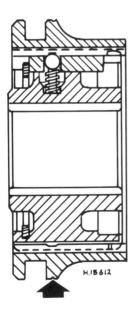

Fig. 6.14 Cross-section of coil spring type 5th synchro unit (Sec 4)

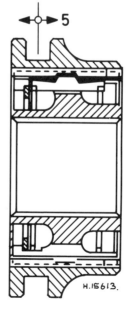

Fig. 6.15 Cross-section of circular spring type 5th synchro unit (Sec 4)

cone, then use a feeler blade to determine the clearance between the dog teeth (see Fig. 6.11). If the clearance is less than 0.5 mm (0.020 in) renew the synchro-ring. If the synchro unit is to be dismantled to renew worn components, first inspect the unit to see whether it incorporates coil or circular type springs.

9   *To dismantle a coil spring type synchro unit,* wrap a cloth round it, mark the hub in relation to the sleeve and then press the hub out of the sleeve. As the hub is ejected so the keys, balls and springs will be displaced (spring guides are provided on the 5th synchro). Renew the components as necessary and then reassemble them by inserting the springs and keys into the hub and, while holding the keys depressed, partially insert the hub into the sleeve. Locate one ball at a time and when all three are fitted, push the hub fully home. Fit the hubs into the sleeves in accordance with the diagrams. Note that the 1st/2nd synchro keys have a chamfer on one corner. Make sure that the chamfer is towards the 2nd gear wheel.

10   *To dismantle a circular spring type synchro unit,* mark the hub in relation to the sleeve then remove the circlip (5th synchro only), push the hub from the sleeve and extract the keys and springs. Renew components as necessary and then reassemble them so that the hub to sleeve relationship is in accordance with the diagrams (Figs. 6.13 and 6.15). Note that the angled ends of the springs must not be in the same key and the springs must point in opposite directions.

11   Commence reassembly of the mainshaft by mounting it vertical in a soft-jawed vice with the rear end uppermost. Lubricate the components as they are assembled.

12   Locate the 2nd gear needle bearing up to the shoulder, followed by 2nd gear and the thrust washer (if fitted).

13   Fit the 2nd synchro-ring on the 2nd gear then press the 1st/2nd synchro unit on the splines with the flanged end of the sleeve towards the rear of the mainshaft.

14   Fit the 1st synchro-ring on the synchro unit followed by the thrust washer (if fitted).

15   Heat the 1st gear needle bearing inner race then quickly tap it fully onto the mainshaft with a length of metal tube.

16   Fit the needle bearing rollers, 1st gear and the thrust washer. To prevent the 1st gear and needle bearing subsequently coming off, temporarily fit a suitable metal tube over the mainshaft and retain with the flange nut.

17   Invert the mainshaft in the vice then fit the 3rd gear needle bearing followed by the 3rd gear and serrated thrust washer (if fitted).

18   Fit the 3rd synchro-ring on the 3rd gear then press the 3rd/4th synchro unit on the splines, grooved end of the sleeve first.

19   Fit the nut to the front of the mainshaft and tighten to the specified torque, then lock by peening the collar into the groove in the shaft.

5   Countershaft and input shaft – dismantling and reassembly

1   Where applicable, pull the taper bearing from the front of the countershaft.

2   Rest the 3rd gear in an open vice with the largest gear uppermost, and press the countershaft out in a downwards direction. Prise out the Woodruff key.

3   Clean all the components in paraffin and wipe dry, then examine them for wear and damage. Renew them as necessary, but note if the taper bearing is worn; only a ball-bearing is available for a replacement.

4   Fit the Woodruff key and press on the gears in reverse order, making sure that the gear shoulders face each other.

5   Pull the bearing from the input shaft and renew if necessary. Refit in reverse order and tighten the nut where applicable.

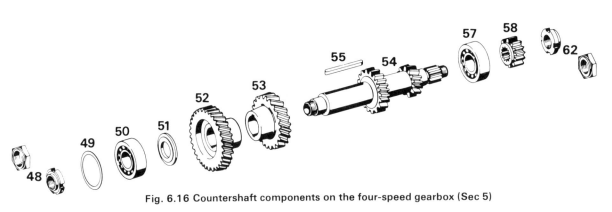

Fig. 6.16 Countershaft components on the four-speed gearbox (Sec 5)

48 Slot nut or hex nut	52 Countershaft helical	55 Woodruff key
49 Compensating washer	gear – constant gear	57 Radial ball-bearing
50 Radial ball-bearing	53 Countershaft helical	58 Reversing gear –
51 Spacing washer (for	gear 3rd gear	countershaft
countershaft gear –	54 Countershaft helical	62 Slot nut or hex nut
constant gear)	gear for 2nd and 1st gear	

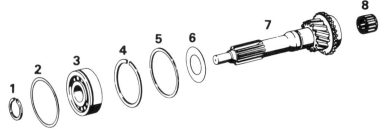

Fig. 6.17 Input shaft components (Sec 5)

1 Circlip	3 Ball-bearing	5 Spacer	7 Input shaft
2 Compensating washer	4 Circlip	6 Oil thrower	8 Needle bearing

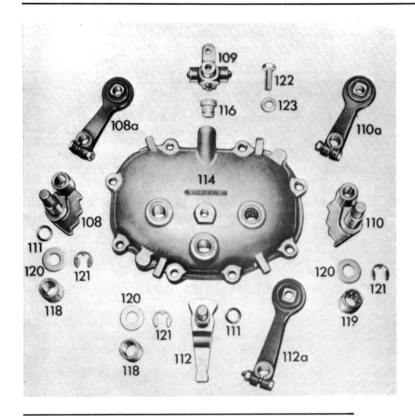

108 Shift rocker for 3rd
and 4th gear
108a Shift lever for 3rd
and 4th gear
109 Locking cage
110 Shift rocker for 1st
and 2nd gear
110a Shift lever for 1st
and 2nd gear
111 O-ring
112 Shift finger for
reverse gear
112a Shift lever for
reverse gear
114 Transmission shift
cover
116 Breather
118 Bushing (bearing
gearshifting shaft 3rd
and 4th gear or reverse
gear)
119 Needle bearing
(bearing gearshifting
lever 1st and 2nd gear)
120 Washer
121 Lockwasher
122 Hex bolt
123 Sheet metal lock or
spring washer

6 Gearshift cover – dismantling and reassembly

1 Mark the shift levers in relation to the shafts then slide them from the splines.
2 Extract the C-clips from the shafts and remove the washers.
3 Pull out the shift rockers and finger.
4 Flatten the locktab (if fitted) then unscrew the central bolt and pull out the locking cage. Note the locating pin in the cover.
5 Clean all the components in paraffin and wipe dry. Examine them for wear and damage and renew them as necessary. If the shaft bearings are worn, drive them out with a soft metal drift and install new ones. Renew the O-ring seals.
6 Reassembly is a reversal of dismantling, but lightly grease the shafts.

7 Casings and bearings – inspection

1 Examine the casings for damage, and check the bearings for wear by spinning them by hand – renew the bearings if roughness or uneven movement is evident.
2 Renew all oil seals and gaskets. To renew the front cover oil seal unbolt the clutch release bearing guide tube, then drive out the seal with a metal tube. The new seal should be driven in flush. Smear sealing compound on the guide tube bolts before inserting them, but do not fully tighten until after the gearbox has been reassembled and the clutch housing fitted.
3 To renew the rear cover oil seal, lever it out then use a block of wood to drive the new seal in flush.
4 Check the speedometer drivegear in the rear cover for wear and renew it if necessary. To remove it use a soft metal drift to drive the shaft through the gear and out of the cover. Note that the sealing ball or plug will be pushed out, but the plug can be levered out first with a screwdriver. Extract the seal by screwing a bolt into it and pulling on the bolt. Refitting is a reversal of removal, with reference to Fig. 6.19, however, before fitting the sealing plug, coat it with sealing compound.

8 Reassembly

1 Insert the countershaft through the casing side aperture and lower it to the bottom.

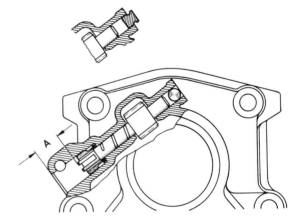

Fig. 6.19 Cross-section of the speedometer drivegear (Sec 7)

A = 19.0 mm (0.748 in)

2 With the 3rd/4th synchro sleeve in the 3rd speed position, insert the mainshaft assembly into the casing.
3 Fit the needle bearing in the input shaft and locate the 4th synchro ring onto the gear cone.

Five-speed version

4 Insert the input shaft and engage it with the mainshaft.
5 While an assistant lifts the mainshaft and input shaft, raise the countershaft and, on tapered roller bearing types, drive it forwards until the bearing is in the casing. Fit the rear (and front, where applicable) countershaft bearings, using metal tubes to drive them into the casing.
6 Fit the oil thrower and bearing on the input shaft then use a metal tube to drive the bearing fully into the casing. Support the mainshaft while fitting the bearing, and make sure that the 4th synchro ring remains in place.
7 Fit the inner circlip to the input shaft.
8 Remove the tube from the mainshaft and fit the rear bearing into the casing using a metal tube while supporting the input shaft.

9   Move the synchro unit sleeves to select two gears at the same time then fit the bearing nut to the front of the countershaft and tighten it to the specified torque. Where applicable peen the nut collar into the shaft groove.

10   Select neutral then fit the bearing endfloat shims and retaining plate to the rear of the casing and tighten the bolts. If the bearing has been renewed, the endfloat of the bearing outer track must be set to between 0 and 0.05 mm (0 and 0.002 in) by using vernier calipers to determine the distances of the bearing circlip and retaining plate shoulder from the mating surface. If applicable, lock the bolts by bending the locktabs.

11   Fit the spacer on the countershaft and press the reverse gear on the splines, then tap the Woodruff key in the groove.

12   Tap the two Woodruff keys into the mainshaft grooves.

13   Using a length of metal tubing, drive the reverse gear onto the mainshaft key, followed by the spacer. The correct thickness of the spacer is dependent on the length of the selector rod in accordance with the following table.

Selector rod coding (on end of fork)	Spacer thickness
Red dot	3.8 mm (0.150 in)
No dot	3.9 mm (0.154 in)
White dot	4.0 mm (0.157 in)

14   Engage the reverse/5th selector rod fork with the sleeve groove on the 5th synchro unit then slide them into the casing and onto the mainshaft. At the same time locate the dog on the selector rod in the casing aperture.

15   Warm the 5th gear needle bearing race (in the hand will suffice) and locate it on the mainshaft against the synchro unit, while pulling the mainshaft rearwards.

16   Locate the synchro-ring on the 5th gear cone then fit the needle bearing and slide the 5th gear on it.

17   Locate the reverse idler gear in the selector fork, then insert the idler shaft through the gear and into the casing.

18   Move the reverse/5th selector rod into its central position and insert the detent ball and spring, having applied a little grease to the components. Drive the holder into the casing to retain.

19   Align the dog with the hole in the selector rod then drive in the roll pin.

20   Fit the intermediate housing, together with a new gasket. Apply sealing compound to the threads of the bolts before inserting them and tightening them finger tight. Note that the locating pin on the reverse idler shaft must face outwards in order to engage the cut-out in the housing.

21   The intermediate housing must be centralised in relation to the intermediate plate before finally tightening the bolts. To do this remove the bearings from the plate, fit the plate to the housing and check that the bearings can be pushed freely into the plate. Re-position the housing as necessary then tighten the outer bolts. Remove the intermediate plate and bearings and tighten the inner bolts.

22   Using a metal tube, drive the 5th gear onto the end of the countershaft.

23   Fit a new gasket to the intermediate plate, having first fitted the bearings, then locate the plate over the mainshaft and countershaft onto the locating pins, insert the bolts and tighten.

24   Temporarily lock the countershaft by selecting two gears at the same time, then fit the nut to the countershaft and tighten to the specified torque. Where applicable peen the nut to lock it.

25   Fit the selector forks to the grooves in the synchro sleeves in the casing side aperture.

Four-speed version

26   Insert the input shaft in the casing and engage it with the front of the mainshaft.

27   Remove the metal tube from the mainshaft then drive the rear bearing onto the mainshaft and into the casing while supporting the input shaft.

28   Invert the gearbox so that the countershaft meshes with the input shaft and mainshaft gears then drive in the front and rear bearings using a metal tube.

29   Select two gears at the same time then fit the nut to the front of the countershaft and tighten it to the specified torque. If applicable, peen the collar into the shaft groove to lock it.

30   Select neutral then fit the bearing endfloat shims and retaining plate to the rear of the casing and tighten the bolts. If the bearing has been renewed, the endfloat of the bearing outer track must be set to

Fig. 6.20 Using vernier calipers to determine the mainshaft rear bearing endfloat shim thickness (Sec 8)

Fig. 6.21 Fitting the rear cover (93) to the four-speed gearbox (Sec 8)

Note the locating dowel (A) and flat on the reverse idler shaft (69)

between 0 and 0.05 mm (0 and 0.002 in) by using vernier calipers to determine the distances of the bearing circlip and retaining plate shoulder from the mating surface. If applicable, lock the bolts by bending the locktabs.

31   Slide the reverse gear onto the rear of the countershaft then, with two gears selected fit the nut and tighten to the specified torque. If applicable peen the collar into the shaft groove to lock it.

32   Insert the reverse selector shaft and at the same time locate the dog on the shaft. Align the holes and drive in the roll pin to secure.

33   Engage the reverse idler gear with the selector fork and insert the idler shaft, tapping it into the casing. Make sure that the flat on the end of the shaft is uppermost. Where a synchroniser brake is fitted the recess must face the countershaft.

34   Using a metal tube drive the reverse gear onto the mainshaft.

35   Fit the selector forks to the grooves in the synchro sleeves in the casing side aperture and engage neutral.

All versions

36   Using a metal tube, drive the speedometer worm drive gear onto the mainshaft with the chamfered end to the rear.

37   Fit the rear cover, together with a new gasket and tighten the bolts evenly to the specified torque.

38   Press the drive flange onto the mainshaft splines and secure by tightening the nut to the specified torque while holding the flange stationary by bolting a metal bar to it. Where applicable lock the nut by peening the collar into the groove.

39 Fit the front cover together with the shims and a new gasket and tighten the bolts. If the input shaft bearing has been renewed the endfloat of the bearing outer track must be set to between 0 and 0.05 mm (0 and 0.002 in). If the countershaft bearing has been renewed the endfloat of the bearing outer track must be set to between 0.07 and 0.15 mm (0.003 and 0.006 in). Use vernier calipers to determine the distances of the cover shoulders, bearing track or bearing circlip from the mating surface, but add the thickness of the compressed gasket to the cover dimensions. Note that the threads of the bolts must be sealed with sealing compound.

40 Position the selector forks and the reverse/5th selector shaft in neutral, then push the reverse/5th shift shaft about 25.0 mm (1.0 in) through the cover.

41 Fit the shift cover, together with a new gasket, while at the same time engaging the reverse/5th finger with the dog, and the selector forks in the rockers. Apply sealing compound on the threads then insert and tighten them.

42 Locate the washer on the reverse/5th shift shaft then fit the circlip.
43 Press the shift lever on the splines in the previously noted position then tighten the clamp bolt.
44 Fill the gearbox with oil to the bottom of the filler plug hole, then tighten the plug.
45 Fit the clutch housing to the front of the gearbox and tighten the nuts. If the clutch release bearing guide tube has been removed, tighten the bolts now.
46 Refit the clutch release arm and bearing, with reference to Chapter 5.

9 Floor gearchange – adjustment

1 Apply the handbrake/parking brake, then jack up the front of the car and support it on axle stands.

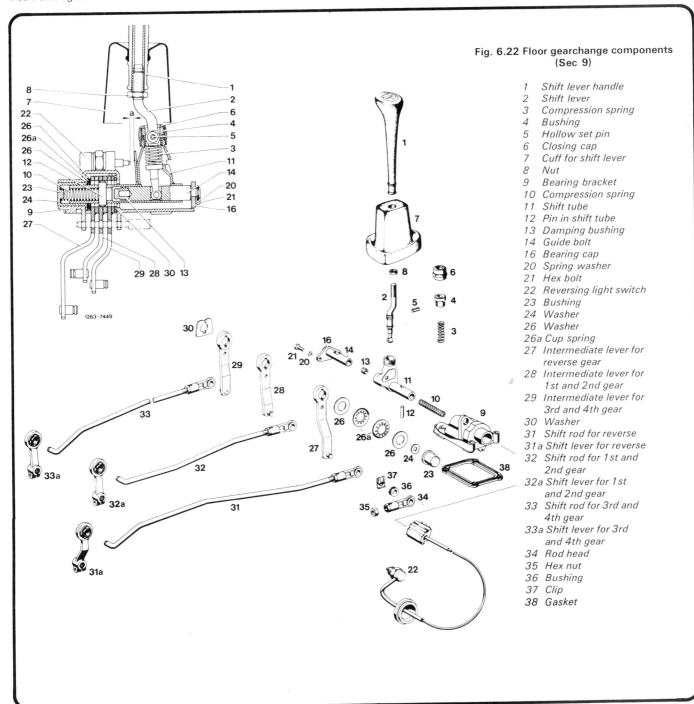

Fig. 6.22 Floor gearchange components (Sec 9)

1 Shift lever handle
2 Shift lever
3 Compression spring
4 Bushing
5 Hollow set pin
6 Closing cap
7 Cuff for shift lever
8 Nut
9 Bearing bracket
10 Compression spring
11 Shift tube
12 Pin in shift tube
13 Damping bushing
14 Guide bolt
16 Bearing cap
20 Spring washer
21 Hex bolt
22 Reversing light switch
23 Bushing
24 Washer
26 Washer
26a Cup spring
27 Intermediate lever for reverse gear
28 Intermediate lever for 1st and 2nd gear
29 Intermediate lever for 3rd and 4th gear
30 Washer
31 Shift rod for reverse
31a Shift lever for reverse
32 Shift rod for 1st and 2nd gear
32a Shift lever for 1st and 2nd gear
33 Shift rod for 3rd and 4th gear
33a Shift lever for 3rd and 4th gear
34 Rod head
35 Hex nut
36 Bushing
37 Clip
38 Gasket

2   Extract the clips and disconnect the rods from the bottom of the floor gearchange.
3   Lock the gearchange levers in neutral by inserting a 6 mm (0.24 in) diameter pin through the hole provided.
4   Move the shift levers into neutral and check the dimensions shown in Figs. 6.23 and 6.24. Reposition the levers on the splines if necessary.

Five-speed models
5   Working inside the car, remove the centre console cover from the

gear lever and push the gear lever fully to the right and forwards. Check that the stop plate and finger are aligned as shown in Fig. 6.25 – if not, reposition the stop plate.
6   Refit the centre console cover.

All models
7   Adjust the lengths of the shift rods so that they enter the levers freely, then fit the clips.
8   Remove the locating pin and lower the car to the ground.

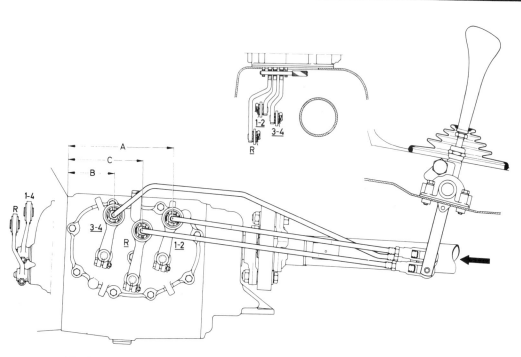

Fig. 6.23 Shift lever neutral setting dimensions on four-speed models (Sec 9)

A   =   142.0 mm (5.59 in)   B   =   58.0 mm (2.28 in)   C   =   111.0 mm (4.37 in)

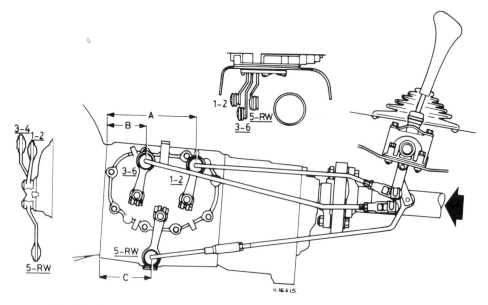

Fig. 6.24 Shift lever neutral setting dimensions on five-speed models (Sec 9)

A   =   168.0 mm (6.61 in)   B   =   86.0 mm (3.39 in)   C   =   95.0 mm (3.74 in)

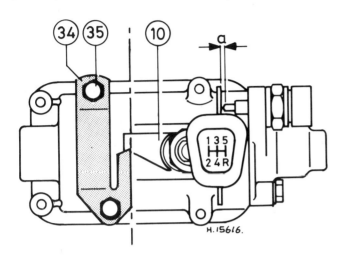

Fig. 6.25 Five-speed gearbox gear lever alignment (Sec 9)

a = 1.5 mm (0.06 in)
10 Stop finger
34 Stop plate
35 Bolt

H.15616.

AUTOMATIC TRANSMISSION

10 General description

The automatic transmission is of four-speed type and includes an oil cooler fitted to the bottom of the radiator.

The transmission incorporates two main components:
(a) A three element hydrokinetic torque converter coupling with a torque multiplication capability.
(b) A torque/speed responsive and hydraulically-operated epicyclic gearbox comprising planetary gearsets providing four forward and one reverse ratio.

Due to the complexity of the automatic transmission unit, if performance is not up to standard, or overhaul is necessary, it is imperative that the unit is tested in the car by a dealer equipped with the special instrumentation required. The content of the following Sections is therefore confined to supplying general information and procedures which can be carried out by the home mechanic.

11 Fluid level checking

1   Position the car on level ground with the handbrake/parking brake applied.
2   With the selector lever in position P run the engine for 2 minutes.
3   With the engine still running, withdraw the dipstick and wipe it clean with a non-fluffy cloth.
4   Re-insert the dipstick fully then withdraw it again. At normal operating temperature the fluid level should be on the maximum mark, but at a fluid temperature of 20 to 30°C (68 to 86°F) the level will be approximately 30.0 mm (1.2 in) below the minimum mark. If necessary top up the level with the correct fluid through the dipstick tube (photo).

5   Re-insert the dipstick and switch off the engine. Note that, when completely filling the transmission with fluid, the selector lever should be moved through all positions three times with the engine idling.

12 Removal and refitting

1   Disconnect the battery negative lead.
2   Jack up the car and support on axle stands. Make sure that there is sufficient working room beneath the car.
3   Place a container beneath the transmission then unscrew the union bolt securing the dipstick tube to the oil pan, and drain the fluid (photo). If necessary, the torque converter can be drained by turning it until the drain plug is located in the housing aperture, and removing the plug. Refit the plug with a new sealing ring when completed.
4   Unscrew the oil cooler feed and return line union bolts and also detach the line brackets from the transmission (photo).
5   Unbolt the cover from the front of the transmission.
6   Remove the propeller shaft, as described in Chapter 7.
7   Detach the oil cooler line brackets from the engine and tie the lines to one side (photo).
8   Unbolt the exhaust bracket from the rear of the transmission.
9   Support the transmission on a trolley jack.
10   Unbolt the rear crossmember from the underbody and transmission then unscrew the nut and remove the mounting rubber (photo).
11   Select P, then disconnect the selector rod from the lever.
12   Unscrew the bolt and pull out the speedometer drive cable (photo).
13   Disconnect the wiring from the kickdown switch (photo).
14   Disconnect the downshift rod (photo).
15   Disconnect the wiring from the inhibitor switch.
16   Unbolt the bracket and disconnect the vacuum hose (photo).
17   Unscrew the three pairs of driveplate bolts from the torque

11.4 Topping-up the automatic transmission fluid

12.3 Dipstick tube-to-oil pan union bolt

12.4 Oil cooler feed and return lines

converter, turning the driveplate as necessary to position the bolts in the front aperture.

18 Slightly lower the transmission then unscrew all the transmission-to-engine bolts.

19 With the help of an assistant, withdraw the transmission from the engine, but make sure that the torque converter remains firmly in contact with the transmission oil pump otherwise it could be damaged. The car must be adequately supported since it will be necessary to rock the transmission to release it.

20 Refitting is a reversal of removal, but first make sure that the torque converter is fully engaged with the oil pump by checking the distance shown in Fig. 6.26 (photo). Fill the unit with the correct fluid and check the level when completely fitted.

12.7 Oil cooler hose connection

---

13 Fluid and filter renewal

1 With the transmission at normal operating temperature position the car on level ground with the handbrake/parking brake applied.

2 Place a container beneath the transmission then unscrew the union bolt securing the dipstick tube to the oil pan and drain the fluid.

3 Turn the crankshaft pulley bolt until the torque converter drain plug is located in the housing aperture then unscrew the plug and drain the fluid. The fluid will be hot, so take the necessary precautions

12.10 Automatic transmission rear crossmember

12.12 Speedometer drive cable connection

12.13 Kickdown switch

12.14 Transmission downshift lever

12.16 Vacuum unit

12.20 Torque converter fully engaged

to avoid scalding. Refit and tighten the drain plug, together with a new washer.
4   Remove the screws and lower the oil pan (photos).
5   Unscrew the cross-head screws and remove the oil filter (photo).
6   Fit the new filter in reverse order, but renew the oil pan gasket and union bolt washers.
7   Using a funnel in the dipstick tube, fill the transmission with the correct grade and quantity of fluid.
8   Check the fluid level, with reference to Section 11.

14 Downshift rod adjustment

1   Adjust the idle speed, as described in Chapter 3.
2   On early models with the downshift rod below the exhaust manifold, allow the engine to idle then disconnect the vacuum hose from the governor on the transmission and stop the engine. Disconnect the downshift rod at the lever, push it fully rearwards, then adjust the length of the rod so that it locates freely on the ball-head.
3   On later models switch off the engine, then disconnect the downshift rod from the lever. Push the lever and downshift rod fully rearwards, and adjust the length of the rod so that it locates freely on the ball-head.

15 Selector linkage adjustment

1   Jack up the front of the car and support on axle stands. Apply the handbrake/parking brake.

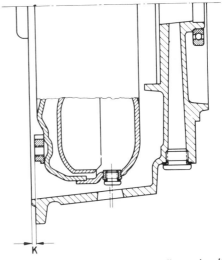

Fig. 6.26 Torque converter installation dimension (Sec 13)

K = 4.0 mm (0.16 in) minimum

13.4A Oil pan corner bolt

13.4B Removing the oil pan

13.5 Filter location on the automatic transmission

Floor change models
2   Disconnect the selector rod from the bottom of the selector lever.
3   Position the selector lever on both the transmission and inside the car to neutral (N).
4   Adjust the length of the selector rod so that it can be reconnected without disturbing the levers.

Steering column change models
5   Disconnect the cable at the transmission lever.
6   Position both the selector lever on the transmission and inside the car to neutral (N).
7   Adjust the outer cable at the locknuts so that the inner cable end can be reconnected without disturbing the levers.
8   The column indicator switch can be adjusted by loosening the retaining screws then switching on the ignition and selecting N. Move the switch so that the N lights up, then tighten the screws.

All models
9   Lower the car to the ground.

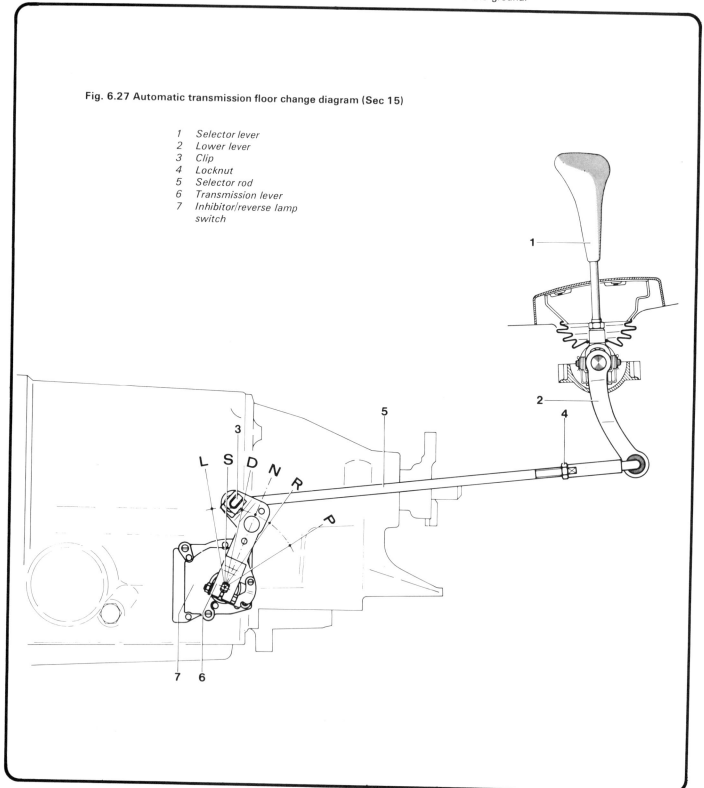

Fig. 6.27 Automatic transmission floor change diagram (Sec 15)

1   Selector lever
2   Lower lever
3   Clip
4   Locknut
5   Selector rod
6   Transmission lever
7   Inhibitor/reverse lamp switch

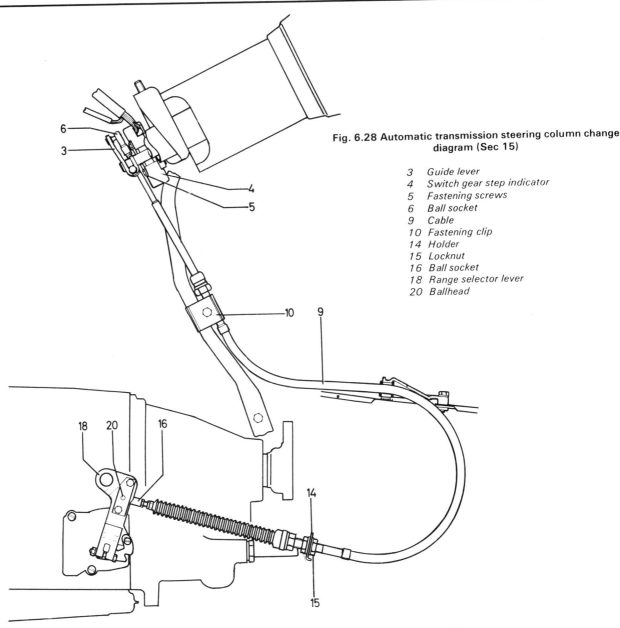

Fig. 6.28 Automatic transmission steering column change diagram (Sec 15)

3   *Guide lever*
4   *Switch gear step indicator*
5   *Fastening screws*
6   *Ball socket*
9   *Cable*
10 *Fastening clip*
14 *Holder*
15 *Locknut*
16 *Ball socket*
18 *Range selector lever*
20 *Ballhead*

16 Starter inhibitor/reverse light switch – adjustment

1   Jack up the front of the car and support on axle stands. Apply the handbrake/parking brake.
2   Select neutral (N) then disconnect the selector rod or cable from the transmission lever.
3   Loosen the switch adjusting screw and insert a 4.0 mm (0.157 in) diameter dowel rod into the special hole. Tighten the screw and remove the dowel rod.
4   Reconnect the selector rod or cable and lower the car to the ground.

17 Shift valve housing – overhaul

In the event of fluid contamination, the shift valve housing should be removed and thoroughly cleaned in addition to the renewal of the fluid and filter.

1   Drain the transmission fluid, with reference to Section 13, and also remove the filter.
2   Select P, then unbolt the shift valve housing from the transmission. Take care only to unscrew the retaining bolts (photos).
3   Place the housing in a clean area then unscrew all but two of the bottom bolts (photo).

Fig. 6.29 Automatic transmission starter inhibitor/reverse light switch (Sec 16)

1   Transmission lever   *5   Dowel rod*
3   Adjusting screw   *6   Clamp nut*
4   Shaft

4   Mount the housing on a fixture (photo) then remove the two bolts and remove the top together with the intermediate plate (photo). Invert the top and plate.

5   Remove the intermediate plate from the top, and note the location of balls and springs (photo).

6   Remove the filter and spring, followed by the two 7 mm diameter balls, the 5.5 mm diameter ball and the spring (photos).

7   Remove the five 5.5 mm balls from the intermediate housing then lift it from the bottom housing (photo).

8   From the bottom housing remove the piston brake shift, the primary pump check valve and spring, the detent valve and spring and the shift pin and spring. Also remove the two 5.5 mm diameter balls and the plastic pin and, where applicable, the detent valve.

9   Remove the intermediate plate and gasket.

10   From the bottom housing remove the pressure valve, one-way throttle valve and the one-way throttle valve releasing end. Also remove the two 5.5 mm diameter balls (photos).

11   Thoroughly clean all the components in paraffin and wipe dry with a lint-free cloth. The channels in the housings are best cleaned with an air line.

12   Commence reassembly by placing the bottom housing on the fixture and fitting the pressure valve, one-way throttle valve, one-way throttle valve releasing end, and the two 5.5 mm diameter balls (photo).

13   Carefully locate the intermediate plate and a new gasket on the bottom housing and clamp together using nuts cut to size (photos). Check the spring-loaded valves for free operation.

14   Locate the two 5.5 mm diameter balls on the intermediate plate (photo).

15   Insert the primary pump check valve into the intermediate housing from below and retain it in the housing with the thumb nail from the top, then lower the intermediate housing onto the gasket and release the valve so that it makes an audible knock onto its seat (photos).

16   Insert the shift pin and spring, the detent valve and spring and the piston brake shift into the intermediate housing. Where applicable, insert the detent valve (photos). Take care not to fit the wrong springs

17.2A Removing the shift valve housing

17.2B View into transmission with shift valve housing removed

17.2C Fluid tubes and seals

17.2D Brake band and servo

17.2E Range selector linkage

17.3 Bottom view of the shift valve housing

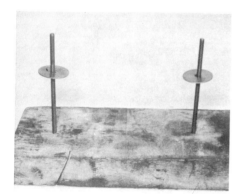

17.4A Fixture for holding the shift valve housing

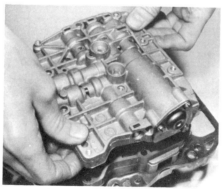

17.4B Removing the top housing

17.5 Removing the intermediate plate from the top housing

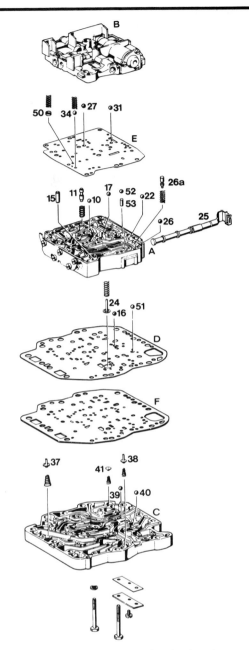

Fig. 6.30 Exploded view of the shift valve housing on all types except 722.112 (Sec 17)

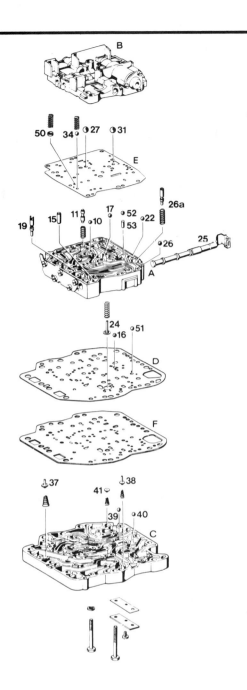

Fig. 6.31 Exploded view of the shift valve housing on type 722.112 (Sec 17)

A	Shift valve housing bottom	25	Range selector valve
B	Shift valve housing top	26	Two-way ball valve
C	Oil distributing plate	26a	Detent valve K2
D	Gasket	27	One-way throttle valve K1
E	Small intermediate plate	31	One-way throttle valve K2
F	Large intermediate plate	34	Pressure relief valve modulating pressure
10	Two-way ball valve	37	Lube pressure valve
11	Shift valve releasing end B2	38	One-way throttle valve B3
15	Piston brake shift 4 to 3	39	Two-way ball valve
16	Check ball valve	40	Two-way ball valve
17	Three-throttle ball valve	41	One-way throttle valve B2
22	Two-way ball valve	50	Filter
24	Check valve primary pump	51	Ball valve
		53	Plastic pin

A	Shift valve housing bottom	26	Two-way ball valve
B	Shift valve housing top	26a	Detent valve K2
C	Oil distributing plate	27	One-way throttle valve K1
D	Gasket	31	One-way throttle valve K2
E	Small intermediate plate	34	Pressure relief valve modulating pressure
F	Large intermediate plate	37	Lube pressure valve
10	Two-way ball valve	38	One-way throttle valve B3
11	Shift valve releasing end B2	39	Two-way ball valve
15	Piston brake shift 4 to 3	40	Two-way ball valve
16	Check ball valve	41	One-way throttle valve B2
17	Three-throttle ball valve	50	Filter
19	Detent valve	51	Ball valve
22	Two-way ball valve	52	Ball valve
24	Check valve primary pump	53	Plastic pin
25	Range selector valve		

17.6A Filter and ball valve location in top housing

– the spring in the top housing with the ball is of 0.6 mm diameter wire whereas the other springs are of 0.45 mm diameter wire.

17 Locate the five 5.5 mm balls in the intermediate housing.

18 In the top housing fit the two 7 mm diameter balls, the 5.5 mm diameter ball and spring and the filter and spring.

19 Locate the intermediate plate on the top housing and hold the two components together. If necessary a feeler blade can be used to compress the springs while the plate is being fitted (photo).

20 Place the top housing on the intermediate housing and insert two bolts finger tight. A feeler blade can be used to compress the springs (photos).

21 Remove the shift valve housing from the fixture, insert the remaining bolts and tighten them evenly (photo).

22 To refit the housing, first screw two long studs into the transmission to act as guides (photo).

23 Using a metal dowel rod inserted through the bottom housing, keep the control valve depressed (photo).

24 Slide the housing onto the guide studs and retain with nuts (photo).

25 Raise the housing and engage the control linkage, then insert and tighten the retaining bolts evenly (photos). Remove the metal dowel.

26 Fit the filter and fill the transmission with fluid, with reference to Section 13.

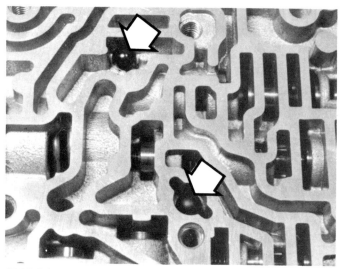

17.6B 7.0 mm diameter ball locations in top housing (arrowed)

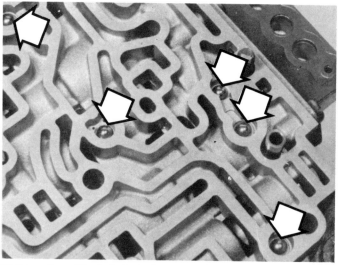

17.7 Location of five balls in the intermediate housing (arrowed)

17.10A Pressure valve location in bottom housing

17.10B One-way throttle valve location in bottom housing

17.10C One-way throttle valve releasing end location in bottom housing

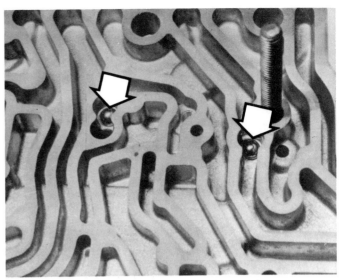

17.10D Ball locations in the bottom housing (arrowed)

17.12 Bottom housing located on fixture

17.13A Intermediate plate and gasket clamped to bottom housing

17.13B Using nuts to clamp the intermediate plate

17.14 The two balls located on the intermediate plate

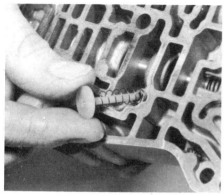

17.15A Inserting the primary pump check valve into the intermediate housing

17.15B Fitting the intermediate housing onto the bottom housing

17.16A Inserting the shift pin and spring in the intermediate housing

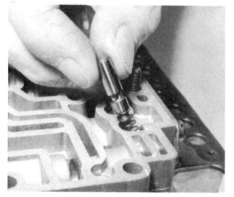

17.16B Inserting the detent valve and spring in the intermediate housing

17.16C Inserting the piston brake shift in the intermediate housing

17.16D Inserting the detent valve in the intermediate housing (arrowed)

17.19 Fitting the intermediate plate to the top housing

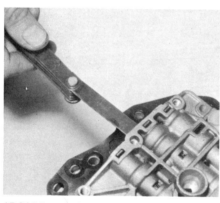

17.20A Locate the top housing on the intermediate housing ...

17.20B ... and insert two bolts

17.21 Top view of the assembled shift valve housing

17.22 Locating studs fitted to the transmission

17.23 Retaining the control valve with a metal dowel (arrowed)

17.24 Fitting the shift valve housing

17.25A Shift valve housing fully fitted

17.25B Control linkage connection (arrowed)

18.3 Fitting the primary pump oil seal

18 Primary pump oil seal – renewal

1   With the engine or transmission removed, lift the torque converter from the front of the transmission. Remove the safety pin first, if fitted.
2   Prise the oil seal from the primary pump with a screwdriver and wipe clean the recess.
3   Drive the new oil seal in squarely, using a metal tube, until flush (photo).
4   Locate the torque converter on the splines while turning it, and check that it is fully entered, with reference to Section 12.
5   Refit the transmission, with reference to Section 12.

ALL TRANSMISSIONS

19 Fault diagnosis – manual gearbox and automatic transmission

Symptom	Reason(s)
Manual gearbox	
Ineffective synchromesh	Worn synchro-rings
Jumps out of gear	Worn gears or synchro units
	Worn selector forks, rockers and detents
Noisy operation	Worn bearings or gears
Difficulty in engaging gears	Worn selector components
	Seized input shaft spigot bearing
	Clutch fault

Automatic transmission
Faults in the automatic transmission are nearly always the result of low fluid level or incorrect adjustment of the selector linkage or downshift rod. Internal faults should be diagnosed by a Mercedes dealer equipped to carry out such work.

Chapter 7 Propeller shaft

Contents

Specifications

Type .... Two-section, tubular with intermediate (centre) bearing, centre universal joint, and end flexible universal joints

Torque wrench settings

	lbf ft	Nm
Flange bolts/nuts	33	45
Rear mounting to underbody	33	45
Rear mounting to transmission	18	24
Sleeve nut	22 to 29	30 to 39
Centre bearing	18	24

1 General description

Drive is transmitted from the manual gearbox or automatic transmission to the final drive unit by means of a two-section tubular propeller shaft incorporating an intermediate (centre) support ball-bearing, centre universal joint, and flexible universal joints at each end of the shaft.

Due to the location of the final drive unit on the underbody the working angles of the universal joints are small, and therefore wear in the joints is likely to be minimal unless very high mileages have been completed. The centre ball-bearing and flexible joints can be renewed, but the centre universal joint is of the sealed type and cannot be serviced.

2 Routine maintenance

1 Every 30 000 miles (48 000 km) check the propeller shaft flange bolts for tightness. At the same time check the flexible universal joint couplings for wear and damage, and renew them if necessary.
2 At the same interval it is also worthwhile checking the centre bearing and universal joint for excessive wear.

3 Propeller shaft – removal and refitting

1 Position the car over an inspection pit or alternatively jack up the front and rear of the car and support it securely on axle stands.
2 Remove the exhaust system, with reference to Chapter 3.
3 Unbolt and remove the guard plate from the underbody.
4 Disconnect the handbrake/parking brake cables and compensating lever mechanism from the underbody, where applicable.
5 Using two large open-ended spanners, unscrew the sleeve nut (approximately two turns) which is located on the front section of the shaft. This will permit the shaft to be slightly compressed to simplify removal. Do not push back the rubber sleeve.
6 Support the transmission on a trolley jack or suitable support then unbolt and remove the rear mounting from the underbody.
7 Unscrew the bolts securing the front and rear flexible couplings to the transmission and final drive (photo).
8 Unscrew the bolts securing the centre bearing to the underbody, and lower the bearing onto an axle stand or suitable support (photo).
9 Mark the two sliding sections of the propeller shaft in relation to each other as a precaution in case the sections are inadvertently separated, otherwise the balance of the shaft may be upset.

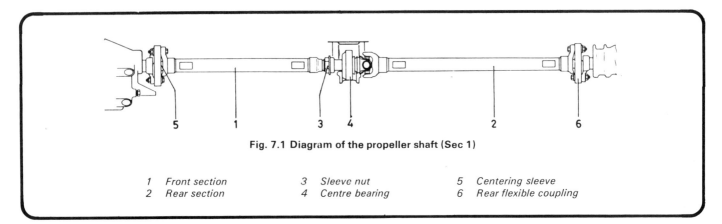

Fig. 7.1 Diagram of the propeller shaft (Sec 1)

1 Front section	3 Sleeve nut	5 Centering sleeve
2 Rear section	4 Centre bearing	6 Rear flexible coupling

3.7 Propeller shaft rear flexible coupling connected to the final drive unit

3.8 Propeller shaft centre bearing

10 Push the rear section of the shaft forwards so that it can be disconnected from the centre pin on the final drive flange.

11 Pull the front section of the shaft from the transmission flange and withdraw the complete unit from under the car. Do not separate the two sections.

12 Unbolt and remove the flexible couplings and, if necessary, remove the centre bearing, with reference to Sections 5 and 4 respectively.

13 To refit the propeller shaft, first fit the centre bearing and flexible couplings, if removed.

14 Fill the centre recesses of the centering sleeves each with 6 grams of high melting-point grease.

15 Locate the front section of the shaft on the transmission flange pin, then push the rear section forwards (sleeve nut still loose) and locate it on the final drive flange pin.

16 Lift the centre bearing into position and fit the bolts finger tight.

17 Insert the coupling bolts (with their heads facing the centre bearing) through the front and rear flanges, fit new self-locking nuts and tighten them evenly to the specified torque.

18 Fit the rear mounting to the underbody and transmission, tighten the bolts, and remove the support.

19 Refit the handbrake/parking brake cables and compensating lever mechanism, with reference to Chapter 9.

20 Rotate the propeller shaft several times to relieve any tension, and allow the front and rear sections to settle, then tighten the sleeve nut to the specified torque.

21 Fully tighten the centre bearing to underbody bolts.

22 Fit the guard plate to the underbody and tighten the bolts.

23 Fit the exhaust system, with reference to Chapter 3.

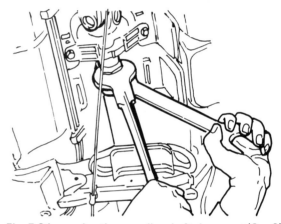

Fig. 7.2 Loosening the propeller shaft sleeve nut (Sec 3)

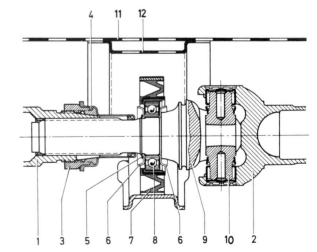

Fig. 7.3 Cross-sectional diagram of the centre bearing (Sec 4)

4 Centre bearing – renewal

1 Remove the propeller shaft, as described in Section 3.

2 Mark the front and rear sections in relation to each other.

3 With the sleeve nut already loosened for removal of the shaft, withdraw the front section.

4 Pull the rubber sleeve from the splines.

5 Extract the circlip using circlip pliers, then remove the cover plate.

6 Using a suitable puller, pull the rubber mounting, together with the bearing, from the universal joint yoke. Remove the inner cover plate.

7 Support the rubber mounting inner bore and, using a metal tube, drive out the bearing.

8 Clean the rubber mounting inner bore then support it on a block of wood and drive in the new bearing using a metal tube on the outer track only. The bearing should be driven in slowly up to the shoulder.

9 Refit the inner cover plate.

10 Mount the universal joint in a soft-jawed vice and locate the bearing and rubber mounting on it with the inner V-fold of the mounting towards the joint (see Fig. 7.3). Using a metal tube on the

1	Front universal shaft	8	Radial ball-bearing
2	Rear universal shaft	9	Yoke
3	Clamping nut	10	Spider with needle bearing
4	Rubber sleeve		and bushing
5	Locking ring	11	Frame floor
6	Protective cap	12	Universal shaft tunnel
7	Universal shaft intermediate		
	bearing		

Fig. 7.4 Removing the rubber sleeve (Sec 4)

Fig. 7.5 Removing the circlip (1) and cover plate (2) (Sec 4)

Fig. 7.6 Removing the rubber mounting with a puller (Sec 4)

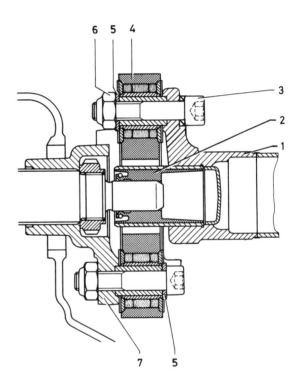

Fig. 7.7 Cross-section of a flexible coupling (Sec 5)

1   Propeller shaft   5   Washer
2   Centering sleeve   6   Self-locking nut
3   Socket-head bolt   7   Transmission flange
4   Flexible coupling

Fig. 7.8 Drill a hole through the old centering sleeve (8)

inner track, drive the bearing fully onto the shaft.
11 Refit the cover plate and retain it with the circlip with the inner crown against the plate.
12 Push the rubber sleeve over the splines.
13 Apply a little grease to the splines then connect the front section of the propeller shaft, making sure that the previously made marks are correctly aligned.
14 Refit the propeller shaft, as described in Section 3

5   Flexible couplings and centering sleeves – renewal

1   Wear or deterioration of the flexible couplings and centering sleeves may cause noise due to the propeller shaft moving off centre and becoming unbalanced. The centering sleeves also incorporate sealing lips which, if worn, will allow grease from the inner cavities to leak out.

Fig. 7.9 ... insert a bar, and lever out the sleeve (Sec 5)

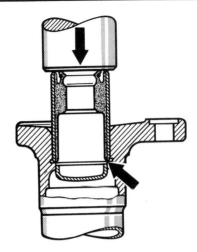

Fig. 7.10 Drive the new sleeve up to the shoulder (arrowed) (Sec 5)

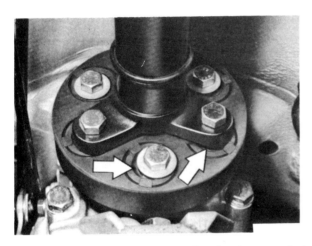

Fig. 7.11 Soft type of flexible coupling fitted to the transmission flange on some models (Sec 5)

Fig. 7.12 Soft type of flexible coupling removed from car (Sec 5)

2 Remove the propeller shaft, as described in Section 3.
3 If the flexible coupling is to be re-used, mark it in relation to the propeller shaft flange.
4 Unscrew and remove the bolts and withdraw the flexible coupling.
5 Mount the propeller shaft in a soft-jawed vice and drill a 10 mm (0.4 in) diameter hole through the centering sleeve approximately 15 mm (0.6 in) from its outer face.
6 Insert a suitable bar through the hole and use two levers to extract the sleeve from the propeller shaft.
7 Clean the recess in the shaft then locate the new sleeve squarely over the bore and drive it in fully, using a metal or wooden block.

8 Locate the flexible coupling on the propeller shaft flange with the previously made marks aligned, if applicable. Insert the bolts (with their heads facing the centre bearing), then fit new self-locking nuts and tighten them evenly to the specified torque. Note that on some models the flexible coupling at the transmission end of the propeller shaft is of a softer design (see Figs 7.11 and 7.12) — this type must always be fitted as shown.
9 Refit the propeller shaft, as described in Section 3. Do not forget to fill the centering sleeve recesses each with 6 grams of high melting-point grease.

6 Fault diagnosis – propeller shaft

Symptom	Reason(s)
Vibration	Worn flexible couplings and centering sleeves Worn centre bearing and rubber mounting Worn sliding sleeve splines Worn centre universal joint
Knock or 'clunk' when taking up drive	Worn centre universal joint Worn sliding sleeve splines
Excessive 'rumble' increasing with road speed	Worn centre bearing

Chapter 8 Final drive and driveshafts

Contents

Specifications

General

Final drive type	Unsprung, attached to rear underbody and suspension crossmember
Driveshaft type	Maintenance-free ball and spider

Final drive ratio

	Ratio	Teeth
250 Saloon:		
Standard	3.69 : 1	48/13
With 15 inch wheels or long body, up to 1981	3.92 : 1	47/12
With 15 inch wheels or long body, 1982 onwards	3.69 : 1	48/13
250 Estate:		
Up to 1981	3.69 : 1	48/13
1982 onwards	3.58 : 1	43/12
280 Saloon:		
Standard	3.58 : 1	43/12
With 15 inch wheels or long body	3.69 : 1	48/13
280 Estate:		
Standard	3.58 : 1	43/12
With 15 inch wheels	3.69 : 1	48/13

Final drive unit oil capacity

1.0 litre 1.8 Imp pt; 1.1 US qt

Driveshaft joint oil quantity

230 grams (8.1 oz)

Torque wrench settings

	lbf ft	Nm
Final drive unit rear mounting to cover	88	119
Final drive unit rear mounting to underbody	22	30
Driveshaft bolt	22	30
Final drive unit front mounting	73	100
Final drive unit rear cover	33	45
Pinion nut (minimum)	132	179

1 General description

The final drive is of unsprung type with the final drive unit attached to the rear underbody and suspension crossmember. Two driveshafts transmit drive from the final drive unit to the rear wheels which are attached to the fully independent rear suspension.

The final drive unit pinion runs in two taper roller bearings which are preloaded using a collapsible spacer. The differential incorporates two planet gears on a single shaft.

The driveshafts are of maintenance-free ball and spider type.

Overhaul of the final drive unit is not covered in this Chapter because special tools and fixtures not normally available to the home mechanic are required.

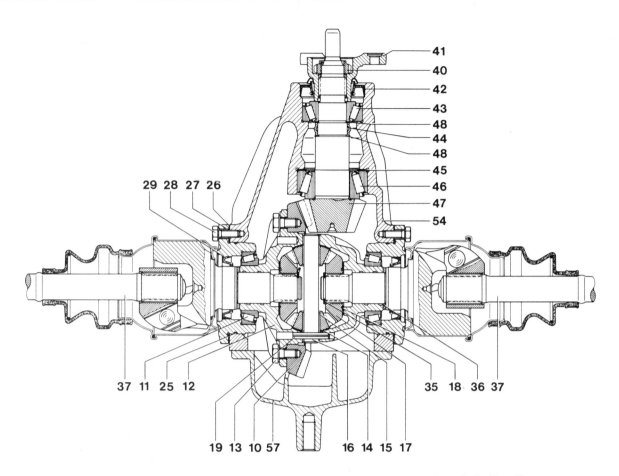

Fig. 8.1 Cross-section of the final drive unit with bearing caps and driveshafts (Sec 1)

10 Ring gear	18 Thrust washer	35 Locking ring	44 Spacing sleeve
11 Tapered roller bearing	19 Clamping sleeve	36 Compensating washer	45 Compensating washer
12 Differential housing	25 Sealing ring	37 Rear axle shaft complete	46 Large tapered roller bearing
13 Hex bolt	26 Compensating washer	40 Locknut	47 Drive pinion
14 Ball washer	27 Bearing cap	41 Universal flange	54 Rear axle housing
15 Differential pinion	28 Hex bolt	42 Radial sealing ring	57 Rear axle end cover
16 Differential pinion shaft	29 Radial sealing ring	43 Small tapered roller bearing	
17 Side gear			

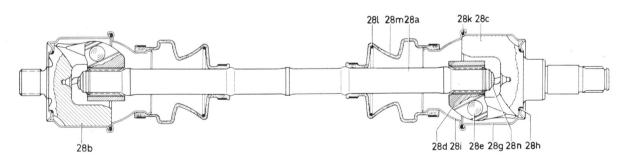

Fig. 8.2 Cross-section of a driveshaft (Sec 1)

28a Driveshaft	28d Spider joint hub	28h Sealing ring	28l Clamping ring
28b Outer spider	28e Ball	28i Stop sleeve	28m Rubber sleeve
28c Inner spider	28g Protective sleeve	28k Sealing ring	28n Stop buffer

2 Routine maintenance

1   Every 10 000 miles (16 000 km) on UK models, and every 15 000 miles (24 000 km) on USA models, check the oil level of the final drive, and top up if necessary. With the filler plug removed the oil level should be at the bottom of the hole with the car on a level surface. If continual topping-up is necessary one of the final drive unit oil seals is probably leaking and should be renewed.

3 Driveshaft – removal and refitting

Note: *If both driveshafts are to be removed it is recommended that the complete final drive unit, together with the driveshafts, is removed, as described in Section 5.*

1   Jack up the rear of the car and support it on axle stands. Chock the front wheels and remove the rear wheels.
2   Place a container beneath the final drive unit then, using a special key, unscrew the drain plug and drain the oil. Refit and tighten the plug when completely drained.
3   Remove the brake caliper, with reference to Chapter 9, but do not disconnect the hydraulic hose. Tie the caliper to one side.
4   Hold the driving flange stationary (insert two wheel bolts and use a lever if necessary) and unscrew the driveshaft bolt and remove the special washer and spacer, if fitted.
5   Using a soft metal drift or puller, force the driveshaft from the rear hub and place it on an axle stand (photo). If the driveshaft cannot be removed completely, despite being compressed to its shortest length, the final drive unit will subsequently need to be unbolted from the crossmember and lowered on one side.
6   Support the final drive unit with a trolley jack then unscrew the bolts securing the rear mounting to the underbody.
7   Clean the final drive rear cover and surrounding components then unbolt and remove the rear cover, together with the mounting.
8   Extract the circlip from the differential side gear, then pull out the driveshaft. Note the location of the spacer and also note that on early models the left- and right-hand driveshafts are identified by an L or R on the inner stub. The driveshafts are 'handed' because of an oil return thread on the seal running surface.
9   Refitting is a reversal of removal, but do not allow the driveshaft to bend excessively, otherwise damage may occur. The circlip thickness must eliminate all endplay. Clean the cover mating surfaces and apply sealing compound. Tighten all bolts to the specified torque and finally fill the final drive unit with oil to the level of the filler hole with the car on level ground.

4 Driveshaft bellows – renewal

1   If the driveshaft bellows are split or damaged they can be renewed. However, special tools are required for opening the inner joint beading and again for remaking the new beading. The use of a press is also required.
2   The parts supplied in the bellows repair kit are shown in Fig. 8.4, but since the necessary tools are not available generally to the home mechanic, it is recommended that the work be entrusted to a Mercedes dealer. The driveshaft must be removed first, as described in Section 3.
3   Note that if the inner driveshaft joint is leaking on the beading, the complete driveshaft must be renewed as there are no service tools for opening and remaking the larger diameter beading.

5 Final drive unit – removal and refitting

1   Jack up the rear of the car and support it on axle stands. Chock the front wheels and remove the rear wheels.
2   Place a container beneath the final drive unit then, using a special key, unscrew the drain plug and drain the oil (photo). Refit and tighten the plug when completely drained.
3   Remove the right-hand brake caliper, with reference to Chapter 9, but do not disconnect the hydraulic hose. Tie the caliper to one side.
4   Working on each side in turn, hold the driving flange stationary (insert the wheel bolts and use a lever if necessary) then unscrew the driveshaft bolt and remove the special washer and spacer, if fitted.

3.5 Removing a driveshaft from the rear hub (left-hand side shown)

Fig. 8.3 Using circlip pliers (1) to extract the driveshaft circlip (26) (Sec 3)

Fig. 8.4 Driveshaft bellows repair kit (Sec 4)

13 Sealing ring   20 Protective sleeve
14 Rubber bellows   22 Sealing ring
18 Stop sleeve   23 Hose clip

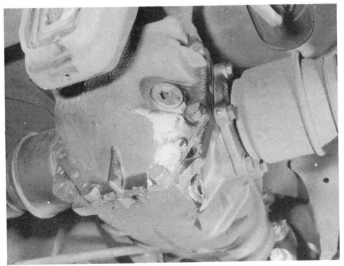

5.2 Final drive unit showing filler and drain plugs

5.8 Final drive unit rear mounting

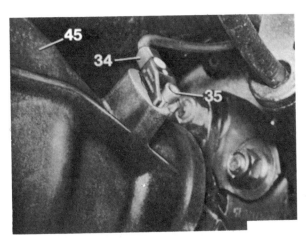

Fig. 8.5 Rpm sensor (34) and retaining bolt (35) on the final drive unit (45) (Sec 5)

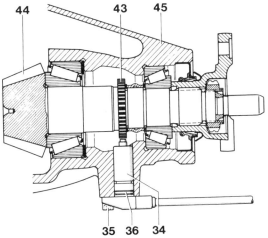

Fig. 8.6 Cross-section of the rpm sensor fitted to some models (Sec 5)

34 Rpm sensor   43 Rotor
35 Screw   44 Pinion
36 O-ring   45 Final drive unit housing

5   Using a soft metal drift or puller, force each driveshaft from the rear hubs and support on axle stands. If the driveshafts cannot be removed completely, despite being compressed to their shortest lengths, remove them later with the final drive unit.
6   Remove the propeller shaft, as described in Chapter 7.
7   Where an rpm sensor is fitted to the final drive unit, unscrew the retaining bolt with an Allen key, remove the sensor and place it to one side.
8   Support the final drive unit with a trolley jack then unscrew the bolts securing the rear mounting to the underbody (photo).
9   Disconnect the handbrake/parking brake cable from the underbody, if necessary.
10 Lower the jack a little and unscrew the nuts securing the final drive unit to the crossmember.
11 With the help of an assistant, lower the final drive unit and driveshafts to the floor and withdraw from under the car. Take care not to damage the driveshaft joints.
12 If required, remove the driveshafts from the final drive unit, with reference to Section 3.
13 Unbolt the rear mounting from the final drive cover. Renew the mounting if it is damaged or has deteriorated.
14 Refitting is a reversal of removal, but tighten all nuts and bolts to the specified torque. Self-locking nuts and bolts should ideally be renewed. Where an rpm sensor is fitted, make sure that the magnetic pick-up is free of any foreign particles. Fill the final drive unit with oil to the level of the filler hole with the car on level ground.

6   Final drive unit pinion oil seal – renewal

1   Remove the propeller shaft, as described in Chapter 7, and drain the oil from the final drive unit.
2   In order that the correct bearing preload is maintained the turning torque of the pinion must now be established. If a torque gauge is not available, wind some string around the flange centre pin and use a spring balance to record the force required to turn the flange slowly. Note that the driveshafts should be horizontal and the brake pads and shoes away from the discs and drums.
3   Hold the flange stationary with a length of bar bolted to two of the bolt holes, then unscrew the pinion nut using a slotted box spanner.
4   Using a puller or slide hammer, draw the flange from the pinion splines.
5   Using a screwdriver, prise the oil seal from the final drive housing.
6   Clean the oil seal seating and the flange. Renew the flange if the oil seal shoulder is worn excessively.
7   Smear a litle oil on the outer edge of the new oil seal and also the sealing lips, then, using a suitable length of metal tube, drive the oil seal squarely into the housing.
8   Locate the flange on the pinion splines and screw on a new pinion nut finger tight.

9 Tighten the pinion nut gradually until the turning torque is the same as that recorded in paragraph 2. Do not overtighten the nut, otherwise the collapsible spacer on the pinion will need to be renewed; and this work must be carried out by a Mercedes dealer. The final tightened torque of the nut must be at least that given in the Specifications, and again, if this cannot be attained, the collapsible spacer must be renewed.
10 Using a blunt cold chisel lock the nut by peening the shoulder into the cut-out on the pinion.
11 Refit the propeller shaft, as described in Chapter 7, and fill the final drive unit with oil to the level of the filler hole with the car on level ground.

7 Final drive unit driveshaft oil seal – renewal

1 Remove the relevant driveshaft, as described in Section 3.
2 Prise out the oil seal with a screwdriver.
3 Clean the oil seal seating and the driveshaft. If the sealing surface on the driveshaft is worn excessively it will be necessary to renew the driveshaft.
4 Smear a little oil on the outer edge and sealing lips of the new oil

seal, then, using a suitable length of metal tubing, drive the seal squarely into the bearing cap or housing. Figs. 8.8, 8.9 and 8.10 show the fitted position of the oil seals and, if an installing tool is not available, the position must be determined using vernier calipers.
5 Refit the driveshaft, with reference to Section 3.

8 Final drive unit rear mounting – renewal

1 Chock the front wheels, then jack up the rear of the car and support it on axle stands.
2 Support the final drive unit on a trolley jack.
3 Unbolt the rear mounting from the underbody.
4 Slightly lower the final drive unit, then unbolt the mounting from the rear cover.
5 Clean the mounting contact areas on the rear cover and underbody.
6 Locate the new mounting on the rear cover, insert the bolts and tighten them evenly to the specified torque.
7 Raise the trolley jack, insert the bolts to the underbody and tighten them evenly.
8 Remove the trolley jack then lower the car to the ground.

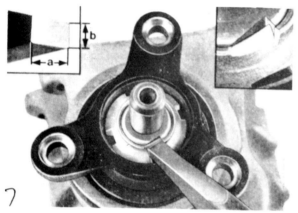

Fig. 8.7 Locking the pinion nut (Sec 6)

Inset shows dimensions of cold chisel

a = 8.0 mm (0.315 in)   *b = 4.0 mm (0.157 in)*

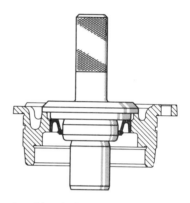

Fig. 8.8 Inserting driveshaft oil seal in early bearing cap (Sec 7)

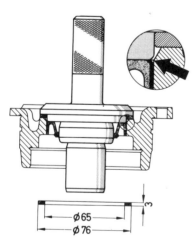

Fig. 8.9 Inserting driveshaft oil seal in later bearing cap (Sec 7)

The spacer must be used with the special tool

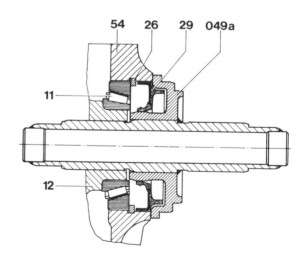

Fig. 8.10 Inserting driveshaft oil seal in final drive housing without bearing caps (Sec 7)

11 Tapered roller bearing
12 Differential housing
26 Circlip

29 Oil seal
049a Installing tool
54 Final drive housing

9   Fault diagnosis – final drive and driveshafts

Symptom	Reason(s)
Noise from final drive unit	Lack of lubricant Worn bearings, crownwheel and pinion Loose or deteriorated final drive unit mountings
Oil leakage from final drive unit	Pinion or driveshaft oil seals worn
Metallic grating noise from driveshafts	Worn driveshaft joints

Chapter 9 Braking system

Contents

Specifications

System type .... Front and rear discs, with drums incorporated in the rear discs for parking brake shoes, vacuum servo assistance, dual hydraulic circuit, cable-operated parking brake

Discs

Type	Solid or ventilated
Front disc thickness:	
New	12.6 mm (0.496 in)
Minimum	10.6 mm (0.417 in)
Front disc run-out (maximum)	0.12 mm (0.005 in)
Rear disc thickness:	
New	10.0 mm (0.394 in)
Minimum	8.3 mm (0.327 in)
Rear disc run-out (maximum)	0.12 mm (0.005 in)
Rear disc drum internal diameter	159.8 to 160.2 mm (6.29 to 6.31 in)

Disc pad lining thickness (new):	**Pre 1979**	**1979 onwards**
Front	15.0 mm (0.6 in)	17.5 mm (0.7 in)
Rear	15.0 mm (0.6 in)	15.5 mm (0.6 in)
Disc pad lining thickness (minimum)	2.0 mm (0.079 in)	

Master cylinder

Bore maximum out-of-round	0.03 mm (0.001 in)

Vacuum servo unit

Boosting factor	approx 3:1

Handbrake/parking brake

Lining thickness:	
New	4.0 mm (0.16 in)
Minimum	1.5 mm (0.06 in)

Torque wrench settings

	lbf ft	Nm
Brake disc to front hub	84	114
Caliper to steering knuckle	84	114
Caliper to trailing arm	66	89
Master cylinder to servo	11	15
Hydraulic line union nut	11	15
Flexible hose union	7	9
Servo unit	11	15
Vacuum line to servo	22	30
Parking brake carrier	36	49
Master cylinder stop screw	3 to 6	4 to 8
Master cylinder plug	11 to 22	15 to 30
Pressure differential switch	11 to 14	15 to 19

1 General description

The braking system is of dual hydraulic circuit type with discs all round. The front and rear hydraulic circuits are operated independently so that, in the event of a failure in one circuit, the remaining circuit still functions.

The disc calipers are of double piston type and are self-adjusting by means of wedged type piston seals which are deformed when the brakes are applied but regain their original shape when the brakes are released.

The cable-operated handbrake/parking brake is of conventional brake shoe type on the rear wheels, the drums being an integral part of the rear brake discs. The shoes are adjusted manually at the intervals given in Section 2.

A vacuum servo unit is fitted between the master cylinder and the footbrake pedal.

The brake fluid reservoir incorporates one or two low fluid warning switches operated by floats.

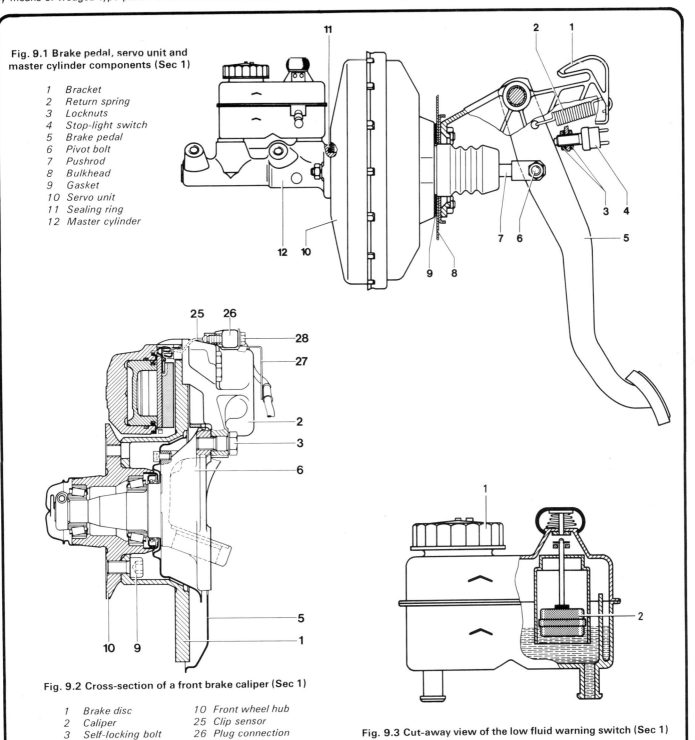

Fig. 9.1 Brake pedal, servo unit and master cylinder components (Sec 1)

1 Bracket
2 Return spring
3 Locknuts
4 Stop-light switch
5 Brake pedal
6 Pivot bolt
7 Pushrod
8 Bulkhead
9 Gasket
10 Servo unit
11 Sealing ring
12 Master cylinder

Fig. 9.2 Cross-section of a front brake caliper (Sec 1)

1 Brake disc
2 Caliper
3 Self-locking bolt
5 Cover plate
6 Steering knuckle
9 Self-locking screw
10 Front wheel hub
25 Clip sensor
26 Plug connection
27 Cable holder
28 Hex. bolt

Fig. 9.3 Cut-away view of the low fluid warning switch (Sec 1)

1 Filler cap   2 Float

2   Routine maintenance

1   Every 10 000 miles (16 000 km) on UK models, and every 15 000 miles (24 000 km) on USA models, check all brake lines for damage and leakage.
2   Check the disc pads and shoes for wear, and renew if necessary.
3   Adjust the handbrake/parking brake.
4   Check the hydraulic fluid level, and top up if necessary.
5   Every 12 months the hydraulic fluid should be renewed.
6   Every 30 000 miles (48 000 km) check the handbrake/parking brake cables and linkage for damage and ease of operation.

3   Disc pads – inspection and renewal

1   Jack up the front of the car and support it on axle stands. Apply the handbrake/parking brake and remove the roadwheels.
2   If wear warning wires are fitted pull the plugs from the connectors (photo).
3   On the Teves type caliper use a small punch to drive out the pad retaining pins. On Bendix and Girling types extract the clips and drive out the retaining pins.
4   Pull the wear warning wires from the pad and also remove the retaining spring.
5   Using pliers push one disc pad and piston into its bore then withdraw the pad. If necessary move it from side to side to loosen any accumulated dust and dirt. Similarly remove the remaining pad (photos).
6   Check each pad for wear and, if the lining thickness is below the minimum thickness given in the Specifications, renew all the disc pads on the front calipers.
7   Brush the dust and dirt from the caliper housing, pistons, disc and pads, but **do not** *inhale it, as it is injurious to health.* Scrape any scale or rust from the disc.
8   Push one of the pistons fully into its bore, apply a little high melting-point **brake** grease to the back and edges of the new pad backplate then insert the pad in the caliper. Similarly insert the second pad.
9   Locate the retaining spring on the pads then insert the pins (photo) and either tap them fully into the caliper (Teves) or fit the clips (Bendix and Girling).
10   Fit the wear warning wires, where applicable.
11   Depress the footbrake pedal several times in order to set the pads in their normal positions.
12   Repeat the procedure described in paragraphs 2 to 11 on the remaining front brake, then fit the roadwheels and lower the car to the ground.
13   Chock the front wheels, jack up the rear of the car and support it on axle stands. Remove the roadwheels.
14   Renew the rear disc pads, as described in paragraphs 2 to 12 (photos). On models with a pressure differential warning indicator on the master cylinder, the warning lamp may light up after removing and fitting disc pads; in which case the reset pin on the master cylinder should be depressed.

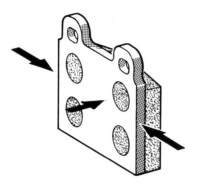

Fig. 9.4 Apply a little brake grease to the surfaces indicated before fitting the disc pads (Sec 3)

3.2 Disconnecting the disc pad wear warning wire plugs

3.5A Removing a front outer disc pad

3.5B Removing a front inner disc pad

3.9 Fitting the disc pad retaining spring and pins

3.14A Removing the rear disc pad retaining pins

3.14B Removing a rear outer disc pad

3.14C Removing a rear inner disc pad

3.14D Rear disc pads correctly fitted

4 Disc caliper – removal, overhaul and refitting

Front
1 Jack up the front of the car and support it on axle stands. Apply the handbrake/parking brake and remove the relevant front roadwheel.
2 Remove the disc pads, as described in Section 3.
3 Remove the brake fluid reservoir filler cap and tighten it down onto a piece of polythene sheeting in order to reduce the loss of fluid in the subsequent operations. Alternatively fit a hose clamp to the caliper flexible hose.
4 Unbolt the bracket securing the pad wear warning cables to the caliper.
5 Loosen the flexible brake hose union at the caliper.
6 Unscrew the mounting bolts and withdraw the caliper from the steering knuckle, then unscrew the caliper from the flexible hose.

Rear
7 Chock the front wheels then jack up the rear of the car and support it on axle stands. Remove the relevant rear roadwheel.
8 Remove the disc pads, as described in Section 3.
9 Remove the brake fluid resevoir filler cap and tighten it down onto a piece of polythene sheeting in order to reduce the loss of fluid in the subsequent operations. Alternatively fit a hose clamp to the caliper flexible hose.

4.10 Flexible hose union on a rear caliper

10 Loosen the flexible brake hose union at the caliper (photo).
11 Unscrew the mounting bolts and withdraw the caliper from the wheel carrier, then unscrew the caliper from the flexible hose.

Overhaul

12 Prise off the dust caps, taking care on the Bendix type not to remove the pressed-on ring. If necessary remove the heat shields.
13 Apply air pressure from a tyre pump to the fluid inlet union on the caliper, hold one piston depressed and eject the opposite one. Very low air pressure is required for this and a foot-operated tyre pump will do the job.
14 Hold a thick rubber pad against the open cylinder, apply air pressure again and eject the second piston. Mark the pistons and their respective cylinders so that they will not be interchanged. A piece of masking tape will be useful for this.
15 Examine the surfaces of the pistons and cylinders for scoring or 'bright' wear areas. If there is any evidence of these, renew the caliper complete. If the pistons are seized or rusted in their bores and cannot be ejected then again the caliper must be renewed complete.
16 If the piston and cylinder are in good condition, carefully pick out the seals from their cylinder grooves and discard them, then obtain a repair kit which will contain new ones and any other renewable items.
17 Manipulate the new seals into position using the fingers only for this work. Use only clean hydraulic fluid or methylated spirit for cleaning.
18 Smear the pistons with hydraulic fluid and insert them into their respective bores. Turn the pistons so that the recesses are at 20° to the bottom of the caliper, as shown in Fig. 9.6 then push them in fully and fit the dust caps.
19 Press on the heat shields and check that the raised part of the piston is at least 0.1 mm (0.004 in) above the surface of the heat shield. If necessary, press the heat shield further into the piston by means of a short bolt and nut located against a plate in the pad aperture of the caliper body. The heat shields for the inner and outer pistons are different and are not interchangeable.
20 Refitting is a reversal of removal, but check that the flexible hose is not twisted when fully tightened, renew the self-locking mounting bolts and tighten them to the specified torque. Finally bleed the hydraulic system, as described in Section 8.

---

5 Brake disc – examination, removal and refitting

1 Remove the disc caliper, as described in Section 4, however, do not disconnect the flexible hose. Support the caliper on an axle stand to prevent straining the hose.
2 Rotate the disc and examine it for deep scoring or grooving. Light scoring is normal, but if excessive the disc should be renewed or alternatively ground by a suitable engineering works.
3 Check that the disc thickness is not less than the specified minimum.

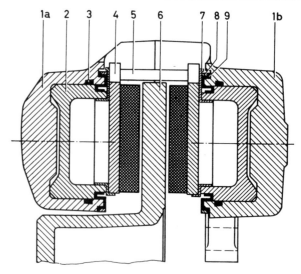

Fig. 9.5 Cross-section of a disc caliper (Sec 4)

1a Outer caliper half	5 Retaining pin
1b Inner caliper half	6 Brake disc
2 Piston	7 Heat shield
3 Piston seal	8 Clamping ring
4 Brake pad	9 Dust cap

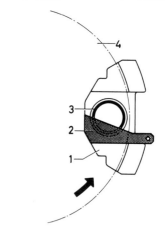

Fig. 9.6 Correct position of the caliper piston recess using a 20° gauge (Sec 4)

1 Caliper	3 Piston
2 Gauge	4 Disc

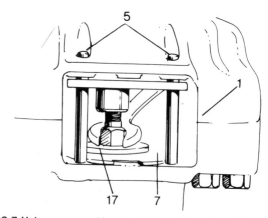

Fig. 9.7 Using a nut and bolt to fit the caliper piston heat shields (Sec 4)

1 Caliper body	17 Nut, bolt and washer for
5 Pad retaining pin	applying pressure to heat
7 Heat shield	shield

4 Using a dial gauge, or metal block and feeler gauges, check that the disc run-out does not exceed the amount given in the Specifications.

Front
5 Remove the front wheel hub, as described in Chapter 11.
6 Screw two bolts in the hub and mount the assembly in a vice with the brake disc uppermost.
7 Using an Allen key, unscrew the bolts and separate the brake disc from the hub.
8 To refit the brake disc first clean the mating surfaces.
9 Locate the disc on the hub, insert new bolts, and tighten them evenly to the specified torque.
10 Refit the hub and disc caliper, with reference to Chapter 11 and Section 4 respectively.

Rear
11 With the handbrake fully released use a soft-headed mallet to tap the brake disc from the rear axle flange.
12 To refit the brake disc first clean the mating surfaces and coat them with a little high melting-point grease. Note that new brake discs are coated with an anti-corrosion paint which must be removed with a solvent before fitting the disc.
13 Locate the brake disc on the rear axle flange, making sure that it is located on the small pin.
14 Refit the disc caliper, with reference to Section 4.

Fig. 9.8 Removing a front brake disc from the hub (Sec 5)

6 Master cylinder – removal, overhaul and refitting

1 Fit a bleed tube to the bleed nipple on one of the front disc calipers with its free end in a container, then depress the footbrake pedal repeatedly until no more fluid emerges. Tighten the bleed nipple.

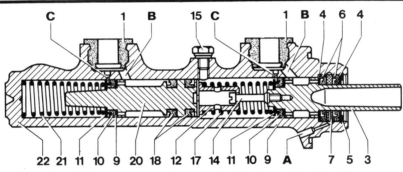

Fig. 9.9 Cross-section of the standard master cylinder (Sec 6)

1 Container plug	7 Intermediate ring	14 Connecting screw	21 Compression spring
3 Piston (primary circuit)	9 Filling washer	15 Stop screw	22 Housing
4 Stop washer	10 Primary sleeve	17 Compression spring	A Leak hole
5 Locking ring	11 Supporting ring	18 Parting sleeve	B Filler hole
6 Secondary and vacuum sleeve	12 Spring retainer	20 Piston (secondary circuit)	C Compensating hole

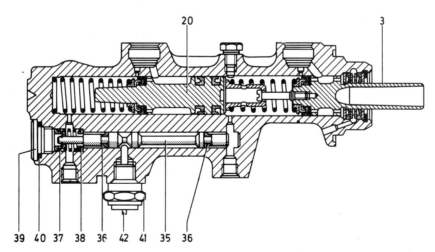

Fig. 9.10 Cross-section of the master cylinder with a pressure differential warning switch (Sec 6)

3 Piston (primary circuit)	36 Ring sleeve	39 Screw	41 Switch
20 Piston (secondary circuit)	37 Spring	40 Sealing ring	42 Release pin
35 Control piston	38 Spring retainer		

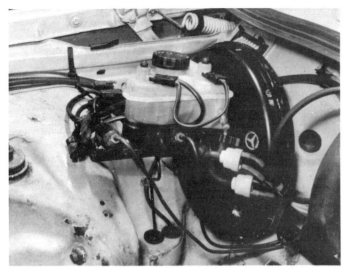

6.3 Brake master cylinder and servo unit showing low fluid warning wires

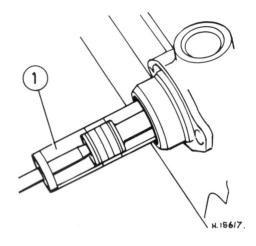

Fig. 9.11 Using an assembly sleeve (1) to fit the pistons to the master cylinder (Sec 6)

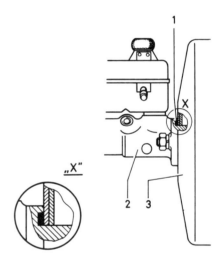

Fig. 9.12 Location of the sealing ring (1) between the master cylinder (2) and servo unit (3) (Sec 6)

2   Transfer the bleed tube to one of the rear disc calipers and similarly drain the rear hydraulic circuit.
3   Disconnect the low fluid warning wiring from the fluid reservoir, using a small screwdriver to release the lugs (photo).
4   Unscrew the union nuts, preferably with a split ring spanner, and disconnect the hydraulic lines from the master cylinder. Cover the line and cylinder apertures with masking tape. On manual gearbox models, disconnect the clutch hydraulic hose from the reservoir.
5   Where applicable, disconnect the wiring from the pressure differential warning switch.
6   Unscrew the nuts and withdraw the master cylinder from the front face of the vacuum servo unit.
7   Prise the sealing ring from the groove in the master cylinder flange.
8   Clean the exterior of the master cylinder.
9   Pull the fluid reservoir out, together with the sealing plugs.
10   Depress the primary piston slightly, then unscrew the stop screw and remove it, together with its seal.
11   Extract the circlip, then withdraw the primary piston, stop washers, secondary and vacuum sleeve and the intermediate ring.
12   Tap the end of the master cylinder on a piece of wood in order to remove the secondary piston and spring.
13   Where applicable, unscrew the pressure differential warning switch, then unscrew the end plug and extract the control piston by tapping the master cylinder on a piece of wood.
14   Unscrew the reservoir filler cap and extract the strainer. Note that the low fluid warning switch cannot be removed from the reservoir.
15   Clean all the components in methylated spirit and examine them for wear and damage. In particular, check the surfaces of the pistons and cylinder bore for scoring and corrosion. If the cylinder bore is worn, renew the complete master cylinder, but if the bore is in good condition obtain a repair kit of seals and, if applicable, pistons.
16   Fit the seals to the pistons, if applicable, using the fingers only to manipulate them into position.
17   Smear a little clean brake fluid on the cylinder bore.
18   If available, fit the primary and secondary piston components to an assembly sleeve, then use a screwdriver to insert them into the cylinder. Alternatively dip the components in brake fluid and insert them carefully, making sure that the seal lips are not trapped.
19   Fit the secondary and vacuum sleeves, together with the intermediate ring and stop washers using either of the methods described in paragraph 18 and retain them by fitting the circlip in the groove.
20   Depress the primary piston slightly, then insert and tighten the stop screw, together with a new seal.
21   Where applicable, dip the pressure differential warning switch control piston in brake fluid and insert it into the cylinder, taking care not to damage the ring sleeves. Insert the end plug with a new sealing ring and tighten.
22   Clean the strainer, then insert it in the reservoir and fit the filler cap.

23   Press the sealing plugs in the master cylinder and fit the reservoir by pushing it into one plug then turning it through 180° and pushing it into the remaining plug.
24   To refit the master cylinder, locate a new sealing ring on the flange then fit the unit to the front of the vacuum servo unit and tighten the nuts.
25   Where applicable, reconnect the pressure differential warning switch wiring.
26   Insert the hydraulic lines and tighten the union nuts.
27   Connect the low fluid warning wiring to the fluid reservoir.
28   Fill the reservoir with brake fluid and bleed the hydraulic system, as described in Section 8.

7   Hydraulic brake lines and hoses – general

1   The brake lines and hoses should be checked for deterioration and damage at the interval given in Section 2 (photo).
2   Examine flexible hoses by bending them and checking for small cracks which, if evident, will mean renewing the hose (photo).
3   Examine the rigid lines for abrasion at points where they run through holes in the bodyframe or where their securing clips are loose. If rust or corrosion is evident, the section of pipe must be renewed. Most garages can make up a new pipe if the old one is taken as a guide.

7.1 Brake line and bracket

7.2 Rear brake flexible hose

4   When renewing a flexible hose, disconnect it first at its union with the rigid line. Then disconnect it from its support bracket and finally unscrew it from the caliper body or connectors as the case may be. Never be tempted to try and unscrew a hose from the wrong end by twisting it round and round.

5   Having fitted a new hose, check that it does not rub against any part of the suspension or tyres. Turn the roadwheels from lock to lock to verify this. Where necessary, the lockplate at the flexible hose support bracket may be moved to give the hose a 'set' away from any adjacent components.

8   Hydraulic system – bleeding

1   If any of the hydraulic components in the braking system have been removed or disconnected, or if the fluid level in the master cylinder has been allowed to fall appreciably, it is inevitable that air will have been introduced into the system. The removal of all this air is essential if the brakes are to function correctly, and the process of removing it is known as bleeding.

2   There are a number of one-man, do-it-yourself brake bleeding kits currently available from motor accessory shops. It is recommended that one of these kits should be used whenever possible as they greatly simplify the bleeding operation and also reduce the risk of expelled air and fluid being drawn back into the system.

3   If one of these kits is not available then it will be necessary to gather together a clean jar and a suitable length of clear plastic tubing which is a tight fit over the bleed screw, and also to engage the help of an assistant.

4   Before commencing the bleeding operation, check that all rigid pipes and flexible hoses are in good condition and that all hydraulic unions are tight. Take great care not to allow hydraulic fluid to come into contact with the vehicle paintwork, otherwise the finish will be seriously damaged. Wash off any spilled fluid immediately with cold water.

5   If hydraulic fluid has been lost from the reservoir due to a leak in the system, ensure that the cause is traced and rectified before proceeding further, or a serious malfunction of the braking system may occur.

6   To bleed the system, clean the bleed screw at the caliper to be bled. If the hydraulic system has only been partially disconnected and suitable precautions were taken to prevent further loss of fluid, it should only be necessary to bleed that part of the system (ie the front brake circuit or the rear brake circuit). However, if the entire system is to be bled, bleed the front circuit, followed by the rear circuit.

7   Remove the filler cap and top up the reservoir with brake fluid to the maximum mark. Periodically check the fluid level during the bleeding operation and top up as necessary.

8   If a pressurised one-man brake bleeding kit is being used fit it to the reservoir in accordance with the manufacturer's instructions, and

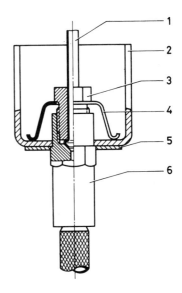

Fig. 9.13 Brake line connection (Sec 7)

1	Rigid brake line	4	Clip
2	Bracket	5	Safety plate
3	Union nut	6	Flexible hose

connect the plastic tubing to one of the front caliper bleed screws. With the free end of the tube in a suitable container unscrew the bleed screw half a turn and allow the fluid to flow out until free of air bubbles, then tighten the bleed screw.

9   If a non-pressurised one-man brake bleeding kit is being used, connect the outlet tube to one of the front caliper bleed screws then open the screw half a turn. If possible position the unit so that it can be viewed from the car, then depress the brake pedal to the floor and slowly release it. The one-way valve in the kit will prevent dispelled air from returning to the system at the end of each stroke. Repeat this operation until clean hydraulic fluid, free from air bubbles, can be seen coming through the tube. Now tighten the bleed screw and remove the outlet tube.

10 If a one-man brake bleeding kit is not available, connect one end of the plastic tubing to one of the front caliper bleed screws and immerse the other end in a jar containing sufficient hydraulic fluid to

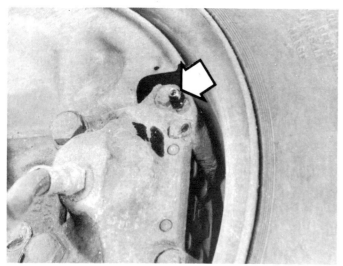

8.10A Rear brake bleed screw location on the caliper (arrowed)

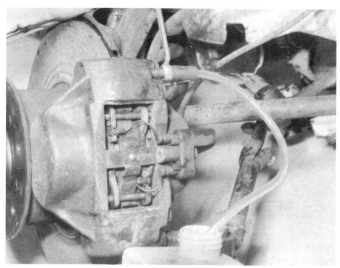

8.10B Brake bleeding kit connected to a front caliper

9 Stop-light switch – removal and refitting

1   The stop-light switch is located on the pedal bracket below the steering column.
2   To remove the switch, disconnect the wires then unscrew the inner locknut and withdraw the switch from the bracket.
3   Refitting is a reversal of removal, but adjust the position of the switch with the locknuts so that the stop-light comes on after 5 to 15 mm (0.2 to 0.6 in) of pedal travel measured at the foot pad. With the pedal fully released there should be a clearance of 6 to 8 mm (0.2 to 0.3 in) between the pedal and the fixed part of the switch.

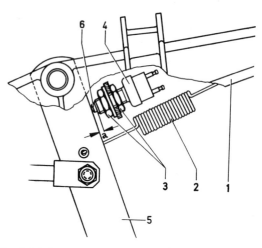

Fig. 9.14 Cross-section of the stop-light switch (Sec 9)

1	Mounting bracket for brake pedal	5	Brake pedal
2	Return spring	6	Contact button
3	Hex. nut		
4	Brake lamp switch	a = adjusting dimension	

10 Brake pedal – removal and refitting

1   Remove the lower facia panel, if necessary.
2   Disconnect the pushrod from the brake pedal by unscrewing the pivot bolt (photo). Remove the bush.
3   Unhook the return spring.
4   Remove the spring clip and withdraw the pedal from the shaft.
5   Refitting is a reversal of removal, but lubricate the shaft with a little grease.

keep the end of the tube submerged (photos). Open the bleed screw half a turn and have your assistant depress the brake pedal to the floor and then slowly release it. Tighten the bleed screw at the end of each downstroke to prevent expelled air and fluid from being drawn back into the system. Repeat this operation until clean hydraulic fluid, free from air bubbles, can be seen coming through the tube. Now tighten the bleed screw and remove the plastic tube.
11 If the entire system is being bled the procedures described above should now be repeated at the remaining front caliper, followed by the rear calipers. Do not forget to recheck the fluid level in the reservoir at regular intervals and top up as necessary.
12 When completed, recheck the fluid level in the reservoir, top up if necessary and refit the cap. Check the 'feel' of the brake pedal which should be firm and free from any 'sponginess' which would indicate air is still present in the system.
13 Discard any expelled hydraulic fluid, as it is likely to be contaminated with moisture, air and dirt which renders it unsuitable for further use.
14 The manufacturer's recommend renewal of the brake fluid every 12 months. To do this syphon all the fluid from the reservoir before adding the new fluid. In order to remove all the old fluid from the calipers remove the disc pads and push the pistons fully into their bores, retaining them with blocks of wood during the bleeding operation.

10.2 Pushrod connection on the brake pedal (automatic transmission model)

11 Handbrake/parking brake – adjustment

1 The handbrake/parking brake requires adjustment when it has to be applied by 5 to 10 notches to hold the vehicle. Right-hand drive models are provided with a pull-out handle in the facia, whereas left-hand drive models have a parking brake pedal.
2 Unscrew one bolt from each of the rear roadwheels then chock the front wheels, jack up the rear of the car and support it on axle stands. Fully release the handbrake/parking brake.
3 Working on each wheel in turn, rotate the wheel until the adjuster is visible through the bolt hole. The hole should be positioned as shown in Fig. 9.15 – use a torch if necessary. Insert a screwdriver and turn the adjuster until the wheel is locked, then back off the adjuster 2 or 3 teeth so that the wheel is just free to rotate without binding (photo).
4 With both rear wheels adjusted, lower the car to the ground and refit and tighten the two bolts.
5 Apply the handbrake/parking brake and count the number of notches necessary to apply it fully. If excessive, adjust the cable by turning the bolt on the equalizer located behind the transmission (photo). Note that the lug on the bolt must always be vertical.

Fig. 9.15 Correct position of bolt hole when adjusting the handbrake/parking brake (Sec 11)

1	Roadwheel	3	Screwdriver
2	Hub	F = front	

12 Handbrake/parking brake shoes – inspection and renewal

1 Remove the rear brake discs, as described in Section 5.
2 Brush the dust from the brake shoes, backplate, adjuster, operating levers and drums, but **do not** inhale it as it is injurious to health. Scrape any rust or scale from the drum inside surfaces.
3 Check the thickness of the linings and, if any are worn down to 1.5 mm (0.06 in), renew them as a set.
4 To remove the shoes, align one of the wheel bolt holes with a shoe steady spring then use a screwdriver to compress the spring, turn it through 90°, and withdraw it (photo). Remove the remaining shoe steady spring in the same manner.
5 Note the position of the return springs then unhook and remove the lower return spring.
6 Pull the bottom of the shoes apart and withdraw them over the axle flange, together with the adjuster and upper return spring (photos).
7 Unhook the upper return spring and remove the shoes from the adjuster.
8 If necessary remove the expander from the control cable by pushing out the clevis pin.
9 Wash the expander in paraffin and wipe dry, then coat the sliding surfaces with high melting-point grease.
10 Connect the expander to the control cable and fit the clevis pin. Trap the pin by pushing the expander against the backplate.
11 Using an Allen key check the tightness of the bolts securing the backplate and carrier housing.

11.3 Adjusting the handbrake/parking brake with a screwdriver

11.5 Handbrake/parking brake equaliser mechanism

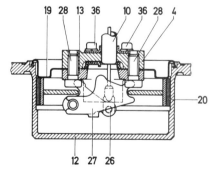

Fig. 9.16 Cross-section of the handbrake/parking brake shoe expander (Sec 12)

4	Wheel carrier	20	Brake shoes
10	Brake cable control	26	Bolt
12	Brake disc	27	Expander
13	Brake carrier	28	Hex. socket bolt
19	Backplate	36	Hex. socket bolt

12.4 Shoe steady spring location for the handbrake/parking brake

12.6A Handbrake/parking brake shoe expander mechanism

12.6B Handbrake/parking brake shoe adjuster

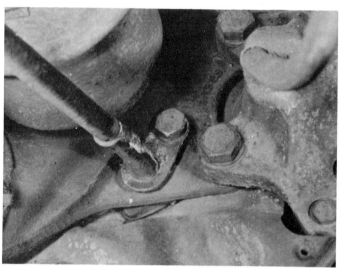

13.15 Rear handbrake/parking brake cable and retaining bolt

12 Lubricate the adjuster with a little high melting-point grease, then set it to its shortest length.

13 Fit the upper ends of the shoes (ie with large slots) to the adjuster so that the adjuster wheel is towards the front of the car, then fit the upper return spring to the inner surfaces of the shoes.

14 Pull the bottom of the shoes apart and locate them over the axle flange, then locate the small slots on the expander.

15 Insert the steady springs and use a screwdriver to hook them onto the backplate by turning them through 90°.

16 Attach the small hook of the lower return spring to the front brake shoe, then attach the large hook to the rear brake shoe.

17 Refit the rear brake discs, as described in Section 5.

18 Adjust the handbrake/parking brake, as described in Section 11.

13 Handbrake/parking brake cables – removal and refitting

1 Chock the front wheels, then jack up the rear of the car and support it on axle stands.

2 Lower the exhaust system onto an axle stand, with reference to Chapter 3.

3 Unbolt and remove the heatshield, where applicable.

4 Unhook the return spring from the wire.

5 Fully unscrew the adjusting bolt, then release the intermediate lever from the underbody and adjusting bracket.

Front cable

6 Extract the split pin and remove the clevis pin securing the front cable to the intermediate lever.

7 Prise off the spring clip securing the cable guide to the crossmember behind the transmission.

8 Working inside the car, remove the trim panel for access to the cable.

9 Disconnect the inner cable from the lever/pedal then prise out the spring clip and disconnect the outer cable.

10 Pull the cable through the rubber grommet from under the car.

11 Refitting is a reversal of removal, but adjust the handbrake/parking brake, as described in Section 11.

Rear cables

12 Disconnect the equaliser from both rear cables.

13 Prise off the spring clips and remove the cables from the underbody brackets.

14 Remove the handbrake/parking brake shoes and expanders, as described in Section 12.

15 Unscrew the bolts from the axle housings and withdraw the cables (photo).

16 Refitting is a reversal of removal. Refer to Section 12 when

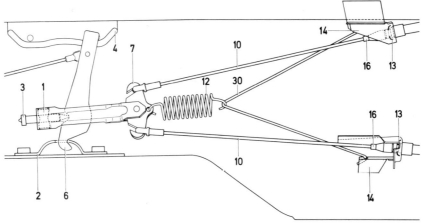

Fig. 9.17 Diagram of the
handbrake/parking brake cables (Sec 13)

1	Adjusting bracket	7	Compensating lever
2	Bearing on frame floor	10	Rear brake cable control
3	Adjusting screw	12	Return spring
4	Guide for intermediate lever	13	Spring clamp
6	Intermediate lever		

14 Bracket for rear brake
    cable control
16 Rubber sleeve
30 Spring holder

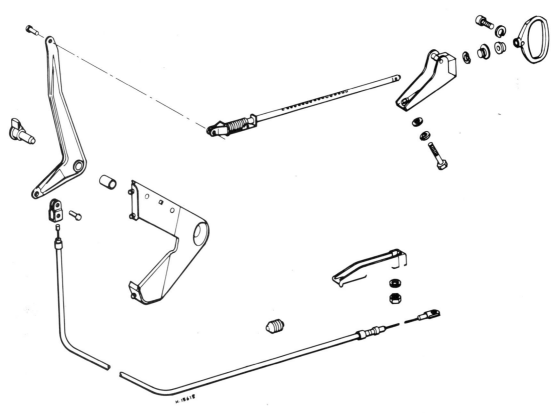

Fig. 9.18 Exploded view of the handbrake lever for RHD models (Sec 14)

refitting the handbrake/parking brake shoe, and adjust the handbrake/parking brake, as described in Section 11.

14 Handbrake lever (RHD models)– removal and refitting

1 Chock the front wheels then jack up the rear of the car and support it on axle stands.

2 Lower the exhaust system onto an axle stand, with reference to Chapter 3.

3 Unbolt and remove the heatshield, where applicable.

4 Unhook the handbrake return spring from the wire.

5 Fully unscrew the cable adjusting bolt, then release the intermediate lever from the underbody and adjusting bracket.

6 Working inside the car, remove the trim panel and disconnect the inner cable from the lever.

7   Unbolt the lever bracket from the side panel and disconnect the top of the lever from the pullrod by extracting the clevis pin.
8   Refitting is a reversal of removal, but adjust the handbrake, as described in Section 11.

15 Parking brake pedal (LHD models) – removal and refitting

1   Chock the front wheels then jack up the rear of the car and support it on axle stands.
2   Lower the exhaust system onto an axle stand, with reference to Chapter 3.
3   Unbolt and remove the heatshield, where applicable.
4   Unhook the parking brake return spring from the wire.
5   Fully unscrew the cable adjusting bolt, then release the intermediate lever from the underbody and adjusting bracket.
6   Turn the steering fully to the left and unscrew the pedal bracket nut from under the wheel arch.
7   Unscrew the bracket nut located in the engine compartment.
8   Working inside the car, remove the trim panel.
9   Disconnect the inner cable from the pedal then prise out the spring clip and disconnect the outer cable.
10 Disconnect the wiring connector and the warning switch wiring.
11 Disconnect the release knob chain from the lever.
12 Unscrew the upper retaining bolt and withdraw the pedal assembly from the car.
13 Refitting is a reversal of removal, but adjust the parking brake, as described in Section 11.

16 Vacuum servo unit – description, removal and refitting

1   The vacuum servo unit is fitted between the footbrake pedal and the master cylinder and provides assistance to the driver when the pedal is depressed. The unit operates by vacuum supplied through a check valve from the inlet manifold. With the foot pedal released vacuum is channelled to both sides of the internal diaphragm, however, when the pedal is depressed one side is opened to the atmosphere resulting in assistance to the pedal effort. Should the vacuum servo develop a fault, the hydraulic system is not affected, but greater effort will be required at the pedal.
2   To test the unit, switch off the engine and depress the footbrake pedal several times to dissipate the vacuum. Now depress the pedal and hold it down, while starting the engine. With the engine idling the vacuum assistance will draw the pedal a short distance toward the floor proving that the unit is functioning correctly.
3   To remove the vacuum servo unit first remove the master cylinder, as described in Section 6.
4   Unscrew the union nut and disconnect the vacuum line.
5   Remove the lower facia panel inside the car.
6   Disconnect the servo pushrod from the footbrake pedal. On early models, unscrew the nut and withdraw the bolt, but on later models extract the clip and withdraw the pin.
7   Unscrew the mounting nuts, then withdraw the servo unit from inside the engine compartment.
8   Refitting is a reversal of removal, but refit the master cylinder with reference to Section 6, making sure that a new sealing ring is fitted between the master cylinder and servo unit.

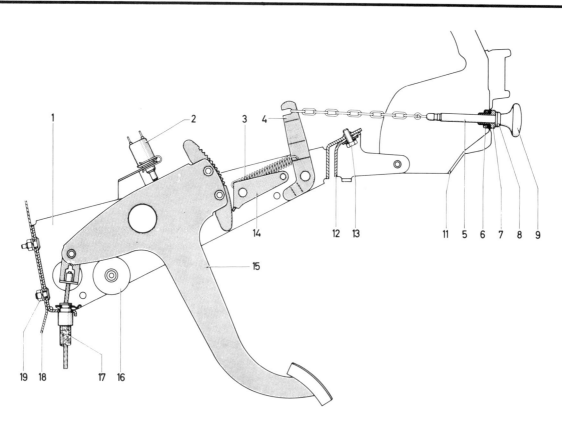

Fig. 9.19 Diagram of the parking brake pedal for LHD models (Sec 15)

1	Bracket	7	Rosette	14	Detent
2	Switch for warning light	8	Stop buffer	15	Pedal
3	Return spring	9	Actuating knob	16	Rubber stop
4	Releasing lever	11	Facia panel	17	Brake control cable
5	Pull rod with chain	12	Holder for facia panel	18	Bulkhead
6	Nut on rosette	13	Bolt	19	Bolt

17 Fault diagnosis – braking system

Symptom	Reason(s)
Excessive pedal travel	Air in hydraulic system
Uneven braking and pulling to one side	Contaminated linings Seized caliper Incorrect tyre pressures
Brake judder	Worn discs Contaminated linings Wear in suspension
Brake pedal feels 'spongy'	Air in hydraulic system Worn master cylinder seals
Excessive effort to stop car	Servo unit faulty Excessively worn disc pad linings Seized calipers Contaminated linings Failure of front or rear hydraulic circuit

Chapter 10 Electrical system

Contents

Specifications

System type
.... 12 volt, negative earth

Battery
Capacity .... 55 amp hr

Alternator
Type .... Bosch: 55 amp or 65 amp

Charging current at engine speed:

Engine 123.920 .... 36 amp at 1040 rpm, 55 amp at 3130 rpm

Engine 123.921 .... 36 amp at 930 rpm, 55 amp at 2760 rpm

Engine 110 (pre March 1980) .... 36 amp at 1040 rpm, 55 amp at 3130 rpm

Engine 110 (March 1980 onwards)
with 55 amp alternator .... 36 amp at 930 rpm, 55 amp at 2760 rpm

Engine 110 (March 1980 onwards)
with 65 amp alternator .... 43 amp at 980 rpm, 65 amp at 2760 rpm

Minimum brush length .... 5 mm (0.197 in)

Starter motor
Type .... Bosch pre-engaged
Rating .... 0.85 kW (1.1 HP), 1.04 kW (1.4 HP) or 1.5 kW (1.95 HP)

Bulbs

	Wattage
Headlamp (halogen)	60/55
Front foglamp (halogen)	55
Direction indicators	21
Direction indicators and side marker	21/5
Stop-lamps	21
Reversing lamps	21
Number plate lamps	5
Tail lamps	10
Front parking lamps	4
Rear foglamp	21
Interior lamp	10
Glove compartment lamp	5
Luggage compartment lamp	10

Torque wrench settings

	lbf ft	Nm
Starter motor	18	25

1 General description

The electrical system is of 12 volt negative earth type. The battery is charged by a belt-driven alternator which incorporates a voltage regulator.

The starter motor is of pre-engaged type where a solenoid moves the drive pinion into engagement with the ring gear before the starter motor is energised.

Although repair procedures are given in this Chapter, it may well be more economical to renew worn components as complete units.

2 Routine maintenance

1 Every 10 000 miles (16 000 km) on UK models, and every 15 000 miles (24 000 km) on USA models, check the function of all electrical components and check the battery electrolyte level. Top up if necessary.

2 At the same time check the wiper blades for wear, and renew if necessary.

3 Battery – removal and refitting

1 The battery is located in the engine compartment on the left-hand side of the bulkhead.

2 Note the location of the leads and, where fitted, unclip the plastic cover from over the positive terminal.

3 Unscrew the clamp bolts and disconnect the negative terminal lead followed by the positive terminal lead (photo).

4 Unscrew the bolts and remove the clamps (photo), then lift the battery from the platform, taking care not to spill any electrolyte on the bodywork.

5 Refitting is a reversal of removal, however do not over-tighten the bolts. Smear the exposed areas of the terminals and clamps with a little petroleum jelly.

4 Battery – maintenance

1 The standard battery incorporates an automatic level device to prevent overfilling. If the electrolyte level is below the maximum mark on the front of the battery, remove the filler caps or cover and add distilled or de-ionized water until the area above the rubber plugs begins to fill with water (photo). This will ensure that the cells are full and the internal plate separators covered with electrolyte.

3.3 Positive battery terminal

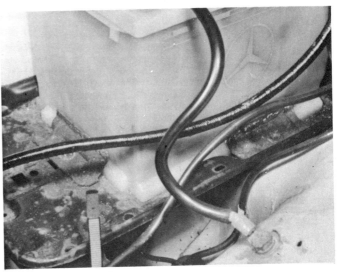
3.4 Battery retaining clamps

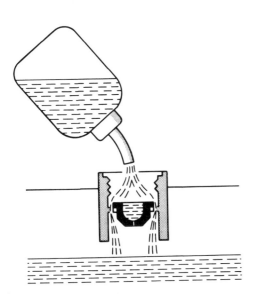
Fig. 10.1 Automatic level device in the battery (Sec 4)

4.1 Topping-up the battery electrolyte level

2   Keep the top of the battery clean to prevent the accumulation of dust and dampness which may cause the battery to become partially discharged over a period of time.

3   Also check the battery clamp and platform for corrosion. If evident, remove the battery and clean the deposits away. Then treat the affected metal with a proprietary anti-rust liquid and paint with the original colour.

4   Whenever the battery is removed it is worthwhile checking it for cracks and leakage. Cracks can be caused by topping-up the cells with distilled water in winter after instead of before a run. This gives the water no chance to mix with the electrolyte, so the water freezes and splits the battery case. If the case is fractured, it may be possible to repair it with a proprietary compound, but this depends on the material used for the case. If electrolyte has been lost from a cell, refer to Section 5 for details of adding a fresh solution.

5   If topping-up the battery becomes excessive and the case is not fractured, the battery is being over-charged and the voltage regulator may be faulty.

6   If the car covers a small annual mileage it is worthwhile checking the specific gravity of the electrolyte every three months to determine the state of charge of the battery. Use a hydrometer inserted through the rubber plugs to make the check, and compare the results with the following table:

	Ambient temperature above 25°C (77°F)	Ambient temperature below 25°C (77°F)
Fully charged	1.210 to 1.230	1.270 to 1.290
70% charged	1.170 to 1.190	1.230 to 1.250
Fully discharged	1.050 to 1.070	1.110 to 1.130

Note that the specific gravity readings assume an electrolyte temperature of 15°C (59°F); for every 10°C (18°F) below 15°C (59°F) subtract 0.007. For every 10°C (18°F) above 15°C (59°F) add 0.007.

7   If the battery condition is suspect, first check the specific gravity of electrolyte in each cell. A variation of 0.040 or more between any cells indicates loss of electrolyte or deterioration of the internal plates.

5   Battery – electrolyte replenishment

1   If the battery is in a fully charged state and one of the cells maintains a specific gravity reading which is 0.040 or more lower than the others, then it is likely that electrolyte has been lost from the cell at some time.

2   Top up the cell with a solution of 1 part sulphuric acid to 2.5 parts of distilled water. If the cell is already fully topped up draw some electrolyte out of it with a hydrometer.

3   When mixing the sulphuric acid and water **never add water to sulphuric acid** – always pour the acid slowly onto the water in a glass container. **If water is added to sulphuric acid it will explode.**

4   Continue to top up the cell with the freshly made electrolyte and then recharge the battery and check the hydrometer readings.

6   Battery – charging

1   In winter time, when heavy demand is placed upon the battery, such as when starting from cold, and much electrical equipment is continually in use, it is a good idea to occasionally have the battery fully charged from an external source at the rate of 3.5 or 4 amps.

2   Continue to charge the battery at this rate until no further rise in specific gravity is noted over a four hour period.

3   Alternatively, a trickle charger at the rate of 1.5 amps can be safely used overnight.

4   Specially rapid 'boost' charges which are claimed to restore the power of the battery in 1 to 2 hours are not recommended, as they can cause serious damage to the battery plates through overheating.

5   While charging the battery, note that the temperature of the electrolyte should never exceed 40°C (104°F)

7   Alternator – maintenance and special precautions

1   Periodically wipe away any dirt which has accumulated on the outside of the unit, and also check that the plug is pushed firmly onto the terminals. At the same time, check the tension of the drivebelt and adjust it, if necessary, as described in Chapter 2.

2   Take extreme care when making electrical circuit connections on the car, otherwise damage may occur to the alternator or other electrical components employing semi-conductors. Always make sure that the battery leads are connected to the correct terminals. Before using electric-arc welding equipment to repair any part of the car, disconnect the battery leads and the alternator multi-plug. Disconnect the battery leads before using a mains charger. Never run the alternator with the multi-plug or a battery lead disconnected.

8   Alternator – removal and refitting

1   Disconnect the battery negative lead.

2   Remove the air cleaner, as described in Chapter 3, and the air conditioning compressor, if applicable (Chapter 12).

3   Prise off the spring clip and pull the multi-plug from the rear of the alternator (photo).

4   Loosen the alternator mounting and adjustment nuts and bolts, then swivel the alternator towards the cylinder block (photo).

5   Slip the drivebelt from the alternator pulley.

6   Unscrew the nut from the pivot bolt and remove the earth strap (photo).

7   Remove the mounting and adjustment bolts together with the spacers, and withdraw the alternator from the engine.

8.3 Alternator multi-plug location

8.4 Alternator mounting bolt locations

8.6 Alternator earth strap location

8.8A Tensioning the alternator drivebelt

8.8B Alternator mounting bracket

8   Refitting is a reversal of removal, but tension the drivebelt by turning the adjustment bolt head, as described in Chapter 2 (photo). Finally check the tightness of the mounting bracket bolts (photos).

9   Alternator and voltage regulator – testing in car

1   To check for the cause of lack of charge to the battery, carry out the following test to verify operation of the regulator.
2   Disconnect the lead from the battery negative terminal.
3   Connect a 0 to 16V voltmeter between the B+ terminal on the alternator and the alternator body.
4   Disconnect the red cable from the B+ terminal and connect a 0 to 60A ammeter between the end of the cable and the terminal.
5   Reconnect the battery negative lead and then bridge the battery terminals with a 55A variable resistor.
6   Start the engine and run it at a constant speed of between 2000 and 3000 rpm.
7   Adjust the current on the load resistor to between 28 and 30A when the voltmeter should indicate between 13.9 and 14.8V. Any deviation from these figures will require immediate attention to the voltage regulator by your dealer.
8   To test the alternator output, switch on the load resistor, set the engine speed to 1300 rpm and at the same time increase the load current to 10A. The charge warning lamp should be out.
9   Repeat the test at 2000 and 6000 rpm, adjusting the load current to 36 and 55A for the 55A alternator, or 43 and 65A for the 65A alternator.
10   Where a fault occurs in an alternator it is not recommended that it is dismantled, but rather that it is overhauled by a Bosch agent or else a new unit is obtained.

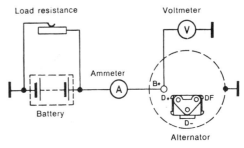

Fig. 10.2 Alternator test circuit (Sec 9)

10   Alternator brushes – removal, inspection and refitting

1   Disconnect the battery negative lead.
2   Remove the air cleaner, as described in Chapter 3, and the air conditioning compressor, if applicable (Chapter 12). Depending on the model it may be necessary to completely remove the alternator.
3   Remove the screws and withdraw the regulator and brush box from the rear of the alternator (photo).
4   If the length of either brush is less than the minimum given in the Specifications, unsolder the wiring and remove the brushes and springs.
5   Wipe clean the alternator slip rings with a fuel-moistened cloth – if they are very dirty use fine glass paper to clean them, then wipe with the cloth (photo).
6   Refitting is a reversal of removal, but make sure that the brushes move freely in their holders.

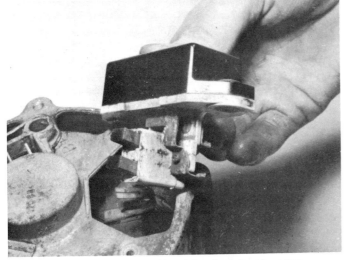

10.3 Removing the regulator and brush box from the alternator

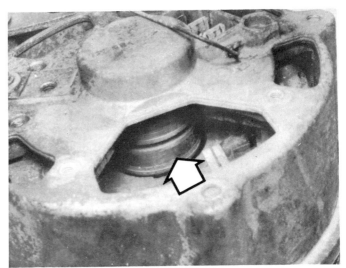

10.5 Alternator slip rings (arrowed)

11 Starter motor – removal and refitting

1 Jack up the front of the car and support on axle stands. Apply the handbrake/parking brake.
2 Disconnect the battery negative lead.
3 Disconnect the wiring from the solenoid by unscrewing the nut to remove the main cable and pulling the control wires from the terminals (photo).
4 Unbolt the starter motor from the intermediate plate and bracket, and withdraw it from under the car (photo). Note that an Allen key is required for the top mounting bolt.
5 Refitting is a reversal of removal but first insert all the bolts finger tight, then fully tighten them.

12 Starter motor – overhaul

1 Failure of the starter motor to operate may be due to factors other than the motor itself. First check that the battery and solenoid terminal connections are tight and clean. Check that the battery is in a high state of charge.
2 The starter motor usually has a very long life and it is normally economically sound to change it for a new or factory reconditioned unit when it fails. However, the brushes and commutator may be serviced, but anything more extensive should be left to your Bosch agent.

11.3 Starter motor solenoid wiring

11.4 Removing the starter motor

12.3 Removing the starter motor solenoid connecting wire

12.4 Removing the starter motor solenoid body and spring

12.5 Unhooking the starter motor solenoid armature

12.7 Removing the starter motor end cap

12.8 Extract the circlip and thrust washer ...

12.9A ... remove the through-bolts ...

12.9B ... and pull off the end cover

12.10 Checking the starter motor brushes

3   To dismantle the starter motor, unscrew the nut and remove the connecting wire from the solenoid (photo).
4   Unscrew the bolts and withdraw the solenoid body and spring from the end bracket (photo).
5   Unhook the solenoid armature from the engagement lever (photo).
6   Remove the mounting bracket, if necessary.
7   Remove the screws and withdraw the end cap (photo).
8   Prise out the circlip and remove the thrust washer (photo).
9   Unscrew the through-bolts and pull off the end cover (photos).
10 Lift the springs and extract the brushes (photo).
11 The drivegear should be examined for wear or damaged teeth (photo). Also inspect the overrunning clutch which should only be able to be turned clockwise when viewed from the pinion gear end. Clean the commutator initially with a fuel-soaked cloth. If the surfaces of the segments are burnt, they can be cleaned with glass paper, **not emery cloth** and the mica insulators then undercut to a depth of between 0.6 and 0.8 mm (0.024 and 0.031 in). If the armature bushes are worn, leave renewal to your dealer. Apply grease to the bushes and reassemble by reversing the dismantling operations. If new brushes are being fitted, check that they slide easily in their holders. Use a piece of wire to retain the springs when inserting the brushes.
12 When the starter motor is reassembled energise the solenoid and check the clearance between the drive pinion face and its stop on the drive end housing. This should be between 1.0 and 4.0 mm (0.04 and 0.16 in).

12.11 Starter motor drivegear

13 Fuses and relays – general

1   The fuses are located in the engine compartment on the right-hand side of the bulkhead (photo). The individual relays are located separately in the wiring harness.
2   Always renew a fuse with one of identical rating and never renew it more than once without finding the source of the trouble (usually a short circuit). Always switch off the ignition before renewing a fuse.
3   Access to the fuses is gained by removing the fusebox cover (2 knobs) – the fuses are held between spring clip terminals.
4   The fuse application is shown on the inside of the cover, but, if necessary, reference may be made to the wiring diagrams at the end of this Chapter.
5   The in-line fuse for the radio is located next to the radio.
6   The relay units are located by the instrument panel or in the engine compartment (photo).

14 Combination switch – removal and refitting

1   Disconnect the battery negative lead.
2   Remove the lower facia panel and disconnect the switch multi-plug (photos).

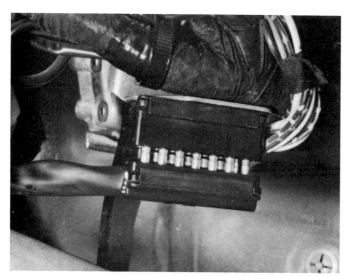

13.1 Fusebox with cover removed

13.6 Relay unit located behind the instrument panel

14.2A Disconnecting the combination switch multi-plug

14.2B Locating pin for the combination switch multi-plug (arrowed)

14.3 Pull off the surround ...

14.4 ... remove the screws ...

14.5 ... disconnect the horn wires ...

14.6A ... and withdraw the combination switch

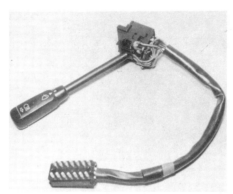

14.6B Combination switch

15.1 Removing a courtesy light switch

3   Pull out the rubber lever surround (photo).
4   Unscrew the cross-head mounting screws (photo).
5   Disconnect the horn wires by loosening the terminal screws (photo).
6   Withdraw the switch while feeding the wiring harness through the aperture (photos).
7   Refitting is a reversal of removal.

15 Courtesy light switch – removal and refitting

1   Open the door and prise the switch from the door pillar (photo).
2   Pull out the wires sufficiently to prevent them springing back into the pillar, then disconnect them from the terminals and remove the switch.
3   Refitting is a reversal of removal.

16 Lighting switch – removal and refitting

1   Disconnect the battery negative lead.
2   Pull off the switch knob.
3   Remove the lower facia panel.
4   Unscrew the nut, withdraw the switch from the rear of the facia panel and disconnect the wiring. Remove the cover.
5   Refitting is a reversal of removal, but make sure that the cover and switch engage the cut-outs in the facia panel.

17 Facia panel/console switches – removal and refitting

1   Disconnect the battery negative lead.
2   Prise out the switch (photo).
3   Pull off the connector and remove the switch.
4   Refitting is a reversal of removal.

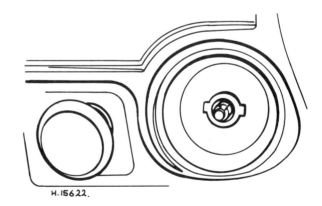

H.15622.

Fig. 10.3 Lighting switch locating lugs (Sec 16)

17.2 Removing a facia panel switch

18.5A Disconnecting the speedometer cable from the instrument panel

18.5B Square section end to the speedometer cable

18.6 Disconnecting a multi-plug from the instrument panel

18.7A Disconnecting the oil pressure line

18.7B End fitting of the oil pressure line

18.8 Front and rear views of the instrument panel

18.9 Both instrument panel multi-plugs (arrowed)

18 Instrument panel – removal and refitting

1   Disconnect the battery negative lead.
2   Remove the lower facia panel.
3   Push out the instrument panel from the rear. Alternatively the lower facia panel can be left in position and a hooked instrument used to extract the instrument panel.
4   Release the speedometer cable from the plastic clips in the engine compartment.
5   Unscrew the knurled nut and disconnect the speedometer cable from the instrument panel (photos).
6   Pull off the wiring multi-plugs and individual wires, noting their location (photo).
7   Unscrew the union nut and disconnect the oil pressure line from the gauge (photos).

8   Withdraw the instrument panel from the facia (photo).
9   Refitting is a reversal of removal (photo).

19 Speedometer cable – removal and refitting

1   Disconnect the speedometer cable from the instrument panel, with reference to Section 17.
2   Jack up the front of the car and support on axle stands. Apply the handbrake/parking brake.
3   Unscrew the retaining bolt from the gearbox/transmission and pull out the speedometer cable.
4   Release the body clips and withdraw the cable.
5   Refitting is a reversal of removal, but make sure that there are no sharp bends in the cable.

20.2 Rear view of the clock

20.8 Rear view of the instrument panel gauges section

20 Instrument panel gauges – removal and refitting

1   Remove the instrument panel, as described in Section 18.

Clock
2   Remove the four cross-head screws and withdraw the clock from the back of the instrument panel (photo).
3   Refitting is a reversal of removal.

Speedometer
4   First remove the clock (paragraph 2).
5   Remove the two cross-head screws, then tilt the speedometer and withdraw it from the instrument panel.
6   Refitting is a reversal of removal, but check that the trip mileage reset lever engages the knob.

Gauges
7   First remove the speedometer (paragraphs 4 and 5).
8   Remove the three cross-head screws (one retaining the instrument lighting potentiometer) (photo).
9   Pull out the potentiometer, then withdraw the gauge assembly.
10   Refitting is a reversal of removal.

21 Headlamp/foglamps – alignment

1   This is a job best left to a service station having the necessary beam setting equipment.
2   In an emergency, the headlight main beams should be adjusted using the adjusting knobs provided, so that the following conditions are complied with.
3   With the car positioned square to and 5.0 m (16 ft) from a screen and the headlight beams on main beam, the light pattern should not project above a horizontal line drawn on the screen at a height equivalent to the light centres on the car.
4   The brightest points of the light pattern should be in direct alignment with the headlamps.
5   The foglamps can be adjusted using the same procedure.

22 Headlamps/foglamps and bulbs – removal and refitting

UK models
1   To remove a headlamp/foglamp bulb open the bonnet and unclip the headlamp unit rear cover (photo).
2   Disconnect the wiring from the bulb, then either release the spring

Fig. 10.4 Removing the clock from the instrument panel (Sec 20)

22.1 Headlamp/foglamp rear cover

clips or turn the bulbholder to extract the bulb (photos). The bulb glass should not be touched with the fingers, however, if it is touched, clean it with methylated spirit.

3   To remove the headlamp unit, first remove the direction indicator lamp, as described in Section 23, then unscrew the unit side mounting screws exposed (photo).

4   Unscrew the inner mounting screws and withdraw the headlamp unit from the car (photo).

5   To dismantle the headlamp, prise off the clips and remove the glass (photos).

6   Remove the surround panel (photo).

7   Release the clips and vacuum adjustment unit and remove the reflectors (photos).

8   Refitting is a reversal of removal.

USA models

9   Sealed beam units are fitted for both the headlamp and foglamp.

10   To remove a unit first unscrew the knurled knobs from inside the engine compartment.

11   Unscrew the inner mounting screws and withdraw the unit to the side until the wiring plugs can be disconnected.

12   Unbolt the parking light/direction indicator unit from the headlamp unit.

13   Refitting is a reversal of removal.

22.2A Disconnecting the headlamp wiring plug

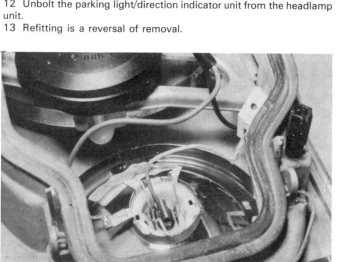

22.2B Foglamp bulb wiring

22.2C Release the clips ...

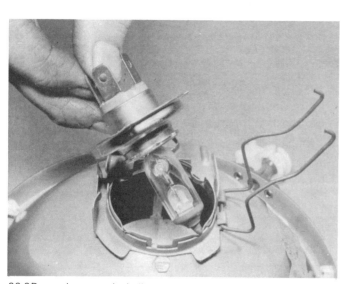

22.2D ... and remove the bulb

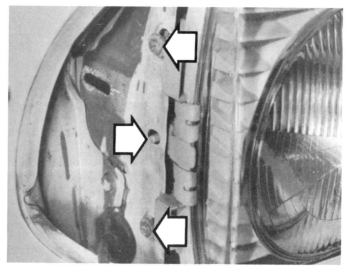

22.3 Headlamp side mounting screws and locating lug (arrowed)

Fig. 10.5 Headlamp for USA models (Sec 22)

1	Foglamp	4	Direction indicator
2	High beam	5	Sidelight
3	Low beam		

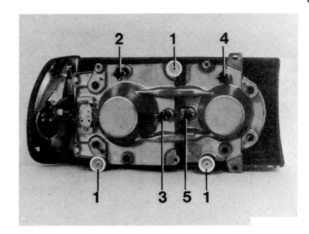

Fig. 10.6 Rear view of the headlamp for USA models (Sec 22)

1	Frame retaining knobs	4	Foglamp height adjustment
2	Headlamp height adjustment	5	Foglamp lateral adjustment
3	Headlamp lateral adjustment		

22.4 Headlamp inner mounting screw

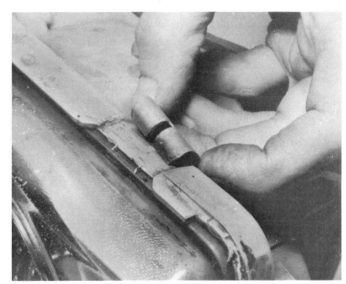

22.5A Prise off the clips ...

22.5B ... and remove the headlamp glass

22.6 Removing the surround panel

22.7A Foglamp mounting clip

22.7B Headlamp mounting clip

22.7C Headlamp pivot

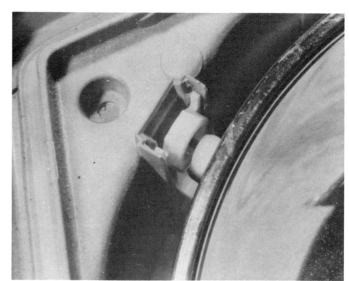

22.7D Headlamp adjustment

22.7E Headlamp vacuum control arm connection

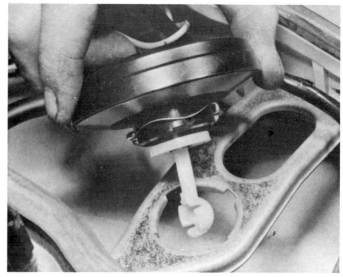

22.7F Headlamp vacuum control unit

23 Lamp bulbs – renewal

Front sidelamps
1 Unclip the headlamp unit rear cover.
2 Pull out the parking lamp holder, then depress and twist the bulb to remove it (photo).

Direction indicator lamp
3 Unscrew the knurled nut in the engine compartment, release the lamp unit from the headlamp brackets, and withdraw the lamp unit (photos).
4 Either pull out the bulbholder or twist it to remove it, then depress and twist the bulb to remove it.

Rear lamp cluster (Saloon models)
5 Unscrew the knurled nuts in the luggage compartment and remove the combined bulbholder (photo).
6 Depress and twist the relevant bulb to remove it.

Rear lamp cluster (Estate models)
7 Loosen only the rear lamp retaining nuts in the luggage compartment, press the lamp rearwards to release it from the body, then remove the nuts and withdraw the lamp.
8 Prise the lug and remove the lamp bracket.
9 Depress and twist the relevant bulb to remove it.

Number plate lamp
10 Open the bootlid/tailgate, remove the screws and withdraw the lampholder (photo).
11 Remove the festoon type bulb from the spring terminals.

Interior lamp
12 Carefully prise the lamp from the headlining (photo).
13 Remove the festoon type bulb from the spring terminals.

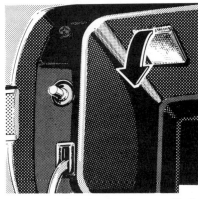

Fig. 10.7 Removing the glovebox lamp and bulb (Sec 23)

Boot lamp
14 Open the boot lid and remove the festoon type bulb from the spring terminals (photo).

Glovebox lamp
15 Prise the lamp from the top of the glovebox and remove the festoon type bulb from the spring terminals.

Hazard switch bulb
16 Prise the hazard switch from the centre console and disconnect the multi-plug.
17 Turn the bulbholder a quarter turn anti-clockwise and withdraw it from the switch, then depress and twist the bulb to remove it.

Heater control bulbs
18 Pull off the heater control knobs and pull the knob illumination bulbs from the centre holders.

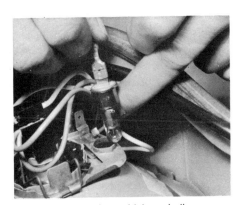

23.2 Removing a front sidelamp bulb

23.3A Unscrew the knurled nut ...

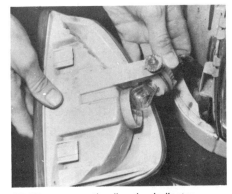

23.3B ... remove the direction indicator lamp, and withdraw the bulbholder

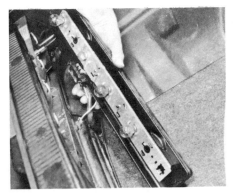

23.5 Removing a rear lamp cluster bulbholder

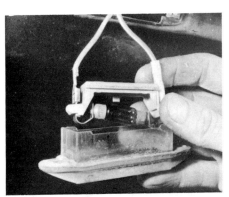

23.10 Removing a number plate lamp bulb

23.12 Removing an interior lamp bulb

19　Pull off the air flap control knob, then unscrew the nuts and withdraw the control cover.
20　Pull out the bulbholders and extract the bulbs.

Ashtray lamp

21　Remove the ashtray, unscrew the two screws and withdraw the top.
22　Pull out the bulbholder and extract the bulb.

Instrument panel bulbs

23　Remove the instrument panel, as described in Section 18.
24　Turn the bulbholder a quarter turn and remove it from the rear of the instrument panel (photos).

Selector lever illumination (automatic transmission models)

25　Remove the selector lever surround, with reference to Chapter 6.
26　Remove the bulbholder and extract the bulb (photo).

24　Windscreen wiper blades – renewal

1　Lift the wiper arm then depress the plastic clip and slide the blade from the arm (photo).

23.14 Removing the boot lamp bulb

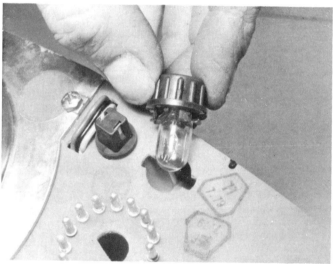

23.24A Removing type A instrument panel bulb

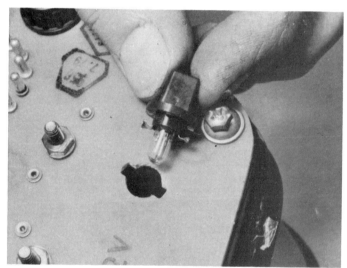

23.24B Removing type B instrument panel bulb

23.26 Automatic transmission selector lever illumination bulb location

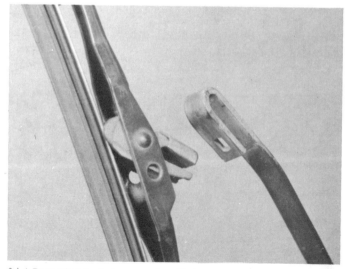

24.1 Removing a windscreen wiper blade

2   If necessary, the puller may be renewed separately by sliding it from the blade and removing the springs.
3   Fit the new blade by reversing the removal procedure.

25 Windscreen wiper arm – removal and refitting

1   Remove the wiper blades, as described in Section 24.
2   Lift the hinged covers (with the arm already in the lifted position), then remove the arm and cover together towards the windscreen (photo).
3   Remove the nut and washer, mark the arm in relation to the spindle, then pull off the arm.
4   Refitting is a reversal of removal.

25.2 Windscreen wiper arm hinged cover

26 Windscreen wiper motor – removal and refitting

1   Remove the wiper arms, as described in Section 25.
2   Remove the plastic heater air intake grilles. To do this, use a narrow screwdriver to push out the clip center pins, prise out the clips and pull the grilles forwards. Remove the cap and nut, where applicable.
3   Remove the screws and push out the clip centre pins, and withdraw the centre panel.
4   Prise the operating rods from the wiper motor crank.
5   Remove the drain tube from the spindle, where applicable.
6   Disconnect the battery negative lead.
7   Disconnect the wiper motor multi-plug from within the engine compartment.
8   Unclip the wiring plug, then unbolt the wiper motor from the centre bracket.
9   Refitting is a reversal of removal.

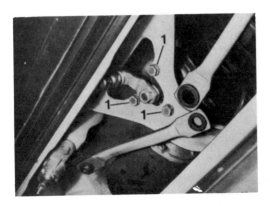

Fig. 10.8 Windscreen wiper motor mounting bolts (1) (Sec 26)

27 Windscreen wiper linkage – removal and refitting

1   Remove the wiper motor, as described in Section 26.
2   Renew the operating rods, then unbolt the spindle assemblies from the bulkhead.
3   Refitting is a reversal of removal.

28 Headlamp wiper motor – renewal and refitting

1   Remove the wiper blade and arm (1 nut).
2   Remove the headlamp unit, with reference to Section 22.
3   Disconnect the battery negative lead.
4   Disconnect the wiring plug from the motor.
5   Unbolt the mounting nuts and withdraw the wiper motor.
6   Refitting is a reversal of removal, but before fitting the wiper blade and arm, switch the motor on then off so that the spindle turns to the 'parked' position.

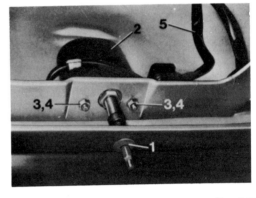

Fig. 10.9 Headlamp wiper motor location (Sec 28)

1 *Grommet*	4 *Spring washers*
2 *Wiper motor*	5 *Wiring harness*
3 *Nuts*	

29 Windscreen washer system – general

1   The windscreen washer system consists of a fluid reservoir located within the engine compartment, an electric pump and the necessary control switch, jets and connecting pipes (photo).
2   Do not use plain water in the system as this can cause corrosion and blockage of the jets. Use a recommended solvent in the water.
3   If a fault occurs, check the circuit fuse, the electrical connections and the fluid pipe attachments.
4   A faulty pump will have to be renewed complete.

29.1 Windscreen washer fluid reservoir, showing the electric pump (arrowed)

30 Radios and tape players (general) – installation

A radio or tape player is an expensive item to buy and will only give its best performance if fitted properly. It is useless to expect concert hall performance from a unit that is suspended from the dash panel on string with its speaker resting on the back seat or parcel shelf! If you do not wish to do the installation yourself there are many in-car entertainment specialists who can do the fitting for you.

Make sure the unit purchased is of the same polarity as the car, and ensure that units with adjustable polarity are correctly set before commencing installation.

It is difficult to give specialist information with regard to fitting, as final positioning of the radio/tape player, speakers and aerial is entirely a matter of personal preference. However, the following paragraphs give guidelines to follow, which are relevant to all installations.

Radios

Most radios are a standardised size of 7 inches wide, by 2 inches deep – this ensures that they wil fit into the radio aperture provided in most cars. If your car does not have such an aperture, then the radio must be fitted in a suitable position either in, or beneath, the dashpanel. Alternatively, a special console can be purchased which will fit between the dashpanel and the floor. These consoles can also be used for additional switches and instrumentation if required. Where no radio aperture is provided, the following points should be borne in mind before deciding exactly where to fit the unit:

(a) *The unit must be within easy reach of the driver wearing a seat belt*

(b) *The unit must not be mounted in close proximity to an electronic tachometer, the ignition switch and its wiring, or the flasher unit and associated wiring*

(c) *The unit must be mounted within reach of the aerial lead, and in such a place that the aerial lead will not have to be routed near the components detailed in the preceding paragraph 'b'*

(d) *The unit should not be positioned in a place where it might cause injury to the car occupants in an accident; for instance, under the dashpanel above the driver's or passenger's legs*

(e) *The unit must be fitted really securely*

Some radios will have mounting brackets provided together with instructions: others will need to be fitted using drilled and slotted metal strips, bent to form mounting brackets – these strips are available from most accessory shops. The unit must be properly earthed, by fitting a separate earthing lead between the casing of the radio and the vehicle frame.

Use the radio manufacturers' instructions when wiring the radio into the vehicle's electrical system. If no instructions are available refer to the relevant wiring diagram to find the location of the radio 'feed' connection in the vehicle's wiring circuit. A 1-2 amp 'in-line' fuse must be fitted in the radio's 'feed' wire – a choke may also be necessary.

The type of aerial used, and its fitted position is a matter of personal preference. In general the taller the aerial, the better the reception. It is best to fit a fully retractable aerial – especially, if a mechanical car wash is used or if you live in an area where cars tend to be vandalised. In this respect electric aerials which are raised and lowered automatically when switching the radio on or off are convenient, but are more likely to give trouble than the manual type.

When choosing a site for the aerial the following points should be considered:

(a) *The aerial lead should be as short as possible – this means that the aerial should be mounted at the front of the car*

(b) *The aerial must be mounted as far away from the distributor and HT leads as possible*

(c) *The part of the aerial which protrudes beneath the mounting point must not foul the roadwheels, or anything else*

(d) *If possible the aerial should be positioned so that the coaxial lead does not have to be routed through the engine compartment*

(e) *The plane of the panel on which the aerial is mounted should not be so steeply angled that the aerial cannot be mounted vertically (in relation to the 'end-on' aspect of the car). Most aerials have a small amount of adjustment available.*

Having decided on a mounting position, a relatively large hole will have to be made in the panel. The exact size of the hole will depend upon the specific aerial being fitted, although, generally, the hole required is of 19 mm (0.75 in) diameter. On metal bodied cars, a 'tank-cutter' of the relevant diameter is the best tool to use for making the hole. This tool needs a small diameter pilot hole drilled through the panel through which the tool clamping bolt is inserted. On GRP bodied cars, a 'hole-saw' is the best tool to use. Again, this tool will require the drilling of a small pilot hole. When the hole has been made the raw edges should be de-burred with a file and then painted, to prevent corrosion.

Fit the aerial according to the manufacturer's instructions. If the aerial is very tall, or if it protrudes beneath the mounting panel for a considerable distance it is a good idea to fit a stay between the aerial and the vehicle frame. This stay can be manufactured from the slotted and drilled metal strips previously mentioned. The stay should be securely screwed or bolted in place. For best reception it is advisable to fit an earth lead between the aerial and the vehicle frame – this is essential for GRP bodied cars.

It will probably be necessary to drill one or two holes through bodywork panels in order to feed the aerial lead into the interior of the car. Where this is the case ensure that the holes are fitted with rubber grommets to protect the cable, and to stop possible entry of water.

Positioning and fitting of the speaker depends mainly on its type. Generally, the speaker is designed to fit directly into the aperture already provided in the car. Where this is the case, fitting the speaker is just a matter of removing the protective grille from the aperture and screwing or bolting the speaker in place. Take great care not to damage the speaker diaphragm whilst doing this. It is a good idea to fit a 'gasket' between the speaker frame and the mounting panel, in order to prevent vibration – some speakers will already have such a gasket fitted.

If a 'pod' type speaker was supplied with the radio, this can be secured to the mounting panel with self-tapping screws.

When connecting a rear mounted speaker to the radio, the wires should be routed through the vehicle beneath the carpets or floor mats – preferably along the side of the floorpan, where they will not be trodden on by passengers. Make the relevant connections as directed by the radio manufacturer.

By now you will have several yards of additional wiring in the car, use PVC tape to secure this wiring out of harm's way. Do not leave electrical leads dangling. Ensure that all new electrical connections are properly made (wires twisted together will not do) and completely secure.

The radio should now be working, but before you pack away your tools it will be necessary to 'trim' the radio to the aerial. If specific instructions are not provided by the radio manufacturer, proceed as follows. Find a station with a low signal strength on the medium-wave band, slowly turn the trim screw of the radio in, or out, until the loudest reception of the selected station is obtained – the set is then trimmed to the aerial.

Tape players

Fitting instructions for cassette stereo tape players are the same as when fitting a radio. Tape players are not usually prone to electrical interference like radio – although it can occur – so positioning is not so critical. If possible the player should be mounted on an 'even-keel'. Also it must be possible for a driver wearing a seat belt to reach the unit in order to change or turn over tapes.

For the best results from speakers designed to be recessed into a panel, mount them so that the back of the speaker protrudes into an enclosed chamber within the car (eg. door interiors or the boot cavity).

To fit recessed type speakers in the front doors first check that there is sufficient room to mount the speakers in each door without it fouling the latch or window winding mechanism. Hold the speaker against the skin of the door, and draw a line around the periphery of the speaker. With the speaker removed draw a second 'cutting' line, within the first, to allow enough room for the entry of the speaker back, but at the same time providing a broad seat for the speaker flange. When you are sure that the 'cutting-line' is correct, drill a series of holes around its periphery. Pass a hacksaw blade through one of the holes and then cut through the metal between the holes until the centre section of the panel falls out.

De-burr the edges of the hole and then paint the raw metal to prevent corrosion. Cut a corresponding hole in the door trim panel – ensuring that it will be completely covered by the speaker grille. Now drill a hole in the door edge and a corresponding hole in the door surround. These holes are to feed the speaker leads though — so fit grommets. Pass the speaker leads through the door trim, door skin and out through the holes in the side of the door and door surround. Refit the door trim panel and then secure the speaker to the door using self-tapping screws. **Note**: If the speaker is fitted with a shield to prevent water dripping on it, ensure that this shield is at the top.

Pod type speakers can be fastened anywhere offering a corresponding mounting point on each side of the car. Pod speakers sometimes offer a better reproduction quality if they face the rear window — which then acts as a reflector — so it is worthwhile to do a little experimenting before finally fixing the speaker.

31 Fault diagnosis — electrical system

Symptom	Reason(s)
Starter fails to turn engine	Battery discharged or defective
	Battery terminal and/or earth leads loose
	Starter motor connections loose
	Starter solenoid faulty
	Starter brushes worn or sticking
	Starter commutator dirty or worn
Starter turns engine very slowly	Battery discharged
	Starter motor connections loose
	Starter brushes worn or sticking
Starter noisy	Pinion or flywheel ring gear teeth badly worn
	Mounting bolts loose
Battery will not hold charge for more than a few days	Battery defective internally
	Electrolyte level too low
	Battery terminals loose
	Alternator drivebelt slipping
	Alternator or regulator faulty
	Short circuit
Ignition light stays on	Alternator faulty
	Alternator drivebelt broken
Ignition light fails to come on	Warning bulb blown or open circuit
	Alternator faulty
Instrument readings increase with engine speed	Voltage stabilizer faulty
Fuel or temperature gauge gives no reading	Wiring open circuit
	Sender unit faulty
	Gauge faulty
Fuel or temperature gauge gives maximum reading all the time	Wiring short circuit
	Gauge faulty
Lights inoperative	Bulb blown
	Fuse blown
	Battery discharged
	Switch faulty
	Wiring open circuit
	Bad connection due to corrosion
Failure of component motor	Commutator dirty or burnt
	Armature faulty
	Brushes sticking or worn
	Armature bearings seized
	Fuse blown
	Wiring loose or broken
	Field coils faulty

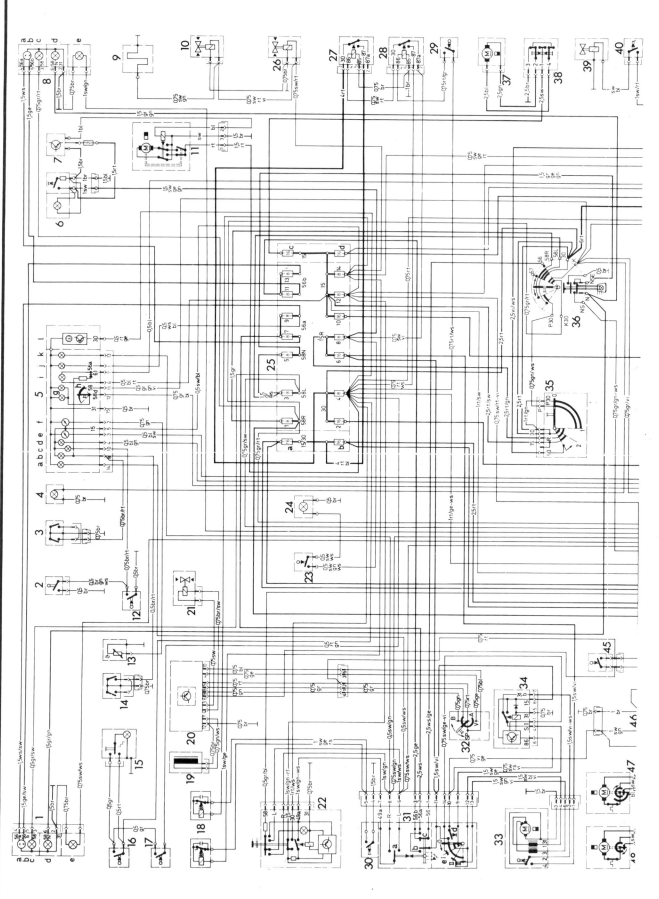

Fig. 10.10 Wiring diagram for UK 250 models (123.026)

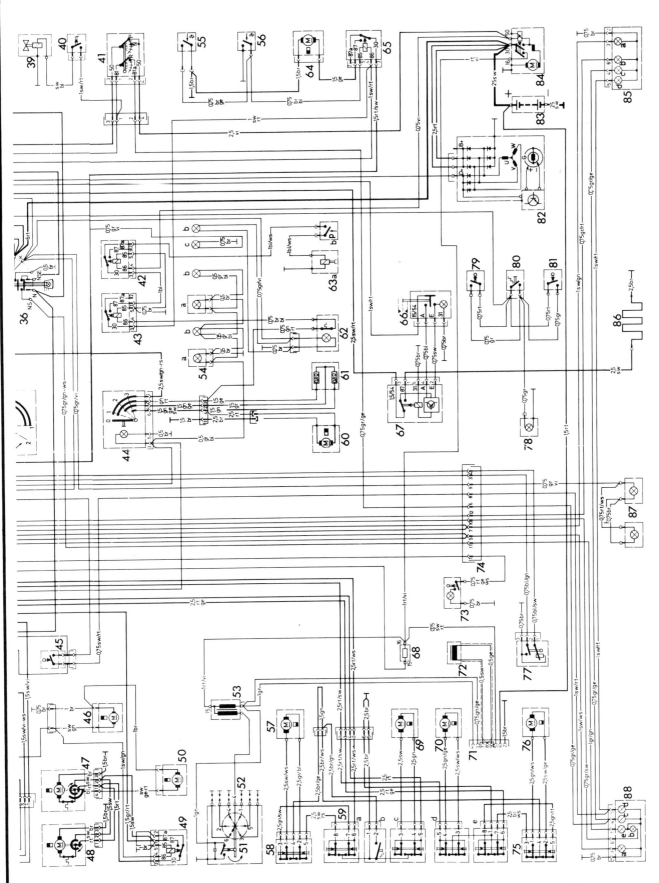

Fig. 10.10 Wiring diagram for UK 250 models (123.026) – continued

Key to wiring diagram for UK 250 models (123.026)

1 Headlight unit, left:
  a High beam
  b Low beam
  c Standing/parking light
  d Foglight
  e Turn signal light
2 Brake fluid indicator light switch
3 Contact sensor, brake pads, front, left
4 Illumination, gate plate*
5 Instrument cluster
  a Turn signal indicator light, left
  b Brake pad wear indicator light
  c Brake fluid and parking brake indicator light
  d Fuel reserve warning light
  e Fuel gauge
  f Coolant temperature gauge
  g Instrument lights
  h Rheostat, instrument lights
  i Charge indicator light
  j High beam indicator light
  k Turn signal indicator light, right
  l Electronic clock
6 Cigar lighter with ashtray illumination
7 Radio*
8 Headlight unit, right:
  a High beam
  b Low beam
  c Standing/parking light
  d Foglight
  e Turn signal light
9 Heater coil, automatic choke
10 Idle fuel cut-out valve II
11 Automatic antenna*
12 Parking brake indicator light switch
13 Temperature sensor, coolant
14 Contact sensor, brake pads, front, right
15 Front dome light w/switch
16 Door contact switch, left
17 Door contact switch, right
18 Horn
19 Sensor Tempomat*
20 Amplifier, Tempomat*
21 Throttle actuator*
22 4-way warning flasher switch/timer
23 Glove compartment light switch
24 Glove compartment light
25 Fusebox
26 Idle fuel cut-out valve I
27 Relay I, window lifts*
28 Relay II, window lifts*

29 Door contact switch, window lifts*
30 Signal system contact
31 Combination switch:
  a Turn signal light switch
  b Passing light switch
  c Dimmer switch
  d Washer switch
  e Switch for wiping speed:
    I Interval wiping
    II Slow wiping
    III Fast wiping
32 Switch, Tempomat*:
  A Off
  V Decel/set
  SP Resume
  B Accel/set
33 Wiper motor
34 Interval wiping timer
35 Ignition starter switch
36 Rotary light switch
37 Sliding roof motor*
38 Switch, electrically operated sliding roof*
39 Solenoid valve, automatic transmission*
40 Kick-down switch*
41 Starter-lockout and back-up light switch*
42 Relay, air conditioner II*
43 Relay, air conditioner I*
44 Blower switch with light
45 Brake light switch
46 Washer pump
47 Wiper motor, headlight, left*
48 Wiper motor, headlight, right*
49 Relay, headlight cleaning system*
50 Washer pump, headlights*
51 Distributor*
52 Spark plugs
53 Ignition coil
54 Illumination:
  a Air deflector control
  b Heater control
  c Switch*
55 Temperature switch 62°C (144°F) dehydrator, air conditioner*
56 Temperature switch 100°C (212°F)*
57 Window lift motor, rear, left*
58 Switch, window, rear, left*
59 Switch cluster, window lifts*:
  a Switch, window, rear, left*

  b Safety switch
  c Switch, window, front, left
  d Switch, window, front, right
  e Switch, window, rear, right
60 Blower motor
61 Pre-resistance, blower motor
62 Temperature control w/lighting, air conditioner*
63a Solenoid clutch, refrigerant compressor*
63b Pressure switch, refrigerant compressor* on 2.6 bar, off 2.0 bar
64 Auxiliary fan*
65 Relay, auxiliary fan*
66 Switch, heated rear window*
67 Time-lag relay, heated rear window
68 Pre-resistance 1.8Ω
69 Window lift motor, front, left*
70 Window lift motor, front, right*
71 Plug socket (diagnosis)
72 TDC transmitter
73 Trunk light
74 Plug connection, cable to rear components
75 Switch, window, rear, right*
76 Window lift motor, rear, right*
77 Fuel gauge sending unit
78 Rear dome light*
79 Door contact switch, rear, left*
80 Rear dome light switch*
81 Door contact switch, rear, right*
82 Alternator w/electronic regulator
83 Battery
84 Starter
85 Tail light unit, right:
  a Turn signal light
  b Tail/parking light
  c Reversing light
  d Brake light
86 Heated rear window*
87 Number plate light
88 Tail light unit, left:
  a Turn signal light
  b Tail/parking light
  c Reversing light
  d Brake light
  e Rear foglight

Special equipment

Wire Colour Code

bl	blue	nf	neutral
br	brown	rs	pink
el	ivory	rt	red
ge	yellow	sw	black
gn	green	vi	purple
gr	grey	ws	white

Example:
Wire designation 1.5 gr/rt
Basic colour gr = grey
Identification colour rt = red
Crosssection of wire 1.5 = 1.5 mm²

Key to wiring diagram for UK 280 models (123.030)

1 Headlight unit, left:
   a High beam
   b Low beam
   c Standing/parking light
   d Foglight
   e Turn signal light
2 Brake fluid indicator light switch
3 Contact sensor, brake pads, front, left
4 Illumination, gate plate*
5 Instrument cluster
   a Turn signal indicator light, left
   b Brake pad wear indicator light
   c Brake fluid and parking brake indicator light
   d Fuel reserve warning light
   e Fuel gauge
   f Coolant temperature gauge
   g Instrument lights
   h Rheostat, instrument lights
   i Charge indicator light
   j High beam indicator light
   k Turn signal indicator light, right
   l Electronic clock
6 Cigar lighter with ashtray illumination
7 Radio*
8 Headlight unit, right:
   a High beam
   b Low beam
   d Foglight
   e Turn signal light
9 Heater coil, automatic choke
10 Idle fuel cut-out valve II
11 Automatic antenna*
12 Parking brake indicator light switch
13 Temperature sensor, coolant
14 Contact sensor, brake pads, front, right
15 Front dome light w/switch
16 Door contact switch, left
17 Door contact switch, right
18 Dual-tone horns (fanfares)
19 Sensor Tempomat*
20 Amplifier, Tempomat*
21 Throttle actuator
22 4-way warning flasher switch/timer
23 Glove compartment light switch
24 Glove compartment light
25 Fusebox
26 Idle fuel cut-out valve I
27 Relay I, window lifts*
28 Relay II, window lifts*
29 Door contact switch, window lifts*

30 Signal system contact
31 Combination switch:
   a Turn signal light switch
   b Passing light switch
   c Dimmer switch
   d Washer switch
   e Switch for wiping speed:
      I Interval wiping
      II Slow wiping
      III Fast wiping
32 Switch, Tempomat*:
   A Off
   V Decel/set
   SP Resume
   B Accel/set
33 Wiper motor
34 Interval wiping timer
35 Ignition starter switch
36 Rotary light switch
37 Sliding roof motor*
38 Switch, electrically operated sliding roof*
39 Solenoid valve, automatic transmission*
40 Kick-down switch*
41 Starter-lockout and back-up light switch*
42 Relay, air conditioner II*
43 Relay, air conditioner I*
44 Blower switch with light
45 Brake light switch
46 Washer pump
47 Wiper motor, headlight, left*
48 Wiper motor, headlight, right*
49 Relay, headlight cleaning system*
50 Washer pump, headlights*
51 Distributor*
52 Spark plugs
53 Ignition coil
54 Illumination:
   a Air deflector control
   b Heater control
   c Switch*
55 Temperature switch 62°C (144°F) dehydrator, air conditioner*
56 Temperature switch 100°C (212°F)*
57 Window lift motor, rear, left*
58 Switch, window, rear, left*
59 Switch cluster, window lifts*:
   a Switch, window, rear, left*

   b Safety switch
   c Switch, window, front, left
   d Switch, window, front, right
   e Switch, window, rear, right
60 Blower motor
61 Pre-resistance, blower motor
62 Temperature control w/lighting, air conditioner*
63a Solenoid clutch, refrigerant compressor*
63b Pressure switch, refrigerant compressor*
   On 2.6 bar, off 2.0 bar
64 Auxiliary fan*
65 Relay, auxiliary fan*
66 Switch, heated rear window*
67 Time-lag relay, heated rear window
68 Pre-resistance 1.8Ω
69 Window lift motor, front, left*
70 Window lift motor, front, right*
71 Plug socket (diagnosis)
72 TDC transmitter
73 Trunk light
74 Plug connection, cable to rear components
75 Switch, window, rear, right*
76 Window lift motor, rear, right*
77 Fuel gauge sending unit
78 Rear dome light*
79 Door contact switch, rear, left*
80 Rear dome light switch*
81 Door contact switch, rear, right*
82 Alternator w/electronic regulator
83 Battery
84 Starter
85 Tail light unit, right:
   a Turn signal light
   b Tail/parking light
   c Reversing light
   d Brake light
86 Heated rear window*
87 Number plate light
88 Tail light unit, left:
   a Turn signal light
   b Tail/parking light
   c Reversing light
   d Brake light
   e Rear foglight

* Special equipment

Wire Colour Code

bl	blue	nf	neutral
br	brown	rs	pink
el	ivory	rt	red
ge	yellow	sw	black
gn	green	vi	purple
gr	grey	ws	white

Example:
Wire designation 1.5 gr/rt
Basic colour gr = grey
Identification colour rt = red
Cross-section of wire 1.5 = 1.5 mm^2

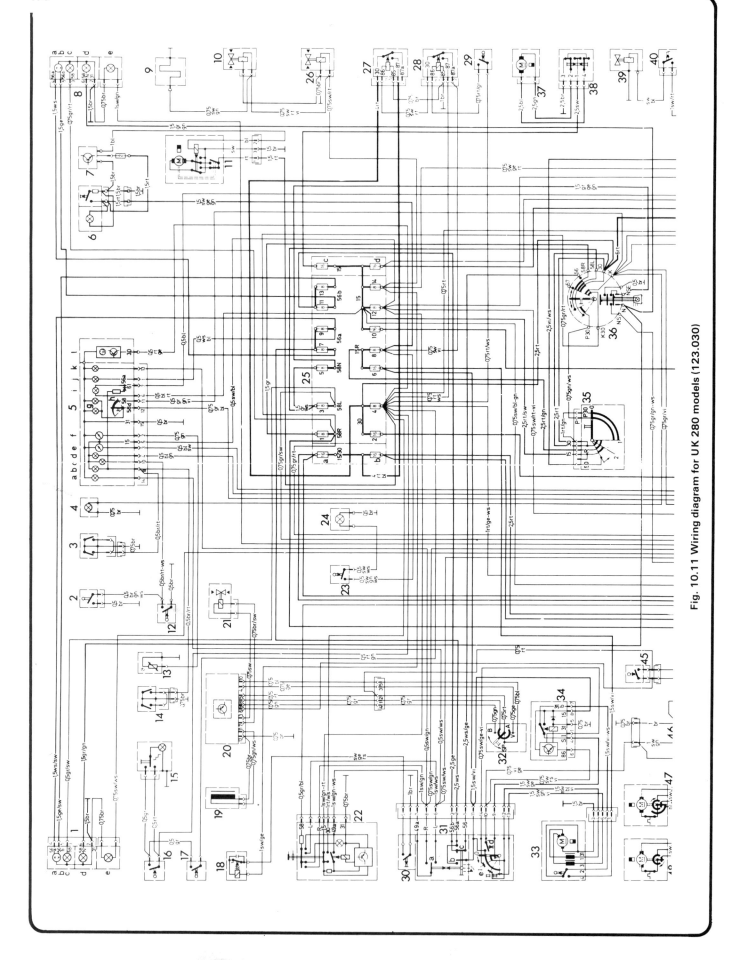

Fig. 10.11 Wiring diagram for UK 280 models (123.030)

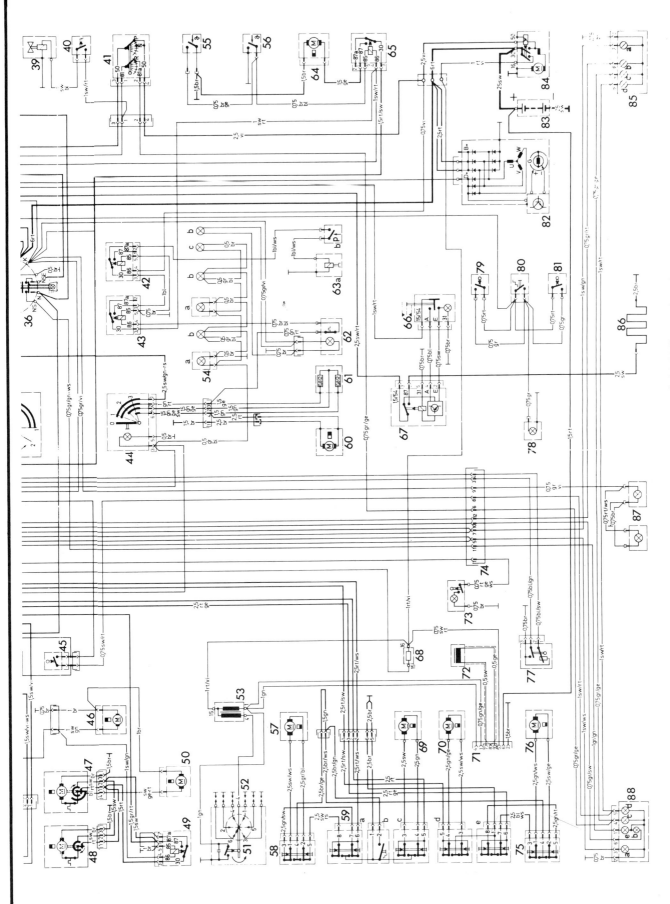

Fig. 10.11 Wiring diagram for UK 280 models (123.030) – continued

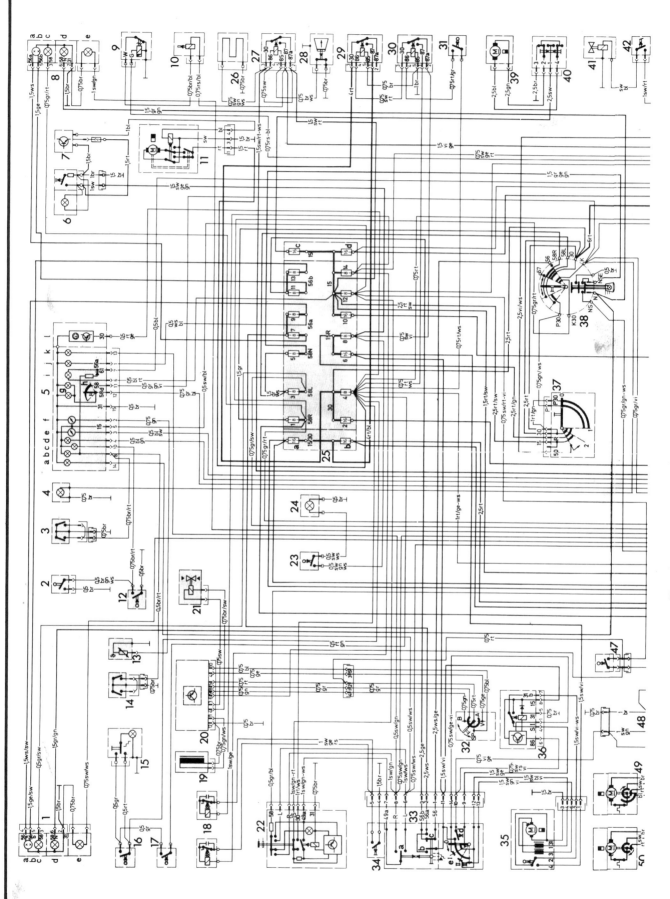

Fig. 10.12 Wiring diagram for UK 280 E models (123.033)

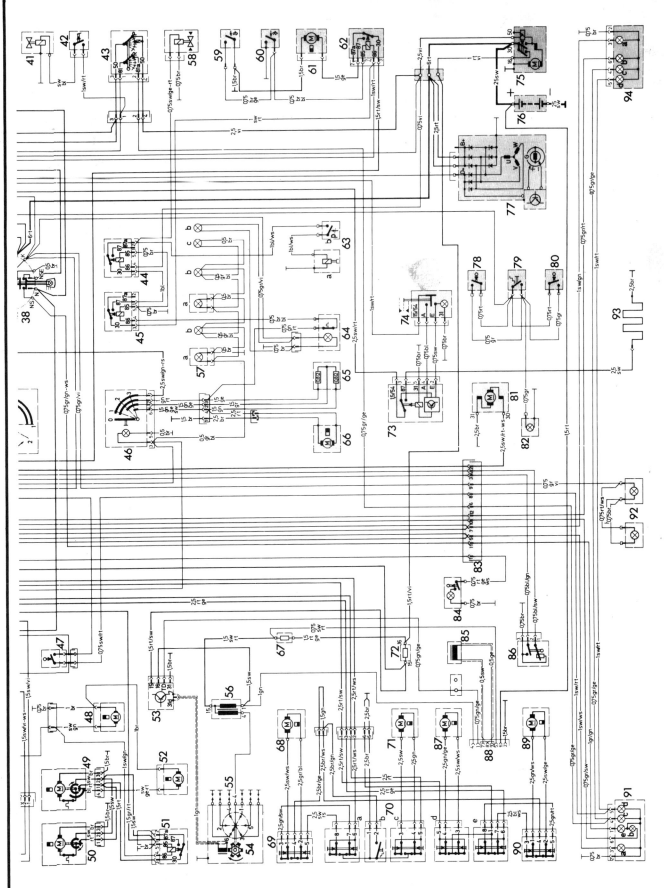

Fig. 10.12 Wiring diagram for UK 280 E models (123.033) – continued

Key to wiring diagram for UK 280 E models (123.033)

1 Headlight unit, left:
  a High beam
  b Low beam
  c Standing/parking light
  d Foglight
  e Turn signal light
2 Brake fluid indicator light switch
3 Contact sensor, brake pads, front, left
4 Illumination, gate plate*
5 Instrument cluster
  a Turn signal indicator light, left
  b Brake pad wear indicator light
  c Brake fluid and parking brake
    indicator light
  d Fuel reserve warning light
  e Fuel gauge
  f Coolant temperature gauge
  g Instrument lights
  h Rheostat, instrument lights
  i Charge indicator light
  j High beam indicator light
  k Turn signal indicator light, right
  l Electronic clock
6 Cigar lighter with ashtray illumination
7 Radio*
8 Headlight unit, right:
  a High beam
  b Low beam
  c Standing/parking light
  d Foglight
  e Turn signal light
9 Thermotime switch
10 Starter valve
11 Automatic antenna*
12 Parking brake indicator light switch
13 Temperature sensor, coolant
14 Contact sensor, brake pads, front, right
15 Front dome light w/switch
16 Door contact switch, left
17 Door contact switch, right
18 Dual-tone horns (fanfares)
19 Sensor Tempomat*
20 Amplifier, Tempomat*
21 Throttle actuator*
22 4-way warning flasher switch/timer
23 Glove compartment light switch
24 Glove compartment light
25 Fusebox
26 Heater coil, warm-up control
27 Relay, fuel pump/warm-up control
28 Safety switch, baffle plate
29 Relay I, window lifts*
30 Relay II, window lifts*
31 Door contact switch, window lifts

32 Switch, Tempomat*:
32 Switch, Tempomat*:
  A Off
  V Decel/set
  SP Resume
  B Accel/set
33 Combination switch
  a Turn signal light switch
  b Passing light switch
  c Dimmer switch
  d Washer switch
  e Switch for wiping speed:
    I Interval wiping
    II Slow wiping
    III Fast wiping
34 Signal system contact
35 Wiper motor
36 Interval wiping timer
37 Ignition starter switch
38 Rotary light switch
39 Sliding roof motor*
40 Switch, electrically operated sliding
  roof*
41 Solenoid valve, automatic
  transmission*
42 Kick-down switch
43 Starter-lockout and back-up light
  switch*
44 Relay, air conditioner II*
45 Relay, air conditioner I*
46 Blower switch with light
47 Brake light switch
48 Washer pump
49 Wiper motor, headlight, left*
50 Wiper motor, headlight, right*
51 Relay, headlight cleaning system*
52 Washer pump, headlights*
53 Transistorized ignition switching unit
54 Ignition distributor, w/o breaker points
55 Spark plugs
56 Ignition coil
57 Illumination:
  a Air deflector control
  b Heater control
  c Switch*
58 Switch-over valve, idle stabilization*
59 Temperature switch 62°C
  (144°F) dehydrator, air conditioner*
60 Temperature switch 100°C (212°F)*
61 Auxiliary fan*
62 Relay, auxiliary fan*
63a Solenoid clutch, refrigerant
  compressor*

63b Pressure switch, refrigerant
  compressor*
  On 2.6 bar, Off 2.0 bar
64 Temperature control w/lighting, air
  conditioner*
65 Pre-resistance, blower motor
66 Blower motor
67 Pre-resistance 0.6Ω
68 Window lift motor, rear, left*
69 Switch, window, rear, left
70 Switch cluster, window lifts*:
  a Switch, window, rear, left*
  b Safety switch
  c Switch, window, front, left
  d Switch, window, front, right
  e Switch, window, rear, right
71 Window lift motor, front, left*
72 Pre-resistance 0.4Ω
73 Time-lag relay, heated rear window*
74 Switch, heated rear window*
75 Starter
76 Battery
77 Alternator w/electronic regulator
78 Door contact switch, rear, left*
79 Rear dome light switch*
80 Door contact switch, rear, right*
81 Fuel pump
82 Rear dome light
83 Plug connection, cable to rear
  components
84 Boot light
85 TDC transmitter
86 Fuel gauge sending unit
87 Window lift motor, front, right*
88 Plug socket (diagnosis)
89 Window lift motor, rear, right*
90 Switch, window, rear, right*
91 Tail light unit, left:
  a Turn signal light
  b Tail/parking light
  c Reversing light
  d Brake light
  e Rear foglight
92 Number plate light
93 Heated rear window*
94 Tail light unit, right:
  a Turn signal light
  b Tail/parking light
  c Reversing light
  d Brake light

* Special equipment

Wire Colour Code

bl	blue	nf	neutral
br	brown	rs	pink
el	ivory	rt	red
ge	yellow	sw	black
gn	green	vi	purple
gr	grey	ws	white

Example:
Wire designation 1.5 gr/rt
Basic colour gr = grey
Identification colour rt = red
Cross-section of wire 1.5 = 1.5 mm²

Key to wiring diagram for USA 280 E models (123.033)

1 Headlight unit, left:
  a High beam
  b Low beam
  c Foglight
  d Standing/parking/side marker light
  e Turn signal light
2 Brake fluid indicator light switch
3 Switch, pressure differential indicator light
4 Parking brake indicator light switch
5 Temperature sensor, coolant
6 Contact sensor, brake pads, front, left
7 Instrument cluster:
  a Turn signal indicator light, left
  b Brake pad wear indicator light
  c Brake fluid and parking brake indicator light
  d Fuel reserve warning light
  e Fuel gauge
  f Coolant temperature gauge
  g Instrument lights
  h Rheostat, instrument lights
  i Charge indicator light
  j High beam indicator light
  k Turn signal indicator light, right
  l Electronic clock
  m Seat-belt warning light
8 Contact sensor, brake pads, front, right
9 Warning buzzer contact
10 Door contact switch, warning buzzer
11 Driver's belt buckle switch
12 Relay, window lifts
13 Headlight unit, right:
  a High beam
  b Low beam
  c Foglight
  d Standing/parking/side marker light
  e Turn signal light
14 Thermo-time switch
15 Warning device
16 Front dome light w/switch
17 Door contact switch, front, left
18 Door contact switch, front, right
19 Dual-tone horns (fanfares)
20 Sensor, cruise control
21 Amplifier, cruise control
22 Actuator, cruise control
23 Starter valve
24 Heater coil, warm-up control
25 Relay, fuel pump/warm-up control
26 Safety switch, baffle plate
27 Sliding roof motor*
28 Fuse, amplifier, automatic climate control
29 Fusebox
30 Illumination, gate plate
31 Glove compartment light switch
32 Glove compartment light
33 Brake light switch
34 Warning flasher switch/timer
35 Signal system contact
36 Combination switch:
  a Turn signal light switch

  b Headlight flasher switch
  c Dimmer switch
  d Washer switch
  e Switch wiping speed:
    I Interval wiping
    II Slow wiping
    III Fast wiping
37 Relay, air conditioner/starter
38 Switch, electrically operated sliding roof*
39 Solenoid valve, automatic transmission*
40 Kick-down switch
41 Starter-lockout and back-up light switch*
42 Dual contact relay
43 Rotary light switch
44 Ignition starter switch
45 Illumination, heater controls
46 Washer pump
47 Switch, cruise control:
  A Off
  V Decelerate/set
  SP Resume
  B Accelerate/set
48 Wiper motor
49 Interval wiping timer
50 Solenoid clutch, refrigerant compressor
51 Ignition distributor, breakerless
52 Spark plugs
53 Transistorized ignition switching unit
54 Ignition coil
55 Relay, auxiliary fan
56 Switch-over valve (fresh/recirculating air flap)
57 Pressure switch, refrigerant compressor On 2.6 bar, Off 2.0 bar
58 Pre-resistance, blower motor
59 Control unit:
  a Temperature selector
  b Pushbutton switch
60 Temperature switch 2°C (36°F)
61 Automatic antenna*
62 Temperature sensor, outside
63 Switch, refrigerant compressor, on/off
64 Relay, separation air conditioner (auxiliary fan) from ignition change-over
65 Pre-resistance 0.6Ω
66 Pre-resistance 0.4Ω
67 TDC transmitter
68 Plug socket (diagnosis)
69 Switch, window, rear, left
70 Window lift motor, rear, left
71 Relay switch-over valve, ignition
72 Vacuum switch 78.5 mbar, refrigerant compressor (DEF and BI-LEVEL)
73 Vacuum switch, 78.5 mbar, refrigerant compressor
74 Switch, automatic antenna*
75 Cigar lighter with ashtray illumination
76 Radio

77 Plug for tester, automatic climate control system
78 Temperature sensor, inside
79 Amplifier, automatic climate control
80 Servo assembly, automatic climate control system
81 Auxiliary water pump for heater, automatic climate control system
82 Temperature switch, On 16°C – Off 26°C (On 61°F, Off 79°F)
83 Temperature switch 62°C (144°F) dehydrator, air conditioner
84 Switch cluster, window lifts:
  a Switch, window, rear, left*
  b Safety switch
  c Switch, window, front, left
  d Switch, window, front, right
  e Switch, window, rear, right
85 Window lift motor, front, right*
86 Switch-over valve, idle stabilization
87 Auxiliary fan
88 Window lift motor, front, right
89 Vacuum switch (BI-LEVEL)
90 Vacuum compressor, 175 mbar, master switch
91 Door contact switch, rear, left
92 Rear dome light switch
93 Door contact switch, rear, right
94 Rear dome light
95 Blower motor
96 Starter
97 Battery
98 Alternator w/electronic regulator
99 Switch-over valve ("BI-LEVEL")
100 Switch-over valve (footwell flaps)
101 Plug connection, cable to rear components
102 Switch, heated rear window
103 Time-lag relay, heated rear window
104 Temperature switch 100°C (212°F)
105 Switch, window, rear, right
106 Window lift motor, rear, right
107 Trunk light
108 Tail light unit, left:
  a Side marker light
  b Turn signal light
  c Tail/parking light
  d Reversing light
  e Brake light
109 Heated rear window
110 Number plate light
111 Fuel gauge sending unit
112 Fuel pump
113 Tail light unit, right:
  a Side marker light
  b Turn signal light
  c Tail/parking light
  d Reversing light
  e Brake light

Special equipment

Wire Colour Code

bl	blue	nf	neutral
br	brown	rs	pink
el	ivory	rt	red
ge	yellow	sw	black
gn	green	vi	purple
gr	grey	ws	white

Example:
Wire designation 1.5 gr/rt
Basic colour gr = grey
Identification colour rt = red
Cross-section of wire 1.5 = 1.5 mm²

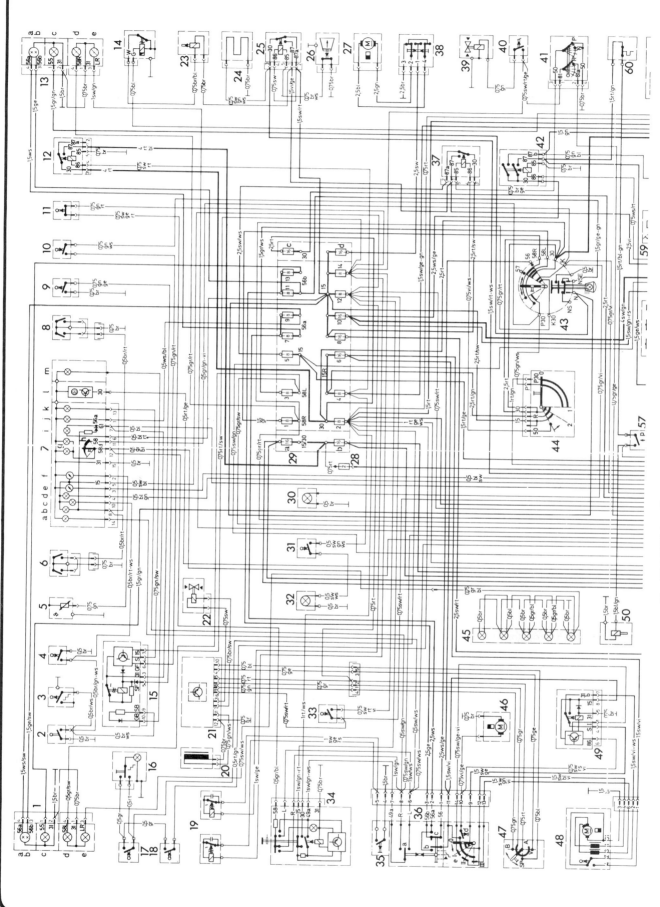

Fig. 10.13 Wiring diagram for USA 280 E models (123.033)

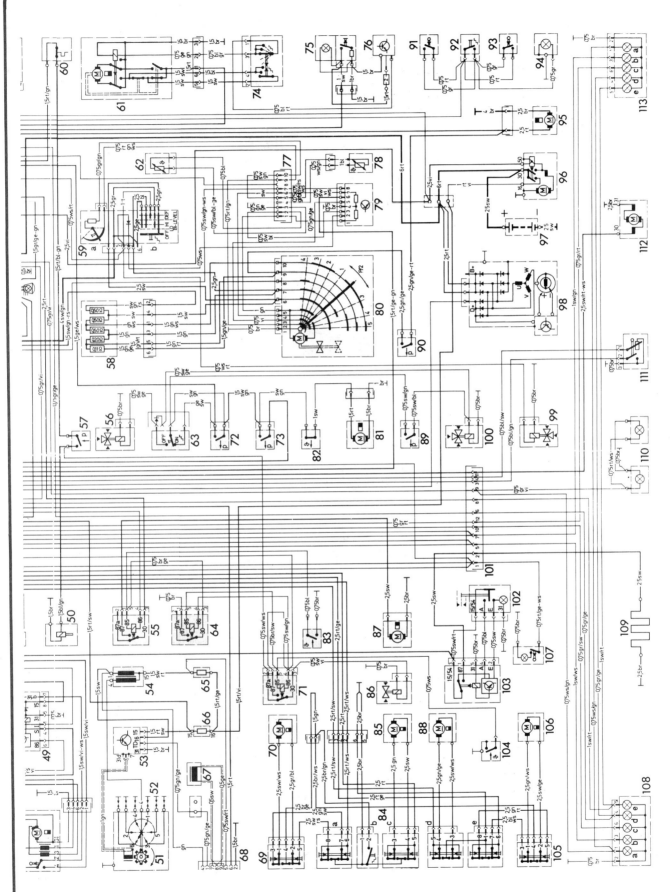

Fig. 10.13 Wiring diagram for USA 280 E models (123.033) – continued

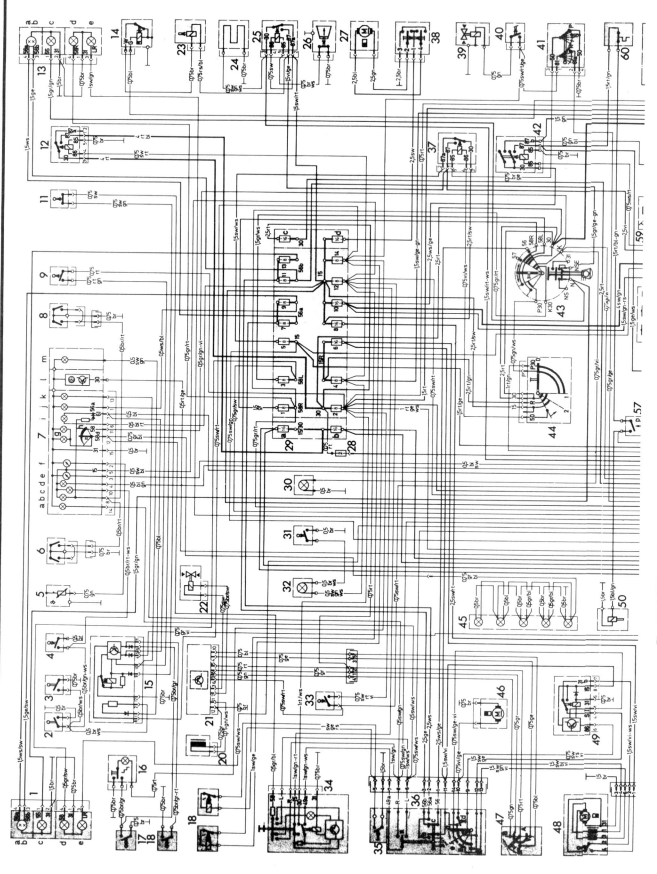

Fig. 10.14 Wiring diagram for USA 280 E/CE models (123.033/053) – 1978/1979

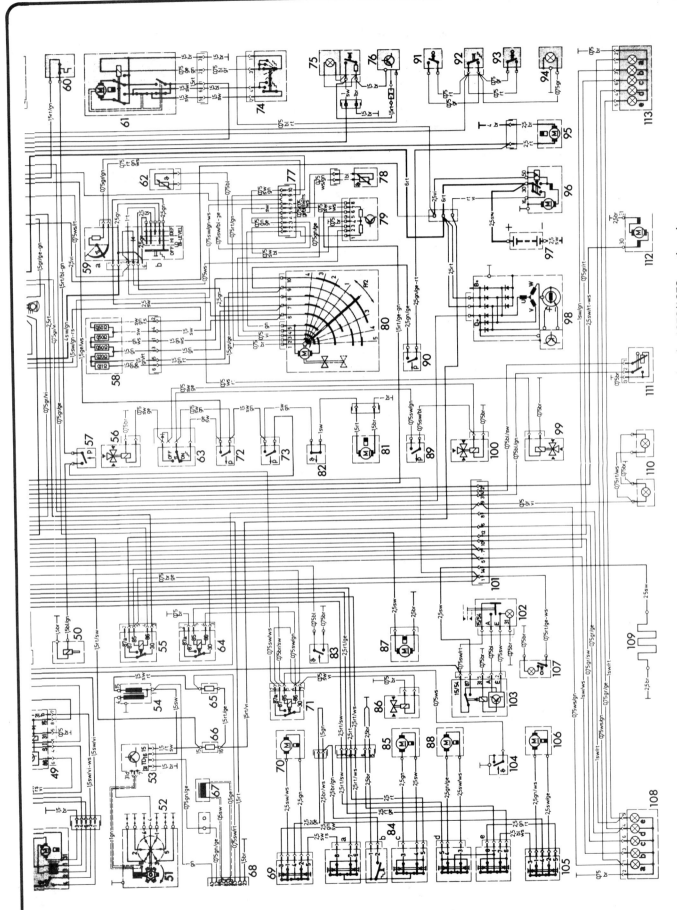

Fig. 10.14 Wiring diagram for USA 280 E/CE models (123.033/053) – 1978/1979 continued

Key to wiring diagram for USA 280 E/CE models (123.033/053) – 1978/1979

1 Headlight unit, left:
- a High beam
- b Low beam
- c Foglight
- d Parking/side marker/standing lamp
- e Turn signal lamp
2 Brake fluid indicator lamp switch I
3 Brake fluid indicator lamp switch II
4 Parking brake indicator lamp switch
5 Temperature sensor, coolant
6 Contact sensor, brake pads, front, left
7 Instrument cluster:
- a Turn signal indicator lamp, left
- b Brake pad wear indicator lamp
- c Brake fluid and parking brake indicator lamp
- d Fuel reserve warning lamp
- e Fuel gauge
- f Coolant temperature gauge
- g Instrument lamps
- h Rheostat, instrument lamps
- i Charge indicator lamp
- j High beam indicator lamp
- k Turn signal indicator lamp, right
- l Electronic clock
- m Seat-belt warning lamp
8 Contact sensor, brake pads, front, right
9 Warning buzzer contact
10 Warning buzzer contact
11 Driver's belt buckle switch
12 Relay, window lifts
13 Headlamp unit, right:
- a High beam
- b Low beam
- c Foglamp
- d Parking/side marker/standing lamp
- e Turn signal lamp
14 Thermotime switch
15 Warning device
16 Front dome lamp w/switch
17 Door contact switch, front, left
18 Door contact switch, front, right
19 Dual-tone horns (fanfares)
20 Sensor, cruise control
21 Amplifier, cruise control
22 Actuator, cruise control
23 Starter valve
24 Heater coil, warm-up control
25 Relay, fuel pump/warm-up control
26 Safety switch, air flow sensor plate
27 Sliding roof motor*
28 Fuse, amplifier, automatic climate control
29 Fusebox
30 Shift gate illumination lamp
31 Glove compartment lamp switch
32 Glove compartment lamp
33 Stop-lamp switch
34 Warning flasher switch/timer
35 Horn contact switch
36 Combination switch:
- a Turn signal lamp switch
- b Headlamp flasher switch
- c Dimmer switch

- d Washer switch
- e Switch wiping speed:
  - I Interval wiping
  - II Slow wiping
  - III Fast wiping
37 Relay, air conditioner/starter
38 Switch, electrically operated sliding roof*
39 Solenoid valve, automatic transmission*
40 Kick-down switch
41 Starter-lockout and reversing lamp switch*
42 Double-pole relay
43 Lighting switch
44 Ignition starter switch
45 Illumination lamps, heater controls
46 Washer pump
47 Switch, cruise control:
- A Off
- V Decelerate/set
- SP Resume
- B Accelerate/set
48 Wiper motor
49 Interval wiping timer
50 Solenoid clutch, refrigerant compressor
51 Ignition distributor, breakerless
52 Spark plugs
53 Transistorized ignition switching unit
54 Ignition coil
55 Relay, auxiliary fan
56 Switch-over valve (fresh/recirculating air flap)
57 Pressure switch, refrigerant compressor
On 2.6 bar, Off 2.0 bar
58 Pre-resistance, blower motor
59 Control unit:
- a Temperature selector
- b Pushbutton switches
60 Temperature switch 2°C (36°F)
61 Automatic antenna
62 Temperature sensor, outside
63 Switch, refrigerant compressor, on/off
64 Relay, separation air conditioner (auxiliary fan) from ignition change-over
65 Pre-resistance 0.6Ω
66 Pre-resistance 0.4Ω
67 TDC transmitter
68 Plug connection (Diagnosis)
69 Switch, window, rear, left
70 Window lift motor, rear, left
71 Relay switch-over valve, ignition
72 Vacuum switch 78.5 mbar, refrigerant compressor (DEF and BI-LEVEL)
73 Vacuum switch, 78.5 mbar, refrigerant compressor
74 Switch, automatic antenna
75 Cigar lighter with ashtray illumination
76 Radio*
77 Plug for tester, automatic climate control system

78 Temperature sensor, inside
79 Amplifier, automatic climate control
80 Servo assembly, automatic climate control system
81 Auxiliary water pump for heater, automatic climate control system
82 Temperature switch, On 16°C – Off 26°C
(On 61°F, Off 79°F)
83 Temperature switch 62°C (144°F) receiver drier, automatic climate control
84 Switch cluster, window lifts:
- a Switch, window, rear, left
- b Safety switch
- c Switch, window, front, left
- d Switch, window, front, right
- e Switch, window, rear, right
85 Window lift motor, front, left
86 Switch-over valve, idle stabilization
87 Auxiliary fan
88 Window lift motor, front, right
89 Vacuum switch (BI-LEVEL)
90 Vacuum switch, 78.5 mbar, master switch
91 Door contact switch, rear, left
92 Rear dome lamp switch
93 Door contact switch, rear, right
94 Rear dome lamp
95 Blower motor
96 Starter
97 Battery
98 Alternator w/electronic regulator
99 Switch-over valve ("BI-LEVEL")
100 Switch-over valve (footwell flaps)
101 Plug connection, cable to rear components
102 Push button switch, heated rear window
103 Time-lag relay, heated rear window
104 Temperature switch 100°C (212°F)
105 Switch, window, rear, right
106 Window lift motor, rear, right
107 Trunk lamp
108 Tail lamp unit, left:
- a Side marker lamp
- b Turn signal lamp
- c Tail/parking lamp
- d Reversing lamp
- e Brake lamp
109 Heated rear window
110 Number plate lamp
111 Fuel gauge sending unit
112 Fuel pump
113 Tail lamp unit, right:
- a Side marker lamp
- b Turn signal lamp
- c Tail/parking lamp
- d Reversing lamp
- e Brake lamp

* Special equipment

Wire Colour Code

bl	blue	nf	neutral
br	brown	rs	pink
el	ivory	rt	red
ge	yellow	sw	black
gn	green	vi	purple
gr	grey	ws	white

Example:
Wire designation 1.5 gr/rt
Basic colour gr = grey
Identification colour rt = red
Cross-section of wire 1.5 = 1.5 mm²

Key to wiring diagram for USA 280 E/CE models (123-033/053) – 1980

1 Headlamp unit, left:
  a   High beam
  b   Low beam
  c   Foglamp
  d   Parking/standing/side marker lamp
  e   Turn signal lamp
2 Brake fluid indicator lamp switch I
3 Brake fluid indicator lamp switch II
4 Parking brake indicator lamp switch
5 Temperature sensor, coolant
6 Contact sensor, brake pads, front, left
7 Instrument cluster:
  a   Turn signal indicator lamp, left
  b   Brake pad wear indicator lamp
  c   Brake fluid and parking brake indicator lamp
  d   Fuel reserve warning lamp
  e   Fuel gauge
  f   Coolant temperature gauge
  g   Instrument lamps
  h   Rheostat, instrument lamps
  i   Charge indicator lamp
  j   High beam indicator lamp
  k   Turn signal indicator lamp, right
  l   Electronic clock
  m   Seat belt warning lamp
  n   Indicator lamp, oxygen sensor
8 Contact sensor, brake pads, front, right
9 Warning buzzer contact
10 Driver's belt buckle switch
11 Oxygen sensor renewal indicator
12 Relay, window lifts
13 Headlamp unit, right:
  a   High beam
  b   Low beam
  c   Foglamp
  d   Parking/standing/side marker lamp
  e   Turn signal lamp
14 Thermotime switch
15 Warning device
16 Front dome lamp w/switch
17 Door contact switch, front left
18 Door contact switch, front right
19 Dual-tone horn (fanfare)
20 Sensor, cruise control system
21 Amplifier, cruise control
22 Actuator, cruise control
23 Starter valve
24 Heater coil, warm-up compensator

25 Relay, fuel pump with electronic speed limiter/warm-up compensator
26 Sliding roof motor*
27 Fusebox
28 Illumination, shift plate
29 Glove compartment lamp switch
30 Glove compartment lamp
31 Stop-lamp switch
32 Warning flasher switch/timer
32 Horn contact
34 Combination switch:
  a   Turn signal lamp switch
  b   Headlamp flasher switch
  c   Dimmer switch
  e   Switch, wiping speed:
     I   Intermittent wiping
     II Slow wiping
     III Fast wiping
35 Relay, air conditioner/starter
36 Switch, electrically operated sliding roof*
37 Solenoid valve, automatic transmission
38 Kick-down switch
39 Starter lockout and reversing lamp switch
40 Lighting switch
41 Ignition starter switch
42 Illumination, heater control
43 Washer pump
44 Switch, cruise control:
  A   Off
  V   Decelerate/set
  SP Resume
  B   Accelerate/set
45 Wiper motor
46 Intermittent wiping timer
47 Ignition distributor, breakerless
48 Spark plugs
49 Transistorized ignition switching unit
50 Ignition coil
51 Overload protection, Lambda
52 Idling speed/full load switch
53 Oxygen sensor
54 Frequency valve, Lambda control
55 Automatic antenna
56 Switch, automatic antenna
57 Relay, Lambda (main relay)
58 Temperature switch 16°C (61°F)
59 Pre-resistance 0.6Ω

60 Pre-resistance 0.4Ω
61 TDC transmitter
62 Plug socket (diagnosis)
63 Switch, window, rear, left
64 Window lift motor, rear, left
65 Switch cluster, window lifts:
  a   Switch, window, rear, left
  b   Safety switch
  c   Switch, window, front, left
  d   Switch, window, front, right
  e   Switch, window, rear, right
66 Window lift motor, front, left
67 Control unit, Lambda control
68 Cigar lighter with ashtray illumination
69 Radio*
70 Door contact switch, rear, left
71 Rear dome lamp switch
72 Door contact switch, rear, right
73 Rear dome lamp
74 Starter
75 Battery
76 Alternator w/electronic regulator
77 Fuel gauge sending unit
78 Plug connection, tail lamp cable harness
79 Switch, heated rear window
80 Time-lag relay, heated rear window
81 Window lift motor, front, right
82 Switch, window, rear, right
83 Window lift motor, rear, right
84 Trunk lamp
85 Tail lamp unit, left:
  a   Side marker lamp
  b   Turn signal lamp
  c   Tail/standing lamp
  d   Reversing lamp
  e   Stop-lamp
86 Heated rear window
87 Number plate lamp
88 Fuel pump
89 Tail lamp unit, right:
  a   Side marker lamp
  b   Turn signal lamp
  c   Tail/standing lamp
  d   Reversing lamp
  e   Stop-lamp

Special equipment

Wire Colour Code

bl	blue	nf	neutral
br	brown	rs	pink
el	ivory	rt	red
ge	yellow	sw	black
gn	green	vi	purple
gr	grey	ws	white

Example:
Wire designation 1.5 gr/rt
Basic colour gr = grey
Identification colour rt = red
Cross-section of wire 1.5 = 1.5 mm²

188

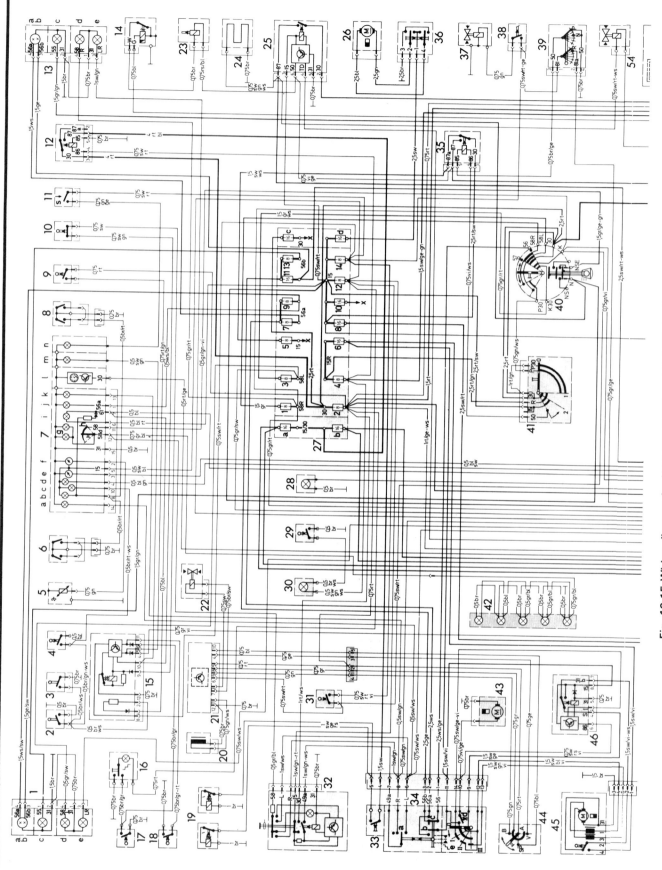

Fig. 10.15 Wiring diagram for USA 280 E/CE models (123-033/053) – 1980

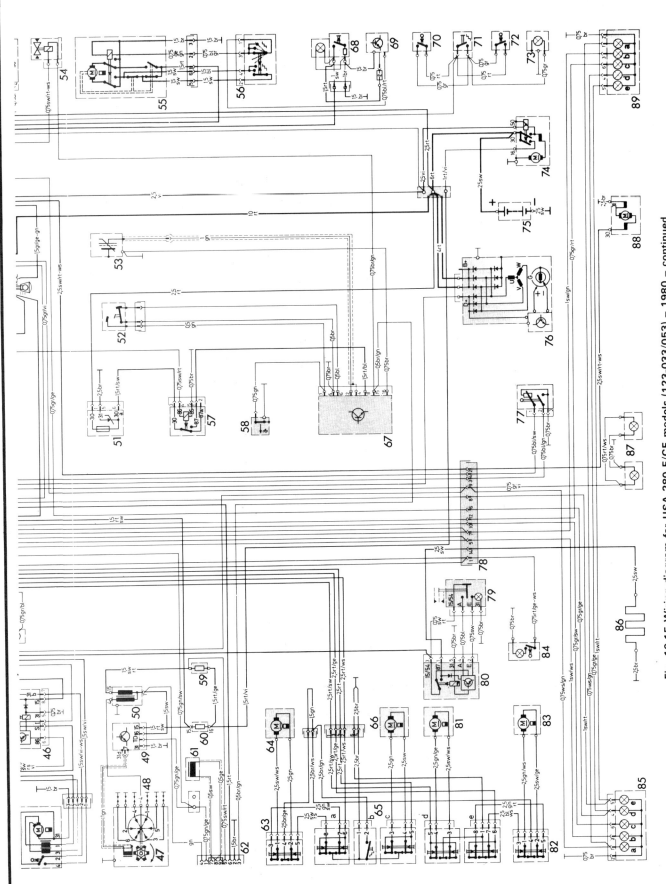

Fig. 10.15 Wiring diagram for USA 280 E/CE models (123-033/053) – 1980 – continued

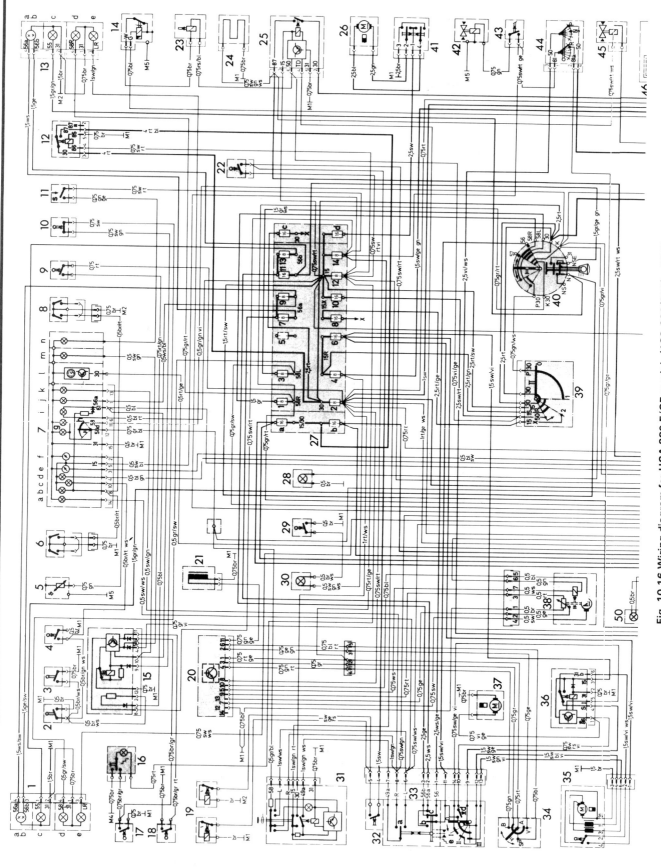

Fig. 10.16 Wiring diagram for USA 280 E/CE models (123-033/053) – 1981

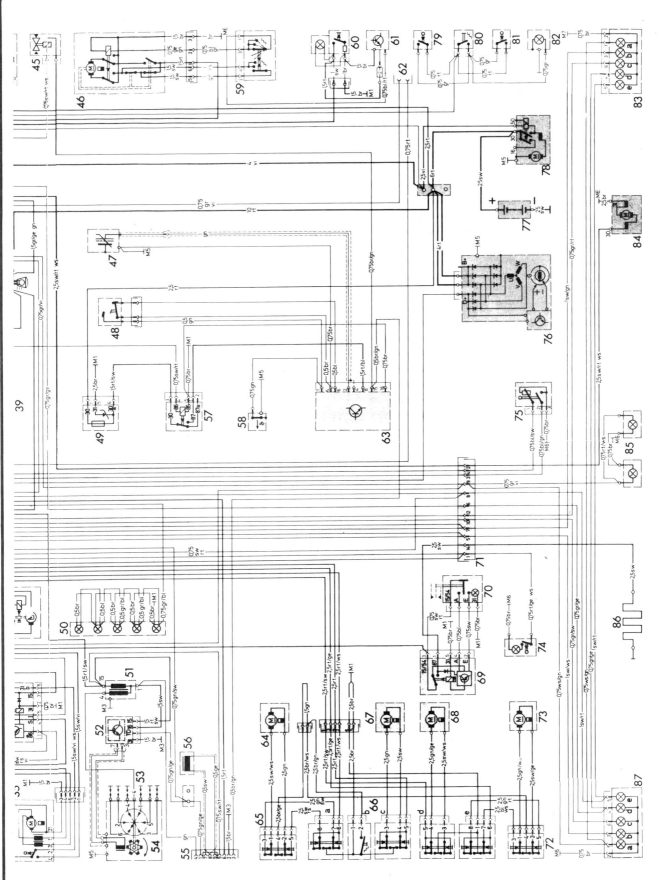

Fig. 10.16 Wiring diagram for USA 280 E/CE models (123-033/053) – 1981 – continued

Key to wiring diagram for USA 280 E/CE models (123-033/053) – 1981

1 Headlamp unit, left:
  a   High beam
  b   Low beam
  c   Foglamp
  d   Parking/standing/side marker lamp
  e   Turn signal lamp
2 Brake fluid indicator lamp switch I
3 Brake fluid indicator lamp switch II
4 Parking brake indicator lamp switch
5 Temperature sensor, coolant
6 Contact sensor, brake pads, front, left
7 Instrument cluster:
  a   Turn signal indicator lamp, left
  b   Brake pad wear indicator lamp
  c   Brake fluid and parking brake
       indicator
  d   Fuel reserve warning lamp
  e   Fuel gauge
  f   Coolant temperature gauge
  g   Instrument lamps
  h   Rheostat, instrument lamps
  i   Charge indicator lamp
  j   High beam indicator lamp
  k   Turn signal indicator lamp, right
  l   Electronic clock
  m   Seat belt warning lamp
  n   Indicator lamp, oxygen sensor
8 Contact sensor, brake pads, front, right
9 Warning buzzer contact
10 Driver's belt buckle switch
11 Oxygen sensor renewal indicator
12 Relay, window lifts
13 Headlamp unit, right:
  a   High beam
  b   Low beam
  c   Foglamp
  d   Parking/standing/side marker lamp
  e   Turn signal lamp
14 Thermotime switch
15 Warning device
16 Front dome lamp w/switch
17 Door contact switch, front right
18 Door contact switch, front left
19 Dual-tone horn (fanfare)
20 Amplifier, cruise control
21 Sensor, cruise control
22 Stop-lamp switch
23 Starter valve

24 Heater coil, warm-up compensator
25 Relay, fuel pump with electronic
   speed limiter/warm-up compensator
26 Sliding roof motor
27 Fusebox
28 Illumination, shift plate
29 Glove compartment lamp switch
30 Glove compartment lamp
31 Warning flasher switch/timer
32 Horn contact
33 Combination switch:
  a   Turn signal lamp switch
  b   Headlamp flasher switch
  c   Dimmer switch
  d   Washer switch
  e   Switch, wiping speed:
       I   Intermittent wiping
       II   Slow wiping
       III Fast wiping
34 Switch, cruise control:
  A   Off
  V   Decelerate/set
  SP Resume
  B   Accelerate/set
35 Wiper motor
36 Intermittent wiping timer
37 Washer pump
38 Actuator, cruise control
39 Ignition starter switch
40 Lighting switch
41 Switch, electrically operated sliding
   roof
42 Solenoid valve, automatic transmission
43 Kick-down switch
44 Starter lockout and backup lamp
   switch
45 Frequency valve, Lambda control
46 Automatic antenna
47 Oxygen sensor
48 Idle speed/full load switch
49 Overload protection, Lambda
50 Illumination, heater controls
51 Ignition coil
52 Transistorized ignition switching unit
53 Spark plugs
54 Ignition distributor, breakerless
55 Plug socket (diagnosis)
56 TDC transmitter

57 Relay, Lambda (main relay)
58 Temperature switch 16°C (61°F)
59 Switch, automatic antenna
60 Cigar lighter with ashtray illumination
61 Radio
62 Connector, electronic radio
63 Control unit, Lambda control
64 Window lift motor, rear left
65 Switch, window, rear, left
66 Switch cluster, window lifts:
  a   Switch, window, rear, left
  b   Safety switch
  c   Switch, window, front, left
  d   Switch, window, front, right
  e   Switch, window, rear, right
67 Window lift motor, front, left
68 Window lift motor, front, right
69 Time-lag relay, heated rear window
70 Switch, heated rear window
71 Plug connection, tail lamp cable
   harness
72 Switch, window, rear, right
73 Window lift motor, rear, right
74 Trunk lamp
75 Fuel gauge sending unit
76 Alternator w/electronic regulator
77 Battery
78 Starter
79 Door contact switch, rear, left
80 Rear dome lamp switch
81 Door contact switch, rear right
82 Rear dome lamp
83 Tail lamp unit, right:
  a   Side marker lamp
  b   Tail/standing lamp
  d   Reversing lamp
  e   Stop-lamp
84 Fuel pump
85 Number plate lamp
86 Heated rear window
87 Tail lamp unit, left:
  a   Side marker lamp
  b   Turn signal lamp
  c   Tail/standing lamp
  d   Reversing lamp
  e   Stop-lamp

* Special equipment

Wire Colour Code
bl   blue
br   brown
el   ivory
ge yellow
gn green
gr grey
nf   neutral
rs   pink
rt   red
sw black
vi   purple
ws white

Example
Wire designation 1.5 gr/rt
Basic colour gr = grey
Identification colour rt = red
Cross-section of wire 1.5 = 1.5 mm²

Ground connections
M1 Main ground
     (behind instrument cluster)
M2 Ground, front, right
     (near headlamp unit)
M3 Ground, wheelhouse, front, left
     (ignition coil)
M4 Ground, dome lamp, front
M5 Ground, engine
M6 Ground, trunk, wheelhouse, left
M7 Ground, trunk, wheelhouse, right

**Key to wiring diagram 280 E models (123.033 from chassis end no 081 279)
and 280 CE models (123.053 from chassis end no 021 430)**

1　Headlamp unit, left:
　a　High beam
　b　Low beam
　c　Parking/standing lamp
　d　Foglamp
　e　Turn signal lamp
2　Brake fluid indicator lamp switch
3　Contact sensor, brake pads, front, left
4　Contact sensor, brake pads, front, right
5　Instrument cluster:
　a　Turn signal indicator lamp, left
　b　High beam indicator lamp
　c　Coolant temperature gauge
　d　Fuel gauge
　e　Fuel reserve warning lamp
　f　Charge indicator lamp
　g　Brake pad wear indicator lamp
　h　Brake fluid and parking brake
　　　indicator lamp
　i　Instrument lamps
　j　Rheostat, instrument lamps
　k　Warning buzzer
　l　Turn signal indicator lamp, right
　m　Electronic clock
6　Cigar lighter with ashtray illumination
7　Radio*
8　Headlamp unit, right
　a　High beam
　b　Low beam
　c　Parking/standing lamp
　d　Foglamp
　e　Turn signal lamp
9　Thermotime switch
10　Starter valve
11　Automatic antenna*
12　Parking brake indicator lamp switch
13　Temperature sensor, coolant
14　Warning buzzer contact
15　Front dome lamp w/switch
16　Door contact switch, front, left
17　Door contact switch, front, right
18　Dual-tone horn (fanfare)
19　Sensor, Tempomat*
20　Amplifier, Tempomat*
21　Actuator, Tempomat*
22　Warning flasher switch/timer
23　Glove compartment lamp switch
24　Glove compartment lamp
25　Fusebox
26　Heater coil, warm-up compensator
27　Relay, fuel pump with electronic speed
　　limiter/warm-up compensator
28　Electromagnetic clutch, refrigerant
　　compressor*

29　Relay I window lifts*
30　Relay II window lifts*
31　Door contact switch, window lifts*
32　Switch, Tempomat*:
　A　Off
　V　Decelerate/set
　SP　Resume
　B　Accelerate/set
33　Combination switch:
　a　Turn signal lamp switch
　b　Hoadlamp flasher switch
　c　Dimmer switch
　d　Washer switch
　e　Switch, wiping speed:
　　I　Intermittent wiping
　　II　Slow wiping
　　III　Fast wiping
34　Horn contact
35　Wiper motor
36　Intermittent wiping timer
37　Ignition starter switch
38　Lighting switch
39　Sliding roof motor*
40　Switch, electrically operated sliding
　　roof*
41　Solenoid valve, automatic
　　transmission*
42　Kick-down switch*
43　Starter lockout and reversing lamp
　　switch*
44　Pressure switch, refrigerant
　　compressor*
　　On 2.6 bar, Off 2.0 bar
45　Relay, air conditioner II*
46　Blower switch with lamp
47　Stop-lamp switch
48　Washer pump
49　Wiper motor, headlamp, left*
50　Wiper motor, headlamp, right*
51　Relay, headlamp cleaning system*
52　Washer pump, headlamps*
53　Transistorized ignition switching unit
54　Ignition distributor, breakerless
55　Spark plugs
56　Ignition coil
57　Illumination:
　a　Air deflector control
　b　Heater control
　c　Switch*
58　Switch-over valve, throttle valve lift
59　Temperature switch 52°C (126°F)
　　receiver drier, air conditioner*
60　Temperature switch 100°C (212°F)*
61　Auxiliary fan*

62　Relay, auxiliary fan*
63　Switch-over valve, fresh/recirculating
　　air flap*
64　Temperature sensor, air conditioner*
65　Temperature selector, air conditioner*
66　Pre-resistance, blower motor
67　Blower motor
68　Pre-resistance 0.6 Ω
69　Window lift motor, rear, left*
70　Switch, window, rear, left*
71　Switch cluster, window lifts*:
　a　Switch, window, rear, left
　b　Safety switch
　c　Switch, window, front, left
　d　Switch, window, front, right
　e　Switch, window, rear, right
72　Window lift motor, front, left*
73　Pre-resistance 0.4
74　Time-lag relay, heated rear window
75　Switch, heated rear window
76　Illumination, shift plate*
77　Starter
78　Battery
79　Alternator w/electronic regulator
80　Door contact switch, rear, right*
81　Rear dome lamp switch*
82　Door contact switch, rear, left*
83　Fuel pump
84　Rear dome lamp*
85　Plug connection, tail lamp cable
　　harness
86　Trunk lamps
87　Fuel gauge sending unit
88　TDC transmitter
89　Window lift motor, front, right*
90　Plug socket (diagnosis)
91　Window lift motor, rear, right*
92　Switch, window, rear, right*
93　Tail lamp unit, left:
　a　Turn signal lamp
　b　Tail/standing lamp
　c　Reversing lamp
　d　Stop-lamp
　e　Rear foglamp
94　Number plate lamp
95　Heated rear window
96　Tail lamp unit, right:
　a　Turn signal lamp
　b　Tail/standing lamp
　c　Reversing lamp
　d　Stop-lamp

*Special equipment

Wire Colour Code

bl	blue
br	brown
el	ivory
ge	yellow
gn	green
gr	grey
nf	neutral
rs	pink
rt	red
sw	black
vi	purple
ws	white

Example:
Wire designation 1.5 gr/rt
Basic colour gr = grey
Identification colour rt = red
Cross-section of wire 1.5 = 1.5 mm²

Ground connections
M1　Main ground (behind instrument
　　cluster)
M2　Ground, front, right (near
　　headlamp unit)
M3　Ground, wheelhouse, front, left
　　(ignition coil)
M4　Ground, dome lamp, front
M5　Ground, engine
M6　Ground, trunk, wheelhouse, left
M7　Ground, trunk, wheelhouse, right

194

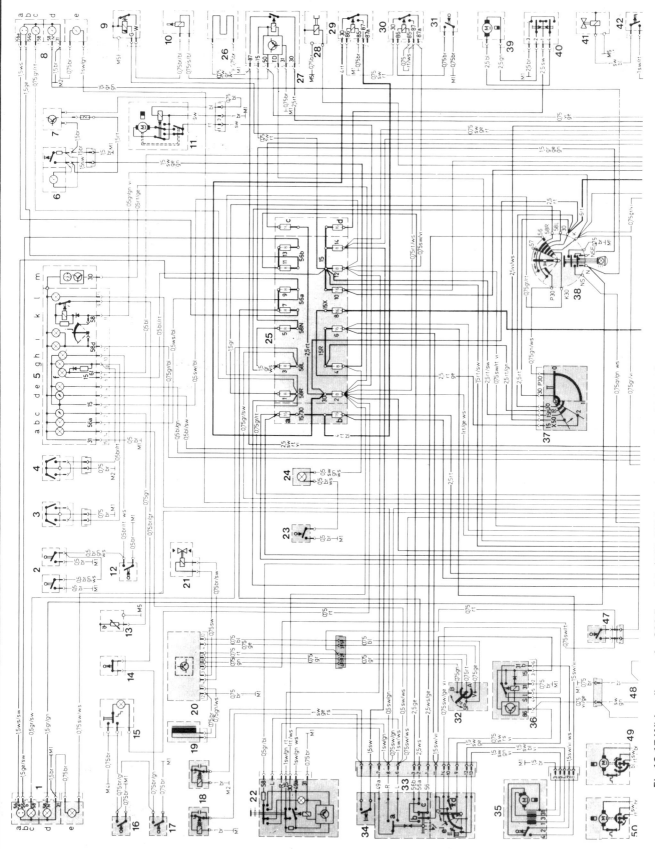

Fig 10.17 Wiring diagram for 280 E models (123.033 from chassis end no 081 279) and 280 CE models (123.053 from chassis end no 021 430)

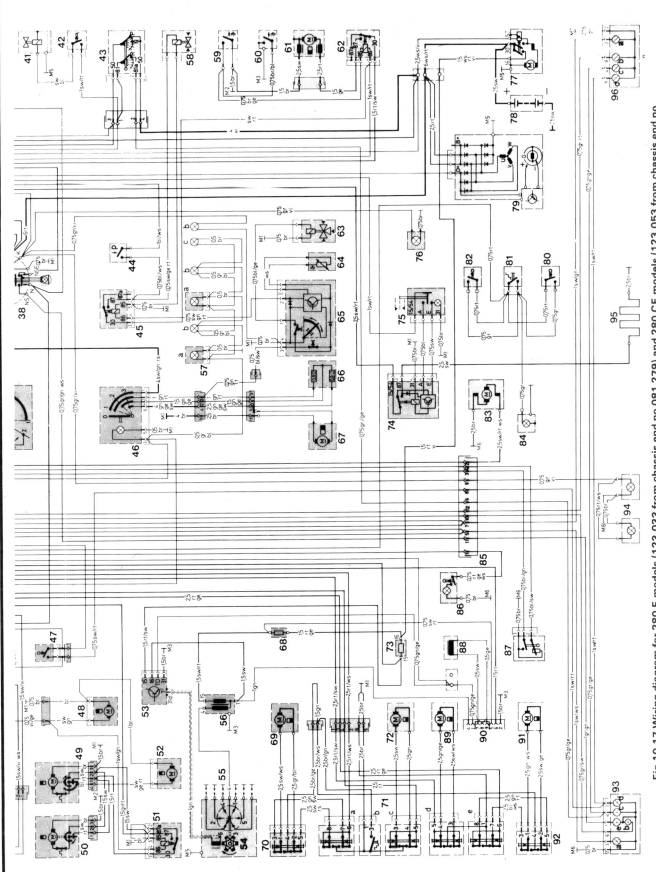

Fig 10.17 Wiring diagram for 280 E models (123.033 from chassis end no 081 279) and 280 CE models (123.053 from chassis end no 021 430) — continued

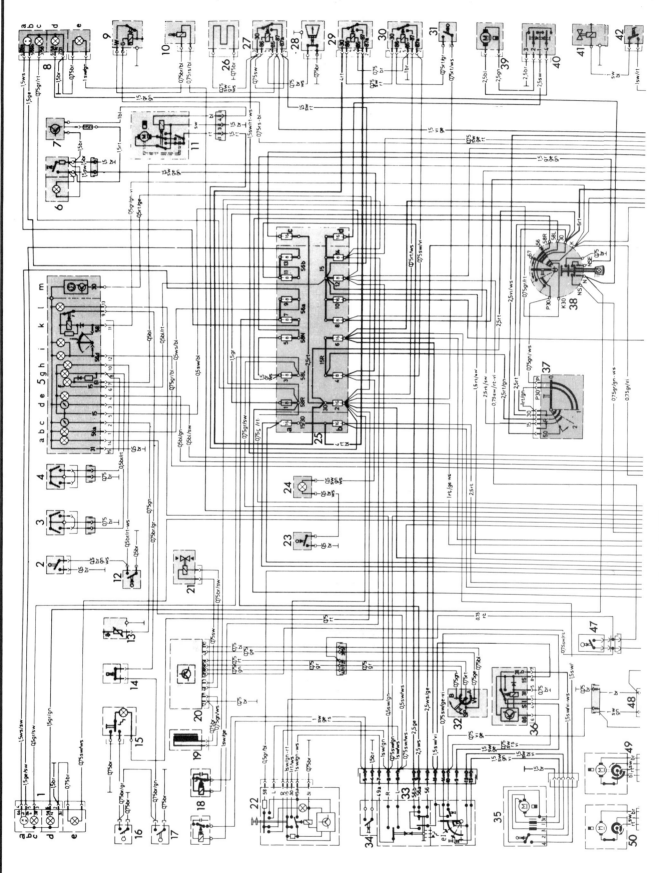

Fig. 10.18 Wiring diagram for 280 TE models (123.093)

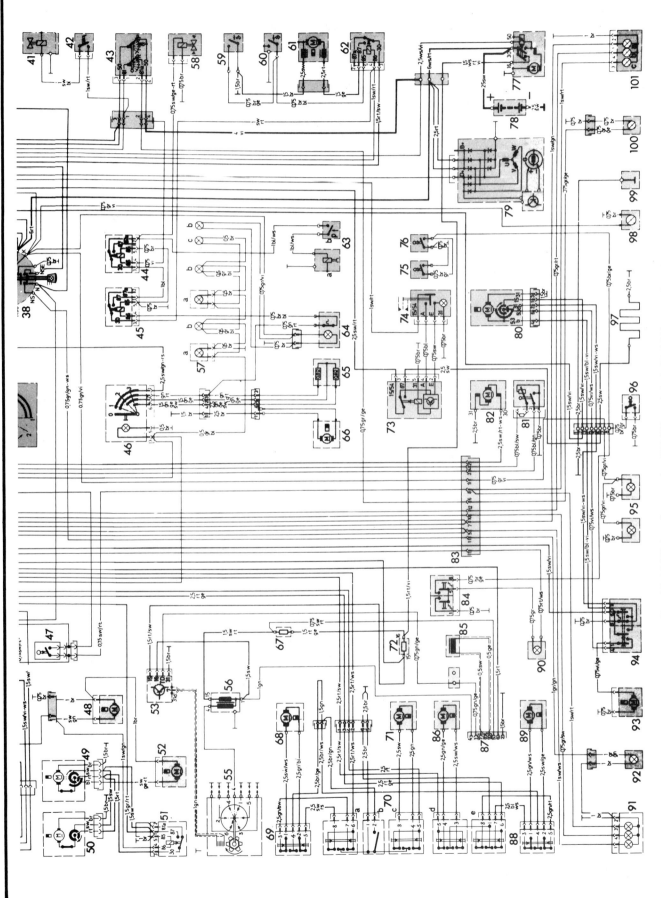

Fig. 10.18 Wiring diagram for 280 TE models (123.093) – continued

Key to wiring diagram for 280 TE models (123.093)

1 Headlight unit, left:
- a High beam
- b Low beam
- c Standing/parking light
- d Foglight
- e Turn signal light
2 Switch brake fluid checkup
3 Contact sensor brake linings, front, left
4 Contact sensor brake linings, front, right
5 Instrument cluster:
- a Turn signal indicator light, left
- b High beam control
- c Coolant temperature gauge
- d Fuel gauge
- e Fuel reserve warning light
- f Charge indicator light
- g Brake pad wear indicator light
- h Brake fluid and parking brake indicator light
- i Instrument lights
- j Rheostat, instrument lights
- k Warning buzzer
- l Turn signal indicator light, right
- m Electronic clock
6 Cigar lighter with ashtray illumination
7 Radio*
8 Headlight unit, right:
- a High beam
- b Low beam
- c Standing/parking light
- d Foglight
- e Turn signal light
9 Thermotime switch
10 Starter valve
11 Automatic antenna*
12 Parking brake indicator light switch
13 Temperature sensor, coolant indicator
14 Warning buzzer contact
15 Front dome light with switch
16 Door contact switch, front, left
17 Door contact switch, front, right
18 Dual-tone horns (fanfares)
19 Cruise control sending unit*
20 Control unit, cruise control*
21 Regulating unit, cruise control*
22 Warning flasher switch/electronic
23 Glove compartment light switch
24 Glove compartment light
25 Fusebox
26 Heater coil, warm-up control
27 Relay, fuel pump/warm-up control
28 Safety switch, baffle plate
29 Relay I window lift*
30 Relay II window lift*

31 Door contact switch window lift*
32 Switch, cruise control*:
- A Off
- V Decel/set
- SP Resume
- B Accel/set
33 Combination switch:
- a Turn signal light switch
- b Passing light switch
- c Dimmer switch
- d Washer switch
- e Switch wiping speed:
  - I Interval wiping
  - II Slow wiping
  - III Fast wiping
34 Signal system contact
35 Wiper motor
36 Interval wiping timer
37 Ignition starter switch
38 Rotary light switch
39 Sliding roof motor*
40 Switch electric sliding roof*
41 Solenoid valve, automatic transmission*
42 Kick-down switch*
43 Starter-lockout and backup light switch*
44 Relay, air conditioner II*
45 Relay, air conditioner I*
46 Blower switch with light
47 Brake light switch
48 Washer pump
49 Wiper motor, headlight, left*
50 Wiper motor, headlight, right*
51 Relay, headlight cleaning system*
52 Washer pump, headlights*
53 Transistorized ignition switching unit
54 Distributor, contactless
55 Spark plugs
56 Ignition coil
57 Illumination:
- a Air switch control
- b Heat control
- c Switch
58 Switch-over valve, idle stabilization*
59 Temperature switch 62°C (124°F) dehydrator, air conditioner*
60 Temperature switch 100°C (212°F)*
61 Auxiliary fan*
62 Relay auxiliary fan*
63a Solenoid clutch, refrigerant compressor*
63b Pressure switch, refrigerant compressor*
   On 2.6 bar, Off 2.0 bar

64 Temperature control with lighting, air conditioner*
65 Pre-resistance, blower motor
66 Blower motor
67 Pre-resistance 0.6 Ω
68 Window lift motor, rear, left*
69 Switch window, rear, left*
70 Switch group window lifts*:
- a Switch window, rear, left
- b Safety switch
- c Switch window, front, left
- d Switch window, front, right
- e Switch window, rear, right
71 Window lift motor, front, left*
72 Pre-resistance 0.4
73 Time-lag relay, heated rear window
74 Switch, heated rear window
75 Door contact switch, rear, right*
76 Door contact switch, rear, left*
77 Starter
78 Battery
79 Alternator with electronic regulator
80 Wiper motor rear door
81 Fuel gauge sending unit
82 Fuel pump
83 Plug connection, cable to rear components
84 Detent switch dome light, rear
85 TDC transmitter
86 Window lift motor, front, right*
87 Plug socket (diagnosis)
88 Switch window, rear, right*
89 Window lift motor, rear, right*
90 Dome light, rear
91 Tail light unit, left:
- a Turn signal light
- b Standing/parking light
- c Braking light
92 Rear foglight
93 Washer pump, rear door
94 Detent switch washer motor/rear door
95 Number plate light
96 Rear door contact switch/rear door lock
97 Heated rear window
98 Illumination, gate plate
99 Ground connection rear door
100 Reversing light
101 Tail light unit, right:
- a Turn signal light
- b Standing/parking light
- c Braking light

* Special equipment

Wire Colour Code

bl	blue	nf	neutral
br	brown	rs	pink
el	ivory	rt	red
ge	yellow	sw	black
gn	green	vi	violet
gr	grey	ws	white

Key to wiring diagram for 280 TE models (123-093 from chassis end no 007 619)

1 Headlamp unit, left:
  a High beam
  b Low beam
  c Parking/standing lamp
  e Turn signal lamp
2 Brake fluid indicator lamp switch
3 Contact sensor, brake pads, front, left
4 Contact sensor, brake pads, front, right
5 Instrument cluster:
  a Turn signal indicator lamp, left
  b High beam indicator lamp
  c Coolant temperature gauge
  d Fuel gauge
  e Fuel reserve warning lamp
  f Charge indicator lamp
  g Brake pad wear indicator lamp
  h Brake fluid and parking brake indicator lamp
  i Instrument lamps
  j Rheostat, instrument lamps
  k Warning buzzer
  l Turn signal indicator lamp, right
  m Electronic clock
6 Cigar lighter with ashtray illumination
7 Radio
8 Headlamp unit, right
  a High beam
  b Low beam
  c Parking/standing lamp
  d Foglamp
  e Turn signal lamp
9 Thermotime switch
10 Starter valve
11 Automatic antenna*
12 Parking brake indicator lamp switch
13 Temperature sensor, coolant
14 Warning buzzer contact
15 Front dome lamp w/switch
16 Door contact switch, front, left
17 Door contact switch, front, right
18 Dual-tone horn (fanfare)
19 Sensor, Tempomat*
20 Amplifier, Tempomat*
21 Actuator, Tempomat*
22 Warning flasher switch/timer
23 Glove compartment lamp switch
24 Glove compartment lamp
25 Fusebox
26 Heater coil, warm-up compensator
27 Relay, fuel pump with electronic speed limiter/warm-up compensator
28 Electromagnetic clutch, refrigerant compressor*
29 Relay I window lifts*
30 Relay II window lifts*
31 Door contact switch, window lifts*

32 Switch, Tempomat*
  A Off
  V Decelerate/set
  SP Resume
  B Accelerate/set
33 Combination switch:
  a Turn signal lamp switch
  b Headlamp flasher switch
  c Dimmer switch
  e Switch, wiping speed
    I Intermittent wiping
    II Slow wiping
    III Fast wiping
34 Horn contact
35 Wiper motor
36 Intermittent wiping timer
37 Ignition starter switch
38 Lighting switch
39 Sliding roof motor*
40 Switch, electrically operated sliding roof*
41 Solenoid valve, automatic transmission*
42 Kick-down switch*
43 Starter lockout and back-up lamp switch*
44 Pressure switch, refrigerant compressor*
  On 2.6 bar, Off 2.0 bar
45 Relay, air conditioner II*
46 Blower switch with lamp
47 Stop-lamp switch
48 Washer pump
49 Wiper motor, headlamp, left*
50 Wiper motor, headlamp, right*
51 Relay, headlamp cleaning system*
52 Washer pump, headlamps*
53 Transistorized ignition switching unit
54 Ignition distributor, breakerless
55 Spark plugs
56 Ignition coil
57 Illumination:
  a Air deflector control
  b Heater control
  c Switch*
58 Switch-over valve, throttle valve lift
59 Temperature switch 52°C (126°F) receiver drier, air conditioner*
60 Temperature switch 100°C (212°F)
61 Auxiliary fan*
62 Relay, auxiliary fan*
63 Switch-over valve, fresh/recirculating air flap*
64 Temperature sensor, air conditioner*
65 Temperature selector, air conditioner*
66 Pre-resistance, blower motor
67 Blower motor

68 Pre-resistance 0.6Ω
69 Window lift motor, rear, left*
70 Switch, window, rear, left*
71 Switch cluster, window lifts*
  a Switch, window, rear, left
  b Safety switch
  c Switch, window, front, left
  d Switch, window, front, right
  e Switch, window, rear, right
72 Window lift motor, front, left*
73 Pre-resistance 0.4Ω
74 Time-lag relay, heated rear window
75 Switch, heated rear window
76 Illumination, shift plate*
77 Starter
78 Battery
79 Alternator w/electronic regulator
80 Intermittent wiping timer, rear door
81 Wiper motor, rear door
82 Fuel gauge sending unit
83 Fuel pump
84 Plug connection, tail lamp cable harness
85 Detent switch, wiper motor, rear door or
  Detent switch, intermittent wiping, rear door
86 TDC transmitter
87 Window lift motor, front, right*
88 Plug socket (diagnosis)
89 Switch, window, rear, right*
90 Window lift motor, rear, right*
91 Rear dome lamp w/switch
92 Tail lamp unit, left:
  a Turn signal lamp
  b Tail/standing lamp
  c Stop-lamp
93 Rear foglamp
94 Washer pump, rear door
95 Detent switch, rear dome lamp or Push-button switch washer pump, rear door
96 Number plate lamp
97 Heated rear window
98 Door contact switch, rear, left*
99 Door contact switch, rear, right*
100 Rear door contact switch
101 Ground connection, rear door
102 Reversing lamp
103 Tail lamp unit, right:
  a Turn signal lamp
  b Tail/standing lamp
  c Stop-lamp

Special equipment

Wire colour Code
bl blue
br brown
el ivory
ge yellow
gn green
gr grey
nf neutral
rs pink
rt red
sw black
vi purple
ws white

Example:
Wire designation 1.5 gr/rt
Basic colour gr = grey
Identification colour rt = red
Cross-section of wire 1.5 = 1.5 mm²

Ground connections
M1 Main ground (behind instrument cluster)
M2 Ground, front, right (near headlamp unit)
M3 Ground, wheelhouse, front, left (ignition coil)
M4 Ground, dome lamp, front
M5 Ground, engine
M6 Ground, trunk, wheelhouse, left
M7 Ground, trunk, wheelhouse, right
M8 Ground, rear door

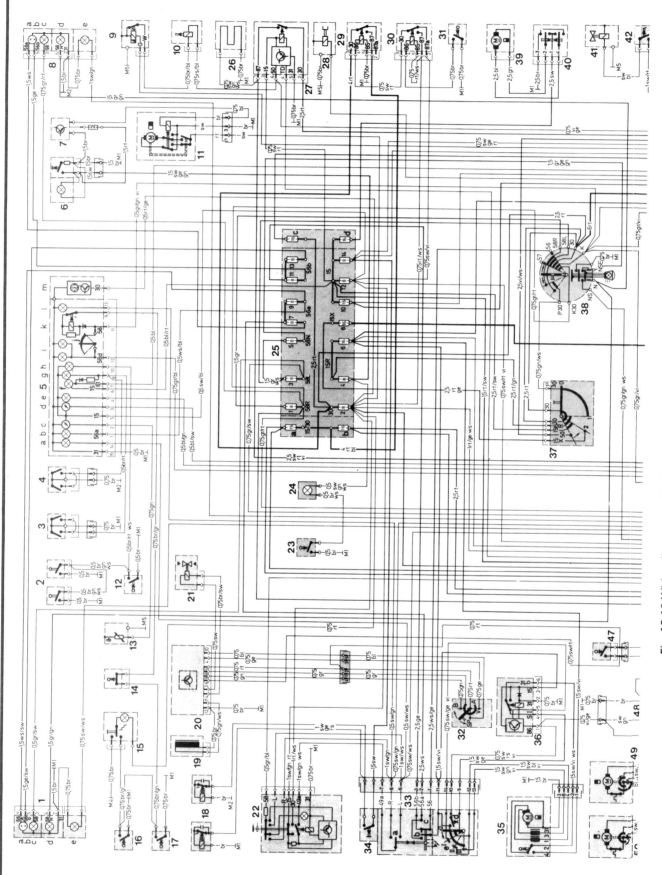

Fig. 10.19 Wiring diagram for 280 TE models (123-093 from chassis end no 007 619)

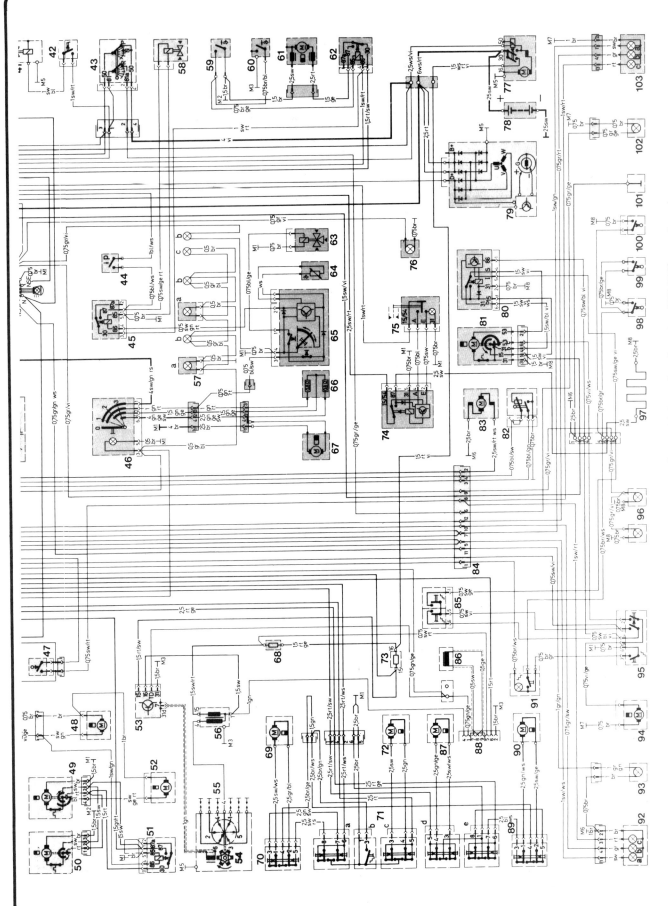

Fig. 10.19 Wiring diagram for 280 TE models (123-093 from chassis end no 007 619) – continued

Chapter 11 Suspension and steering

Contents

Specifications

Front suspension

Type	Independent with coil springs, upper and lower control arms, telescopic shock absorbers and a stabiliser bar
Wheel bearing endplay	0.01 to 0.02 mm (0.0004 to 0.0008 in)
Camber	-0° 20′ to +0° 10′
Caster	8° 15′ to 9° 15′
Maximum caster difference left and right	0° 30′
Toe-in	0° 15′ to 0° 35′ or 2.0 to 4.0 mm (0.08 to 0.016 in)

Rear suspension

Type	Independent with coil springs, semi-trailing arms, telescopic shock absorbers and a stabiliser bar
Wheel bearing endplay	0.04 to 0.06 mm (0.0016 to 0.0023 in)
Camber	-0° 20′ to +0° 20′
Toe-in/out	0.5 mm (0.02 in) toe-out to 1.0 mm (0.04 in) toe-in

Steering

Type	Recirculating ball with safety collapsible column, power steering
Power steering fluid capacity	1.5 litre; 2.6 Imp pt; 1.6 US qt
Safety tube length:	
Manual steering	368.5 to 369.5 mm (14.51 to 14.55 in)
Power steering	321.5 to 322.5 mm (12.66 to 12.70 in)
Power steering pump drivebelt tension	10.0 mm (0.4 in) deflection midway between pulleys under firm thumb pressure

Wheels

Type	Pressed-steel or alloy
Size:	
Standard	5½J x 14 H2 or 6J x 14 H2
Special	5½J x 15 H2

Tyres

Size	175SR14, 175HR14, 195/70HR14, 185HR15	
Pressures (cold) lbf/in² (kgf/cm²):	**Front**	**Rear**
Standard Saloons and Coupes	28 (2.0)	31 (2.2)
Special Saloons	36 (2.5)	43 (3.0)
Long Saloons	31 (2.2)	37 (2.6)
Standard Estates	28 (2.0)	31 (2.2)
Special Estates	33 (2.3)	46 (3.2)

Note: For sustained high speed use add 1.5 lbf/in² (0.1 kgf/cm²) for every 6 mph (10 kph) above 100 mph (160 kph)

Torque wrench settings

Front suspension

	lbf/ft	Nm
Shock absorber lower mounting	14	19
Stabiliser bar end bolt	48	65
Stabiliser bar mounting clamp	14	19
Upper control arm	59	80
Lower control arm	132	179
Balljoint:		
Upper	30	41
Lower	59	80
Support tube	25	34
Hub nut screw	10	14
Spring seat	14	19

Rear suspension

	lbf/ft	Nm
Shock absorber lower mounting	33	45
Stabiliser bar mounting:		
With spring washers	14	19
Without spring washers	22	30
Stabiliser bar link:		
Metal	33	45
Plastic	22	30
Self-levelling strut:		
Upper mounting	22	30
Lower mounting	33	45
Hose union	14	19
Balljoint	48	65
Pressure reservoir hollow screw	31	42
Self-levelling pump	9	12
Self-levelling controller	33	45
Rear suspension front mounting	88	119
Semi-trailing arm	88	119
Rear suspension rear mounting:		
To floor	22	30
To final drive	88	119

Steering

	lbf/ft	Nm
Track rod end	30	41
Steering gear	51 to 59	69 to 80
Pitman arm:		
M22	103 to 132	140 to 179
M24	118 to 147	160 to 199
Steering arm	59	80
Steering wheel	59	80
Steering column:		
Upper mounting	7	9
Lower mounting	18	24
Power steering pump	25	34

1 General description

The front suspension is of independent coil spring type incorporating upper and lower control arms, support arms and telescopic shock absorbers. A stabiliser bar is attached to the upper control arms, and all suspension mounting points are of rubber. The steering knuckle is attached to the control arms by sealed balljoints. The adjustable front wheel bearings are of taper-roller type.

The rear suspension is of independent type incorporating semi-trailing arms, coil springs and telescopic shock absorbers. Some models are equipped with a hydropneumatic self-levelling system operating on the rear suspension only. All suspension points are of rubber, and the rear wheel bearings are of adjustable taper-roller type. A stabiliser bar is fitted.

The steering is of recirculating ball type with a safety collapsible column. Power steering is standard on all models.

2 Routine maintenance

1 Every 10 000 miles (16 000 km) on UK models, and every 15 000 miles (24 000 km) on USA models, check all joints and rubbers for wear, both on the steering and suspension.
2 Check the tyres for wear and damage and rotate their position.
3 Check the power steering and suspension level control fluid levels, and top up if necessary.
4 Check all steering and suspension fastenings for tightness.

3 Front coil spring – removal and refitting

1 Working in the engine compartment unscrew the locknuts from the relevant shock absorber upper mountings and remove the washer and mounting rubber.
2 Apply the handbrake then jack up the front of the car and support it on axle stands. Remove the roadwheel.
3 Fit a spring compressor to the coil spring (photo). To do this first compress the spring with a trolley jack beneath the lower control arm, then fit the compressor over 9 of the coils.
4 Lower the control arm and withdraw the coil spring from the car, together with the upper rubber mounting.
5 Remove the rubber mounting with a screwing motion, then release the compressor, if necessary.
6 Clean the upper and lower coil seats and make sure that the drain holes in the lower seat are not obstructed.
7 Refitting is a reversal of removal, but make sure that the lower end of the coil spring enters the special channel in the lower seat. Tighten the shock absorber locknuts with the weight of the car on the suspension.

3.3 Front coil spring

4.2 Front shock absorber upper mounting locknuts

4   Front shock absorber – testing, removal and refitting

1   A quick method of testing a shock absorber is to push down the relevant front corner of the car, then release it and note the number of oscillations before the body stops moving. The body should rise, then stop moving on the downward motion. A more accurate method is described later.

2   Working in the engine compartment unscrew the locknuts from the shock absorber upper mounting and remove the washer and mounting rubber (photo). Do not allow the centre rod to rotate when unscrewing the locknuts.

3   Apply the handbrake, then jack up the front of the car and support it on axle stands. Remove the roadwheel.

4   Pull the upper sections of the shock absorber from the body.

5   Unbolt the shock absorber from the lower control arm.

6   Remove the components from the shock absorber with reference to Figs. 11.1, 11.2 or 11.3.

7   Compress the shock absorber sections to the internal stop or until additional resistance is felt (according to type) and compare the dimensions as shown in Fig. 11.4. If the dimensions are outside the specified limits, renew the shock absorber.

8   Refitting is a reversal of removal, but renew the mounting rubbers, if necessary.

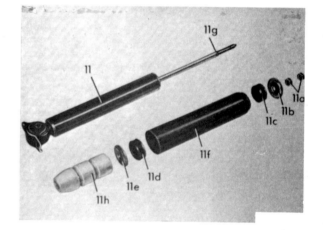

Fig. 11.1 Components of type A front shock absorber (Sec 4)

11	Shock absorber body	11e	Washer
11a	Nuts	11f	Protective sleeve
11b	Washer	11g	Circlip
11c	Upper mounting rubber	11h	Supplementary spring
11d	Lower mounting rubber		buffer

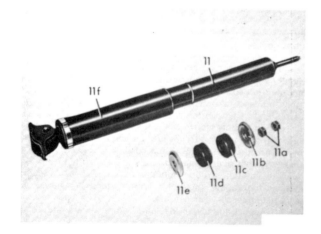

Fig. 11.2 Components of type B front shock absorber (Sec 4)

Key as Fig. 11.1

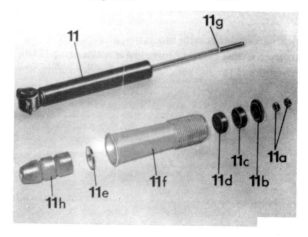

Fig. 11.3 Components of type C front shock absorber (Sec 4)

Key as Fig. 11.1

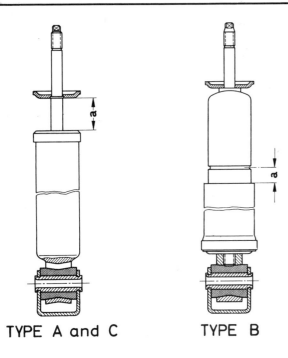

TYPE A and C   TYPE B

Fig. 11.4 Front shock absorber testing (Sec 4)

Type A and C: a = 0 to 32.0 mm (0 to 1.26 in)
Type B: a = 0 to 20.0 mm (0 to 0.8 in)

5 Front stabiliser bar – removal and refitting

1   Apply the handbrake/parking brake then jack up the front of the car and support it on axle stands positioned beneath the lower control arms. Remove the front roadwheels.
2   Unscrew the mounting bolts from each end of the stabiliser bar. Note the position of the washers and mounting rubbers.
3   Remove the brake master cylinder and servo unit, as described in Chapter 9.
4   If necessary, remove the coolant hoses (drain cooling system first, as described in Chapter 2), linkage, vacuum lines and wiring to gain access to the stabiliser bar.
5   Unscrew the mounting nuts on the bulkhead and remove the clamps.

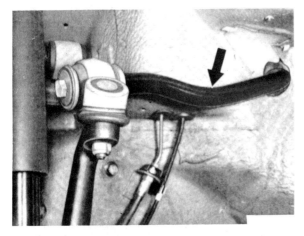

Fig. 11.5 Correct fitting of the front stabiliser bar (Sec 5)

6   Pull the split rubbers from the stabiliser bar and remove the end covers from the body.
7   Withdraw the stabiliser bar from one side of the car. Remove the mounting rubbers from each end of the bar.
8   Check the mounting rubbers for deterioration and renew them, if necessary.
9   Refitting is a reversal of removal, but make sure that the bends on the bar are as shown in Fig. 11.5, and that the recesses in the clamps are located over the lugs on the mounting rubbers. Delay fully tightening the mounting nuts and bolts until the full weight of the car is on the suspension.

6 Front suspension assembly – removal and refitting

1   Remove the front shock absorber and coil spring, as described in Sections 4 and 3 respectively.
2   Unscrew the nut from the track rod end and use a separator tool to detach the track rod end from the steering knuckle.
3   Disconnect the brake flexible hose and disc pad wear warning wiring from the brake caliper, with reference to Chapter 9.
4   Unbolt the support tube from the underbody.
5   Support the suspension assembly on a trolley jack.
6   Mark the lower control arm inner eccentric bolt discs in relation to the crossmember, then unscrew the nut and remove the discs and bolt.
7   Unscrew the bolt securing the stabiliser bar to the upper control arm. Note the position of the washers and rubbers.
8   Working in the engine compartment, unscrew the nut and drive out the upper control arm inner pivot bolt. Note which way round the bolt is fitted.
9   Withdraw the suspension assembly from the car,
10 Check the mounting rubbers for deterioration and, if necessary, renew them, with reference to Sections 8, 9 and 10.
11 Refitting is a reversal of removal, with reference to Sections 3 and 4 as necessary. Bleed the brake hydraulic system, as described in Chapter 9. Delay fully tightening the mounting nuts and bolts until the full weight of the car is on the suspension. Have the front wheel alignment, in particular the camber setting, checked by a Mercedes dealer.

7 Front hub and bearings – removal, refitting and adjustment

1   Jack up the front of the car and support it on axle stands. Apply the handbrake/parking brake and remove the roadwheel.
2   Tap off the hub grease cap and remove the radio interference suppressor contact spring (photo).
3   Remove the disc caliper, as described in Chapter 9, but do not disconnect the flexible hose. Tie the caliper to one side.
4   Using an Allen key, loosen the bolt then unscrew the clamp nut.

7.2 Radio interference suppressor contact spring on the front hub

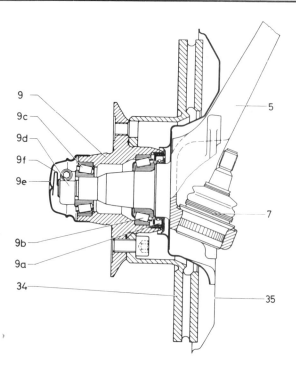

Fig. 11.6 Cross-sectional diagram of the front hub (Sec 7)

5	Steering knuckle	9d	Hub nut (clamp nut)
7	Lower balljoint		
9	Front hub	9e	Grease cap
9a	Oil seal	9f	Contact spring
9b	Inner bearing	34	Brake disc
9c	Outer bearing	35	Backplate

5   Slide the front hub and disc from the stub axle, if necessary using a suitable puller.
6   If the inner bearing race has remained on the stub axle, remove it with a puller and remove the oil seal.
7   If necessary, separate the brake disc from the hub, as described in Chapter 9.
8   Remove the outer bearing race and roller cage.
9   Prise out the oil seal and remove the inner bearing race and roller cage.
10 Using a soft metal drift drive the outer races from the hub.
11 Wash the components in paraffin and wipe dry. Examine them for wear and damage and renew them as necessary. If the surfaces of the bearing races and rollers show signs of excessive wear or pitting renew them.
12 Using a suitable metal tube drive the outer races fully into the hub.
13 Pack the inner bearing race and rollers with lithium based grease and locate it in the hub.
14 Smear a little sealing compound around the outer edge of the oil seal then press it squarely into the hub. Smear a little grease around the sealing lips.
15 Pack the hub approximately one third full with grease around the inner surfaces.
16 Pack the outer bearing race and rollers with lithium based grease and locate it in the hub.
17 Fit the brake disc to the hub, with reference to Chapter 9.
18 Slide the hub, disc and bearings onto the stub axle and screw on the clamp nut.
19 Refit the disc caliper, with reference to Chapter 9.

Adjustment

20 If necessary, lever the disc pads away from the brake disc so that the disc can be rotated freely.
21 Tighten the clamp nut by hand as far as possible while rotating the brake disc, then back it off $\frac{1}{3}$ of a turn and strike the end of the stub axle with a wooden mallet to release any tension. Tighten the clamp bolt with an Allen key.

22 Using a dial gauge, check that the wheel bearing end play is as given in the Specifications.
23 Fit the radio interference suppressor contact spring, then fill the grease cap with grease to the shoulder and tap it firmly onto the hub.
24 Refit the roadwheel and lower the car to the ground.

8   Steering knuckle – removal, overhaul and refitting

1   Jack up the front of the car and support on axle stands. Apply the handbrake/parking brake and remove the roadwheel.
2   Unbolt the steering arm from the bottom of the steering knuckle.
3   Remove the disc caliper, as described in Chapter 9, but do not disconnect the flexible hose. Tie the caliper to one side.
4   Remove the front hub, as described in Section 7.
5   Support the lower control arm with a trolley jack, then unscrew the nut from the upper balljoint and use a separator tool to detach the upper control arm (photo).
6   Unscrew the nut from the lower balljoint and use a separator tool to detach the steering knuckle from the lower control arm.
7   Unbolt the backplate from the steering knuckle.
8   Check the balljoints for excessive wear which is evident if the ball-pin has end play. If the sealing rubbers are damaged they can be renewed, but the clip ends on the upper balljoint must always face forwards, and the joints must be filled with fresh grease before fitting the rubbers.
9   If the lower balljoint is worn excessively it can be renewed. Grip the steering knuckle in a soft-jawed vice with the lower face uppermost, then drive out the balljoint using a metal tube. Drive in the new balljoint in a similar manner. Do not attempt to re-use removed balljoints.
10 If the upper balljoint is worn excessively the complete upper control arm must be renewed.
11 Refitting is a reversal of removal. Refit the front hub with reference to Section 7. Tighten nuts and bolts to the specified torque.

8.5 Steering knuckle upper balljoint

9   Front upper control arm – removal and refitting

1   Jack up the front of the car and support on axle stands positioned beneath the lower control arms.
2   Unscrew the nut from the upper balljoint and use a separator tool to detach the upper control arm from the steering knuckle. Tie the knuckle to one side.
3   Unscrew the bolt securing the stabilizer bar to the upper control arm. Note the position of the washers and rubbers.
4   Working in the engine compartment, unscrew the nut and drive out the inner pivot bolt (photo). Note which way round the bolt is fitted.
5   Withdraw the upper control arm from the car.

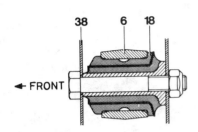

Fig. 11.7 Cross-section of the front upper control arm inner bearing (Sec 9)

6   Upper control arm   38   Body
18 Rubber bearing

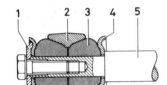

Fig. 11.8 Cross-section of the stabiliser mounting on the front upper control arm (Sec 9)

1   Cone washer   4   Washer
2   Upper control arm   5   Stabiliser bar
3   Rubber bearings

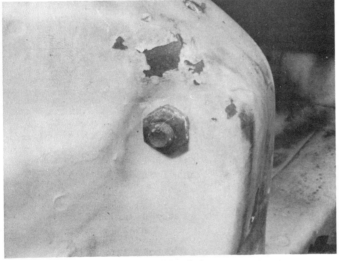

9.4 Front upper control arm inner pivot bolt

6   Check the control arm for damage. If the rubber bushes are worn they can be renewed using a suitable piece of metal tubing, a long bolt and nut, and spacers. Dip the new bush in soapy water to assist installation and make sure that the bush is fitted the correct way round, as shown in Fig. 11.7.

7   Refitting is a reversal of removal, but delay fully tightening the nuts and bolts until the full weight of the car is on the suspension. Finally check the front wheel alignment, as described in Section 31.

10 Front lower control arm – removal and refitting

1   Remove the front shock absorber and coil spring, as described in Sections 4 and 3.
2   Unscrew the nut from the track rod end and use a separator tool to detach the track rod end from the steering knuckle.

3   Unbolt the rear of the support tube from the underbody.
4   Mark the lower control arm inner eccentric bolt discs in relation to the crossmember, then unscrew the nut and remove the discs and bolt.
5   Unscrew the nut from the steering knuckle lower balljoint and use a separator tool to detach the lower control arm.
6   Withdraw the lower control arm, together with the support tube.
7   Unbolt the coil spring seat from the lower control arm.
8   Mark the support tube in relation to the lower control arm, then unscrew the joint bolt and separate the two components.
9   Check the two mountings and lower balljoint for wear and damage. If the balljoint is worn renew the complete lower control arm. Check the control arm for damage and distortion.
10 To renew the support tube rollers, prise out the cups and rubbers and locate the new parts in the control arm.
11 To renew the inner mounting rubbers, first prise out the old ones using a drill and hacksaw, if necessary, to cut the rubbers free. Clean the bore, then dip the new rubbers in soapy water and press them into the control arm with a vice, making sure that the outer lugs are in the vertical plane.
12 Refitting is a reversal of removal, but delay fully tightening the nuts and bolts until the full weight of the car is on the suspension. Finally check the front wheel alignment, as described in Section 31.

11 Front suspension support tube – removal and refitting

1   Remove the front shock absorber and coil spring, as described in Sections 4 and 3.
2   Mark the lower control arm inner eccentric bolt discs in relation to the crossmember, then unscrew the nut and remove the discs and bolt.
3   Unbolt the rear of the support tube from the underbody.

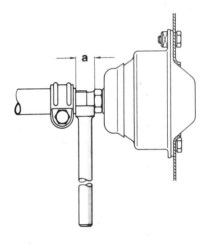

Fig. 11.9 Using a gauge to adjust the support tube to its initial setting (Sec 11)

a = 14.0 mm (0.55 in)

4   Unbolt the coil spring seat from the lower control arm.
5   Mark the support tube in relation to the lower control arm, then unscrew and remove the joint bolt.
6   Pull the lower control arm from the crossmember, swivel it forward and withdraw the support tube.
7   Check the support tube for wear and damage. Use a straight-edge to check that the tube is not distorted. There should be no play in the rear balljoint mounting, but the tube must be free to turn smoothly with the joint held stationary.
8   To renew the joint, first note the position of the ball-pin, then loosen the clamp bolt and unscrew the ball-pin and joint. Screw the new joint to the same position – the setting should be approximately as given in Fig. 11.9.
9   Refitting is a reversal of removal, but delay fully tightening the nuts and bolts until the full weight of the car is on the suspension. Finally check the front wheel alignment, as described in Section 31, in particular the caster angle which is adjustable at the support tube.

12 Rear shock absorber – testing, removal and refitting

1 Refer to Section 4, paragraph 1 for testing the shock absorber.
2 Remove the rear seat cushion and backrest, as described in Chapter 12.
3 Jack up the rear of the car and support it with axle stands positioned beneath the outer ends of the trailing arms. Chock the front wheels.
4 Prise out the access cover and unscrew the locknuts from the shock absorber upper mounting. Remove the washer and rubber.
5 Working under the car, unscrew the lower mounting bolts (photo) and lower the shock absorber from the semi-trailing arm.

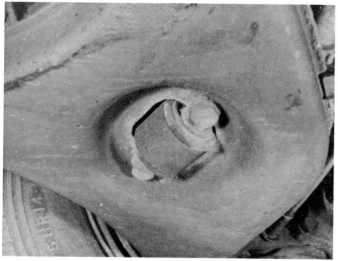

12.5 Rear shock absorber lower mounting

6 Remove the components from the shock absorber, with reference to Figs. 11.10 or 11.11.
7 Compress the shock absorber sections to the internal stop or until additional resistance is felt (according to type) and compare the dimensions as shown in Fig. 11.12. If the dimensions are outside the specified limits, renew the shock absorber.
8 Refitting is a reversal of removal, but renew the mounting rubbers, if necessary. Tighten the upper mounting lower locknut to the end of the thread and then tighten the upper locknut.

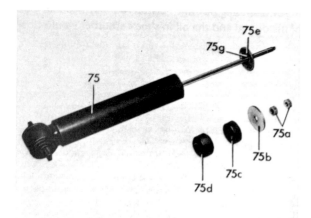

Fig. 11.10 Components of type A rear shock absorber (Sec 12)

75	Shock absorber body	75d	Lower mounting rubber
75a	Nuts	75e	Washer
75b	Washer	75f	Protective sleeve
75c	Upper mounting rubber	75g	Circlip

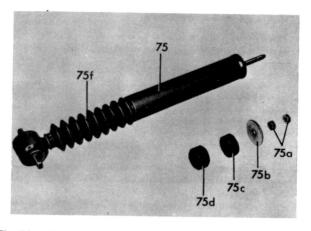

Fig. 11.11 Components of type B rear shock absorber (Sec 12)

Key as Fig. 11.10

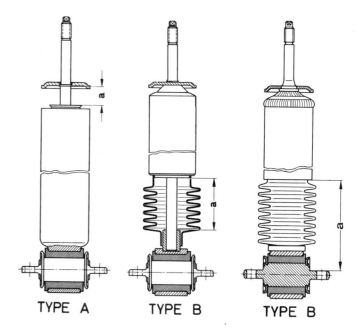

TYPE A   TYPE B   TYPE B

Fig. 11.12 Rear shock absorber testing (Sec 12)

Type A: a = 0 to 32.0 mm (0 to 1.26 in)
Type B: a = 82.0 to 105.0 mm (3.23 to 4.13 in) or:
Type B: a = 137.0 to 147.0 mm (5.39 to 5.79 in)

13 Rear stabiliser bar – removal and refitting

1 Jack up the rear of the car and support on axle stands. Chock the front wheels.
2 On models with rear suspension level control unscrew the nuts and disconnect the control link, after noting its position.
3 Remove the rear roadwheels.
4 Unscrew the nuts securing the ends of the stabiliser bar to the links and pull out the links (photo).
5 Unbolt the mounting clamps from the underbody and remove the mounting plates and rubbers (photo).
6 Disconnect the exhaust mounting rubbers and lower the rear exhaust onto an axle stand.
7 Withdraw the stabiliser bar from the car.
8 Check the mounting rubbers for deterioration and renew them, if necessary.

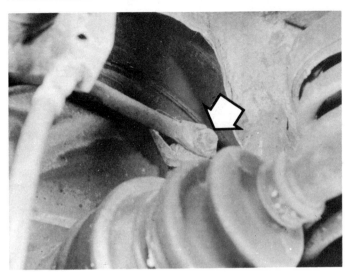

13.4 Rear stabiliser bar-to-link joint (arrowed)

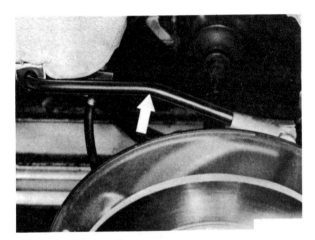

Fig. 11.13 Correct fitting of the rear stabiliser bar (Sec 13)

9   Refitting is a reversal of removal, but make sure that the bends on the bar are as shown in Fig. 11.13. Delay fully tightening the mounting nuts and bolts until the full weight of the car is on the suspension. On level control models have the rear body level checked by a Mercedes dealer.

14 Rear coil spring – removal and refitting

1   Remove the rear shock absorber (Section 12) or spring strut (automatic level control models).
2   Fit a spring compressor to the coil spring. To do this compress the spring as far as possible with a trolley jack beneath the semi-trailing arm, then fit the compressor over 5 of the coils.
3   Lower the semi-trailing arm sufficiently to withdraw the rear coil spring, together with the upper rubber mounting.
4   Remove the rubber mounting and release the compressor, if necessary.
5   Clean the upper and lower coil seats.
6   Refitting is a reversal of removal, but make sure that the lower end of the coil spring enters the special channel in the semi-trailing arm. Tighten the shock absorber locknuts with the weight of the car on the suspension.

15 Rear suspension assembly – removal and refitting

1   Jack up the rear of the car and support it on axle stands. Chock the front wheels and remove the rear wheels.
2   Remove the exhaust system, as described in Chapter 3.

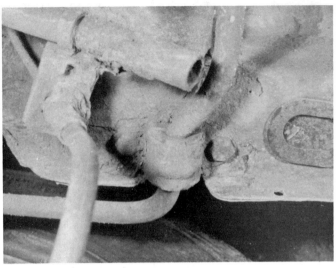

13.5 Rear stabiliser mounting clamp

3   Where applicable, unbolt the heat shield from the underbody, then remove the handbrake/parking brake cables, with reference to Chapter 9.
4   Also referring to Chapter 9, disconnect the hydraulic flexible hoses from the rear calipers and seal the apertures with masking tape.
5   Remove the propeller shaft, as described in Chapter 7.
6   Remove the rear coil springs, as described in Section 14.
7   Unscrew the nuts securing the ends of the rear stabiliser bar to the links and pull out the links.
8   Where applicable, disconnect the rpm wiring from behind the rear seat backrest and pull it downwards.
9   Support the rear suspension assembly with a trolley jack.
10 Unbolt the front support brackets from the underbody.
11 Unbolt the rear mounting bracket behind the final drive unit from the underbody.
12 Lower the rear suspension assembly and withdraw it from the car.
13 Refitting is a reversal of removal, but tighten nuts and bolts to the specified torque, and always renew the self-locking bolts for the rear mounting. Bleed the brake hydraulic system, as described in Chapter 9, and also adjust the handbrake/parking brake.

16 Rear semi-trailing arm – removal and refitting

1   Remove the rear suspension assembly, as described in Section 15.
2   Remove the driveshaft, with reference to Chapter 8.
3   Unscrew the nuts and drive out the mounting bolts then withdraw the semi-trailing arm from the crossmember (photo).

16.3 Rear semi-trailing arm pivot bolt

4   If necessary, the mounting rubbers may be removed using a metal tube, long bolt, nut and spacers. The new rubbers can be fitted using the same method, but first dip them in soapy water and insert them from the outer surface of the semi-trailing arm.

5   Refitting is a reversal of removal, with reference to Chapter 8 and Section 15 of this Chapter, but delay fully tightening the semi-trailing arm mounting bolts until the weight of the car is on the suspension.

17 Rear hub and bearings – removal, refitting and adjustment

1   Chock the front wheels, then jack up the rear of the car and support it on axle stands.

2   Remove the rear brake disc, as described in Chapter 9. Though not essential it is also recommended that the handbrake/parking brake shoes are removed.

3   Unscrew the bolt from the centre of the driving flange (photo) and remove the spacer, if fitted.

4   Push the driveshaft inwards from the flange and tie it to one side.

5   Using a small punch release the peening from the slot nut on the inner end of the flange.

6   Hold the flange stationary by bolting a bar to it, then use a slotted box spanner to unscrew the slot nut.

7   Prise out the spacer and oil seal.

8   Drive out the driving flange using a mandrel or slide hammer, and remove the inner bearing race and collapsible spacer.

9   Prise the outer oil seal from the hub.

10 Using a soft metal drift, drive the outer races from the hub.

11 Remove the outer bearing race from the driving flange with a suitable puller.

12 Wash the components in paraffin and wipe dry. Examine them for wear and damage, and renew them as necessary. If the surfaces of the bearing races and rollers show signs of excessive wear or pitting renew them. Note that the driving flanges are handed, as they incorporate an oil return spiral, and they are marked R (right) or L (left) on the flange shoulder.

13 Using a metal tube drive the outer bearing race onto the driving flange. Similarly drive the outer races into the hub.

14 Apply a little sealing compound to the seat on the hub then drive the new oil seal into position using a block of wood.

15 Pack the inner bearing races and rollers with lithium based grease, and also fill the hub inner cavity between the outer races with grease.

16 Locate a new collapsible spacer on the driving flange and insert the flange into the hub.

17 Slide the inner bearing race onto the flange and tap it up to the collapsible spacer with a metal tube.

18 Apply a little sealing compound to the seat in the hub then drive in the new oil seal with a metal tube.

19 Fit the spacer and screw on the slot nut hand tight.

20 Hold the flange stationary and tighten the slot nut until the end play is as given in the Specifications. Use a dial gauge or feeler gauge

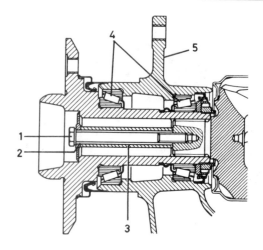

Fig. 11.14 Cross-sectional diagram of the rear hub (Sec 17)

1	Driveshaft bolt	4	Bearings
2	Washer	5	Hub
3	Sleeve		

and fixed block to check the end play. If the slot nut is overtightened the collapsible spacer must be renewed before making a further adjustment.

21 Lock the slot nut by peening at two points.

22 Refit the driveshaft then insert the bolt (and new spacer, if fitted) and tighten it to the specified torque.

23 Refit the handbrake/parking brake shoes and brake disc, with reference to Chapter 9, and lower the car to the ground.

18 Rear suspension front mounting – renewal

1   Chock the front wheels, then jack up the rear of the car and support it on axle stands.

2   Support the crossmember with a trolley jack.

3   Unbolt the mounting plate from the underbody and crossmember (photo).

4   Extract the mounting rubber by pushing it out a little then using two screwdrivers to prise it out.

5   Dip the new mounting rubber in soapy water and push it into the crossmember. If difficulty is experienced, use a long bolt and nut with spacers to pull it into position.

6   Refit the mounting plate and tighten the bolts.

7   Lower the car to the ground.

17.3 Removing the rear driveshaft bolt from the rear hub

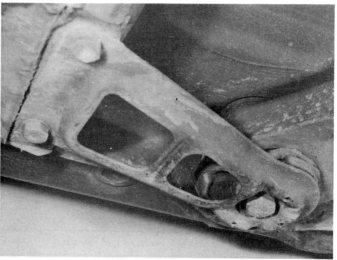

18.3 Rear suspension front mounting

Fig. 11.15 Prising out the rear suspension front mounting (Sec 18)

19 Automatic level control – general

1   Certain models are fitted with an automatic level control system which regulates the rear ride height of the car hydraulically. The system incorporates two struts fitted in place of the rear shock absorbers, and each strut is connected to its own pressure reservoir. A pump on the engine supplies the hydraulic fluid and the ride height is adjusted by a level controller attached to the rear stabiliser bar. The pressure reservoirs incorporate a gas-filled section which maintains the pressure during the deflection of the suspension.

2   On the 110 engine the pressure pump is driven from the front of the exhaust camshaft, but on the 123 engine it is driven from the front of the auxiliary shaft.

3   If the system develops a fault it should be checked by a Mercedes dealer, since a pressure gauge and special adaptors are required.

4   When filling the system, top up the reservoir to the maximum mark then run the engine at fast idling speed for approximately 1 minute with one or two persons, or an equivalent weight, in the rear luggage compartment. Stop the engine and top up the level. Note that, with the car fully loaded and the engine running, the level will drop to the minimum mark.

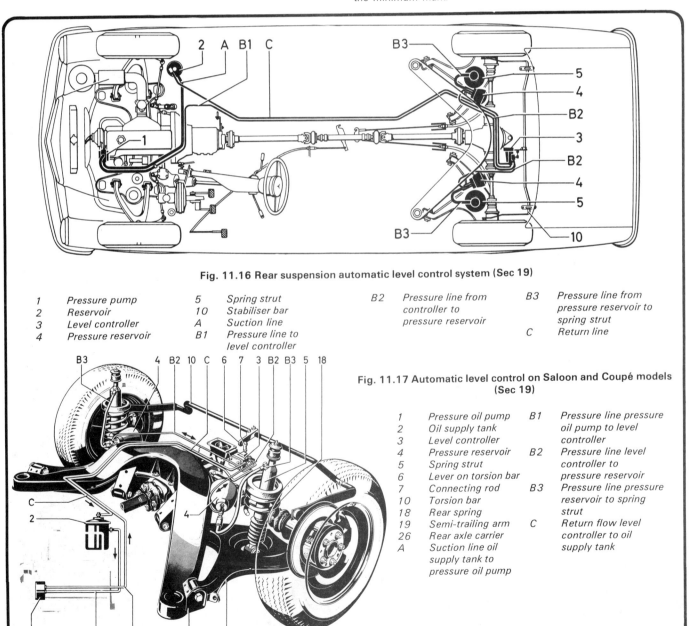

Fig. 11.16 Rear suspension automatic level control system (Sec 19)

1	Pressure pump	5	Spring strut
2	Reservoir	10	Stabiliser bar
3	Level controller	A	Suction line
4	Pressure reservoir	B1	Pressure line to level controller

B2   Pressure line from controller to pressure reservoir

B3   Pressure line from pressure reservoir to spring strut

C   Return line

Fig. 11.17 Automatic level control on Saloon and Coupé models (Sec 19)

1	Pressure oil pump	B1	Pressure line pressure oil pump to level controller
2	Oil supply tank		
3	Level controller		
4	Pressure reservoir	B2	Pressure line level controller to pressure reservoir
5	Spring strut		
6	Lever on torsion bar		
7	Connecting rod	B3	Pressure line pressure reservoir to spring strut
10	Torsion bar		
18	Rear spring		
19	Semi-trailing arm	C	Return flow level controller to oil supply tank
26	Rear axle carrier		
A	Suction line oil supply tank to pressure oil pump		

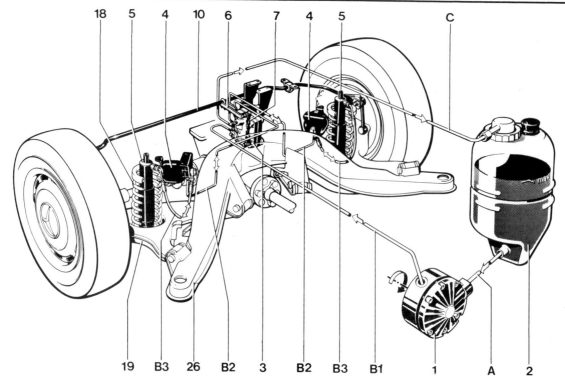

Fig. 11.18 Automatic level control on Estate models (Sec 19)

1	Pressure oil pump	7	Connecting rod	B1	Pressure line pressure oil pump to level controller
2	Oil supply tank	10	Torsion bar	B2	Pressure line level controller to pressure reservoir
3	Level controller	18	Rear spring		
4	Pressure reservoir	19	Semi-trailing arm	B3	Pressure line pressure reservoir to spring strut
5	Spring strut	26	Rear axle carrier		
6	Lever on torsion bar	A	Suction line oil supply tank to pressure oil pump	C	Return line level controller to oil supply tank

5 Removal and refitting of the system components is straightforward, but any adjustment of the ride height should be made by a Mercedes dealer.

20 Steering wheel – removal and refitting

1 On early models pull the complete horn pad from the steering wheel, but on later models prise the motif from the centre of the pad with a screwdriver.

2 With the front wheels straight-ahead mark the steering wheel and inner column in relation to each other.

3 Engage the steering lock, if necessary, and unscrew the nut or countersunk screw (photo). An Allen key is required for the countersunk screw. Experience has shown that the screw may be extremely difficult to remove, even to the point where the complete column must be removed and mounted in a vice.

4 Pull the steering wheel from the splines on the column (photo).

5 Refitting is a reversal of removal, but tighten the nut/screw to the specified torque.

20.3 Removing the steering wheel countersunk screw with an Allen key

20.4 Removing the steering wheel from the column splines

21 Steering column – removal, overhaul and refitting

1 Remove both lower facia panels, with reference to Chapter 12.

2 Remove the steering wheel, as described in Section 20.

3 Remove the instrument panel, as described in Chapter 10.

4 On automatic transmission models with steering column shift, disconnect the linkage.

5 Remove the steering lock, as described in Section 23.

6 Using an Allen key, unscrew the clamp bolt at the bottom of the column (photo).

7 Unscrew the column lower mounting nuts (photo), and remove the heater hose bracket, if applicable.

8 Disconnect the combination switch wiring plug.

9 Unscrew the column upper mounting nuts then lower the column and withdraw it (photo). Take care not to damage the corrugated safety tube and, to ensure correct refitting, mark the tube and inner column in relation to each other.

10 Remove the combination switch with reference to Chapter 10. Also remove the support ring.

11 Remove the spacer, grip ring, spring and ball-bearing on early models or remove the grip ring, spring, support and ball-bearing on later models from the bottom of the column (photo).

12 Extract the circlip from the top of the inner column and remove the ring and ball-bearing (photo). Withdraw the inner column.

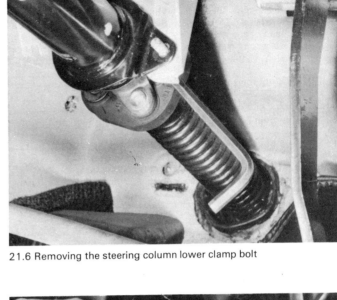

21.6 Removing the steering column lower clamp bolt

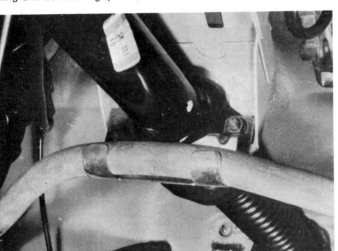

21.7 The steering column lower mounting

21.9 Removing the steering column

21.11 Bottom view of the steering column

21.12 Top view of the steering column

13 Using the inner column and suitable packing drive the bearing outer races from the outer column.

14 Wash all the components in paraffin and wipe dry. Examine them for wear and damage and renew them as necessary. In particular check the ball-bearing surfaces for pitting and deterioration.

15 When reassembling the column press the grip ring fully against the spring with a metal tube, and lubricate the bearings with a little grease.

16 Refitting is a reversal of removal.

22 Column coupling and corrugated tube – removal and refitting

1   Remove both lower facia panels, with reference to Chapter 12.

2   Working in the engine compartment, use an Allen key to unscrew both clamp bolts from the coupling to the steering gear (photo). Push the coupling fully against the steering gear. If applicable, first remove the guard plate.

3   Working inside the car use an Allen key to unscrew the clamp bolt at the bottom of the column on the coupling.

4   Push the coupling down then withdraw it from the car, taking care not to damage it (photo). If necessary, remove the convoluted rubber sleeve from the body.

5   Refitting is a reversal of removal, but lubricate the sealing ring at the bottom of the tube with a little grease and make sure that the coupling clamp bolts are located in the special grooves, where applicable.

23 Steering lock – removal and refitting

Note: *If the steering lock is defective and cannot be operated, the complete column must be removed, as described in Section 21, and the locking pin drilled out.*

1   Remove both lower facia panels, with reference to Chapter 12.

2   Remove the instrument panel, with reference to Chapter 10.

3   Pull the plug connector from the switch on the lock (photo).

4   Bend back the tabs and remove the key surround from the facia (photo).

5   On early models use a hooked instrument to pull the plastic cap from the lock.

6   On later models insert the ignition key and turn it to position 'I', then insert some 1.25 mm (0.05 in) diameter wire in the locking cylinder cut-out, unscrew the cap and remove the locking cylinder (photo). Remove the wire then turn the key to position 'O' and remove it. Remove the cap then re-insert the key to position 'I' and refit the locking cylinder in the housing while pushing down the detent. Disconnect the contact plug.

7   On all models loosen the steering lock clamp bolt.

8   With the ignition key in position 'I', depress the locking pin with a

23.4 Steering column safety corrugated tube

23.3 Disconnecting the plug from the ignition switch

22.2 Steering gear coupling

23.4 Removing the key surround

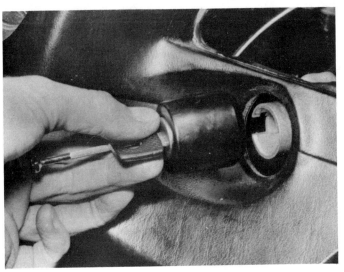

23.6 Removing the lock cylinder

23.8 Steering lock locking pin (arrowed)

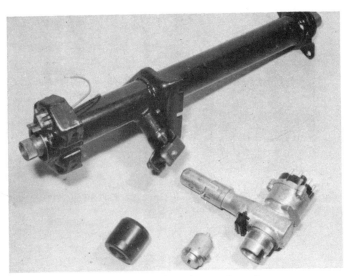

23.9 The steering lock removed from the steering column

23.10 Inner view of the locking cylinder

small screwdriver and slightly turn the lock, now turn the key to position 'O' and remove it (photo).

9 Withdraw the steering lock from the column (photo).

10 With the key in position 'I' remove the contact switch or locking cylinder as applicable (photo).

11 Refitting is a reversal of removal.

24 Steering gear (manual) — removal, overhaul and refitting

1 Set the front wheels in the straight-ahead position.

2 Working in the engine compartment, unscrew the coupling clamp bolts with an Allen key and slide the coupling from the steering gear.

3 Jack up the front of the car and support it on axle stands. Apply the handbrake/parking brake.

4 Extract the split pins and unscrew the nuts securing the drag link and track rod end to the steering gear drop arm (Pitman arm). Use a separator tool to release the link and arm.

5 Unscrew the self-locking nut and use a puller to remove the drop arm from the steering gear after marking the arm in relation to the sector shaft.

6 Unscrew the mounting bolts and withdraw the steering gear downwards.

7 Clean the steering gear with paraffin and wipe dry.

8 Unscrew the adjusting locknut and the cover bolts, then turn the adjusting screw clockwise and at the same time withdraw the cover and gasket. Pull out the sector shaft.

9 Extract the circlip, unscrew the ring nut and the adjusting ring and remove them. A pin wrench will be needed for this job on early models.

10 Remove the steering worm/nut/ball cage assembly.

11 Using a small puller, extract the outer bearing track from the steering box.

12 Remove the oil seal.

13 Extract the bearing inner races from the worm shaft. If the bearings are to be used again, tape the bearing together with its outer track; do not mix them up.

14 Check for wear or damage in all the components. The worm/nut/ball assembly can only be renewed as a complete unit.

15 Clean out the interior of the steering box and prepare for reassembly.

16 Commence reassembly by pressing the outer track of the lower bearing into the steering box.

17 Press the outer track of the upper bearing into the adjusting ring.

18 Heat the inner races of the bearings to 80°C (176°F) in hot oil and fit them to the worm.

19 Locate the ball cage in the lower bearing outer track.

20 Fit the worm and nut.

21 Fit the new oil seal to the adjusting ring.

22 Fit the upper ball-bearing cage to the worm.

23 Using a piece of thin plastic tubing fitted to the worm shaft as a

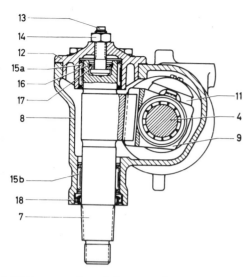

Fig. 11.19 Cross-section of the manual steering gear (Sec 24)

4	Worm	14	Locknut
7	Sector shaft	15a	Bearing
8	Housing	15b	Bearing
9	Nut	16	Circlip
11	Ball guide tubes	17	Washer
12	Cover	18	Seal
13	Adjusting screw		

Fig. 11.20 Removing the sector shaft (7) from the housing (8) (Sec 24)

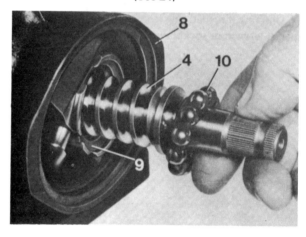

Fig. 11.21 Removing the worm (4), nut (9) and ball cage (10) from the housing (8) (Sec 24)

protection for the oil seal lips, push the adjusting ring into position and then screw it in several turns.

24 Remove the temporary protection sleeve and tighten the adjusting ring until the worm can just be turned, but stiffly.

25 Coat the threads of the ring nut with a thread locking compound and screw the ring into the gearbox.

26 At this stage, adjust the steering worm. To do this, tighten the adjusting ring (using the pin wrench if necessary) until all endfloat just disappears and yet the worm turns easily. Without moving the position of the adjusting ring, fully tighten the ring nut. Fit the circlip.

27 Fit the adjuster screw, spacer and locking ring into the recess in the end of the sector shaft. Any play between the adjuster screw head at the recess in the shaft should be eliminated by changing the spacer washer for a thicker one.

28 Fit the sector shaft into the steering box so that the centre tooth of the shaft engages in the centre gap of the worm nut.

29 Fit a new gasket to the flange of the steering box; fit the top cover by winding the adjuster screw through the cover. Fit and tighten the cover bolts.

30 Screw the locknut onto the adjuster screw, but do not tighten it.

31 Slide a protective sleeve (or tape) over the exposed splines of the sector shaft and then fit the shaft oil seal using a piece of tubing as a drift.

32 Fill the steering box with the correct quantity of the specified oil.

33 Now adjust the sector shaft endfloat. To do this, turn the steering to the centre position. This position can be determined by unscrewing the filler plug and observing that the centre point of the worm nut is directly under the plug hole. A dimple is made in the worm nut to indicate this.

34 Wind a cord round the splines of the sector shaft and attach it to a spring balance. Now check the force required to move the sector shaft off its central position. This should be between 5 and 7 kgf (11 and 15 lbf), as shown on the spring balance. Turn the adjuster screw until the adjustment is correct and then tighten the locknut without altering the adjustment.

35 Refit the filler plug.

36 Refitting is a reversal of removal, but tighten the nuts and bolts to the specified torque. Make sure that the steering wheel and gear are in their central positions before sliding the coupling into place. Check that on full lock the drop arm or idler arm contacts the stops on the crossmember. If not, the track rod lengths may be unequal and should be checked, as described in Section 31.

25 Steering idler – removal, overhaul and refitting

1 Apply the handbrake/parking brake then jack up the front of the car and support it on axle stands.

2 Extract the split pins and unscrew the nuts securing the drag link and track rod end to the steering idler. Use a separator tool to release the link and arm.

3 Unscrew the self-locking nut from the bottom of the idler and remove the washer.

4 Lift out the idler arm, noting the position of washers and dust caps.

5 Remove the bushes from the idler using a soft metal drift as necessary.

6 Clean all the components and check them for wear.

7 Refitting is a reversal of removal, but lubricate the bushes with oil and tighten the nuts to the specified torque.

26 Track rod and drag link – removal and refitting

1 Jack up the front of the car and support it on axle stands. Apply the handbrake/parking brake. If removing a track rod, remove the relevant roadwheel.

2 Extract the split pins and unscrew the nuts.

3 Using a separator tool release the tapered ball-pins from the arms (photo). Additionally, when removing the drag link, disconnect the damper (photo). Note the position of washers and covers.

4 Refitting is a reversal of removal, but check the front wheel alignment, as described in Section 31.

26.3A Removing a track rod end with a separator tool

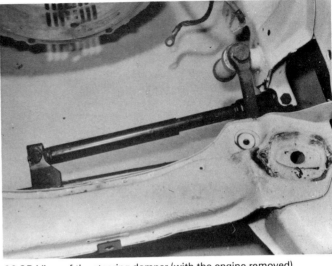

26.3B View of the steering damper (with the engine removed)

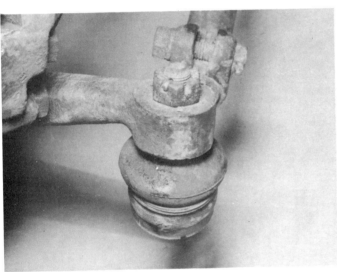

27.3 Track rod end connected to the steering arm

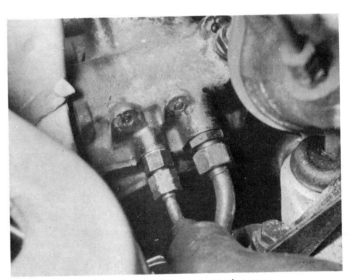

28.3A Hydraulic line unions on the power steering gear

27 Track rod ends – testing and renewal

1   To test a track rod end balljoint, jack up the front of the car and support it on axle stands. Apply the handbrake/parking brake.
2   Attempt to turn the front wheel by hand alternately in opposite directions. If any play is evident check each balljoint to determine which one is worn.
3   Remove the roadwheel. Extract the split pin and unscrew the nut (photo).
4   Using a separator tool, release the track rod end from the steering arm.
5   Loosen the clamp bolt and unscrew the track rod end, noting the exact number of turns necessary to remove it.
6   Screw the new track rod end to the identical position and tighten the clamp bolt.
7   Refit the track rod end to the steering arm, tighten the nut, and lock with a new split pin.
8   Finally check the front wheel alignment, as described in Section 31.

28 Power steering gear – removal and refitting

1   The removal and refitting procedures are similar to those described in Section 24 for the manual steering gear with the

28.3B Power steering gear

29.2 Power steering pump hydraulic fluid reservoir

30.2A Power steering pump showing upper pivot bolt (arrowed)

30.2B Power steering pump drivebelt tension bolt

30.6 Checking the power steering pump drivebelt tension

following exceptions:
2   Syphon the fluid from the pump reservoir.
3   Unscrew the hose unions from the steering gear and plug the openings to prevent the ingress of dust and dirt (photos).
4   After refitting the power steering gear bleed the hydraulic system, as described in Section 29.

29 Power steering system – bleeding

1   Check the security of all hoses and unions.
2   Fill the pump reservoir to the level mark with the correct hydraulic fluid (photo).
3   Start the engine and turn the steering lock to lock several times.
4   Stop the engine then repeat the procedure given in paragraphs 2 and 3 once more.
5   Finally stop the engine and refit the reservoir cap.

30 Power steering pump – removal and refitting

1   Syphon the fluid from the pump reservoir.
2   Loosen the upper pivot bolt and the nut on the front of the adjustment bolt (photo).
3   Turn the adjustment bolt to releaase the tension, then slip the

drivebelt from the pulley.
4   Remove the pivot and adjustment bolts, and withdraw the steering pump from the engine.
5   If necessary unscrew the nut and use a puller to remove the pulley.
6   Refitting is a reversal of removal, but first check the plastic bushes on the mounting bracket and renew them, if necessary. Tension the drivebelt as given in the Specifications (photo) and finally bleed the hydraulic system, as described in Section 29.

31 Wheel alignment – checking and adjusting

1   Accurate wheel alignment is essential for good steering and slow tyre wear. Before checking it, make sure that the car is only loaded to kerbside weight and that the tyre pressures are correct.
2   Position the car on level ground with the wheels straight-ahead, then roll the car backwards 4 m (12 ft) and forwards again.
3   Using a wheel alignment gauge check that the front wheels are aligned for toe-in as given in the Specifications.
4   If adjustment is necessary loosen the clamp bolts on both track rods and turn the track rods equally until the setting is correct. Note that the length of both track rods between ball-pin centres must be equal. Tighten the clamp bolts.
5   Checking of camber and castor angles requires special instruments and this work should be entrusted to a Mercedes dealer.

The camber angle on the front wheels is adjusted by the eccentric bolts on the inner ends of the lower control arms. The castor angle is adjusted by lengthening or shortening the front suspension support tubes.

32 Roadwheels and tyres – general

1   Clean the insides of roadwheels whenever they are removed and,

where applicable, remove any rust and repaint them.
2   At the same time remove any flints or stones which may have become embedded in the tyres and also examine the tyres for damage and splits. Check the tread depth and renew the tyres, if necessary.
3   The wheels should be balanced when new tyres are fitted and rebalanced halfway through the life of the tyres to compensate for loss of rubber.
4   Check and adjust the tyre pressures regularly and make sure that the dust caps are correctly fitted. Do not forget to check the spare tyre.

33 Fault diagnosis – suspension and steering

Symptom	Reason(s)
Excessive play in steering	Worn track rod end or drag link balljoints
	Worn suspension balljoints
	Steering gear worn or requiring adjustment
Wanders or pulls to one side	Incorrect wheel alignment
	Worn steering or suspension balljoints
	Incorrect tyre pressures
	Faulty shock absorbers
Heavy or stiff steering	Seized steering or suspension balljoint
	Incorrect wheel alignment
	Low tyre pressures
	Lack of lubricant in steering gear
	Faulty power steering system
Wheel wobble and vibration	Wheels out of balance or damaged
	Faulty shock absorbers
	Worn hub bearings
	Worn steering or suspension balljoints
Excessive tyre wear	Incorrect wheel alignment
	Faulty shock absorbers
	Incorrect tyre pressures
	Wheels out of balance
	Worn steering or suspension balljoints

Chapter 12 Bodywork and fittings

Contents

1 General description

The bodyshell is of all-steel welded construction incorporating a safety cell passenger compartment and impact absorbing front and rear sections. Body styles include Saloon, Coupe and Estate versions, and features include a sliding roof and vacuum-operated central locking system. The sliding roof may be either manual or electric, the latter incorporating a manual override for emergency use (photos).

2 Maintenance – bodywork and underframe

1 The general condition of a vehicle's bodywork is the one thing that significantly affects its value. Maintenance is easy but needs to be regular. Neglect, particularly after minor damage, can lead quickly to further deterioration and costly repair bills. It is important also to keep watch on those parts of the vehicle not immediately visible, for instance the underside, inside all the wheel arches and the lower part

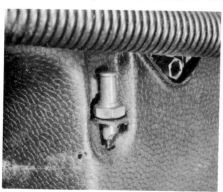

1.1A Electric sliding roof emergency key

1.1B Using a socket spanner to operate the electric sliding roof emergency key

1.1C Electric sliding roof emergency cable unit

of the engine compartment.

2   The basic maintenance routine for the bodywork is washing — preferably with a lot of water, from a hose. This will remove all the loose solids which may have stuck to the vehicle. It is important to flush these off in such a way as to prevent grit from scratching the finish. The wheel arches and underframe need washing in the same way to remove any accumulated mud which will retain moisture and tend to encourage rust. Paradoxically enough, the best time to clean the underframe and wheel arches is in wet weather when the mud is thoroughly wet and soft. In very wet weather the underframe is usually cleaned of large accumulations automatically and this is a good time for inspection.

3   Periodically, it is a good idea to have the whole of the underframe of the vehicle steam cleaned, engine compartment included, so that a thorough inspection can be carried out to see what minor repairs and renovations are necessary. Steam cleaning is available at many garages and is necessary for removal of the accumulation of oily grime which sometimes is allowed to become thick in certain areas. If steam cleaning facilities are not available, there are one or two excellent grease solvents available which can be brush applied. The dirt can then be simply hosed off.

4   After washing paintwork, wipe off with a chamois leather to give an unspotted clear finish. A coat of clear protective wax polish will give added protection against chemical pollutants in the air. If the paintwork sheen has dulled or oxidised, use a cleaner/polisher combination to restore the brilliance of the shine. This requires a little effort, but such dulling is usually caused because regular washing has been neglected. Always check that the door and ventilator opening drain holes and pipes are completely clear so that water can be drained out. Bright work should be treated in the same way as paintwork. Windscreens and windows can be kept clear of the smeary film which often appears, by adding a little ammonia to the water. If they are scratched, a good rub with a proprietary metal polish will often clear them. Never use any form of wax or other body or chromium polish on glass.

3   Maintenance — upholstery and carpets

1   Mats and carpets should be brushed or vacuum cleaned regularly to keep them free of grit. If they are badly stained remove them from the vehicle for scrubbing or sponging and make quite sure they are dry before refitting. Seats and interior trim panels can be kept clean by wiping with a damp cloth. If they do become stained (which can be more apparent on light coloured upholstery) use a little liquid detergent and a soft nail brush to scour the grime out of the grain of the material. Do not forget to keep the headlining clean in the same way as the upholstery. When using liquid cleaners inside the vehicle do not over-wet the surfaces being cleaned. Excessive damp could get into the seams and padded interior causing stains, offensive odours or even rot. If the inside of the vehicle gets wet accidentally it is worthwhile taking some trouble to dry it out properly, particularly where carpets are involved. *Do not leave oil or electric heaters inside the vehicle for this purpose.*

4   Minor body damage — repair

The photographic sequences on pages 230 and 231 illustrate the operations detailed in the following sub-sections.

Repair of minor scratches in bodywork

If the scratch is very superficial, and does not penetrate to the metal of the bodywork, repair is very simple. Lightly rub the area of the scratch with a paintwork renovator, or a very fine cutting paste, to remove loose paint from the scratch and to clear the surrounding bodywork of wax polish. Rinse the area with clean water.

Apply touch-up paint to the scratch using a fine paint brush; continue to apply fine layers of paint until the surface of the paint in the scratch is level with the surrounding paintwork. Allow the new paint at least two weeks to harden: then blend it into the surrounding paintwork by rubbing the scratch area with a paintwork renovator or a very fine cutting paste. Finally, apply wax polish.

Where the scratch has penetrated right through to the metal of the bodywork, causing the metal to rust, a different repair technique is required. Remove any loose rust from the bottom of the scratch with

a penknife, then apply rust inhibiting paint to prevent the formation of rust in the future. Using a rubber or nylon applicator fill the scratch with bodystopper paste. If required, this paste can be mixed with cellulose thinners to provide a very thin paste which is ideal for filling narrow scratches. Before the stopper-paste in the scratch hardens, wrap a piece of smooth cotton rag around the top of a finger. Dip the finger in cellulose thinners and then quickly sweep it across the surface of the stopper-paste in the scratch; this will ensure that the surface of the stopper-paste is slightly hollowed. The scratch can now be painted over as described earlier in this Section.

Repair of dents in bodywork

When deep denting of the vehicle's bodywork has taken place, the first task is to pull the dent out, until the affected bodywork almost attains its original shape. There is little point in trying to restore the original shape completely, as the metal in the damaged area will have stretched on impact and cannot be reshaped fully to its original contour. It is better to bring the level of the dent up to a point which is about $\frac{1}{8}$ in (3 mm) below the level of the surrounding bodywork. In cases where the dent is very shallow anyway, it is not worth trying to pull it out at all. If the underside of the dent is accessible, it can be hammered out gently from behind, using a mallet with a wooden or plastic head. Whilst doing this, hold a suitable block of wood firmly against the outside of the panel to absorb the impact from the hammer blows and thus prevent a large area of the bodywork from being 'belled-out'.

Should the dent be in a section of the bodywork which has a double skin or some other factor making it inaccessible from behind, a different technique is called for. Drill several small holes through the metal inside the area — particularly in the deeper section. Then screw long self-tapping screws into the holes just sufficiently for them to gain a good purchase in the metal. Now the dent can be pulled out by pulling on the protruding heads of the screws with a pair of pliers.

The next stage of the repair is the removal of the paint from the damaged area, and from an inch or so of the surrounding 'sound' bodywork. This is accomplished most easily by using a wire brush or abrasive pad on a power drill, although it can be done just as effectively by hand using sheets of abrasive paper. To complete the preparation for filling, score the surface of the bare metal with a screwdriver or the tang of a file, or alternatively, drill small holes in the affected area. This will provide a really good 'key' for the filler paste.

To complete the repair see the Section on filling and re-spraying.

Repair of rust holes or gashes in bodywork

Remove all paint from the affected area and from an inch or so of the surrounding 'sound' bodywork, using an abrasive pad or a wire brush on a power drill. If these are not available a few sheets of abrasive paper will do the job just as effectively. With the paint removed you will be able to gauge the severity of the corrosion and therefore decide whether to renew the whole panel (if this is possible) or to repair the affected area. New body panels are not as expensive as most people think and it is often quicker and more satisfactory to fit a new panel than to attempt to repair large areas of corrosion.

Remove all fittings from the affected area except those which will act as a guide to the original shape of the damaged bodywork (eg headlamp shells etc). Then, using tin snips or a hacksaw blade, remove all loose metal and any other metal badly affected by corrosion. Hammer the edges of the hole inwards in order to create a slight depression for the filler paste.

Wire brush the affected area to remove the powdery rust from the surface of the remaining metal. Paint the affected area with rust inhibiting paint; if the back of the rusted area is accessible treat this also.

Before filling can take place it will be necessary to block the hole in some way. This can be achieved by the use of zinc gauze or aluminium tape.

Zinc gauze is probably the best material to use for a large hole. Cut a piece to the approximate size and shape of the hole to be filled, then position it in the hole so that its edges are below the level of the surrounding bodywork. It can be retained in position by several blobs of filler paste around its periphery.

Aluminium tape should be used for small or very narrow holes. Pull a piece off the roll and trim it to the approximate size and shape required, then pull off the backing paper (if used) and stick the tape over the hole; it can be overlapped if the thickness of one piece is insufficient. Burnish down the edges of the tape with the handle of a screwdriver or similar, to ensure that the tape is securely attached to the metal underneath.

Bodywork repairs – filling and re-spraying

Before using this Section, see the Sections on dent, deep scratch, rust holes and gash repairs.

Many types of bodyfiller are available, but generally speaking those proprietary kits which contain a tin of filler paste and a tube of resin hardener are best for this type of repair. A wide, flexible plastic or nylon applicator will be found invaluable for imparting a smooth and well contoured finish to the surface of the filler.

Mix up a little filler on a clean piece of card or board – measure the hardener carefully (follow the maker's instructions on the pack) otherwise the filler will set too rapidly or too slowly.

Using the applicator apply the filler paste to the prepared area; draw the applicator across the surface of the filler to achieve the correct contour and to level the filler surface. As soon as a contour that approximates to the correct one is achieved, stop working the paste – if you carry on too long the paste will become sticky and begin to 'pick up' on the applicator. Continue to add thin layers of filler paste at twenty-minute intervals until the level of the filler is just proud of the surrounding bodywork.

Once the filler has hardened, excess can be removed using a metal plane or file. From then on, progressively finer grades of abrasive paper should be used, starting with a 40 grade production paper and finishing with 400 grade wet-and-dry paper. Always wrap the abrasive paper around a flat rubber, cork, or wooden block – otherwise the surface of the filler will not be completely flat. During the smoothing of the filler surface the wet-and-dry paper should be periodically rinsed in water. This will ensure that a very smooth finish is imparted to the filler at the final stage.

At this stage the 'dent' should be surrounded by a ring of bare metal, which in turn should be encircled by the finely 'feathered' edge of the good paintwork. Rinse the repair area with clean water, until all of the dust produced by the rubbing-down operation has gone.

Spray the whole repair area with a light coat of primer – this will show up any imperfections in the surface of the filler. Repair these imperfections with fresh filler paste or bodystopper, and once more smooth the surface with abrasive paper. If bodystopper is used, it can be mixed with cellulose thinners to form a really thin paste which is ideal for filling small holes. Repeat this spray and repair procedure until you are satisfied that the surface of the filler, and the feathered edge of the paintwork are perfect. Clean the repair area with clean water and allow to dry fully.

The repair area is now ready for final spraying. Paint spraying must be carried out in a warm, dry, windless and dust free atmosphere. This condition can be created artificially if you have access to a large indoor working area, but if you are forced to work in the open, you will have to pick your day very carefully. If you are working indoors, dousing the floor in the work area with water will help to settle the dust which would otherwise be in the atmosphere. If the repair area is confined to one body panel, mask off the surrounding panels; this will help to minimise the effects of a slight mis-match in paint colours. Bodywork fittings (eg chrome strips, door handles etc) will also need to be masked off. Use genuine masking tape and several thicknesses of newspaper for the masking operations.

Before commencing to spray, agitate the aerosol can thoroughly, then spray a test area (an old tin, or similar) until the technique is mastered. Cover the repair area with a thick coat of primer; the thickness should be built up using several thin layers of paint rather than one thick one. Using 400 grade wet-and-dry paper, rub down the surface of the primer until it is really smooth. While doing this, the work area should be thoroughly doused with water, and the wet-and-dry paper periodically rinsed in water. Allow to dry before spraying on more paint.

Spray on the top coat, again building up the thickness by using several thin layers of paint. Start spraying in the centre of the repair area and then, using a circular motion, work outwards until the whole repair area and about 2 inches of the surrounding original paintwork is covered. Remove all masking material 10 to 15 minutes after spraying on the final coat of paint.

Allow the new paint at least two weeks to harden, then, using a paintwork renovator or a very fine cutting paste, blend the edges of the paint into the existing paintwork. Finally, apply wax polish.

5 Major body damage – repair

Where serious damage has occurred, or large areas need renewal due to neglect, it means certainly that completely new sections or panels will need welding in and this is best left to professionals. If the damage is due to impact, it will also be necessary to completely check the alignment of the bodyshell structure. Due to the principle of construction, the strength and shape of the whole car can be affected by damage to one part. In such instances the services of a Mercedes agent with specialist checking jigs are essential. If the body is left misaligned, it is first of all dangerous as the car will not handle properly, and secondly uneven stresses will be imposed on the steering and possibly engine and transmission, causing abnormal wear or complete failure. Tyre wear may also be excessive.

6 Maintenance – bodywork and fittings

1   Every 12 500 miles (20 000 km) lubricate the door hinges with multi-purpose grease using a grease gun with a pointed adaptor end. At the same time on Estate models lubricate the tailgate hinges with engine oil. Also lubricate the door strikers and catch with a little grease.

2   Oil the bonnet hinges and stays, cable, lock and safety catch. Apply a little grease to the lock catch.

3   Where folding exterior mirrors are fitted, disengage the mirror and oil the hinge, then grease the detent clip before reassembling the mirror.

4   Clean all door weatherseals at the same time.

5   Every 30 000 miles (48 000 km) check that all the body drain channels are clear.

6   Every 12 months lubricate the sliding roof rails and check the drain channels using compressed air from an air line or tyre pump. At the same time check the underbody for damage and corrosion, in particular the condition of the underseal. Apply new underseal and carry out repairs as necessary.

Fig. 12.1 Folding exterior mirror lubricating points (Sec 6)

7 Bonnet – removal and refitting

1   Fully open the bonnet and place some cloth pads beneath the two rear corners.

2   Disconnect the windscreen washer tube at the T-piece, release the clip and pull out the tube.

3   Mark the location of the hinge bolts on the bonnet with a pencil, then loosen them several turns (photo).

4   With the help of an assistant, support the bonnet then remove the bolts and lift the bonnet from the car.

5   Refitting is a reversal of removal, but set the hinges to their original positions before tightening the bolts. Check that the bonnet is central within its aperture and aligned correctly with the surrounding bodywork (Fig. 12.2). Note that the lower edge at the front of the bonnet should align with the upper edge of the turn signal lamp cut-outs.

7.3 Bonnet hinge bolts

8.1 Removing the lower facia panel

6   To adjust the bonnet longitudinally loosen the hinge bolts, reposition the bonnet, then tighten the bolts. To adjust the height, loosen the locknuts and turn the rubber stops under the front of the bonnet as required, then tighten the locknuts.

Fig. 12.2 Correct bonnet alignment (Sec 7)

8   Bonnet lock cable – removal and refitting

1   Remove the lower facia panel (photo).
2   Unbolt the bonnet release lever from the side panel and disengage the cable.

Fig. 12.3 Cable attachment to bonnet lock (Sec 8)

3   Working in the engine compartment release the cable from the bracket and plastic straps, then pull it from the clips near the lock.
4   Disconnect the cable from the lock by loosening the locknuts and pushing the pin from the clip.
5   Withdraw the cable from the car.
6   Refitting is a reversal of removal, but when completely fitted adjust the cable at the locknuts to eliminate the free play.

9   Boot lid – removal and refitting

1   Remove both number plate lamps, as described in Chapter 10.
2   Remove the boot light and switch, as described in Chapter 10.
3   With the battery already disconnected, unclip the wiring and withdraw it from the boot lid.
4   Place some cloth pads beneath the boot lid corners.
5   Mark the location of the hinge bolts with a pencil, then loosen them several turns (photo).
6   With the help of an assistant, support the boot lid then remove the bolts and lift the boot lid from the car.
7   Refitting is a reversal of removal, but align the bolts with the previously made marks before tightening them. Check that the boot lid is central within its aperture and aligned with the surrounding bodywork. Make sure that the boot lid seats correctly onto the weatherseal – if necessary adjust the boot lid within its aperture by loosening the hinge bolts, and adjust it onto the weatherseal by adding or taking away spacers from the striker.

9.5 Boot lid hinge

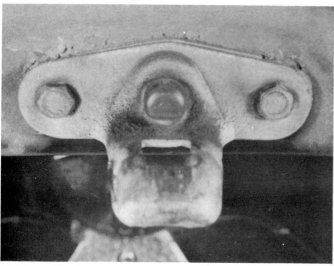

10.5 Boot lid striker

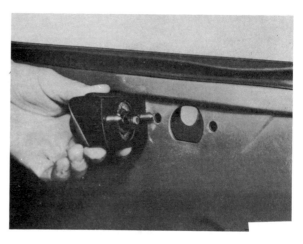

Fig. 12.4 Removing the boot lid lock (Sec 10)

10 Boot lid lock – removal and refitting

1   Open the boot lid and unscrew the lock nuts. Remove the washers.
2   Withdraw the lock from the rear panel.
3   Prise the plastic cover from inside the rear panel.
4   Unscrew the bolt and withdraw the lower lock section through the cover aperture. Disconnect the central locking links, if applicable.
5   Refitting is a reversal of removal. Make sure that the striker engages the lock correctly (photo).

11 Tailgate (Estate models) – removal and refitting

1   Remove the rear compartment light with reference to Chapter 10, but do not disconnect the wiring.
2   Unscrew the retaining screws and withdraw the rear roof panel from the clips.
3   With the battery disconnected, disconnect the wiring from the terminal block on the roof and unclip the harness.
4   Where applicable remove the rear mounted speakers and disconnect the wiring.
5   Disconnect the rear window washer tube and, where applicable, the central locking vacuum lines.
6   Support the tailgate, then prise out the spring clips and disconnect the gas-filled springs from the hinges.
7   Mark the location of the hinge bolts with a pencil then loosen them several turns.
8   With the help of an assistant, support the tailgate then remove the bolts and lift the tailgate from the car.
9   Refitting is a reversal of removal, but align the bolts with the previously made marks before tightening them. The wiring should be connected as shown in Fig. 12.5. Check that the tailgate is central within its aperture and aligned with the surrounding bodywork. Adjustment can be made by loosening the hinge bolts and repositioning the tailgate so that it is level with the surrounding bodywork or a maximum of 1.0 mm (0.04 in) lower.
10 To adjust the striker, slightly loosen the striker and side stop screws, close the tailgate so that it is level with, or a maximum of 1.0 mm (0.04 in) lower than the surrounding bodywork, then open the tailgate and tighten the screws. If necessary spacers can be added or taken away from under the striker or side stops.

12 Tailgate window (Estate models) – removal and refitting

1   Remove the rear wiper arm, as described in Chapter 10.
2   Unscrew the locking knob and remove the tailgate trim panel (6 screws).

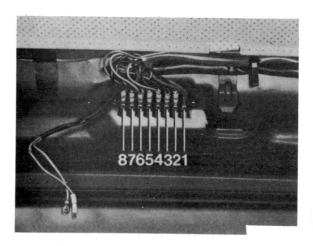

Fig. 12.5 Tailgate wiring diagram (Sec 11)

1	Light brown (earth)	5	Black/purple/white
2	Black/purple	6	Black
3	Black/blue/purple	7	Grey/purple
4	Purple/white	8	Brown/grey

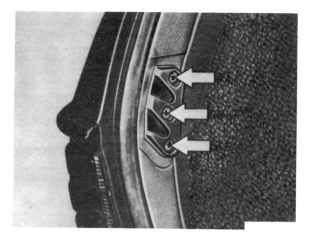

Fig. 12.6 Tailgate side stop screws (Sec 11)

3 Remove the screw from the inner handle cover and remove the cover.
4 Lift the panel from the clips.
5 Release the clip and remove the wiper spindle grommet from the window.
6 Disconnect the two wires from the heated back window.
7 Unscrew the wiper motor mounting bolts and suspend the motor away from the window.
8 With the help of an assistant prise up the weatherseal and press out the window from the inside.
9 Apply sealant to the window groove and insert a cord into the weatherseal.
10 Locate the window over the aperture and have an assistant press lightly while the cord is pulled to position the weatherseal on the tailgate flange. The remaining refitting procedure is a reversal of removal, but centralise the wiper spindle in the glass before tightening the mounting bolts.

Fig. 12.7 Tailgate wiper spindle grommet clip (Sec 12)

13 Tailgate gas-filled spring (Estate models) — removal and refitting

1 Open the tailgate and remove the rear compartment light, with reference to Chapter 10, however, do not disconnect the wiring.
2 Unscrew the retaining screws and withdraw the rear roof panel from the clips.
3 Support the tailgate then prise out the spring clip and extract the pin from the hinge.
4 Using an Allen key unscrew the front mounting bolt. If there is no access hole in the headlining, carefully pull the headlining away.
5 Withdraw the spring from the rear.
6 Refitting is a reversal of removal.

14 Door inner trim panel — removal and refitting

Saloon and Estate models
1 Unscrew the locking knob from the top of the panel and fully close the window.
2 Prise the plastic insert from the window regulator handle, move it towards the knob and remove it — not on electric windows (photo).
3 Note the position of the handle, then remove it together with the escutcheon (except electric windows).
4 Prise out and remove the interior door handle cover (photo). Disconnect the switch on electric window models.
5 Remove the surround (1 screw) followed by the armrest upper mounting screw (photos).
6 Remove the lower screws and withdraw the armrest.
7 Remove the two screws and withdraw the lock surround (photo).
8 On the rear door remove the ashtray, then prise up the cam and lift out the ashtray housing.
9 Using a wide-bladed screwdriver prise the trim panel from the door. Insert the screwdriver adjacent to the clips to prevent damage to the panel.

10 Lift the trim panel from the upper clips and withdraw it from the door (photos). On front doors note that the inner hook must be disconnected, and on rear doors make sure that the clip by the ashtray is released.

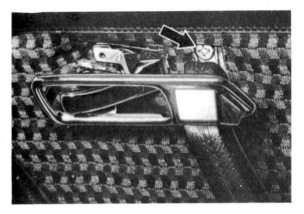

Fig. 12.8 Arm rest upper mounting screw (Sec 14)

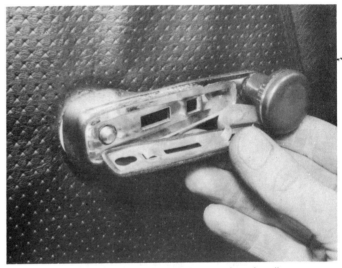

14.2 Removing the insert from the window regulator handle

14.4 Prise out the interior door handle cover ...

Coupé models

11 Remove the screws and withdraw the cover plate from the end of the door above the lock. Also remove the small bezel.

12 Where applicable, prise the plastic insert from the window regulator handle, move it towards the knob and remove it.

13 With the window shut note the position of the handle then remove it together with the escutcheon (except electric windows).

14 Remove the locking lever cover (1 screw).

15 Prise the interior handle cover out then remove the screw and withdraw the surround.

16 Remove the screws and withdraw the armrest.

17 Using a wide-bladed screwdriver prise the trim panel from the door. Insert the screwdriver adjacent to the clips to prevent damage to the panel. Note that there are additional clips at the front of the panel.

18 Lift the rear of the panel from the clips, at the same time prising it out from the locking lever.

19 Lift the front of the panel to disconnect the inner hook, then withdraw it from the door.

All models

20 If necessary, peel the polythene sheet from the door, taking care not to tear it.

21 Refitting is a reversal of removal, but make sure that the retaining clips are correctly aligned before pressing them into the door.

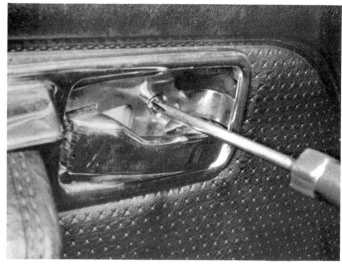

14.5A ... then remove the surround ...

14.5B ... and arm rest

14.7 Removing the lock surround

14.10A Front door inner trim panel hook

14.10B Front door with the inner trim panel removed

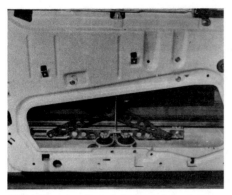

15.2A Showing the window regulator arms in the front door

15.2B The window regulator arm clips are located behind the lifting channel

15.2C Window regulator retaining bolts

15 Window regulator (manual) – removal and refitting

1 Remove the door inner trim panel and polythene sheet, as described in Section 14.

Front door
2 On Saloon models lower the window and prise the clips from the lift arms, then raise the window and support it with a block of wood. Remove the arms from the channel then unbolt the regulator and withdraw it through the aperture (photos).
3 On Coupé models lower the window and remove the screws from the lifting rail, then raise the window and support it with a block of wood. Unbolt the regulator and withdraw it through the aperture.

Rear door
4 Lower the window and remove the screws from the lifting rail, then raise the window and support it with a block of wood.
5 Unbolt the regulator and withdraw it through the aperture.

Front and rear doors
6 Refitting is a reversal of removal.

16 Window regulator (electric) – removal and refitting

1 Remove the door inner trim panel and polythene sheet, as described in Section 14.
2 Lower the window then disconnect the battery negative lead.
3 Unscrew the bolts securing the lifting rail to the glass channel.
4 Raise the window and support it with a block of wood.
5 Identify the electric wires for position then disconnect them from the terminals.
6 On the rear door remove the rear window channel screws and push the channel forwards.
7 Unscrew the bolts/nuts and withdraw the regulator through the aperture together with the motor.
8 Refitting is a reversal of removal, but if necessary adjust the lower travel of the window by loosening the bolt and positioning the stop pad on the regulator arm as required.

17 Front door window – removal and refitting

1 Remove the window regulator, as described in Sections 15 or 16.

Saloon and Estate models
2 Position the window in the apertures and unscrew the lifting rail bolts.
3 Prise the inner and outer seals from the top of the door. First remove the exterior mirror from the left-hand door and the inner cover from the right-hand door. Also prise off the moulding.
4 Lift the rear of the window, tilt it forward and withdraw it from the top of the door.
5 Refitting is a reversal of removal, but before tightening the rail bolts, fully lower the window, press it forward into the channel and at

Fig. 12.9 Stop pad bolt on the electric window regulator (Sec 16)

Fig. 12.10 Removing the front door window (Sec 17)

the same time press the lifting rail to the rear, then tighten the bolts. Fully raise the window and loosen the rear channel bolts. Press the window rearward into the channel then tighten the bolts.

Coupé models
6 Prise the inner seal from the top of the door.
7 Unscrew and remove the top and bottom stops from the rear window channel.
8 Unscrew the bottom nut and top bolt and remove the rear window channel.
9 Remove the screws and withdraw the rear guide wedge.
10 Lift the window rearward from the door.

11 Refitting is a reversal of removal, but adjust it as follows. Adjust the front guide retainer so that it **lightly** contacts the weatherstrip with the door closed. Check that, with the window closed, the front edge is aligned with the guide retainer – if necessary adjust the upper stops, channels and lifting rail as required. Lateral adjustment is made at the guide pins. With the window fully open the upper edge must be flush with the seals – adjustment is made at the stop on the window lifting rail. Adjust the guide wedge so that it contacts the rear edge of the window. Finally apply a little anti-corrosion grease to the window channels.

18 Rear door window – removal and refitting

1 Remove the window regulator, as described in Sections 15 or 16.
2 Unscrew the bolts and withdraw the rear window channel.
3 Prise the inner and outer seals from the top of the door. First prise off the moulding.
4 Lift the front of the window and withdraw it from the top of the door.
5 Refitting is a reversal of removal, but adjust the rear channel as required.

19 Rear door fixed glass – removal and refitting

1 Remove the window regulator, as described in Sections 15 or 16.
2 Unscrew the bolt and screw, and remove the retaining channel.
3 Withdraw the fixed glass and rubber forward from the door.
4 Refitting is a reversal of removal.

20 Door – removal and refitting

1 Open the door to its fullest extent and support its lower edge on jacks or blocks covered with rags.
2 Disconnect the check strap from the body pillar (photo).
3 If the car is fitted with electric windows, disconnect the electrical leads.
4 Mark the position of the hinge plates on the door frame edge and then unbolt and remove the hinge screws (photo). Lift the door from the car.
5 Refitting is a reversal of removal and, if the hinges are bolted back into their original positions, door alignment should be correct. If adjustment is required to lift or lower the door or to make the door panel flush with the body panels, slacken the hinge bolts and move the door as necessary. Check that the gap round the edge of the door is equal on both sides and at the top.
6 Adjustment of the striker plate on the body pillar will affect the door closure and also the flush appearance of the door edge with the body panel or pillar adjacent to it. The striker plate can be set by releasing the retaining screws so that it moves stiffly and then closing the door (photo). This will position the door closure point. Open the door carefully and fully tighten the screws. If necessary, shims can be removed or inserted behind the striker plate to ensure positive closure. Sometimes it is an advantage to adjust the door so that its locking edge is 1.0 mm (0.04 in) proud of the rear door panel or body panel to reduce wind noise.

21 Door check strap – removal and refitting

1 Remove the trim panel, as described in Section 14, and peel the polythene sheet from the area by the check strap.
2 Extract the small retainer and tap the pin from the door pillar.
3 Unscrew the bolts and nut and withdraw the check strap from the door.
4 Refitting is a reversal of removal, but lubricate the moving parts with a little grease.

22 Front door exterior handle – removal and refitting

Saloon and Estate models
1 Prise the grommet from the edge of the door and unscrew the cross-head screws (photo).

20.2 Door check strap

20.4 Door hinge

20.6 Door striker

22.1 Front door exterior handle retaining screws

24.2A Door remote control handle

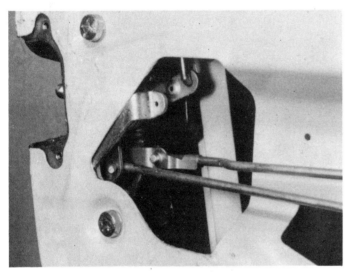

24.2B Operating rods on the front door lock

24.4 Front door lock and retaining screws

2   Push the handle forward, pull the grip, and withdraw the handle assembly.

3   Before refitting the handle, screw in the front mounting screw leaving approximately the thickness of the sheet metal.

4   Pull the grip and insert the handle so that the operating rod enters the lock. If necessary tighten the front screw, and adjust the drive pin clearance to 1.0 mm (0.04 in) using an Allen key.

5   Tighten the rear screws and insert the grommet.

Coupé Models

6   The procedure is identical to that described in paragraphs 1 to 5 except that access to the rear screws is gained by removing the cover at the top of the door and prising back the weatherseal.

23 Rear door exterior handle – removal and refitting

1   Prise back the weatherseal and unscrew the rear screw.

2   Push the handle forward, pull the grip and withdraw the handle assembly.

3   Before refitting the handle screw in the front mounting screw leaving approximately the thickness of the sheet metal.

4   Pull the grip and insert the handle, then push in the grip so that the drive screw engages. If necessary tighten the front screw, and adjust

the drive screw clearance to 1.0 mm (0.04 in) by loosening the locknut.

5   Tighten the rear screw and fit the weatherseal.

24 Front door lock – removal and refitting

1   Remove the trim panel, as described in Section 14.

2   Mark the position of the remote control handle then remove it by unscrewing the cross-head screws and disconnecting the operating rods (photos).

3   Remove the exterior handle, as described in Section 22.

4   Remove the cross-head screws and withdraw the lock downward through the aperture (photo).

5   Refitting is a reversal of removal. If necessary adjust the remote control handle to eliminate all play.

25 Rear door lock – removal and refitting

1   Remove the trim panel, as described in Section 14.

2   Disconnect the remote control linkage from the door lock then remove the remote control handle and linkage.

3   On models equipped with electric windows or side impact

This sequence of photographs deals with the repair of the dent and paintwork damage shown in this photo. The procedure will be similar for the repair of a hole. It should be noted that the procedures given here are simplified — more explicit instructions will be found in the text

In the case of a dent the first job — after removing surrounding trim — is to hammer out the dent where access is possible. This will minimise filling. Here, the large dent having been hammered out, the damaged area is being made slightly concave

Now all paint must be removed from the damaged area, by rubbing with coarse abrasive paper. Alternatively, a wire brush or abrasive pad can be used in a power drill. Where the repair area meets good paintwork, the edge of the paintwork should be 'feathered', using a finer grade of abrasive paper

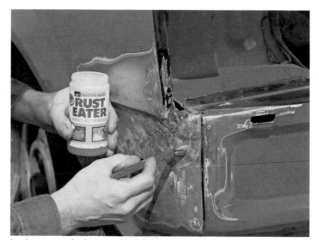

In the case of a hole caused by rusting, all damaged sheet-metal should be cut away before proceeding to this stage. Here, the damaged area is being treated with rust remover and inhibitor before being filled

Mix the body filler according to its manufacturer's instructions. In the case of corrosion damage, it will be necessary to block off any large holes before filling — this can be done with aluminium or plastic mesh, or aluminium tape. Make sure the area is absolutely clean before ...

... applying the filler. Filler should be applied with a flexible applicator, as shown, for best results; the wooden spatula being used for confined areas. Apply thin layers of filler at 20-minute intervals, until the surface of the filler is slightly proud of the surrounding bodywork

Initial shaping can be done with a Surform plane or Dreadnought file. Then, using progressively finer grades of wet-and-dry paper, wrapped around a sanding block, and copious amounts of clean water, rub down the filler until really smooth and flat. Again, feather the edges of adjoining paintwork

The whole repair area can now be sprayed or brush-painted with primer. If spraying, ensure adjoining areas are protected from over-spray. Note that at least one inch of the surrounding sound paintwork should be coated with primer. Primer has a 'thick' consistency, so will find small imperfections

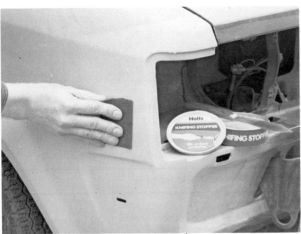

Again, using plenty of water, rub down the primer with a fine grade wet-and-dry paper (400 grade is probably best) until it is really smooth and well blended into the surrounding paintwork. Any remaining imperfections can now be filled by carefully applied knifing stopper paste

When the stopper has hardened, rub down the repair area again before applying the final coat of primer. Before rubbing down this last coat of primer, ensure the repair area is blemish-free — use more stopper if necessary. To ensure that the surface of the primer is really smooth use some finishing compound

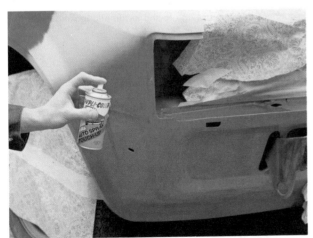

The top coat can now be applied. When working out of doors, pick a dry, warm and wind-free day. Ensure surrounding areas are protected from over-spray. Agitate the aerosol thoroughly, then spray the centre of the repair area, working outwards with a circular motion. Apply the paint as several thin coats

After a period of about two weeks, which the paint needs to harden fully, the surface of the repaired area can be 'cut' with a mild cutting compound prior to wax polishing. When carrying out bodywork repairs, remember that the quality of the finished job is proportional to the time and effort expended

reinforcements, remove the window regulator, as described in Sections 15 or 16.

4 Remove the cross-head screws and withdraw the lock downwards through the aperture.

5 Refitting is a reversal of removal.

26 Tailgate lock (Estate models) – removal and refitting

1 With the tailgate open unscrew the locking knob and remove the tailgate trim panel (6 screws).

2 Remove the screw from the inner handle cover and remove the cover, then lift the trim panel from the clips.

3 Remove the screws and withdraw the bottom rail.

4 Remove the cross-head screw from the inner handle.

5 Pull the switch plug from the right-hand side of the lock and disconnect the locking rod from the left-hand side of the lock.

6 On models equipped with central locking disconnect the linkage from the vacuum unit.

7 Unscrew the lock mounting bolts and press the lock lever to its locked position. The lock can now be withdrawn through the aperture.

8 Refitting is a reversal of removal, but carry out the following adjustments. On models equipped with central locking adjust the vacuum unit so that the linkage has no play when unlocked. The exterior handle free play should be 1.0 mm (0.04 in) – if necessary operate the safety plunger, then insert a screwdriver through the upper bolt hole to position the lock correctly. Finally insert the bolt and tighten it.

27 Exterior mirror – removal and refitting

1 If it is found that vibration is causing the exterior mirror to alter its setting, the mirror must be removed complete and the clamp screw tightened.

2 The glass can be renewed simply by prising it from the mirror head with a plastic or wooden lever.

3 To remove the mirror complete, push the small plastic lock out of the mirror control handle using a small screwdriver and withdraw the handle.

4 Pull off the cover plate to expose the three mirror fixing screws. Extract the screws and remove the mirror.

5 Refitting is a reversal of removal.

28 Fuel filler flap – removal and refitting

1 Open the flap and lever out the cap retainer.

2 Unbolt the flap from the body.

3 Refitting is a reversal of removal, but make sure that the seals are fitted correctly between the flap and the body.

29 Sliding roof – adjustment

Electrically-operated sunroof

1 Remove the headlining from the sliding roof, then loosen the slide bracket bolts and press the brackets inward while keeping the roof central in its opening. Tighten the bolts.

2 To adjust the front height, loosen the slide rail screws and turn the slotted adjustment screws until the front edge is level with, or up to 1.0 mm (0.04 in) lower than the roof panel when shut. Tighten the slide rail screws.

3 To adjust the rear height, close the sliding roof, then loosen the nut and turn the adjustment plate with a screwdriver until the rear edge is level with, or up to 1.0 mm (0.04 in) higher than the roof. Tighten the nut.

4 Refit the headlining.

Manually-operated sunroof

5 Remove the headlining from the sliding roof, then loosen the slide bracket bolts and press the brackets inward while keeping the roof central in its opening. Tighten the bolts.

6 To adjust the stop rods, loosen the nuts and position the sliding roof so that it is in good contact with the front seal, then tighten the

nuts. Half open the roof, loosen the stop rod screws, and adjust so that the lever will operate with the roof in any position.

7 To adjust the front height, loosen the slide rail screws and turn the slotted adjustment screws until the front edge is level with, or up to 1.0 mm (0.04 in) lower than the roof panel when shut. Tighten the slide rail screws.

8 To adjust the rear height turn the screws on the rear brackets until the rear edge is level with or up to 1.0 mm (0.04 in) higher than the roof.

9 Refit the headlining. If the end lever rattles it can be lowered a little using a strip of felt.

Fig. 12.11 Rear height adjustment on the electrically-operated sunroof (Sec 29)

30 Seats – removal and refitting

Front seat (driver's)

1 Set the seat in the highest position and push it fully forwards.

2 Disconnect the return spring.

3 Unscrew the bolt and pull out the slide rail.

4 Unscrew the rear guide rail bolts.

5 Where applicable, on Saloon models without height adjustment, remove the bolt from the bracket at the side (photo).

6 Set the seat in the lowest position and push it fully rearwards.

7 Unscrew the front guide rail bolts and, on Coupé models, disconnect the vacuum line to the automatic locking system.

8 Lift the seat from the car.

9 Refitting is a reversal of removal.

Front seat (passenger's)

10 With the seat pushed fully forwards unscrew the bolt and pull out the slide rail.

11 Unscrew both bolts from the side bracket.

12 Push the seat fully rearwards, unscrew the front guide rail bolts (photo), and lift the seat from the car.

13 Refitting is a reversal of removal.

Rear seat and backrest (Saloon models)

14 Push the safety catch and lift out the cushion – do not unfold the armrest.

15 Unscrew the backrest lower bolts, then unfold the armrest and unscrew the centre lower bolt.

16 Withdraw the backrest upwards to release the upper fixings.

17 Refitting is a reversal of removal.

Rear seat and backrest (Estate models)

18 Push down the locking lever and fold the cushion forwards.

19 Push the rod safety catches and lift out the cushion.

20 Prise out the plastic covers, unscrew the bolts, and withdraw the backrest from the car.

21 Refitting is a reversal of removal.

30.5 Driver's seat side bracket

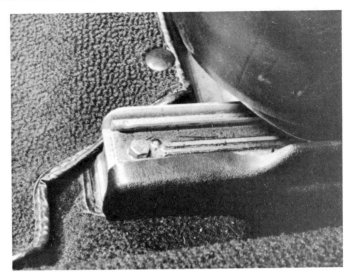

30.12 Passenger's seat front guide rail bolt

31 Windscreen and rear window – removal and refitting

Windscreen

1 Prise the inner mouldings from the trim, leaving the upper moulding in position.
2 Release the inner rubber surround using a blunt screwdriver.
3 With the help of an assistant carefully press out the windscreen from the inside and remove it from the car.
4 Prise the corner pieces and mouldings from the rubber surround, then ease the surround from the windscreen.
5 Clean the body aperture, rubber surround and windscreen.
6 Fit the rubber surround to the windscreen, then dip the mouldings and corner pieces in warm soapy water and fit them to the surround.
7 Cut a piece of cord greater in length than the periphery of the windscreen, dip it in soapy water and insert it in the surround channel.
8 Apply an 8 mm (0.3 in) thick bead of sealant to the vertical pillars of the aperture.
9 Offer the windscreen to the aperture with the cord ends at the centre bottom, and press while the assistant pulls the cord to locate the surround on the flange.
10 Refit the inner mouldings.
11 Inject sealing compound between the surround and windscreen/body on the outside, then remove any excess compound.

Rear window

12 The procedure is similar to that described in paragraphs 1 to 12, but in addition the heater wiring must be disconnected and the trim removed from the rear pillars.

32 Rear quarter window – removal and refitting

Coupé models

1 Remove the rear seat, as described in Section 30.
2 Remove the cover plate (3 screws), regulator handle or electric switch, trim and quarter panel.
3 Unbolt the shell cover and access covers, then disconnect the intermediate lever at the guide plate.
4 Unbolt the guide rail and lift the window forwards from the car.
5 Refitting is a reversal of removal, but adjust the window as necessary by loosening the relevant bolts.

Estate models

6 The procedure is similar to that described in Section 31, except that the relevant trim panels must first be removed.

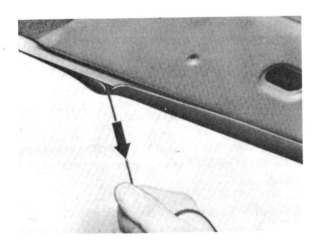

Fig. 12.12 Method of fitting the windscreen (Sec 31)

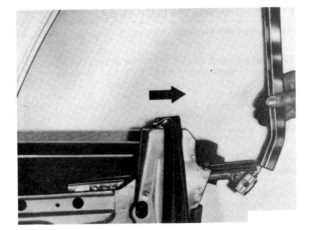

Fig. 12.13 Removing the rear quarter window (Sec 32)

Fig. 12.14 Rear quarter window regulator mounting bolts –
manual (Sec 33)

34 Facia panel – removal and refitting

1   Remove the glove compartment, as described in Section 35.
2   Remove both trim panels from beneath the facia panel.
3   Prise out the windscreen inner mouldings.
4   Remove the screws and unhook the loudspeaker covers, then unscrew the bolts from the facia.
5   Remove the instrument panel, as described in Chapter 10.
6   Press off the light switch control knob, and unscrew the nut to release the switch.
7   Disconnect the chain from the handbrake lever, or disconnect the handgrip, as applicable.
8   Disconnect the left and right vent hoses.
9   Detach the fresh air flap lever and disconnect the fresh air hoses.
10   Disconnect the glove compartment light switch wires.
11   Disconnect the loudspeaker wires, if applicable.
12   Lift the facia panel so that the defroster jets slide from the heater box, then withdraw the panel from the car.
13   Refitting is a reversal of removal.

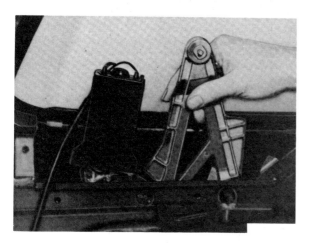

Fig. 12.15 Removing the electric rear quarter window regulator
(Sec 33)

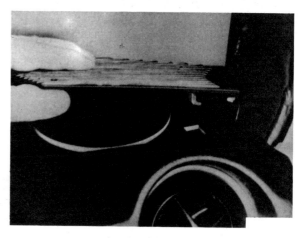

Fig. 12.16 Removing the loudspeaker covers from the facia
(Sec 34)

33 Rear quarter window regulator – removal and refitting

1   Remove the rear quarter trim panel.

Manual regulator

2   Remove the access cover (4 screws) then prise off the clip and disconnect the intermediate lever at the guide plate.
3   Raise the window and support it with a piece of wood.
4   Unscrew the bolts and withdraw the regulator through the aperture.
5   Refitting is a reversal of removal.

Electric regulator

6   Push out the rocker switch and disconnect the wiring plug. Also disconnect the motor wiring from the terminal block, but first identify them for position.
7   Unscrew the screws and remove both access covers.
8   Unbolt and remove the shell cover.
9   Prise off the clip and disconnect the intermediate lever at the guide plate.
10   Unscrew the regulator mounting nuts, lower the window, then withdraw the regulator upwards.
11   Refitting is a reversal of removal.

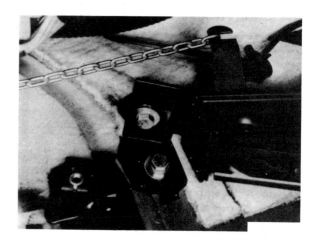

Fig. 12.17 Handbrake lever and chain (Sec 34)

35 Glove compartment and lid – removal and refitting

1 Remove the striker (2 screws) and prise out the studs.
2 Press out the light and disconnect the plug.
3 Pull the glove compartment from the facia panel.
4 Remove the cross-head screws from the lid and unscrew the slotted nuts using a suitable screwdriver.
5 Turn the lock pin on the outer edge of the lid vertical, withdraw it and disconnect the stop bracket. The lock pin has a lock on one side only, so if it cannot be removed it should be turned through 180°.
6 Lift the inner lid and withdraw the outer lid, then withdraw the inner lid and stop bracket.

7 If necessary the lock may be removed by compressing the cams with pincers. Note that the top face of the lock is marked 'oben'.
8 Refitting is a reversal of removal.

36 Centre console – removal and refitting

1 Remove both front well mats.
2 Prise out the outer switches or covers and remove the cross-head screws. Remove the cover.
3 Remove the ashtray and frame, and disconnect the plugs.
4 Remove the carpet liner, then unscrew the front screws from the gearshift lever cover, lift the cover slightly and push up the hazard

Fig. 12.18 Glove compartment lid lock pin (Sec 35)

Fig. 12.19 Centre console rear mounting bolt (Sec 36)

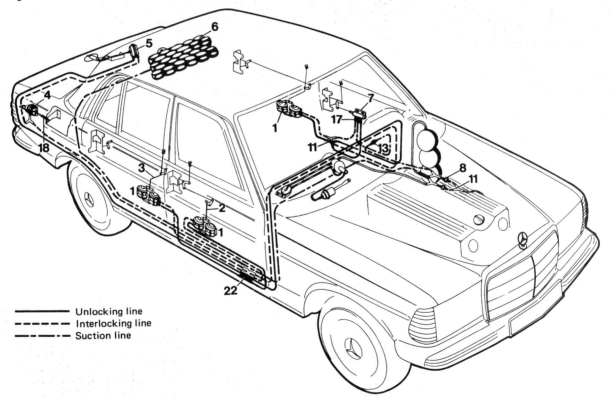

———— Unlocking line
– – – – Interlocking line
– · – · – Suction line

Fig. 12.20 Central locking system (Sec 39)

1 Vacuum element (driver's and rear doors)	4 Vacuum element (flap for tank filler neck)	6 Vacuum supply tank	13 Check valve
2 Control rod (front passenger door)	5 Vacuum element (trunk lid)	7 Vacuum switch	17 Connection
3 Control rod (rear doors)		8 Check valve	18 Compression spring
		11 Three-way distributor	22 Four-way distributor

36.4 Disconnecting plugs and wiring from the centre console

36.5 Removing the gearshift lever cover from the centre console

warning light switch so that the plugs can be disconnected (photo).
5   Pull the gearshift lever cover from the centre console (photo).
6   Remove the radio.
7   Pull off the heater control knobs, then unscrew the nuts.
8   Pull off the heater lever knob and withdraw the cover. Disconnect the light wire.
9   Remove the screws from the front tunnel and the rear bolts from the centre console. Also remove the screw from the tray.
10   Raise the rear of the centre console and withdraw it from the facia panel – hold the end of the console to prevent it spreading apart.
11   Refitting is a reversal of removal.

37 Bumpers – removal and refitting

Front
1   Loosen the bracket mounting nuts and withdraw the bumper forwards (photo).
2   Refitting is a reversal of removal, but on standard models apply soapy water to the rubber side covers and, on deluxe models, make sure that the bumper engages the side brackets.

Rear
3   On Estate models first remove the lens from the reversing light and foglight, disconnect the wiring and remove the reflectors.
4   On all models unscrew the mounting nuts and withdraw the bumper rearwards (photo).
5   Refitting is a reversal of removal, but on standard models apply soapy water to the rubber side covers and, on deluxe models, make sure that the bumper engages the side brackets.

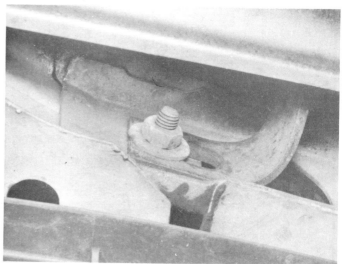

37.1 Front bumper mounting bracket

38 Rear shelf (Saloon models) – removal and refitting

1   Remove the rear seat backrest, as described in Section 30.
2   Remove the two screws from the first aid kit tray, lift the front of the tray, and withdraw it from the shelf.
3   Lift the centre of the rear shelf and withdraw it forwards.
4   Refitting is a reversal of removal.

39 Central locking system – general

The central locking system uses vacuum from the engine to automatically lock all doors, the boot lid and the fuel tank flap when the driver's door is locked. The layout of the system is shown in Fig. 12.20.

Vacuum from the engine inlet manifold is stored in the vacuum tank in the rear compartment and is channelled to the various

37.4 Rear bumper mounting bracket

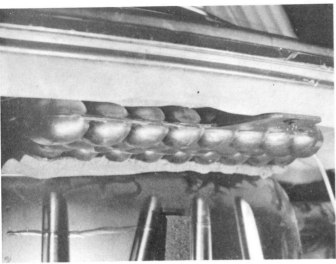

39.2A Central locking system vacuum tank located in the luggage compartment

39.2B Central locking vacuum elements in the front door

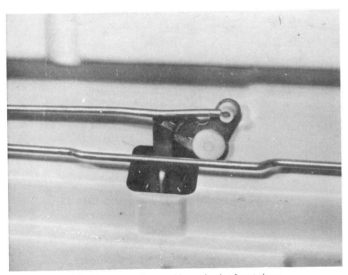

39.2C Central locking operating rod lever in the front door

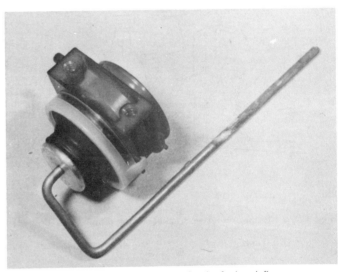

39.2D Central locking system element for the fuel tank flap

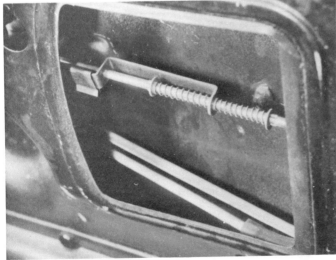

39.2E Central locking system operating rod for the boot lid lock

elements by a switch on the driver's door (photos). The vacuum tank permits the car to be locked up to ten times with the engine stopped, after which the car may be locked manually if required (eg if the engine cannot be started).

40 Heater motor – removal and refitting

1   Remove the lower facia panel and pull the plug from the heater motor.
2   Remove the screw, lift the contact plate and disconnect the series resistance wires, after noting their location.
3   Unscrew the flange bolts and withdraw the heater motor.
4   Refitting is a reversal of removal.

41 Heater unit – removal and refitting

1   Remove the front well mats and the lower facia panel.
2   Remove the centre console, as described in Section 36.
3   Position the front seats fully rearwards.
4   Drain the cooling system, as described in Chapter 2.
5   Disconnect the heater hoses in the engine compartment (photo).
6   Remove the glovebox, as described in Section 35, then disconnect

41.5A Heater water valve in the engine compartment

41.5B Heater water valve connecting hose

41.10 Heater unit showing cable connection

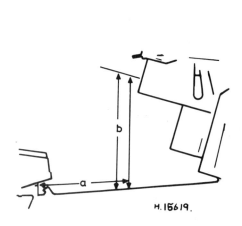

Fig. 12.21 Heater unit lower bracket setting dimensions (Sec 41)

$a = 165.0$ mm (6.5 in) $b = 217.0$ mm (8.5 in)

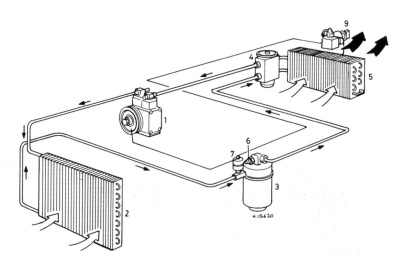

Fig. 12.22 Air conditioning components (Sec 43)

1 Compressor	5 Evaporator
2 Condenser	6 Temperature switch
3 Dehydrator	7 Pressure switch
4 Expansion valve	9 Temperature regulator

the glovebox light switch wires.

7   Remove the screws and withdraw the rear compartment air ducts and the air ducts on the transmission tunnel.

8   Disconnect the air supply hose from the heater and detach the fresh air flap lever.

9   Unbolt the support from the transmission tunnel and unscrew the bolt from the facia.

10   Disconnect the plug and all wiring connectors, also disconnect the control cables (photo).

11   Unscrew the upper mounting nuts and lower mounting bolts.

12   Close the fresh air flap then lower the heater from the defroster nozzle and withdraw it rearwards, together with the water tubes.

13   Refitting is a reversal of removal, but first lubricate the defroster nozzle with soapy water. The lower bracket should be set as shown in Fig. 12.21. Fill the cooling system with reference to Chapter 2.

42 Heater matrix – removal and refitting

1   Remove the heater, as described in Section 41.

2   Prise off the clamps and unscrew the screws, then remove the heater cover.

3   Pull off the rubber seals and remove the remaining clamps, then withdraw the heater matrix assembly.

4   Lift out the matrix and remove the seals from the end tubes.

5   Refitting is a reversal of removal.

43 Air conditioning system – precautions and maintenance

1   Never disconnect any part of the air conditioning refrigerant circuit unless it has been evacuated by a qualified refrigeration engineer.

2   Where the system components obstruct other mechanical operations, then it is permissible to unbolt their mountings and move them to the limit of their flexible hose deflection, but **do not** disconnect the hoses. If there is still insufficient room to carry out the required work then the system must be discharged before disconnecting and removing the components. On completion of the work, have the system recharged.

3   Regularly check the condenser for clogging with flies or dirt, and, if necessary, clear it with a water hose or air line.

4   Regularly check the tension of the compressor drivebelt. The belt deflection should be 10.0 mm (0.4 in) at the centre point of its longest run. If adjustment is required loosen the pulley screw, then turn the adjustment bolt on the bracket as necessary and tighten the pulley screw.

Conversion factors

Length (distance)

Inches (in)	X	25.4	= Millimetres (mm)	X 0.0394	= Inches (in)
Feet (ft)	X	0.305	= Metres (m)	X 3.281	= Feet (ft)
Miles	X	1.609	= Kilometres (km)	X 0.621	= Miles

Volume (capacity)

Cubic inches (cu in; in^3)	X	16.387	= Cubic centimetres (cc; cm^3)	X 0.061	= Cubic inches (cu in; in^3)
Imperial pints (Imp pt)	X	0.568	= Litres (l)	X 1.76	= Imperial pints (Imp pt)
Imperial quarts (Imp qt)	X	1.137	= Litres (l)	X 0.88	= Imperial quarts (Imp qt)
Imperial quarts (Imp qt)	X	1.201	= US quarts (US qt)	X 0.833	= Imperial quarts (Imp qt)
US quarts (US qt)	X	0.946	= Litres (l)	X 1.057	= US quarts (US qt)
Imperial gallons (Imp gal)	X	4.546	= Litres (l)	X 0.22	= Imperial gallons (Imp gal)
Imperial gallons (Imp gal)	X	1.201	= US gallons (US gal)	X 0.833	= Imperial gallons (Imp gal)
US gallons (US gal)	X	3.785	= Litres (l)	X 0.264	= US gallons (US gal)

Mass (weight)

Ounces (oz)	X	28.35	= Grams (g)	X 0.035	= Ounces (oz)
Pounds (lb)	X	0.454	= Kilograms (kg)	X 2.205	= Pounds (lb)

Force

Ounces-force (ozf; oz)	X	0.278	= Newtons (N)	X 3.6	= Ounces-force (ozf; oz)
Pounds-force (lbf; lb)	X	4.448	= Newtons (N)	X 0.225	= Pounds-force (lbf; lb)
Newtons (N)	X	0.1	= Kilograms-force (kgf; kg)	X 9.81	= Newtons (N)

Pressure

Pounds-force per square inch (psi; lbf/in^2; lb/in^2)	X	0.070	= Kilograms-force per square centimetre (kgf/cm^2; kg/cm^2)	X 14.223	= Pounds-force per square inch (psi; lbf/in^2; lb/in^2)
Pounds-force per square inch (psi; lbf/in^2; lb/in^2)	X	0.068	= Atmospheres (atm)	X 14.696	= Pounds-force per square inch (psi; lbf/in^2; lb/in^2)
Pounds-force per square inch (psi; lbf/in^2; lb/in^2)	X	0.069	= Bars	X 14.5	= Pounds-force per square inch (psi; lbf/in^2; lb/in^2)
Pounds-force per square inch (psi; lbf/in^2; lb/in^2)	X	6.895	= Kilopascals (kPa)	X 0.145	= Pounds-force per square inch (psi; lbf/in^2; lb/in^2)
Kilopascals (kPa)	X	0.01	= Kilograms-force per square centimetre (kgf/cm^2; kg/cm^2)	X 98.1	= Kilopascals (kPa)

Torque (moment of force)

Pounds-force inches (lbf in; lb in)	X	1.152	= Kilograms-force centimetre (kgf cm; kg cm)	X 0.868	= Pounds-force inches (lbf in; lb in)
Pounds-force inches (lbf in; lb in)	X	0.113	= Newton metres (Nm)	X 8.85	= Pounds-force inches (lbf in; lb in)
Pounds-force inches (lbf in; lb in)	X	0.083	= Pounds-force feet (lbf ft; lb ft)	X 12	= Pounds-force inches (lbf in; lb in)
Pounds-force feet (lbf ft; lb ft)	X	0.138	= Kilograms-force metres (kgf m; kg m)	X 7.233	= Pounds-force feet (lbf ft; lb ft)
Pounds-force feet (lbf ft; lb ft)	X	1.356	= Newton metres (Nm)	X 0.738	= Pounds-force feet (lbf ft; lb ft)
Newton metres (Nm)	X	0.102	= Kilograms-force metres (kgf m; kg m)	X 9.804	= Newton metres (Nm)

Power

Horsepower (hp)	X	745.7	= Watts (W)	X 0.0013	= Horsepower (hp)

Velocity (speed)

Miles per hour (miles/hr; mph)	X	1.609	= Kilometres per hour (km/hr; kph)	X 0.621	= Miles per hour (miles/hr; mph)

Fuel consumption*

Miles per gallon, Imperial (mpg)	X	0.354	= Kilometres per litre (km/l)	X 2.825	= Miles per gallon, Imperial (mpg)
Miles per gallon, US (mpg)	X	0.425	= Kilometres per litre (km/l)	X 2.352	= Miles per gallon, US (mpg)

Temperature

Degrees Fahrenheit = (°C x 1.8) + 32   Degrees Celsius (Degrees Centigrade; °C) = (°F - 32) x 0.56

*It is common practice to convert from miles per gallon (mpg) to litres/100 kilometres (l/100km),
where mpg (Imperial) x l/100 km = 282 and mpg (US) x l/100 km = 235

Index

Printed by
Haynes Publishing Group
Sparkford Yeovil Somerset
England